D0322433

306.7
HAL

Outspoken Women

The 1960s: the era of the sexual revolution and the 'second wave of feminism'. Bras were burnt, hemlines rose dramatically, women's sexuality was released from the male-defined boundaries behind which it had been fenced, and women's writing on sexual and feminist issues boomed like it never had before . . . or had it?

Outspoken Women: An anthology of women's writing on sex, 1870–1969 brings together the non-fictional writings of British women on sexual attitudes and behaviour nearly a hundred years *prior* to 'second-wave' feminism. Studying the period from the supposedly prudish Victorian era, to the sexual revolution of the 1960s, this comprehensive study reveals a neglected tradition of British women's writing.

The excerpts analysed here come from polemics, works of advice, surveys, essays and *belles lettres*, and the authors, including famous and lesser-known figures, provide a diverse range of perspectives, and include social Darwinists, sexologists, psychoanalysts, VD campaigners, as well as women writing about their own lives and experiences.

Hall's remarkable book is an engaging examination of this fascinating subject and provides students and scholars with an invaluable source of primary material.

Lesley A. Hall is an archivist at the Wellcome Library and an honorary lecturer at University College London. She has published widely on gender and sexuality, and is the founder of the H-Histsex discussion list.

Women's and Gender History
Edited by June Purvis

Emmeline Pankhurst: A Biography
June Purvis

Child Sexual Abuse in Victorian England
Louise A. Jackson

Crimes of Outrage: Sex, Violence and Victorian Working Women
Shani D'Cruze

Feminism, Femininity and the Politics of Working Women: The Women's Co-operative Guild, 1880s to the Second World War
Gillian Scott

Gender and Crime in Modern Europe
Edited by Margaret L. Arnot and Cornelie Usborne

Gender Relations in German History: Power, Agency and Experience from the Sixteenth to the Twentieth Century
Edited by Lynn Abrams and Elizabeth Harvey

Imaging Home: Gender, 'Race' and National Identity, 1945–64
Wendy Webster

Midwives of the Revolution: Female Bolsheviks and Women Workers in 1917
Jane McDermid and Anna Hillyar

No Distinction of Sex? Women in British Universities 1870–1939
Carol Dyhouse

Policing Gender, Class and Family: Britain, 1850–1945
Linda Mahood

Prostitution: Prevention and Reform in England, 1860–1914
Paula Bartley

Sylvia Pankhurst: Sexual Politics and Political Activism
Barbara Winslow

Votes for Women
Edited by June Purvis and Sandra Holton

Women's History: Britain, 1850–1945
Edited by June Purvis

The Women's Suffrage Movement: A Reference Guide, 1866–1928
Elizabeth Crawford

Women and Teacher Training Colleges 1900–1960: A Culture of Femininity
Elizabeth Edwards

Women, Work and Sexual Politics in Eighteenth-Century England
Bridget Hill

Women Workers and Gender Identities, 1835–1913: The Cotton and Metal Industries in England
Carol E. Morgan

Women and Work in Britain Since 1840
Gerry Holloway

Women's History: Britain, 1700–1850
Edited by Hannah Barker and Elaine Chalus

The Women's Suffrage Movement in Britain and Ireland: A Regional Survey
Elizabeth Crawford

Outspoken Women

An anthology of women's writing on sex, 1870–1969

Edited by
Lesley A. Hall

HILLCROFT COLLEGE
LEARNING RESOURCES
SOUTH BANK
SURBITON
SURREY KT6 6DF

Routledge
Taylor & Francis Group

LONDON AND NEW YORK

First published 2005
by Routledge
2 Park Square, Milton Park, Abingdon, Oxon OX14 4RN

Simultaneously published in the USA and Canada
by Routledge
270 Madison Ave, New York, NY 10016

Routledge is an imprint of the Taylor & Francis Group

© 2005 Lesley A. Hall

Typeset in Garamond Book
by Keystroke, Jacaranda Lodge, Wolverhampton
Printed and bound in Great Britain
by Antony Rowe Ltd, Chippenham, Wiltshire

All rights reserved. No part of this book may be reprinted or
reproduced or utilised in any form or by any electronic,
mechanical, or other means, now known or hereafter invented,
including photocopying and recording, or in any information
storage or retrieval system, without permission in writing
from the publishers.

British Library Cataloguing in Publication Data
A catalogue record for this book is available from the British Library

Library of Congress Cataloging in Publication Data
Outspoken women : British women writing about sex, 1870–1969 :
an anthology / edited by Lesley A. Hall. – 1st ed.
       p. cm. – (Women's and gender history)
     Includes bibliographical references.
1. Sex customs–Great Britain–History–19th century.   2. Sex customs–Great
Britain–History–20th century.   3. Sex instruction literature–Great
Britain–History.   4. Women social reformers–Great Britain–Biography.
5. Women authors, English–19th century–Biography.   6. Women authors,
English–20th century–Biography. 7. Sex role in literature. I. Hall, Lesley A.
II. Series.
   HQ18 .G7098 2005
   306.7'082'09410904–dc22

ISBN 0–415–25371–3 (hbk)
ISBN 0–415–25372–1 (pbk)

ả

Contents

Acknowledgements   vii

Introduction   1

1 The Victorians, 1870–1901   11
   Marriage   13
   Desire, pleasure and satisfaction   16
   Heterosexual relationships outside marriage   19
   Prostitution and venereal disease   22
   Birth control   31
   Ignorance and sex education   34

2 The suffrage era, 1902–1918   37
   Marriage   38
   Desire, pleasure and satisfaction   44
   Heterosexual relationships outside marriage   49
   Same-sex relationships, celibacy, and singleness generally   54
   Prostitution and venereal disease   61
   Birth control   73
   Ignorance and sex education   79

3 The Stopes era, 1918–1929   95
   Marriage   97
   Desire, pleasure and satisfaction   108
   Heterosexual relationships outside marriage   116

Same-sex relationships, celibacy, and singleness generally   123
Prostitution and venereal disease   135
Birth control   142
Ignorance and sex education   153

4 The Depression and war, 1930–1945   167
Marriage   168
Desire, pleasure and satisfaction   179
Heterosexual relationships outside marriage   190
Same-sex relationships, celibacy, and singleness generally   206
Prostitution and venereal disease   217
Birth control   225
Ignorance and sex education   237

5 Sex in the Welfare State, 1945–1969   251
Marriage   253
Desire, pleasure and satisfaction   261
Heterosexual relationships outside marriage   271
Same-sex relationships, celibacy, and singleness generally   283
Prostitution and venereal disease   289
Birth control   295
Ignorance and sex education   300

Appendix: Biographical notes on authors   310
Further reading   324
Bibliography of works cited   326
Index   334

ã

Acknowledgements

I should like to thank my colleagues at the Wellcome Library for the History and Understanding of Medicine, where much of the research for this volume was done. In particular, I should like to thank Reader Services, and Simon Jones and the Library Services Team, who all bore competently and cheerfully my orders for never-before consulted stack materials, photocopying orders of some magnitude, etc. This sort of thing makes an immense difference.

Gratitude in great measure also goes to the team of transcribers who greatly eased my burdens: Cathy Doggrell, Joyce Forde, Helena Hilton, Alexandra Iglesias, Derek Scoins, Tim Stentiford and Stella Stevani.

I should also like, as usual, to thank my partner Ray McNamee, who has put up with the increasing encroachments of my collection of works on sex by women and my preoccupation with this project.

I am also extremely grateful to my friends for support, encouragement and suggestions during the time I have been thinking about and editing this book.

Thanks are due to the following for permission to quote copyright material as specified: Duff Hart-Davis for Mary Borden's *The Technique of Marriage*; Mark Bostridge and Rebecca Williams, literary executors of Vera Brittain; David Higham Associates for Margaret Cole's *Marriage Past and Present*; the Holtby Estate for Winifred Holtby's *Women and a Changing Civilisation*; Jim Kornitzer for Margaret Kornitzer, *The Modern Woman and Herself*; Andrew Malleson for Joan Malleson's *Any Wife or any Husband, by 'Medica'*; Mrs Jean Faulks for Ethel Mannin's essay 'Sex and the Child'; Mrs Lois Godfrey for Naomi Mitchison's works; Clairemond Ltd for Claire Rayner's *Parent's Guide to Sex Education*; Mrs Harriet Ward for excerpts from works by Dora Russell; the Galton Institute for works by Marie Stopes; H. Beric Wright for Helena Wright's works; Dr Elisabeth Schoenberg and Mrs Mary Burke for Rosalie Taylor, *Inside Information on Sex and Birth Control*; Dr Richard Pankhurst for Christabel Pankhurst, *The Great Scourge*. Material from Barbara Bennett and Susan Isaacs, *Health and Education in the Nursery*, used by kind permission of the Taylor and Francis Group. Extracts from Clemence Dane, *The Woman's Side*, published by Herbert Jenkins Ltd, London, 1926, reproduced by permission of Pollinger Ltd and the Proprietor. Extracts from Elizabeth Draper, *Birth Control in the Modern World*, reproduced by permission of Penguin Books Ltd. Extracts from Margaret Leonora Eyles, *Commonsense about Sex, The New Commonsense about Sex*, and *Unmarried but Happy*, originally published by Victor Gollancz, reproduced by permission of the Orion Publishing Group. Extracts from *Women of the Streets* by C. H. Rolph (ed.) published by Secker and Warburg and extracts from *Orphans of the Living* by Diana Dewar, published by Hutchinson, are used by permission of The Random House Group Limited. Every effort has been made to contact copyright holders but in several cases it has proved impossible to ascertain who these are.

Introduction

This reader focuses specifically on women writing about sex, critiquing existing social arrangements, suggesting changes, and formulating concepts of female sexuality, in Britain, from the later nineteenth century to the rise of the 'permissive society' during the 1960s.

It initially seemed to the activists of the 'second wave' of feminism which arose in the late 1960s that they were originating debates, but there were later discovered, following delvings into 'herstory', to have been lively questions many decades previously, in this area as in others.[1] Although a number of important works have demonstrated how significant a range of questions on sexual issues were to the rise of 'first-wave' feminism,[2] it has still been possible for otherwise well-informed historians to allege that these questions were sidelined in favour of educational and career issues and political enfranchisement.[3]

As late as 1970, Constance Rover in *Love, Morals and the Feminists* (1970) claimed that the leaders of the earlier women's movement 'subscribed to conventional morality', instead of making 'a more concerted effort to restructure society'.[4] Sheila Jeffreys, in *The Spinster and Her Enemies*,[5] overturned this perception of the first-wave feminists as prudish adherents of conventional moral standards, instead depicting a passionate critique of hegemonic masculine sexual attitudes and behaviour, and rejection of heterosexuality. However, Jeffreys' championing of this particular subversive tradition led her to be unduly dismissive of other women making a case for reformed, even revolutionized, models of sexuality and claiming the right to female sexual pleasure.[6] It should be apparent from the texts excerpted that placating men was quite the antithesis of what figures such as Stella Browne or Dora Russell, or even Marie Stopes, were interested in doing.

The historiography of the development of a scientific discourse on sexuality in the late nineteenth and early twentieth centuries has so far been inclined to overlook the contribution of women. Much of the emphasis has been on the role of sexology in creating homosexual identities, and debates on whether this was an emancipatory strategy,[7] medical policing by labelling,[8] or a complex phenomenon of interaction between men developing a sense of homosexual identity and doctors interested in the 'problem'.[9] On the whole, the extent to which women's protest against man-made institutions such as prostitution and marriage opened up the possibility of critiquing the existing understanding of sex, in particular, assumptions about 'the natural', has been neglected.[10]

Part of the problem with the perception of the role of women's writing in this field, as in others, is the question of mode and genre, and what genres are seen as part of the genealogy. The history of sexology, in a quest to establish the respectable and scientific credentials of a field still regarded somewhat askance, placed most weight on scientific, medical and legal treatises or articles in learned journals by men with the appropriate professional qualifications. Women, however, were working in a range of modes and genres – polemic literature, religious discourse, works of popular instruction, essays, social surveys, textbooks for social workers. Many of these are not considered as contributing to the development of ideas, instead being conceived of as either having a specific campaigning intent, or as popularizing the Big Ideas originated by Big Male Thinkers.[11]

In fact, many women were using these various forms to express and develop ideas that were radical and overturned many male-dominated assumptions. They were often writing from detailed personal knowledge of women's lives and feelings. Knowledge was gained from working in the growing number of professions for women, such as medicine, social work, educational psychology and psychoanalysis, with voluntary organizations of various kinds both providing services such as birth control clinics and lobbying for better provisions, and as 'agony aunts', formal and informal. They were also able to draw on individual experiences of their own, and of friends and associates. One of the most renowned works on sexual matters by a woman in the twentieth century, Marie Stopes's best-selling marriage manual *Married Love*, was based on Stopes's researches in the sexological literature, along with self-observation and discussions with other women about their sexual experiences and responses; and in it she solicited further research data, in particular on the periodicity of female desire.

This volume provides evidence that, far from sex having been something ladies (especially British ladies) did not discuss prior to the sexual revolution of the 1960s, there was a substantial and important tradition well into the 1950s of women writing about female sexuality from an implicitly, if not explicitly, feminist perspective. These women were working within a variety of different traditions, from the polemic essay and the medical tract to the marriage manual and the social survey, and indeed several works cross any simplistic generic boundaries. They present female perspectives on prostitution, venereal diseases, marriage, alternatives to marriage, female sexual pleasure, birth control, sex education, and female homosexuality. Works which predominantly focused on one of these topics frequently addressed the others as well and a distinct holism of vision is apparent.

The women themselves were very diverse. Underlying similarities can often be discovered across startling differences of religious or political views, affiliations to or dissent from the suffrage movement, and so forth. Few, if any, of these writers defended prostitution, or wrote from a perspective of the desirability of regulation. The fact that they were speaking out on sex at all placed these women in a vulnerable position, and even when their messages seem, from today's perspective, to be promoting an extremely conservative agenda, they were advancing arguments, or discussing questions, which many people found abhorrent. Just breaching the silence, to expatiate on the evils of the system of sexual ignorance, to mention the consequences in disease of a system which assumed prostitution was a necessary and ineradicable evil, to condemn the double standard of morality which punished women for crimes for which men escaped any penalty, was a radical act.

Many connections can be discerned between particular women, as well as their references back to a tradition established by early pioneers such as Josephine Butler and Annie Besant. They cited one another's works (even those who anathematized Marie Stopes's arrogance praised the good her writings were doing). A distaff genealogy via the Malthusian (later the New Generation) League can be traced, as well as connections through the suffrage movement, pacifism during the Great War, left-wing politics and the expanding birth control movement of the 1920s. Clusters were associated with the outspoken maverick feminist journal *The Freewoman*, overlapping with the women who joined the British Society for the Study of Sex Psychology, who overlapped with the developing British school of psychoanalysis and with social hygiene groups such as the British Social Hygiene Council. The Women's Cooperative Guild was closely involved in the 1920s' struggle for birth control advice in welfare clinics and in setting up clinics during the 1920s and 1930s. The Federation of Progressive Societies and Individuals, established in the early 1930s, and its Sex Reform Group in particular, included names also associated with the birth control and abortion campaigns, the struggles for sexual enlightenment, and protests against the banning of Radclyffe Hall's *The Well of Loneliness*. Personal contacts can also be identified: Stella Browne, to take one example, encountered Annie Besant and other by then elderly Malthusian pioneers, was a member of the Freewoman group, an early joiner of the

BSSSP, along with Cicely Hamilton, Norah March, and Constance Long, toiled unacknowledged for the Workers' Birth Control Group, spoke to numerous local Women's Cooperative Guilds, was thanked in the acknowledgements of Winifred Holtby's *Woman and a Changing Civilisation* and wrote a short but heartfelt appreciation after Holtby's early death: similar connections could with very little effort be traced.[12]

Works selected were published in Britain, by British citizens either from the UK or the Dominions. There is not much difference apparent between writers from different regions: it is hard to detect any specific Scottish dimension shared by Isabel Hutton, Janet Chance, and Naomi Mitchison, or that their Jewish background had any obvious influence on the works of Charlotte Haldane, Helena Wright or Rose Hacker. Stella Browne left Canada very early in life and in 1915 defined herself as a 'female Briton'.[13] Ettie Hornibrook (née Rout), however, does reveal a different approach to issues of sexually transmitted diseases, uninflected by the Josephine Butler tradition, and owing much more to the more stringent policing of sexual morals noticeable in the white settler colonies of the Antipodes.[14] She is perhaps the only voice raised in defence of some form of regulation of prostitution, though some women advocated *egalitarian* measures of compulsion in respect of venereal disease treatment.

One compelling but often unanswerable question is that of the sexuality of the writers themselves. Marie Stopes's rather chequered sexual history (early disappointed affair with a Japanese scientist, hints of warm emotions towards other women, relatively late first marriage terminated by annulment at her suit for non-consummation, second marriage happy for a while, her husband's giving her *carte blanche* to seek satisfaction with other men, her string of *amitiés amoureuses*, or perhaps more, in later life) has been documented in several biographies. Isabel Hutton's autobiography, *Memories of a Doctor in War and Peace*, raises a number of intriguing questions rather than providing answers. Barbara Evans's biography of Helena Wright, *Freedom to Choose*, indicates that while for most of her career as a sex adviser Wright framed her writings within a discourse of the better preservation of monogamous wedlock, she and her husband had an 'open marriage'. Less disjunction between life and published opinions can be seen in the writings of Naomi Mitchison – whose own frank memoirs, written late in life, describe both her and her husband's extreme initial sexual ignorance (illuminated, as for so many, by Stopes's *Married Love*) and their later open marriage – and those of Dora Russell. However, in very few cases can any definite evidence be adduced for lesbianism or bisexuality. Constance Long's partner was the Jungian analyst Beatrice Hinkle, and Clemence Dane is also known to have had a female partner, to whom her novel *Regiment Of Women* was dedicated. Plausible claims can be made that Stella Browne was bisexual, moving from a position of 'affairs between women predominantly heterosexual' to a concept of an innate bisexuality, but this requires a close analysis of her scattered writings.[15]

These were the writers: who were the audience? It is often assumed that the readers of popular sex manuals were largely middle class, although the copious surviving correspondence received by Marie Stopes indicates that she reached (in some cases via her articles in the popular press) a very much more complex social range. Several texts were specifically directed towards the lower classes, perceived as in particular need of enlightenment and instruction. Leonora Eyles considered that unfortunately women of the lower classes would not read pamphlets, but Pearl Jephcott found considerable enthusiasm for the works of the British Social Hygiene Council among the working-class girls she studied. There was probably a considerable difference between the more socially conscious and politically active women of the working classes, for example, those in the Women's Cooperative Guild, and those who were completely downtrodden and apathetic. A number of works included in this volume gave a voice to women of the silenced classes, e.g. the Women's Cooperative Guild's *Maternity: Letters from Working Women* and Stopes's *Mother England*, while an almost ethnographic approach to prostitution links the 1916 *Downward Paths* to the Wolfenden-era *Women of the Streets*, via the unfortunately never-published 'participant observation' of the prostitutes of Coram Street, Bloomsbury, undertaken by Sybil Neville-Rolfe during the Great War.[16]

The 'Whiteness' of both writer and audience is implicit in all these texts: issues of 'race' in terms of ethnic difference, rather than the use of 'racial' in its early twentieth-century eugenic sense of the 'better breeding' of the British themselves, are sparse until the 1950s, and tend to be confined to occasional cautions against cross-cultural marriage. However, although many of these works seem very specifically white and British and highly ethnocentric, several of them were translated not only into other European languages but into those of the Empire and of other cultures undergoing modernization during the early twentieth century.[17] Stopes, indeed, received letters not only from Europeans domiciled all over the Empire but also from a substantial number of non-ethnically European correspondents.

Changes over time are one element represented within this volume, but considerable continuities persisted and are evident. Many of the most influential works went on being reissued over a lengthy period: Stopes was still taking an active interest in revising new editions of her works during the 1950s in the light of the latest ideas.[18]

When originally planning this volume, the names of several pioneering periodicals significant for stimulating debate on sexual questions from the woman's angle immediately sprang to mind: *The Shield*, the journal of the Ladies' National Association against the Contagious Diseases Acts, later the Association of Moral and Social Hygiene; Margaret Shurmer Sibthorpe's *Shafts: A Journal for Women and the Working Classes* of the 1890s; the *Freewoman* launched by Dora Marsden in 1911; the rather obscure and hard to locate *Urania* with its agenda of radical celibacy and eradication of gender difference. However, if these were included, as they had a strong claim to be, what about the numerous other periodicals in which women were arguing, either in their columns or in letters to the editor, on similar issues? What about *The Malthusian* and its later incarnation *The New Generation*? *The Adult*, the journal of the Legitimation League of the 1890s? Or Lady Rhondda's Equality Feminist *Time and Tide*? Or other contemporary weeklies and fortnightlies of the inter-war years in which questions of birth control, censorship, women's role, 'sexual inversion' were being discussed, with women – several of them represented in this selection – taking an active and articulate part? And how about the dissemination of ideas about birth control, sexual enlightenment of children, women's right to sexual pleasure, and so forth in the pages of mainstream women's magazines? (Leonora Eyles, a number of whose works are excerpted, spent some years as an 'agony aunt' and occasional columnist for *Modern Woman*: this clearly inflects the tone of her other writings.) Not to mention the role of determined woman journalists in getting sympathetic articles on such controversial topics as abortion and lesbianism into women's magazines in the 1940s and 1950s. This soon came to look like a whole project in itself, particularly when the interactive nature of the periodical press is taken into account, with its letter columns, its various question and answer features enabling a much more intimate relationship with the readership (although Stopes can be seen to have expanded and modified the text of *Married Love* in response to reader feedback,[19] this can very seldom be tracked in the case even of popular and best-selling books).

Principles of selection and editing

So much material was discovered in the course of putting this volume together that rather stringent conditions of selection had to be applied. This volume cannot hope to be exhaustive, but it is hoped that it will stimulate readers to follow up some of the paths suggested or implied. Fiction has been excluded, as have autobiography and memoirs, and evidence given to various official and non-official investigations. Only extracts from books and pamphlets have been included, though this does include collections of essays and articles. The question of journals and periodicals and the reasons for excluding these have been addressed above.

Stringency similarly had to be applied in selecting the topics to focus on: those eventually settled upon were:

- *Marriage*: this was central, given that nearly all discussions about sexual relations took marriage as their touch-stone: the effect of prostitution on marriage, the impact of premarital sexual activity on subsequent wedlocked relationships, inter-war 'free love' advocates largely positioned this as 'open marriage', a central relationship with excursions, rather than a free-for-all, and pair-bonds between single women were seen as emotionally congruent to heterosexual marriage. However, marriage itself was dealt with largely in two modes:
  - as it is: the difficulties and problems; divorce;
  - as it could be: recommendations for its improvement, utopian visions of a transcendent monogamy.

- *Desire, pleasure, and satisfaction*:
  - the existence and nature of female desire;
  - how to bring about female sexual pleasure and satisfaction.

- *Heterosexual relations outside the marital relationship*: premarital sex, illegitimacy, seduction and coercion, extramarital affairs, free love, 'promiscuity' and friendships:
  - observations about the existence and prevalence of these, both coercive and consensual;
  - opinions as to whether desirable or not.

- *Same-sex relationships, single women and celibacy*: these seemed to be related so closely, both as representing women (theoretically at least) outside heterosexual relationships, and because there was increasing discussion of friendship, its rewards, dangers and appropriate management, in the lives of single women.

- *Prostitution and venereal disease*:
  - analyses of the problem of prostitution;
  - observations of prostitutes and prostitution;
  - the problem of venereal diseases.

- *Birth control, including abortion*:
  - the desirability of restricting births;
  - whether artificial means of undertaking this were desirable;
  - the problem of abortion;
  - problems with birth control.

- *Sexual ignorance and the need for sex education*:
  - sexual ignorance and its dangers;
  - the desirability of, and strategies for, sex education.

The material has further been grouped chronologically into five periods as follows:

- *The Victorian era*: from approximately the inception of the campaign against the Contagious Diseases Acts of the 1860s to the death of Queen Victoria.
- *The suffrage years*: 1901 to the limited enfranchisement of women in 1918.
- *The Stopes era*: the 1920s, which saw tensions between a new vision of emancipated sex with contraception and continuing older social purity/hygiene views.
- *The Depression and war*: the 1930s have been considered a period of occlusion for feminism, a notion not borne out by the numerous texts from the period bearing on the various topics delineated above and often taking a very radical perspective.
- *Sex in the Welfare State, 1945–1969*: a period which, compared to the inter-war years, seems somewhat regressive, but with some underlying hints of changes to come.

There is an appendix of biographical information on the women whose works have been excerpted. In some cases these are well-known figures about whom much has been written, others are quite obscure and little can be discovered about them. There is also a bibliography of the works excerpted with full publication details: short titles only are given in the text. Some suggestions for further background reading are also given.

In editing the extracts, an ellipsis of 3 dots indicates words omitted within a sentence. An ellipsis of 4 dots indicates the omission of sentence(s) within a paragraph. An ellipsis of 4 dots within square brackets indicates that paragraph(s) have been omitted within a longer passage. It is hoped that in all cases the sense of the material in question has been retained. The numbers in square brackets refer to the page number of the original text.

Notes

1 See e.g. Sheila Rowbotham, *Hidden from History: 300 Years of Women's Oppression and the Fight against It* (London: Pluto Press, 1973); Dale Spender, *Women of Idea and What Men Have Done to Them, from Aphra Behn to Adrienne Rich* (London: Routledge and Kegan Paul, 1982); Barbara Taylor, *Eve and the New Jerusalem: Socialism and Feminism in the Nineteenth Century* (London: Virago, 1983).

2 Lucy Bland, *Banishing the Beast: English Feminism and Sexual Morality, 1885–1914* (London: Penguin, 1995); A. James Hammerton, *Cruelty and Companionship: Conflict in Nineteenth-Century Married Life* (London: Routledge, 1992); Karen Hunt, *Equivocal Feminists: The Social Democratic Federation and the Woman Question 1884–1911* (Cambridge: Cambridge University Press, 1996); Claudia Nelson and Ann Sumner Holmes (eds), *Maternal Instincts: Visions of Motherhood and Sexuality in Britain, 1875–1925* (London: Macmillan Press, 1997); Mary

Lyndon Shanley, *Feminism, Marriage, and the Law in Victorian England, 1850–1895* (Princeton, NJ: Princeton University Press, 1989); Judith R. Walkowitz, *Prostitution and Victorian Society: Women, Class and the State* (Cambridge and New York: Cambridge University Press, 1980); Judith R. Walkowitz, *City of Dreadful Delight: Narratives of Sexual Danger in Late-Victorian London* (London: Virago, 1992).

3 Angus McLaren, *Twentieth-Century Sexuality: A History* (Oxford: Blackwell, 1999), p. 205; Alan Hunt, *Governing Morals: A Social History of Moral Regulation* (Cambridge: Cambridge University Press, 1999), p. 205.

4 Constance Rover, *Love, Morals and the Feminists* (London: Routledge and Kegan Paul, 1970), p. 48.

5 Sheila Jeffreys, *The Spinster and Her Enemies: Feminism and Sexuality 1880–1930* (London: Pandora Press, 1985).

6 Bland, *Banishing the Beast*, presents a much more nuanced picture; see also Lesley A. Hall, 'Feminist Reconfigurations of Heterosexuality in the 1920s', in Lucy Bland and Laura Doan (eds), *Sexology in Culture: Labelling Bodies and Desires* (Cambridge: Polity Press, 1998), pp. 135–149.

7 Edward M. Brecher, *The Sex Researchers* (London: André Deutsch, 1970) and Paul Robinson, *The Modernization of Sex: Havelock Ellis, Alfred Kinsey, William Masters and Virginia Johnson* (New York: Harper and Row, 1976).

8 Michel Foucault, *History of Sexuality, Vol. 1: An Introduction* (Harmondsworth: Penguin, 1981, first published in French 1978); Jeffrey Weeks, *Coming Out: Homosexual Politics in Britain from the Nineteenth Century to the Present* (London: Quartet, 1977) and *Sex, Politics and Society: The Regulation of Sexuality since 1800* (London: Longman, 1981).

9 Lucy Bland and Laura Doan (eds), *Sexology in Culture: Labelling Bodies and Desires* (Cambridge: Polity Press, 1998); Harry Oosterhuis, *Stepchildren of Nature: Krafft-Ebing, Psychiatry, and the Making of Sexual Identity* (Chicago: University of Chicago Press, 2000); Vernon A. Rosario (ed.), *Science and Homosexualities* (London: Routledge, 1997).

10 Lesley A. Hall, 'Hauling Down the Double Standard: Feminism, Social Purity and Sexology in Late Nineteenth Century Britain', *Gender and History* (2004), 16 (1): 36–56.

11 Similar phenomena can be discerned in the occlusion of women as contributors to the emergence of history as a professional discipline: Mary Spongberg, *Writing Women's History Since the Renaissance* (Basingstoke: Palgrave, 2002); their role in literary developments and movements from the eighteenth century onwards: Norma Clarke, *The Rise and Fall of the Woman of Letters* (London: Pimlico, 2004), Ann Ardis, *New Women, New Novels: Feminism and Early Modernism* (New Brunswick, NJ: Rutgers University Press, 1990); Jo-Ann Wallace, 'The Case of Edith Ellis', in Hugh Stevens and Caroline Howlett (eds), *Modernist Sexualities* (Manchester: Manchester University Press, 2000), pp. 13–40; their place in numerous fields of science: M. Julian, 'Women in Crystallography', in G. Kass-Simon and P. Farnes (eds), *Women of Science: Righting the Record* (Bloomington, IN: Indiana University Press, 1990), pp. 335–383; Mary Creese, 'British Women of the Nineteenth and Twentieth Centuries who Contributed to Research in the Chemical Sciences', *British Journal for the History of Science* (1991), 24: 275–305; Pnina Abir-Am and Dorinda Outram (eds), *Uneasy Careers and Intimate Lives: Women in Science 1789–1979* (New Brunswick, NJ: Rutgers University Press, 1987); Lesley A. Hall, 'Chloe, Olivia, Isabel, Letitia, Harriette, Honor and Many More: Women in Medicine

and Biomedical Science, 1914–1945', in Sybil Oldfield (ed.), *This Working-Day World: Women's Lives and Cultures in Britain 1914–1945* (London: Taylor and Francis, 1994), pp. 192–202; their role in the early days of establishing psychoanalysis, Suzanne Raitt, 'Early British Psychoanalysis and the Medico-Psychological Clinic', *History Workshop Journal* (2004), 58: 63–85; and in making changes to the US political process in the years after the grant of suffrage, Kristi Andersen, *After Suffrage: Women in Partisan and Electoral Politics before the New Deal* (Chicago: University of Chicago Press, 1996). If women do it, somehow whatever it is does not really 'count' as whatever the activity is defined as.

12 See Lesley A. Hall, *Strong Red Rag: The Life and Times of Stella Browne, Feminist Sex Radical* (London: I. B. Tauris, forthcoming).

13 F. W. Stella Browne, Letter 'Reflections of a (Female) Briton', *The Malthusian*, 40, January 1916: 10–11.

14 Philippa Levine, *Prostitution, Race and Politics: Policing Venereal Disease in the British Empire* (London: Routledge, 2003).

15 Long's relationship with Hinkle, and their theories on gender, are mentioned in Lois W. Banner, *Intertwined Lives: Margaret Mead, Ruth Benedict and their Circle* (New York: Alfred A. Knopf, 2003), pp. 229, 491; Dane's relationship with 'E. A.' are mentioned both in the entry for her in the *Oxford Dictionary of National Biography*, and in the obituary in *The Times*, 29 Mar. 1965, p. 14; on Stella Browne, see Lesley A. Hall, '"I Have Never Met the Normal Woman": Stella Browne and the Politics of Womanhood', *Women's History Review* (1997), 6: 157–182, also *Strong Red Rag* (forthcoming).

16 Sybil Neville-Rolfe, 'Autobiographical Notes', *Social Biology and Welfare* (London: George Allen & Unwin, 1949), pp. 27–29.

17 Peter Eaton and Marilyn Warnick, *Marie Stopes: A Checklist of her Writings* (London: Croom Helm, 1977), mention translations of *Married Love* and *Wise Parenthood* into Arabic, Chinese, and Hindi as well as several European languages; *Enduring Passion* was translated into Gujarati, and it is by no means clear whether this constitutes an exhaustive list.

18 Personal information from the late James McGibbon, who was her editor at the time.

19 Lesley A. Hall, '"A Deep Debt of Gratitude for your Heroic Frankness": Marie Stopes, Marriage Advice, and Readers' Reactions', in Bruno Wanrooij (ed.), *La Mediazione Matrimoniale: Il terzo (in)comodo in Europa fra Otto e Novecento* (Rome: Edizioni di Storia e Letteratura, 2004), pp. 323–336.

Chapter One

≥&

The Victorians, 1870–1901

Introduction

During the late nineteenth century women began to criticize existing sexual arrangements within society as being for the benefit of men only, whether in the laws relating to marriage or in the widespread existence of prostitution. There were many causes for women's dissatisfaction with marriage: while from 1857 a man could divorce his wife for simple adultery, a wife could only divorce her husband for adultery plus another matrimonial offence such as cruelty, desertion, sodomy or incest, while there were campaigns for women's right to own property and to have custody of their children, and even protests against the presumption that a husband could not rape his wife.

Criticism of the existing male-defined state of affairs became particularly explosive after the introduction of the Contagious Diseases Acts (CD Acts) during the 1860s, which were intended to control the extremely high levels of venereal diseases in the army and navy by the compulsory medical examination, followed by incarceration until 'cured' if found to be infected, of women believed to be prostitutes in a number of 'designated districts' around port and garrison towns. This blatant articulation of the differential standard of sexual morality applied to men and women, and its imposition of intrusive physical examination and virtual imprisonment upon women who were not criminals, raised substantial protests on a number of grounds. The protest by women was spearheaded by the Ladies' National Association for the Repeal of the Contagious Diseases Acts, under the leadership of the charismatic Josephine Butler.

Women were also increasingly gaining access to education and professional training which gave them additional authority in speaking out on these matters. While the major theme of this period is the attack on the double standard of sexual morality from the perspective that both men and women should adhere to the standard required of women, a number of voices, for example, those of women involved with the early birth control organization, the Malthusian League, took a more positive view of the potential of sex to be a rewarding experience for women, and advocated the use of contraception, not merely as beneficial to a woman's health by decreasing the number and frequency of pregnancies, but also as facilitating healthy sexual relations.

The campaign against the CD Acts evolved into a much wider 'social purity' movement aimed at the moral regeneration of society. While historians have demonstrated that this was a complex phenomenon which cannot be mapped into conventional political divisions or analysed in simplistic terms of 'repression', 'liberation' or 'protection of the vulnerable', there was a continuing thread within it strongly opposed to the sexual exploitation of women, and the way in which women were placed at a disadvantage by existing social conventions equating 'innocence' with 'ignorance'.

While there were obvious differences between 'social purity' and 'freethought' perspectives, with strong appeals to Christianity and the use of religious rhetoric by one, and the use of discourses of 'reason' and 'the natural' by the other, there were also significant similarities of opinion on certain issues. Prostitution and other manifestations of the sexual double standard were deplored by both camps, and both agreed in principle about the need for the sexual enlightenment of the young with 'healthy knowledge', though there might be differences on the content of this enlightenment. The iniquities of the marriage system and the adverse position in which it placed women were critiqued across the spectrum, even if the social purity camp was unwilling to reject formal marriage in favour of free unions. Even in the freethought camp, 'free love' was conceptualized not as promiscuity, but as a higher form of monogamy untainted by the strictures of church and state. Only towards the end of the century, in the essays of Edith Lees Ellis, a particularly radical figure, did the possibility of sexual experimentation even tentatively and obliquely emerge.

Other recommended resources

Evidence given to Royal Commission on the Contagious Diseases Acts, 1870, *The Shield* (journal of the Ladies' National Association for the Repeal of the CD Acts, later the Association of Moral and Social Hygiene) and journals of the other social purity bodies, *Shafts* (edited by Margaret Shurmer Sibthorp), *The Malthusian*, *The Adult* (journal of the Legitimation

League, initially formed to fight for the rights of the illegitimate, but soon became concerned with a range of sexually radical questions).

Marriage

Discussions of marriage frame it within what becomes a common dichotomy: the evils of marriage as so often manifested in contemporary society, and an idealistic vision of what the committed monogamous relationship might be in better conditions. The question of the termination of unsatisfactory unions was also argued, pro and con.

Josephine Butler, Social Purity, *1879*

[9] Marriage does not transform a man's nature, nor uproot habits that have grown with his years: the licentious imagination continues its secret blight, though the outward conduct may be restrained. The man continues to be what he was, selfish and unrestrained, though he may be outwardly moral in deference to the opinion of that 'society' which, having previously excused his vices, now expects him to be moral. And what of that other being, his partner – his wife – into whose presence he brings the secret consciousness, it may be the hideous morbid fruits, of his former impurity? Can any man, with any pretension to true manliness, contemplate calmly the shame – the cruelty – of the fact that such marriages are not exceptional, especially in the upper classes?

Annie Besant, Marriage, *1882*

[13] A married woman loses control over her own body; it belongs to her owner, not to herself; no force, no violence, on the husband's part in conjugal relations is regarded as possible by the law; she may be suffering, ill, it matters not; force or constraint is recognised by the law as rape, in all cases save that of marriage . . . no rape can be committed by a husband on a wife; the consent given in marriage is held to cover the life, and if – as sometimes occurs – a miscarriage or premature confinement be brought on by the husband's selfish passions, no offence is committed in the [14] eye of the law, for the wife is the husband's property, and by marriage she has lost the right of control over her own body. The English marriage law sweeps away all the tenderness, all the grace, all the generosity of love, and transforms conjugal affection into a hard and brutal legal right.

[40] [H]usband and wife should be placed on a perfect equality in asking for a divorce: at present if husband and wife be living apart, no amount of

adultery on the husband's part can release the wife; if they be living together, a husband may keep as many mistresses as he will, and provided that he carefully avoid any roughness which can be construed into legal cruelty, he is perfectly safe from any suit for dissolution of marriage. Adultery alone, when committed by the husband, is not ground for a dissolution of marriage; it must be coupled with some additional offence before the wife can obtain her freedom. But the husband can obtain a dissolution of marriage for adultery committed by the wife, and he can further obtain money damages from the co-respondent.

[48] [F]acility of divorce will entirely sweep away those odious [49] suits for 'restitution of conjugal rights' which occasionally disgrace our courts. If a husband and wife are living apart, without legal sanction, it is now open to either of them to bring a suit for restitution of conjugal rights . . . . It is difficult to understand how any man or woman, endued with the most rudimentary sense of decency, can bring such a suit, and, after having succeeded, can enforce the decision. We may hope that, as sexual morality becomes more generally recognised, it will be seen that the essence of prostitution lies in the union of the sexes without mutual love; when a woman marries for rank, for title, for wealth, she sells herself as veritably as her poorer and more unfortunate sister; love alone makes the true marriage, love which is loyal to the beloved, and is swayed by no baser motive than passionate devotion to its object. When no such love exists, the union which is marriage by law is nothing higher than legalised prostitution: the enforcement on an unwilling man or woman of conjugal rights is something even still lower, it is legalised rape.

[59] [L]oyalty of one man to one woman is . . . the highest sexual ideal. The more civilized the nature the more durable and exclusive does the marriage union become.

Jane Clapperton, Scientific Meliorism, *1885*

[157] If I . . . ask – 'What has marriage been to you?' she replies at once – 'A disappointment! But,' she explains, 'I was a dreamer in my youth, a pure idealist. I married without any *real* knowledge of what life is, or is meant to be. I throw no blame upon my husband. He is practical, a man of the world; not always, nay seldom *sympathetic*, but kind to me, and outwardly we are a united couple. In the inner depths of my own consciousness lies the fact that marriage has been a bitter disappointment; but I am wholly ignorant of whether the *cause of this* lies in my objective experience, or my romantic expectations. It may be, I freely admit, that I have looked for *too much*, rather than that the relation has yielded me

too little.' The personal question *she* would gladly solve, I must not dwell upon.

The point of grave importance for us is, that under the fair surface of decorous married life, there exists in this country in hundreds and thousands of cases a vacuum, I mean a space, empty and void of real, substantial happiness.

[311] Truth, simplicity, justice, must form the threefold basis of a better system of things in which asceticism will be put aside as false to the facts of adult human nature, and *early marriage* will be everywhere encouraged and facilitated. Simplicity will take the place of luxury in domestic living, and happiness will be aimed at instead of magnificence and show. Justice will give freedom within the marriage bond itself, creating outward or legal conditions that are neither immoral nor lax. But sufficiently elastic to permit of retrieving the errors of youth, and honestly or openly retracing steps that have converged to mutual dissatisfaction and misery rather than to mutual comfort and peace.

Marriage, as it exists, is, in hundreds of thousands of cases, an artificial sham . . . . But why do we hold divorce in disgust and disrespect? Is it not because we have ourselves defiled it, and made its conditions odious? When its conditions are made reasonable and pure we shall respect it as necessary to general happiness.

Edith Lees Ellis, 'A Noviciate for Marriage', c. 1892

[14] The mere word of the clergyman or the registrar sanctions, and even sanctifies in the eyes of convention, what is in the majority of unions adultery on the man's side and a plunge into animalism on the woman's side. Repression and excess meet in the name of Love, and the bread and wine which life rarely offers more than once to a man and a woman as a veritable sacrament are devoured gluttonously upon the altar steps. To prevent unhappy marriages is surely a saner method than to facilitate divorce after souls and bodies may have become permanently injured through the orthodox experiment which begins after legal marriage.

Ellice Hopkins, The Power of Womanhood, 1899

[143] Whilst the sight is so familiar of wives with health broken down and life made a burden, possibly even premature death incurred, by their being given no rest from the sacred duties of motherhood, to say nothing of the health of the hapless child born under such circumstances, can we wonder that the modern woman often shows a marked distaste to marriage and looks upon it as something low and sensual?

[176] [O]ur girls need to be taught not only that there is nothing derogatory in the married relation to the freest and fullest independence of character, but surely . . . [177] they need to be taught the sanctity of marriage – those first principles which hitherto we have taken for granted, but which now, like everything else, is thrown into the crucible and brought into question. They need definite teaching as to the true nature of marriage; that it is no mere contract to be broken or kept according to the individual contractor's convenience . . . but a sacramental union of love and life, with sacramental grace given to those who will seek it to live happily and endure nobly within its sacred bounds – a union so deep and mystical that even on its physical side our great physiologists are wholly at a loss to account for some of its effects; a union of which permanence is the very essence, as on its permanence rests the permanence and stability of the whole fabric of our life.

[221] It is becoming an impossibility for intelligent women with a knowledge of physiology and an added sense of their own dignity to accept the lower moral standard for men, which exposes them to the risk of exchanging monogamy for a peculiarly vile polygamy – polygamy with its sensuality, but without its duties – bringing physical risks to their children and the terrible likelihood of an inherited moral taint to their sons.

Desire, pleasure and satisfaction

Malthusian freethinkers such as Besant and Clapperton argue the benefits of sexual activity from a relatively old-fashioned model of sexual pleasure as 'natural', healthy and desirable. However, Blackwell, though positioned much more towards the social purity end of the spectrum, deploys her medical qualifications and expertise to plead for the existence of an autonomous female desire, as powerful as, though different from, that of the male

Elizabeth Blackwell, Counsel to Parents on the Moral Education of their Children, *1882*

[52] Physical passion is not in itself evil, on the contrary it is an essential part of our nature. It is an endowment which like every other *human* faculty, has the power of high growth. It possesses that distinctive human characteristic – receptivity to mental impressions. These impressions blend so completely with itself, as to change its whole character and effect; and it thus becomes an ennobling or degrading agent in our lives.

[75] [U]nder the effect of training to a moral life and the action of public opinion, a great body of women in our own country constantly lead a virtuous life, frequently in spite of physical instincts as strong as those of men, and always in spite of mental instincts still more powerful. That the feeling of sex regarded as a mental passion is even stronger in women that in men, must be evident to all who give to the word strength its true signification – the signification of mental as well as physical phenomena, in proportion to the powers of the individual. The demands of women are greater than those of men, they desire more and more the thought and devotion of those they love. They often display a persistent fidelity, terrible in its earnestness, when they have had the misfortune to become attached to an unworthy object. The weak virtue of the mass of women, exposed to constant temptation, indicates the insatiable craving of the woman's heart for love.

Jane Clapperton, Scientific Meliorism, *1885*

[150] They are not simply responsive. It is their nature to throw out tender tentacles of human feeling, and to follow these with candid word and generous action. Now, there is nothing culpable in this, nor is it even dangerous, where [151] refinement exists, and where there have been inculcated the two modern sentiments-love of truth and justice . . . . But in a society, where the question of marriage is made too prominent, such girls are never able to be free and natural.

[321] [A]n early moderate stimulation of the female sexual organs (after puberty is reached) tends, by the law of exercise promoting development of structure, to make parturition in mature life easy and safe; and that the healthy functional and emotional life of the marriage union is the best preventive of hysteria, chlorosis, love melancholy, and other unhappy ailments to which our young women are cruelly and barbarously exposed, and which, I do not hesitate to say, make them in many cases feel their youth to be an almost *insufferable* martyrdom.

Annie Besant, The Law of Population, *1889*

[28] Celibacy is not natural to men or to women: all bodily needs require their legitimate satisfaction, and celibacy is a disregard of natural law. The asceticism which despises the body is a contempt of nature, and a revolt against her; the morality which upholds virginity as the type of womanly perfection is unnatural; to be in harmony with nature, men and women should be husbands and wives, fathers and mothers, and until nature

17

evolves a neuter sex celibacy will ever be a mark of imperfection. Very clearly has nature marked celibacy with disapproval; the average life of the unmarried is shorter than the average life of the married; the unmarried have a less vigorous physique, are more withered, more rapidly aged, more peevish, more fanciful [. . .]

[29] The same fact holds good as regards married and unmarried women. A long train of formidable diseases results from celibacy – such as spermatorrhœa in the male, chlorosis and hysteria in the female – and no one who desires society to be happy and healthy should recommend late marriage as a cure for the social evils around us.

Elizabeth Blackwell, The Human Element in Sex, 1894

[14] The physical pleasure which attends the caresses of love is a rich endowment of humanity, granted by a beneficent Creative Power. There is nothing necessarily evil in physical pleasure. Though inferior in rank to mental pleasure, it is a legitimate part of our nature . . . . The sexual act itself, rightly understood in its compound character, so far from being a necessarily evil thing, is really a divinely created and altogether righteous fulfilment of the conditions of present life. This act, like all human acts, is subjected to the inexorable rule of moral law. Righteous use brings renewed and increasing satisfaction to the two made one in harmonious union. Unrighteous use produces satiety, coldness, repulsion and misery.

[49] Those who deny sexual feeling to women, or consider it so light a thing as hardly to be taken into account in social arrangements, confound appetite and passion; they quite lose sight of this immense spiritual force of attraction, which is distinctly human sexual power, and which exists in so very large a proportion in the womanly nature. The impulse towards maternity is an inexorable but beneficent law of woman's nature, and it is a law of sex.

The different form which physical sensation necessarily takes in the two sexes, and its intimate connection with and development through the mind (love) in women's nature, serve often to blind even thoughtful and painstaking persons, as to the immense power of sexual attraction felt by women.
[. . . .]

[50] The affectionate husbands of refined women often remark that their wives do not regard the distinctively sexual act with the same intoxicating physical enjoyment that they themselves feel, and they draw the conclusion that the wife possesses no sexual passion. A delicate wife will often confide to her medical adviser . . . that at the very time when marriage love seems to unite them most closely, when her husband's welcome kisses and

caresses seem to bring them into profound union, comes an act which mentally separates them, and which may be either indifferent or repugnant to her. But it must be understood that it is not the special act necessary for parentage which is the measure of the compound moral and physical power of sexual passion. It is the profound attraction of one nature to the other which marks passion; and delight in kiss and caress – the love-touch – is physical sexual expression as much as the special act of the male.
[. . . .]

[T]he severe and compound suffering experienced by many widows who were strongly attached to their lost partners is also well known to the physician; and this is not [51] simply a mental loss that they feel, but an immense physical deprivation. It is a loss which all the senses suffer, by the physical as well as moral void which death has created.

Although physical sexual pleasure is not attached exclusively, or in women chiefly, to the act of coition, it is also a well-established fact that in healthy loving women, uninjured by the too frequent lesions which result from childbirth, increasing physical satisfaction attaches to the ultimate physical expression of love. A repose and general well-being result from this natural occasional intercourse.

Heterosexual relationships outside marriage

These are discussed under various headings. Josephine Butler complicates the category of 'prostitute' by pointing out that there might be women who, though not strictly chaste, are not prostitutes by any reasonable understanding of the meaning of the term. The question of 'free love' is debated, though even a radical freethinker like Besant points out the disadvantages in society as it existed. Blackwell introduces the theme of the benefits of healthy companionship between the young of both sexes. Edith Ellis argues for experimentation, but in the interests of an improved monogamy.

Josephine Butler, The Constitution Violated, 1871

[93] [I]n virtue of this [94] non-definition of a prostitute, the policeman and justice of the peace ride rampant at their pleasure throughout all that immense border land of humble society which lies between the confessed prostitute and absolute virtue. All the objections which we have urged against these Acts, with respect to the unconstitutional method by which they decide whether a woman is a prostitute or not, are intensified tenfold by the absence from the Acts of any definition as to what constitutes prostitution. A justice of the peace is therefore set to decide the question

of fact as to a woman's character, in which decision there are involved, as we have shown, most grievous consequences; and he is set to do this with absolutely no guide as to what is the thing which he is to determine the woman to be or not to be, no guide either from the Acts in question, or from the concurrent unanimity of society at large. The result of this is, and must be, that the definition of what a prostitute is, gradually falls into the hands of the policeman who accuses her; a grievous and lamentable consequence of this law, which constitutes one of its greatest oppressions, whereby the whole operation of the law degenerates into mere hunting in the streets by policemen of women suspected by them of unchastity.

[137] In the laws of England there is one great and unique defect . . . . [138] The laws of most other countries make the seduction of any woman under twenty-one a misdemeanour; but our laws, to the disgrace of Englishmen, allow the seduction of any child over twelve. If a villain can persuade the dispensers of the law that he can show that there was consent on the part of the child whom he ruined, he is free.

Elizabeth Blackwell, Counsel to Parents on the Moral Education of their Children, 1882

[97] Now, in the young and growing nature, sex may be richly satisfied by spiritual refreshment and refined companionship. Conjugal relations are not necessary to the very young in attaining true delight in sex. On the contrary, false relations are an outrage. They violently destroy the gradual unfolding of mental and physical joys, which alone produces exquisite and lasting delight. A large amount of honourable companionship between young men and women is of the utmost advantage in [98] strengthening and ennobling young man and womanhood.

Annie Besant, Marriage, 1882

[33] Two disadvantages, however, attach to unlegalised unions; first, the woman has to face social disapprobation, although of late years, as women have been coming more to the front, this difficulty has been very much decreased, for women have begun to recognise the extreme injustice of the laws, and both men and women of advanced views have advocated great changes in the marriage contract. The second disadvantage is of a more serious character: the children proceeding from an unlegalised union do not have the same rights as those born in legal wedlock.

[40] Judicial separation is a direct incentive to licentiousness and secret sexual intercourse; the partially divorced husband, refused any recognised

companion, either indulges in promiscuous lust, to the ruin of his body and mind, or privately lives with some woman whom the law forbids him to marry and whom he is ashamed to openly acknowledge. Meanwhile the semi-divorced wife can obtain no relief, and is compelled to live on, without the freedom of the spinster or the widow, or the social consideration of the married woman. She can only obtain freedom by committing what [41] the law and society brand as adultery.

Catherine Booth, The Iniquity of State Regulated Vice, 1884

[12] I read some paragraphs taken from the report of a debate in the House of Commons, which made me doubt my eyesight, with respect to the age at which female children should be answerable for their own ruin. I could not help the blood rushing to my temples with indignant shame. I could not help rubbing my eyes and reading again and saying, do my eyes deceive me? Could this ever have happened in the House of Commons in England? Oh! my God, are we come to this? I did not think we were so low as this – that one member should suggest that the age of these inno- [13] cents should be heightened to 14, and that another suggested it should be not so high. Another that it should be reduced to 10, and oh! my God, pleaded that it was hard for a man – *HARD* – *for a man!* – having a charge brought against him, not to be able to plead the consent of a child like that . . . . But what is to become of the little girls of poor unprotected widows? Of the little girls of the working classes of this country?

Edith Lees Ellis, 'A Noviciate for Marriage', c. 1892

[12] A noviciate in relation to marriage . . . . would be more coercive to the socially trained conscience of intelligent men and women than rash sensual episodes or haphazard pre-marital relationships. The ethical conscience of a community which countenances a man having one or many mistresses who can be flung aside for a 'moral' relationship in legal marriage, must be either asleep or devoid of the sense alike of humour and of tragedy. The vulgarities of prostitution and casual intimacies will surely be exchanged sooner or later, for rational and self-respecting experiments in the arts of living and loving.

[21] The noviciate experiment is not advocated in the hope that 'free love,' as it is miscalled, should take the place of monogamy in the community, but that true freedom and sincerity shall be encouraged in order that actual monogamy may have a chance to try its fate among a people who worship

it as an ideal, but whose feet are far from its temple. Nothing but open experiments and perfect sincerity as to results can rid us of pruriency and cant in this matter. Woman's economic freedom, her training in the full knowledge of sex, her insistence on her value, as a human being first and a sex being afterwards, her resolution not to sell herself in legal or illegal unions, may lead her to risk experiments, but no longer to countenance hypocrisy and uncleanness.

Ellice Hopkins, The Power of Womanhood, *1899*

[181] [T]he sooner we realize for ourselves and our girls that any relaxation of the marriage bond will in its disastrous consequences fall upon us, and not upon men, the better . . . . It is the man who is the more variable in his affections than [182] the woman; more constant as she is by nature, as well as firmly anchored down by the strength of her maternal love. It is therefore on the woman that any loosening of the permanence of the marriage tie will chiefly fall in untold suffering . . . . If we want to study the innate misery to women arising from the relaxation of the married tie, or transient unions, we had better read Professor Dowden's *Life of Shelley* – misery not the result of public stigma, for there was no such stigma in the circle in which Shelley moved, but misery brought about by the facts themselves, and producing state of things which Matthew Arnold could only characterize by the untranslatable French word '*sale.*'
[. . .]
  I confess it does fill me with sardonic laughter to find this oldest and stalest of all experiments, this oldest and flattest of failures, paraded as a brand new [183] and original panacea for all the woes of our family life, – woes which, if nobly borne, at least make 'perfect through suffering.'

Prostitution and venereal disease

Prostitution is where it all starts: in the voicing of protests against the attitudes encoded in the Contagious Diseases Acts of the 1860s. From this develops an extensive critique of a system privileging a certain model of male sexuality. Writers also address the dreadful conditions of the prostitute's life.

Josephine Butler, The Constitution Violated, *1871*

[32] In answer to our objections to these Acts, it is utter vanity and folly in any one to plead that they apply only to women who are prostitutes. Can

it be supposed that there is any man in England so foolish as to think that the safeguards of English law exist for the sake of [33] the guilty only? They exist for the sake of the innocent, who may be falsely accused, as well to protect them when accused, as to lessen the chances of unjust accusation. And can it be supposed that we are so blind as ever to be able to fancy that it is impossible that under this law an innocent woman may be accused? On the contrary, it is obvious that the question of a woman's honour is one in which mistaken accusations are peculiarly likely to occur.

[34] The Acts require no witness against the woman except the policeman, who, though he must substantiate on oath his own belief that the woman is a prostitute, is not bound to produce on oath what the grounds of that belief are. If the justice of the peace is satisfied with this substantiation, the woman is condemned under the Act.

The honour therefore of every woman is by this law intrusted to two men, the one the justice of the peace and the other the policeman, who, let it be carefully observed, is expressly hired by Government for the one stated object of detecting unchaste women.

[91] The attempt to define a prostitute is as difficult as it is . . . to fix on that point at which a man may be stamped as an immoral character. Nevertheless, if the purification of society were the object of these laws, instead of the protection of one sex against the other, it would be possible, for legal purposes, to define prostitution, although the definition might be arbitrary. But for the purposes of this law, which does not aim at the purification of society, but only at the protection of one sex against the other, it is absolutely necessary that definitions should be avoided, and that the wholesale treatment of the weaker sex should be carried on in a maze of indefiniteness and arbitrary selection.

Josephine Butler, Some Thoughts on the Present Aspect of the Crusade against the State Regulation of Vice, *1874*

[15] Men have imposed on women a stricter rule in morality than they have imposed on themselves, or are willing themselves to obey. This may be to some extent the secret of the unwillingness to many men to see women laying siege in earnest to the great instituted iniquity; they fear lest a discovery of practice as well as theory, too lax to be defended by the least thoughtful, should come to the light, and disturb the social order, or rather disorder, which men have hitherto ordained . . . . [16] Those who thus judge have missed the Christian ideal in the picture they have presented to their own imaginations of the perfection either of true womanhood or true manhood . . . . The way in which even good men, professing to be

23

believers in Jesus of Nazareth, judge this matter, the way in which they cling to their unequal judgments of unchaste men and unchaste women, and continue to separate, by an impassable barrier, the lapsed among women from the pure or the so-called pure; the way in which they dread any probing of the subject, and deprecate the direct action, and the searching and purifying influence of enlightened women in the matter, is so un-Christlike, so unholy, that it calls for the most stern and constantly-repeated rebuke.

Josephine Butler, Social Purity, *1879*

[5] The root of the evil is the unequal standard in morality; the false idea that there is one code of morality for men and another for women, which has prevailed since the beginning, which was proclaimed to be false by Him who spoke as the Son of God, and yet which grew up again after his time in Christian communities, endorsed by the silence of the Church itself, and which has within the last century been publicly proclaimed as an axiom by almost all the governments of the civilized and Christian world.

This unequal standard has more or less coloured and shaped the whole of our social life. Even in lands where a high degree of morality and attachment to domestic life prevails, the measure of the moral strictness of the people is too often the bitterness of their treatment of the erring *woman*, and of her alone. Some will tell me that this is the inevitable rule, and that [6] the sternest possible reprobation of the *female* sinner, as being the most deeply culpable, has marked every age and all teaching in which the moral standard was high. No! – not every age, nor all teaching! There stands on the page of history one marked exception; and, so far as I know, one only – that of Christ.

[8] We never hear it carelessly or complacently asserted of a young woman that '*she* is only sowing her wild oats.' This is not a pleasant aspect of the question; but let us deal faithfully with it. It is a fact, that numbers even of moral and religious people have permitted themselves to accept and condone in man what is fiercely condemned in woman.

And do you see the logical necessity involved in this? It is that a large section of female society has to be told off – set aside, so to speak, to minister to the irregularities of the excusable man. That section is doomed to death, hurled to despair; while another section of womanhood is kept strictly and almost forcibly guarded in domestic purity. Thus even good and moral men have so judged in regard to the vice of sexual immorality as to concede in social opinion *all* that the male profligate can desire.

[21] Is it not time that the woman's voice should be heard in this matter – that she should have a veto upon that immoral claim which men have passed on to their descendants, generation after generation, to the sacrifice, in the interests of impurity, of vast armies of her sisters, women born with capacities, as others, for honourable relationships and spiritual perfecting? Women *have* at last spoken, thanks be to God!

[31] The whole cruelty of the law falling on their own sex for the fancied preservation of the health of men, woke up the womanhood of this land . . . . Never till the woman's public defiance of this law, and of the Government which made it, was heard – never till this sacred cry of revolt was uttered aloud, did this war against impurity begin in earnest. How then should I be silent on this topic? . . . . [32] No amount of 'rescue work' among women, no quiet propagandism of social purity among men, would ever have excited this hostility. The opposition we meet is a cheering token – a proof that we have struck a vital point in the evil thing.

Elizabeth Blackwell, 'Rescue Work in Relation to Prostitution and Disease', 1881

[115] First. By prostitution is meant mercenary and promiscuous sexual intercourse, without affection and without mutual responsibility.

Second. Its object is on one side pecuniary gain, on the other side the exercise of physical lust. It is the conversion of men into brutes and of women into machines.

Third. So far from its being necessary to humanity, it is the destruction of humanity. It is the production of disease, of gross physical cruelty, of moral death.

Lastly. It should be checked by legislative enactment, and destroyed by social opinion.

[. . . .]

[116] I speak of the conversion of soulless lust into a business traffic – of the system of brothels, procurers, and so-called Contagious Diseases Acts – the system which provides for, not checks, vice. I solemnly declare that so far from this system being a necessary part of society, it is the greatest crime that can be committed against our common humanity.

[127] A law which makes it a legal offence for an individual suffering from venereal disease to hold sexual intercourse with another person, and a ground for separation, is positively required in order to establish a true principle of legislation, a principle of just equality and responsibility which will educate the moral sense of the rising generation and protect

the innocent. Any temporary inconveniences which might arise before the wisest methods of administering the law had been established by experience, would be as nothing compared with the elevating national influence of substituting a right method of dealing with the diseases of vice for the present unjust and evil method.

Elizabeth Blackwell, Counsel to Parents on the Moral Education of their Children, *1882*

[44] The women more directly involved in this widespread evil of licentiousness are the women of the poorer classes of society . . . . The extreme danger of moral degradation, in those classes of young women, who constitute such an immense preponderance of the female population, is at once evident. These women are everywhere, interlinked with every class of society. They form an important part (often the larger female portion) of every well-to-do household. They are the companions and inevitable teachers of infancy and childhood. They often form the chief, or only female influence which meets the young man in early professional, business, or even college life. They meet him in every place of public amusement, in his walks at night, in his travels at home and abroad. By day and by night, the young man away from home is brought into free intercourse, not with women of his own class, but with poor working girls and women, who form the numerical bulk of the female population, who are found in every place, and ready for every service. Educated girls are watched and guarded. The young man meets them in rare moments only, under supervision, and generally under unnatural restraint; but the poor girl he meets constantly, freely, at any time and place. Any clear-sighted person who will quietly observe the way in which female servants (for instance) regard very young men, their superiors in station, can easily comprehend the dangers of such association . . . . [45] The customs of civilized nations practically consider poor women as subjects for a life so dishonourable, that a rich man feels justified in ostracising wife, sister, or daughter, who is guilty of the slightest approach to such life. It is the great mass of poor women who are regarded as (and sometimes brutally stated to be) the subjects to be used for the benefit of the upper classes. Young and innocent men, it is true, fall into vice or are led into it, or are tempted into it by older women, and are not deliberate betrayers. But the rubicon of chastity once passed, the moral descent is rapid, and the preying upon the poor soon commences. The miserable slaves in houses of prostitution are the outcasts of the poor. The young girls followed at night in the streets are the honest working girl, the young servant seeking a short outdoor relief to her dreary life, as well as the unhappy fallen girl, who has become in her turn the seducer.

[50] Of the multitude of those who fall into vice, many ultimately marry, and with injured moral qualities and corrupted tastes, become the creators of poor men's homes. The rest drift into a permanent life of vice. The injurious effects of unchastity upon womanly character already noted, can be studied step by step, to their complete development in that great class of the population – the recognised prostitutes. Their marked characteristics are recklessness, sloth and drunkenness . . . . Unchaste women become a most dangerous class of the community. To these bad qualities is added another, wherever, as in France, this evil life is accepted as a part of society, pro- [51] vided for, organized, or legalized; this last result of confirmed licentiousness, is a hardness of character, so complete, so resistent of all improving influences, that the wisest and gentlest efforts to restore, are utterly hopeless before the confirmed and hardened prostitute.

Catherine Booth, The Iniquity of State Regulated Vice, *1884*

[5] [E]very true woman in England, who will really examine the question, must feel bound to give her influence towards the repeal of these abominable Acts. I have been told, and I dare say our friends on the platform have been told, that it is a disgrace for a woman to meddle with this question. But I say if measures are passed which are so obnoxious that it is a disgrace and abomination to discuss them – the [6] odium of such disgrace rests with those who instituted them.

[7] We cannot degrade women without degrading men. We find wherever woman has been regarded merely as the instrument of man's pleasure or gain, there, men are low and mean and sensual, and I was going to say devilish . . . . And I was also going to say that I thanked God it was so, because justice is the foundation of all real improvement. We have as much right to be considered as men – and perhaps future generations will find out that we are quite as important in the scale of being. I sometimes smile when I hear of 'Woman's influence on Society,' as if woman were not part of society, and in this country, at all events, the larger [8] half . . . . If all the women had been of my mind these laws would never have taken effect. I would have fought against them while I had a drop of blood left in my body . . . . No police officer or magistrate should ever have made me submit to them. I admire the women who have thrown themselves from buildings in preference to submitting to them, and I believe that these women will prove to have been pioneers in this movement for moral purity. We know the truest test of a nation's moral condition, is the sanctity or profanity of its treatment of women – we know this, and therefore I say

that any measures or laws which tend to break down those great barriers which God has placed around the natural modesty of woman are the greatest outrages which can be perpetrated on any people.

Jane Clapperton, Scientific Meliorism, 1885

[303] The awful fact that in London alone there are upwards of eighty thousand prostitutes, reveals how far distant we are as yet from the national adoption of such sex relations as would be worthy the name of a *pure monogamy*; and this other startling fact, that as civilization advances, this great evil does not diminish but increases, and in this nineteenth century is fatally corrupting the merest children, calls for a thorough sifting of this hideous subject, and an exposing of the forces that underlie the painful social condition. Miss Ellice Hopkins' work amongst ladies is strikingly significant. It shows that we are rapidly approaching the conscious epoch of evolution, and that even the strong sentiment of delicacy, admirable though it be, will no longer permit humanity to close its eyes to truth, however ghastly.

Annie Besant, The Law of Population, 1889

[27] The more marriage is delayed, the more prostitution spreads. It is necessary to gravely remind all advocates of late marriage that men do not and will not live single; and all women, and all men who honour women, should protest against a teaching which would inevitably make permanent that terrible social evil which is the curse of civilisation, and which condemns numbers of unhappy creatures to a disgraceful and revolting calling. Prostitution is an evil which we should strive to eradicate not to perpetuate, and late marriage, generally adopted, would most certainly perpetuate it. The state of the streets of our large towns at nightfall is the result of deferred marriage, and marriage is deferred owing to the ever-increasing difficulty of maintaining a large family in anything like comfort.

Elizabeth Blackwell, 'Purchase of Women: the Great Economic Blunder', c. 1890

[156] It may be urged that women 'consent' to be purchased, and that therefore there is a radical difference between the purchase of the bodies of men and women, which the anti-slavery movement has pronounced illegal, and the purchase of women by men which we are now considering. The sophistry of such evasion will be apparent if the question of 'consent'

and the specious hypocrisy generally involved in freedom of contract be closely examined. Freedom of contract can only take place between those who in certain essential particulars are equals.

[159] It is now a fact that in every large city, no woman with any pretension to natural attractiveness can fail to meet a purchaser. There are men who think it neither shame nor wrong to purchase for shillings or pounds, as the case may be, a temporary physical gratification, without reflection upon the inevitable results, individual and social, of their temporary action. The knowledge that money may be gained so easily, spreads from woman to woman. The contrast between the ease with which the wages of sin may be gained, and the laborious, even crushing methods of honest industry, becomes an ever present and burning temptation to working women.

It is undoubtedly true that the numerical excess of women in Great Britain, with other economic facts, intensifies most heavily upon women the grinding pressure of our present industrial system. All rescue workers seeking to help their fallen sisters are constantly confronted with the appalling answer, 'Give [160] me work; I cannot starve.'

[161] The great army of domestic servants, whether in public or private dwellings, are surrounded by constant temptations to supplement their wages or relieve their monotonous labour by selling themselves. When we remember the conditions under which the vast mass of servants have grown up, the exposures and privations of their homes, their undeveloped mental state in relation to social duties, the exhausting work upon which the majority of them enter in hotels, lodging-houses, struggling households, or the special danger of rich, careless establishments, and realize both the condition under which their service drags on and the natural instincts of the human being, then it is easy to understand why to a frightfully increasing extent they yield to the solicitations to which they are exposed. The five shillings gained at night becomes an important addition to scanty wages, the stolen pleasures an intoxicating relief to drudgery.

[166] The woman, however 'fallen,' is still a human being with its desperate clinging to life. Let it be realized what is involved in thousands of women living to the age of three-score years and ten, who must feed themselves three times a day, and provide lodging, clothing, and the satisfaction of all human needs by the repeated sale of their bodies, thousands of women, with all the craving and ever active necessities of the human being, bodies and souls to be kept alive by the money of their buyers, and who are compelled to use every art of corruption to find the fresh purchasers through whom they have learned to live – women to whom lust and drink rapidly become a second nature, and sloth and

falsehood habitual; women driven on by ceaseless material needs to lower and lower phases of misery and vice, in whom a bitterness is engendered that revenges itself on the weakness and innocence of youth, tempting the lad when the adult ceases to purchase; women who – terrible fact – finally losing their own marketable value, and scourged by their own daily recurring needs, throw away the last remnants of womanly instinct, and drag down young girls into their hell of life.

[Harriet Nokes], Thirty-Two Years in a House of Mercy, *1895*

[89] [I]t is grossly and cruelly unfair to others – to take a girl from the streets, put her into a Refuge or Home for a few weeks, and because she behaves quietly, to suppose that she is a changed character. It is a fearful risk, and hence I have come to think Short Homes, as they are called, are grievous mistakes. I am speaking, of course, of girls who have lived in open sin, for ever so short a time, not of those who have had what is called a first fall. But some of these cases turn out upon investigation to be by no means a first fall, or, if it be so, there is sometimes a very depraved mind at the back of it.

[93] It must be remembered that a large number of these unfortunate girls do not *mean* to earn their living: idleness brings many of them to their ruin, and the low state of morality in which they are brought up makes them look upon the streets as always a possible way of gaining a livelihood.

[95] [W]hat shall be said of the broken hearts and despairing lives of girls, ruined and flung aside at fifteen, sixteen, and eighteen years of age. Here is a bright, pretty-faced child, of fourteen-and-a-half, brought to us: she is a mother! No one who has not witnessed it can dream of what the miserable consequences are (often for life), physically and mentally, to girls of this age, and the baby face of the poor little mother looks at you with pathetic eyes, which seem to say, 'How shall I understand?'

Ellice Hopkins, The Power of Womanhood, *1899*

[30] [W]hile we have this social code, which is in direct violation of the moral law, we may set on foot any number of Rescue Societies, Preventive Agencies, Acts for the Legal Protection of the Young, etc., but all our efforts will be in vain . . . . The tacitly accepted necessity for something short of the moral law for men will – again I say it – work out with the certainty

of a mathematical law a degraded and outcast class, with its disease, its insanity, its foul contamination of the young, its debasement of manhood, its disintegration of the State, its curse to the community.

Birth control

Birth control – or at least discussion of it – remains largely anathema in Victorian Britain. However, a number of Malthusian freethinkers advance a case for the desirability of the practice, on grounds of maternal health and the benefits of sexual activity as well from the 'classic' neo-Malthusian economic argument. Although figures from the social purity end of the spectrum tend to regard contraception as merely an incitement to further lustful exploitation of women by men, by the end of the century they are also making a case for the limitation of the family, though through marital continence and female control over marital intercourse.

Jane Clapperton, Scientific Meliorism, *1885*

[174] There is in the general or popular mind of the present day a tolerably correct estimate of the importance of this appetite . . . and by a few thoughtful individual minds one of the *greatest* and most *pressing* problems is plainly seen to be – How shall this function be exercised during the whole period of virile life, without injury to society and with all due regard to personal dignity and purity? To those reformers who perceive that human intelligence has found a means by which to subjugate the law of population and regulate the birth-rate, an enormous obstacle is, in their minds, swept away.

[177] Not animalism alone, but animalism combined with philoprogenitiveness will be the complex force to bring into the world the coming generations, and two results will follow. The inestimable blessing of parental love and parental responsibility, *assumed by choice*, will be the outward heritage of all, and inwardly, the new race will by inheritance partake of natures that are broader and fuller than the type of man in whom the pure and tender love of children has no existence, and animality dominates sociability.

[334] [S]ince, by careful use of artificial checks, parentage, and hence the propagation of disease, may be avoided, all adult individuals of ordinary public morality or conscientiousness are free to marry, as spontaneous impulse dictates. *Eugenics* is *not* the primary consideration in marriage.

31

Annie Besant, The Law of Population, 1889

[24] No words can add strength to this statement, proving the absolute right of women to complete repose from sexual disturbance during this slow recovery of the normal condition of the womb. Many a woman in fairly comfortable circumstances suffers from lack of knowledge of physical laws, and from the reckless English disregard of all conjugal prudence . . . . [I]t is only a perverted moral sense which leads men and women to shut their eyes to these sad consequences of over-large families, and causes them thus to disregard the plainest laws of health. Sexual intemperance, the over-procreation of children, is as immoral as intemperance in drink.

[31] It is clearly useless to preach the limitation of the family and to conceal the means whereby such limitation may be effected. If the limitation be a duty, it cannot be wrong to afford such information as shall enable people to discharge it.

There are various prudential checks which have been suggested, but further investigation of this intricate subject is sorely needed . . . . The main difficulty in the way is the absurd notion that prudential checks are obscene, and very few doctors have the courage to face the odium that would arise from a frank treatment of the subject. Some medical men do, at the present time, recommend the use of checks to their female patients, but even these would hesitate ere they openly dealt with the subject. The consequence of this unfortunate state of things is that much doubt hangs over the efficacy of the checks proposed . . . .

[32] The complete ignorance of their own bodies, which is supposed to be a necessary part of 'female modesty', makes necessary a preliminary word on the mechanism of the womb and the process of fertilisation. The passage leading from the exterior of the body to the mouth of the womb varies from four to five inches. At its upper end, projecting into it, is the mouth of the womb, which is normally closed by two thick lips; so that the womb may be regarded as a bag with its mouth kept shut by an india-rubber ring. Now, fertilisation depends on the active element, the spermatozoa, from the male reaching the ova (eggs) of the female, and this can only occur by the spermatozoa making their way through the mouth of the womb into its interior cavity. This mouth opens slightly from time to time during sexual excitement, and thus makes it possible for the spermatozoa to work their way in. If then the mouth of the womb can be kept closed, or in any way guarded, no fertilisation can take place.

Under these circumstances the most reliable checks are those which close the passage into the womb. Of these there are three useful kinds; the soluble pessary, the india-rubber pessary, and the sponge.

[38] It is . . . objected that preventative checks are 'unnatural' and 'immoral'. 'Unnatural' they are not: for the human brain is nature's highest

product, and all improvements on irrational nature are most purely natural: preventive checks are no more unnatural than every other custom of civilisation . . . . But 'immoral'. What is morality? It is the greatest good of the greatest number. It is immoral to give life where you cannot support it. It is immoral to bring children into the world when you cannot clothe, feed, and educate them. It is immoral to crowd new life into already over-crowded houses, and to give birth to children wholesale, who never have a chance of healthy [39] life. Conjugal prudence is most highly moral, and those who endeavor to vilify and degrade these means in the eyes of the public, and who speak of them as 'immoral' and 'disgusting', are little aware of the moral responsibility they incur thereby. As already shown, to reject preventive intercourse is in reality to choose the other three true population checks – poverty, prostitution, and celibacy . . .

But the knowledge of these scientific checks, would, it is argued, make vice bolder, and would increase unchastity among women by making it safe. Suppose that this were so, it might save some broken hearts and some deserted children; men ruin women and go scatheless, and then bitterly object that their victims escape something of public shame. And if so, are all to suffer, so that one or two already corrupt in heart may be preserved from becoming corrupt in act?

Ellice Hopkins, The Power of Womanhood, 1899

[143] I have stood aghast at the advice given by Christian mothers, often backed up by a doctor whom they affirm to be a Christian man, in order to save the health of the wife or limit the increase of the family. The heads of the profession, in England, I believe, are sound on this point, a conference having been held some years ago by our leading medical men to denounce all such 'fruits of philosophy'[1] as physically injurious and morally lowering. [. . . .]

[L]et us women silently band together to preserve the sanctity of the family, of the home, and sternly to bar out the entrance of all that defileth – all that sensualizes her men and enfeebles their self-mastery, all that renders the heart of her women too craven to encounter the burdens of being the mothers of a mighty race, flowing out into all the lands to civilize and Christianize, and 'bear the white man's burthen.'

1   This alludes to the birth control tract, Charles Knowlton's *Fruits of Philosophy*, an edition of which was published by Charles Bradlaugh and Annie Besant, who were tried for obscenity (though acquitted).

Ignorance and sex education

The attack on ignorance as not necessarily any guarantee of innocence is mounted. Already the problem arises of parents who are unable to provide the instruction required, and the question of who, in that case, should do so. This is another of the areas in which the similarities between social purity and freethought can be discerned: both camps are for enlightenment and against obscurantism in the name of a cloistered 'virtue'.

Elizabeth Blackwell, 'Rescue Work in Relation to Prostitution and Disease', 1881

[120] [A]ny efforts that can be made to teach personal modesty to the little boys and girls in our Board schools all over the country form a powerful influence to prevent prostitution. Attention to sexual moralty [*sic*] in educational establishments everywhere, in public and private schools and colleges, amongst young men and young women, is [121] of fundamental importance.

Elizabeth Blackwell, Counsel to Parents on the Moral Education of their Children, 1882

[67] Although direct and impressive instruction and guidance in relation to sex is not only required by the young, but is indispensable to their physical and moral welfare, yet the utmost caution is necessary in giving such guidance, in order that the natural susceptibilities of the nature be not wounded. It is a point on which youth of both sexes are keenly sensitive, and any want of tact in addressing the individual, or any forcible introduction of the subject, where the previous relations of parent and child have not produced the trust and affectionate mutual respect, which would render communication on all serious subjects of life, a rational sequence in their relations, may do harm instead of good. Where the con- [68] science of the parent has only been awakened late in life to this high duty to the child, the attempt to approach the subject with the young adult is often deeply resented by both boy and girl. In such case the necessary counsel may be better given by a stranger – by the physician who will speak with acknowledged authority, or by some book of impressive character, when such an one (much needed) shall have been prepared. That this is a very imperfect fulfilment of parental duty, is true; but it is often all that the parent can attempt, where the high and important character of sex has not been understood at the outset of family life, and thus not guided the past education of the children.

Jane Clapperton, Scientific Meliorism, 1885

[182] But the clear and definite teaching regarding this emotion should be, that love is essentially noble, having nothing to conceal, nothing to fear, nothing to be ashamed of, and it is *only* when mixed with some anti-social feeling, such as jealousy or tyranny . . . that there *is* something to excite in us a sense of shame . . . .

[183] But are such lessons required? I think I hear my reader ask, and is it not to take the bloom, the modesty, the delicate refinement off a maiden's mind to speak to her of love at all? I reply – it is possible to treat the whole subject with refinement; and if this is not done, the vulgar aspects of the question are certain to be forced upon minds unfurnished with true ideas to counteract the false.

Edith Lees Ellis, 'A Noviciate for Marriage', c. 1892

[11] In the future, sexual knowledge will form part of every educational scheme, and the study of Eugenics will be as important in a school curriculum as botany or Euclid. To learn about Love as a botanist [12] learns about flowers may later save human beings mistakes which a sentimental or chaotic view of passion incurs. Physiological needs, romantic desires, and Nature's imperatives demands confuse the novice in the art of Love and often make 'sin' out of mere ignorance. If monogamy is to be the form of evolved sexual relationship it is time we tried every device to obtain the substance and not be any longer content to remain with the shadow.

[13] As a preliminary step we must educate boys and girls in the art of love, and teach them how to approach cleanly and honestly the physical facts of sexual life in experiments which imply neither laxity nor barter.

[18] In face of the fact that marriage differs from other relationships only on its physical side, girls are taught that it is unwomanly to discuss sexual questions with their future husbands. It is a matter of everyday knowledge that a large proportion of brides marry still with no clear idea of the sexual function which they promise to fulfil. They marry in the stage of romance and girlish enthusiasm . . . . In the unwedded girl's idealised love-world nothing is even sanely virile. Brusqueness or brutality is not imaginable in marriage, which only presupposes romantic love . . . . Young girls who enter marriage with this equipment, and without even a true theoretical knowledge of sexual life, are often as much shocked and unnerved by the virility of true manhood as if they had been caught in their sleep by the coarse paws of a satyr.

[Harriet Nokes], Thirty-Two Years in a House of Mercy, *1895*

[89] It is by *living with them* that you get to know the awful depths of *ignorance*, as well as sin, you have to deal with.

Chapter Two

ৰ

The suffrage era, 1902–1918

Introduction

The suffrage movement has sometimes occluded the diverse range of causes for which women were campaigning at the beginning of the twentieth century, and for which, in fact, many saw the vote as necessary but not sufficient in itself to achieve reform. Prevailing concerns about venereal diseases and eugenic anxieties were deployed by women to articulate feminist agendas around marriage, motherhood and morality. Prostitution remained a burning issue. Dissatisfaction with women's status within marriage and the glaring inequality of the divorce laws continued. Issues around birth control were beginning to be voiced, both in the oblique form of arguments that women should bear no more children than their health and energies could bear, with fewer and healthier children better than a larger number who died or were sickly, and more direct advocacy of the use of contraception. The desirability of sex education was increasingly being advocated, and strategies as to how it might be undertaken suggested. A discourse of radical celibacy as a reasoned response to the inequity of existing heterosexual relations was advanced by a number of writers. Some women also began to criticize simplistic attitudes of moral superiority to male lust prevalent in some sections of the suffrage movement, and to suggest a politics in which sexual pleasure might play a part. A few radical individuals such as Edith Lees Ellis and Stella Browne engaged openly with issues of same-sex desire and relationship. Through the agency of the Women's Cooperative Guild the voices of working-class women were enabled to be heard, both in evidence to the Royal Commission on Marriage and Divorce, and in the 1915 volume *Maternity: Letters from Working Women*.

Other recommended resources

The Royal Commission on Marriage and Divorce (which reported in 1912) not only took evidence from women, it was the first Royal Commission to include women as members, a precedent followed by the Royal Commission on Venereal Diseases (appointed 1913, reported 1916). The (non-official, but with much establishment support) National Birth-Rate Commission set up by the National Council of Public Morals included some of the women whose writings are excerpted here, and heard evidence from others, and it produced several reports, including *Youth and Sex*, on sex education, and one on the cinema and its moral implications, as well as on the birth rate and the question of contraception. *The Freewoman* (1911–1912) was a radical if short-lived feminist journal, and the journals of the several suffrage organizations, if not so daringly radical in their recommendations, frequently mentioned the inegalitarianism of the laws relating to sexual offences, the problem of venereal diseases, criticisms of marriage, etc.[1] A rather rare journal, *Urania*, advanced arguments that the existing differences between the two sexes were less stable and eternal than assumed.

Marriage

The themes of the dark side of marriage as it exists, and the potential for a transcendent new form of monogamy, underlie discussions of marriage at this time. Opinions differ about the indissolubility of unions. A belief in the necessity of greater female power within marriage, however, is common to all these writers. The deleterious effects on marriage of extreme ignorance in brides of what awaits them are becoming an established theme.

Frances Swiney, The Awakening of Women, *1908*

[214] Easy-going divorce laws simply imply a growing selfish disinclination on the part of individuals to submit to unpleasant restraint for the sake of others, either for the body politic or for the ulterior cause of morality. It is again a question of suffering. A choice between personal relief and the general weal, between individual sacrifice and unbridled laxity . . . .

---

1   Leslie Garner, *Stepping Stones to Women's Liberty: Feminist Ideas in the Women's Suffrage Movement* (London: Heinemann, 1984).

[215] We cannot, as advocated by many talented but specious writers, run the fearful risk of trying experimental marriages. Whatever hinders marriage, grounded on a basis of love and mutual respect, is hostile to morality; but if marriage is encouraged and consummated, the most rigid limitations should be placed on divorce, as the very foundations of society are dependent for their stability on the purity and inviolability of family ties and obligations. The sacredness of the marriage bond must be kept inviolable.

Cicely Hamilton, Marriage as a Trade, 1909

[35] If it be granted that marriage is . . . essentially a trade on the part of woman – the exchange of her person for the means of subsistence – it is legitimate to inquire into the manner in which that trade is carried on, and to compare the position of the worker in the matrimonial market with the position of the worker in any other market. Which brings us at once to the fact – arising from the compulsory nature of the profession – that it is carried on under disadvantages unknown and unfelt by those who earn their living by other methods.

[253] The custom of regarding one half of the race as sent into the world to excite desire in the other half does not appear to be of real advantage to either moiety, in that it has produced the over-sexed man and the over-sexed woman, the attitude of mind which sneers at self-control. Such an attitude the establishment of marriage for woman upon a purely voluntary basis ought to go far to correct; since it is hardly conceivable that women, who have other careers open to them and by whom ignorance is no longer esteemed as a merit, will consent to run quite unnecessary risks from which their unmarried sisters are exempt. When the intending wife and mother no longer considers it her duty to be innocent and complacent, the intending husband and father will learn, from sheer necessity, to see more virtue in self-restraint.

Margaret Stephens, Woman and Marriage, 1910

[59] A man and woman filled with love for each other seek – though the aim itself may be unconscious – to create some living symbol of their love, and are thus drawn into union by the natural physical means provided. For conjugal love, although first born in the soul as an inspiration, and then entering the heart as a passion, finally reaches the body as a desire for unity . . . . [60] This material or physical side of it, when properly treated from the beginning, can be so ennobled, so elevated, that it becomes, as it were,

the natural outcome of this human love. On the other hand, it can be so improperly treated from the beginning that appalling disease of mind as well as of body may result. Improper treatment may be due to want of thought or sheer ignorance in some cases, and to want of heart and to gross selfishness in others.

On all sexual matters the decision should rest on the justly and considerately formed judgement of the wife. Of all her rights there is surely none so evident as this personal right; and if she be healthy enough to possess the unperverted instinct of sex, or wise enough to understand and sympathise with its possession by others, she will never be unnecessarily churlish over this privilege, while on the other hand, she will take care that the boundary of moderation is not overstepped.

Olive Schreiner, **Woman and Labour,** *1911*

[25] [T]he direction in which the endeavour of woman to readjust herself to the new conditions of life is leading to-day, is not towards a greater sexual laxity, or promiscuity, or to an increased self-indulgence, but toward a higher appreciation of the sacredness of all sex relations, and clearer perception of the sex relation between man and woman as the basis of human society . . . . [26] [I]t will lead to a closer, more permanent, more emotionally and intellectually complete and intimate relation between the individual man and woman. And if in the present disco-ordinate transitional stage of our social growth it is found necessary to allow of readjustment by means of divorce, it will not be because such readjustments will be regarded lightly, but rather, as when, in a complex and delicate mechanism moved by a central spring, we allow in the structure for the readjustment and regulation of that spring, because on its absolute perfection of action depends the movement of the whole mechanism.

Lucy Re-Bartlett, **The Coming Order,** *1911*

[24] One morality for the two sexes requires that man shall come to marriage as pure as woman – can woman find the strength for saying 'No' when he does not? Again, one morality requires a fidelity in the husband after marriage equal to that of the wife – can woman find the strength for separation when this is not observed?

Once more we repeat that the duty of this period is a special duty – the duty of sternness, which pertains to times of war. The beauty of forgiveness and mercy is not forgotten, nor the purity and spirituality which may well accompany them. But this is not the moment for gentleness if a purer social order is to be established.

[53] Why is it that marriage so often lowers love – that the love of husband and wife is nearly always less exquisite, less poetical, than the love which reigns in the days of engagement? Blessed exceptions there are where the love grows higher in the married life, but in most cases though the tie may grow closer, it does not grow higher. Rarely do we find reverence. Commonplaceness is the more usual atmosphere, even with the relatively happy people – bitterness in the case of the unhappy.

The reason for this is to be found in the unsatisfied *souls* of most married people – not even the happy ones have usually sufficient scope for honouring themselves and their wedded mates. And the reason, in turn, of this insufficient scope to honour may be found in most cases, as we can see if we reflect well, in the imperfect ordering of the sexual life. On this side of marriage the physical is generally allowed to assume too great a prominence – is not sufficiently held in balance by the spiritual. But how is this balance, so delicate and so difficult, to be fitly held? It will only be possible to hold it with even a degree of equilibrium when the new standard of service is fully established as a standard at least – when it is clearly recognised that this is the principle which *should* govern, and all divergence is called clearly and simply wrong.

Christabel Pankhurst, The Great Scourge, *1913*

[63] [W]hat women have not known is that marriage as a physical union is (apart from the natural risk of childbirth, which also they foresee) a matter of appalling danger to women.

The danger of marriage is due to the low moral standard and the immoral conduct of men. Men before marriage, and often while they are married, contract sexual disease [64] from prostitutes and give this disease to their wives.

[65] What women must realise is that sexual disease communicated to them by their husbands is the cause of the special ailments and the poor health by which so many women are afflicted. Women are not naturally invalids, as they have been taught to believe. They are invalids because they are the victims of the sexual diseases known as syphilis and gonorrhoea. [. . . .]

[66] Never again must young women enter into marriage blindfolded. From now onwards they must be warned of the fact that marriage is intensely dangerous, until such time as men's moral standards are completely changed and they become as chaste and clean-living as women.

Mary Scharlieb, What It Means to Marry, *1914*

[34] [O]ne of the worst features of present-day society is the eagerness with which not only girls who are ignorant and inexperienced, but also their mothers, who ought to know better, hail with satisfaction an engagement to any man who is in a position to give a suitable home to a wife.

[57] The husband and wife whose union is looked upon as indissoluble, and whose respect for their mutual bond is reinforced by a sane and vigorous public opinion, are in the best position to perfect their characters. No one is perfect; everyone likes his own way, and no one holds exactly the same views as do his fellows; hence disagreements and breaches of peace. In married life, however, there is constant daily adjustment of mutual imperfections, and in the necessary consideration for differing standpoints, political, religious, and social, much is gained. Do we not constantly see that [58] mutual influence, both conscious and uncon- scious, and still more mutual discipline, painful though this may be, produce a fineness of character and a perfection of self-control that are invaluable aspects for the race as well as for the individuals primarily concerned?

The greatest benefits of marriage are not always found in the so-called 'happy marriages.' The best results may be looked for where pain and sorrow have wrought their refining and strengthening work . . . .

[59] Permanence of union and indissolubility of marriage ought to be the ideal reverenced by society, sanctioned by law and inculcated by education

Lucy Re-Bartlett, Sex and Sanctity, *1914*

[10] Women especially are frequently ignorant of their own nature until it is too late, and this ignorance is far more often the cause of conjugal misery than any faultiness of law. Marriage to-day, in short, is entered upon with a blindness which would be thought mad in any other undertaking, and until this can be changed, no law can do very much to better things.

[63] In the past, woman's way of preserving her ideality has often lain in abstracting herself partially, that is to say with her mind and heart, from all that part of the sexual relation which she found unlovely. And the insult that she offered to man as well as to herself by such division of her life, man has very often felt, and the patronage which this type of woman has sometimes let herself feel for man, has often been answered by man in a bitterness and contempt for woman. The woman of to-day who can

understand no such splitting off of ideality – whose faith is high enough to let her both feel and passionately affirm that there is no part of life which cannot and should not be beautiful – this woman, it may be, points to a long and arduous path, but she also 'opens gates'. There is no part of life any longer shut out from the scheme of beauty – from the possibility of being folded in its light.

Edith Lees Ellis, 'The Love of Tomorrow', c. 1914–1915

[5] It is more than probable that the evolved relationship of the future will be monogamy – but a monogamy as much wider and more beautiful than the present caricature of it as the sea is wider and more delicious than a frog-pond. The lifelong faithful love of one man for one woman is the exception and not the rule. The law of affinity being as a subtle and indefinable as the law of gravitation, we may, by and by, find it worth while to give it its complete opportunity in those realms where it can manifest most potently. We are on the wrong bridge if we imagine that licence is the easiest way to freedom, or laxity to beauty. The bridge which will bear us must be strong enough to support us while experiments are tried.

Edith Lees Ellis, 'Marriage and Divorce', c. 1914–1915

[33] The time has come to educate sanely, to emancipate woman economically, to purify and yet enlarge love from a mere sex function into a humanised spiritual function . . . . [I]t is possible that marriage in the future may become a fine domestic experiment in lovely living . . . . Puritans often forget that the expressions of love are individual and diversified, so that even what we call sensual hunger may be diverted or satisfied in very subtle ways if narrow domesticity or insane jealousy do not bar the way. The economic dependence of woman and the sexual gluttony of man, the traditional but false idea that possession in persons is legitimate . . . may gradually open the way to a saner and [34] cleaner enterprise in what may be rationally termed a 'free marriage' rather than the much-abused term of 'free love.'

Mary Scharlieb, The Seven Ages of Woman, 1915

[66] Formerly it was by no means uncommon for unfortunate brides to say that they had been shocked by learning *after marriage* the facts of married life that they ought to have known before marriage. Weird stories were told of women who had gone through the ceremony of mar- [67] riage and

who, after months had passed, were still wives only in name, because they had been unable to understand, or to consent to, their husbands' lawful demands. It is quite possible – nay, it is even desirable – that young girls should learn much physiology, and even the physiology of the reproductive organs, without in any way understanding how such knowledge may personally apply to themselves; but the personal application of knowledge which is most undesirable for the adolescent is an absolute necessity for the prospective bride. No girl ought to be permitted to promise to undertake duties which she does not understand.

Edith Lees Ellis, 'Semi-Detached Marriage', c. 1915

[27] If monogamy is to be the relationship of the future it will have to widen its doors, subjugate its jealousies, and accept many modern devices for spiritualising physical passion. By this is not meant that the senses are to be depleted, but, rather, enlarged and transformed. The lust of the flesh will give place to the passion of the flesh, and two made utterly one will not imply either rape, gluttony, or personal absorption, but the using of personal devotion for larger than individual ends. In a noviciate for marriage, and in experiments after marriage which are within law and order, many nerve-wearing and heart-rending experiences might [28] be saved . . . .

Property in persons is near its doom . . . . When the artificial characteristics of male and female drop away, and human beings of both sexes are allowed the full liberty of their personalities, marriage will become a sacrament and cease to be a sacrilege.

Desire, pleasure and satisfaction

There is a gradually developing recognition of the female potential for sexual desire and pleasure, and the concept that sexual activity may have physical and emotional benefits besides its reproductive aspect. However, it is also argued that many women do not 'fall' through sexual desire but from a complex of other factors.

Maud Churton Braby, Modern Marriage, and How to Bear It, 1908

[50] It is a well-known physiological fact that numbers of women become insane in middle life who would not have done so if they had enjoyed the ordinary duties, pleasures and preoccupations of matrimony – if their women's natures had not been starved by an unnatural celibacy.

Cicely Hamilton, Marriage as a Trade, *1909*

[24] When – if ever – the day of woman's complete social and economic independence dawns upon her, when she finds herself free and upright in a new world where no artificial pressure is brought to bear upon her natural inclinations or disinclinations, then, and then only, will it be possible to untwist a tangled skein and judge to what extent and what precise degree she is swayed by those impulses, sexual and maternal, which are now, to the exclusion of every other [25] factor, presumed to dominate her existence. And not only to dominate, but to justify it.

Margaret Stephens, Woman and Marriage, *1910*

[56] Some young women possess [the instinct of sex] in as great, and in rare cases even a greater degree; but in the majority of average healthy women before marriage it lies in a more or less dormant condition, and occasionally is altogether absent. And dormant things suddenly aroused require an understanding, forewarned and so forearmed, to control and guide them.

Olive Schreiner, Woman and Labour, *1911*

[26] [S]ex [27] and the sexual relation between man and woman have distinct æsthetic, intellectual, and spiritual functions and ends, apart entirely from physical reproduction . . . . [T]hat union has in it latent, other, and even higher forms, of creative energy and life-dispensing power, and . . . its history on earth has only begun.

Lucy Re-Bartlett, The Coming Order, *1911*

[34] That there are many sensual women in the world is all too true, but we maintain that there is an infinitely larger number of whom the chief factor working in sex relationship is the heart. And their hearts lead women astray, and make them weak and wicked, just as the senses do [35] with men . . . . Often in woman, even in the women who are most weak, there is no other temptation that than of giving. This is pleasure, but it is not sensual pleasure, and if egoistic, it is at least a higher form of egoism. But most women cannot put all this into words, and partly from *amour propre*, and partly because they really do not understand any better, men too often imagine that all these women are moved by the senses as they are themselves.

[39] Let woman grasp some of these things, then – that passion is power, and she cannot afford to do away with it. That if she does, she becomes simply an incomplete person, out of the running. That passion will not pull her down, but only sensuality. That she can recognise sensuality instantly by its limitation of her higher powers. That passion, on the contrary, will develop her higher powers if she will but turn it in every direction, uniting passions of mind and soul to those of the heart – ideals to affections. That understanding passion in this way, as simply intensity, it is illogical and weak to wish to exclude it from any special department, such as her love for man. That she should wish to carry the same vitality and entirety into this expression as she has into every other. And that when she is entire, she safely can. For the spiritual and mental forces working in her then will balance the affectional, and with fidelity on all sides, she will have no need to deny any of those elements which only together make a completed whole.

Mary Scharlieb and F. Arthur Sibly, Youth and Sex, 1913

[12] One of the Phenomena of adolescence is the dawn of the sexual instinct. This frequently develops without the child knowing or under-standing what it means. More especially is this true of young girls whose home life has been completely sheltered.
[. . . .]
[14] [I]n the case of the great majority of girls there are . . . impulses having their origin in the yet immature and misunderstood sex impulse which cause the young woman herself annoyance and worry although she is as far from understanding their origins as her elders may be
[. . . .]
[15] All natural instincts implanted in us by Him who knew what was in the heart of man are in themselves right and good, but the exercise of these instincts may be entirely wrong in time or in degree. The sexual instinct, the affinity of boy to girl, the love of adult man and woman, are right and holy when exercised aright.

Downward Paths, 1916

[30] The links in the chain that connect premature sexual experience of all kinds with prostitution are many and strong. Most obvious is the breakdown of the habit of cleanly self-respect of body and mind, which forms so strong a barrier against vicious habits and promiscuity in the decently nurtured man and woman. Quite as serious is the habit of submission to physical demands of the opposite sex which evolves from upbringing in these squalid homes. It is borne out again and again by

our life histories, that mere animal toleration, coupled with financial helplessness, and the entire absence from her surroundings of older persons whom she can trust or respect, is as dangerous to a woman as definite desires.

The effect of premature experience on the sexual instinct itself is more difficult to estimate. Does it produce an abnormal stimulation, which leads a woman to seek satisfaction for her needs in promiscuity, and thus carries her on to take advantage of man's paying capacity? Or does it produce a sort of anaesthesia, a blunting of normal sensations which makes sexual relations a matter of callous indifference? The medical evidence on this point is very scanty, but the researches of those who have investigated this subject (e.g. Prof. [31] Freud and his school) tend to show that premature experiences, especially if of violent nature, produce perversions and disturbances of the sexual feelings, which form the basis of many neuroses in adults.

It is, however, a fact of common experience amply borne out by this enquiry, that early familiarity with sexual matters makes even normal impulses infinitely harder to control. The normal girl, brought up in a wholesome atmosphere, feels and manifests innumerable impulses that are really of sexual origin, but is commonly without definite and conscious desire for sex relationships.

[58] Nearly all who come into contact with prostitutes at the beginning of their career are agreed that sensuality has very little influence in determining their choice . . . . [59] [T]here are in every class girls who either by faulty training or congenital disposition are possessed by uncontrollable promiscuous passions which they must gratify however much it distresses their relatives and even themselves. As such impulses are usually strong at the onset of puberty . . . . and subside again to quiescence until re-awakened by stimulation, commonly in marriage, and are obviously at their most dangerous point when the character is still undeveloped, this, too, is largely a question of the management of adolescence. And it is to be remarked that even in cases of nymphomania the woman would very probably not choose a regular life of prostitution were she not forced into it on discovery by exclusion from other occupations.

F. W. Stella Browne, Sexual Variety and Variability among Women, 1917

[4] I believe that the conventional estimate of women's sexual apathy and instinctive monandry is not true.

[. . . .]

[5] The sexual emotion in women is not, taking it broadly, weaker than in men. But it has an enormously wider range of variation; and much greater diffusion, both in desire and pleasure, all through women's organisms. And thirdly, arising from these two characteristics of variability and diffusion, it is extremely liable to aberrations and perversions, which I believe, under constant social and religious repression of normal satisfaction, have often developed to a pathological extent, while sometimes remaining almost entirely subconscious.

The variability of the sexual emotion in women is absolutely basic and primary. It can never be expressed or satisfied by either patriarchal marriage or prostitution. It is found in the same woman as between different times, and in different individuals . . . .

[6] It is this variety and variability of the sexual impulse among women, which would militate against any real promiscuity, if women were all economically secure and free to follow their own instincts, and to control their maternal function by the knowledge of contraceptives (a most important part of women's real emancipation). Most people are apt to under-rate the real strength of desire, and at the same time, to exaggerate its indiscriminate facility. I submit that, though few women are absolutely monandrous, still fewer are really promiscuous.

[8] Diffusion of the sexual emotions in women is not merely physiological: it extends throughout the imaginative and emotional life . . . . This diffusion is the main cause of the greater slowness and complexity of the sexual processes in women. Finally it makes the traditional masculine over-estimate of, and insistence on anatomical virginity, the most ridiculous superstition in the world. Even if we consider sexual ignorance and intactitude as a woman's highest charm, and virtue – the unruptured hymen is no guarantee of this ignorance and intactitude. It may co-exist with the most varied, and even perverted, sex experience . . . .

The diffused sexuality of women, again, is the enemy of very abrupt transformations and transitions: no social order which took this fact adequately into consideration, could tolerate the present forms of marriage, with the outrage on decency and freedom alike involved in the ideas of 'conjugal rights'.

No woman has been given her full share of the beauty and the joy of life, who has not been very gradually and skilfully initiated into the sexual relation.

[10] [A] certain amount of self-excitement, and solitary enjoyment, seems inevitable in any strongly developed sexual life, and is indisputably much safer, and more consonant with humanity in refinement, than the so-called safety-valve of prostitution.

Heterosexual relationships outside marriage

At this period there are significant comments on the prevalence of seduction and the preventable factors that lead up it. A few voices are making a case for some form of sexual experimentation before marriage, as ultimately beneficial to this union, although concerns are still being expressed about the personal and social perils of 'free love'.

Louisa Martindale, Under the Surface, *c. 1908*

[70] Amongst the hundreds of cases I have come in contact with in my profession, I have been struck with the [71] helplessness of the young girl, the physical paralysis that creeps over her; her utter ignorance of the result of her acquiescence, and her faith in the man she believes is in love with her. She has been trained from her earliest years in the very qualities which make her an easy prey to the professional seducer or procurer.

Frances Swiney, The Awakening of Women, *1908*

[218] There is actually, at the present moment, no law in England or Ireland against incest, though this hideous form of immorality is of frequent occurrence amongst the lowest classes . . . .

Young children and girls, victims to brutal lust, are by no means well protected by legal enactments. The laws affecting their interests are notoriously unjust, giving every benefit of the doubt to the male offender. Cases of indecent assaults on young girls are more especially dismissed without thorough investigation by our callous law-givers.

Seduction, again, is judged by the same debased double code of morality. The woman suffers, the man escapes free. Now, when one considers that the male offender is, as a rule, senior in age and superior in education, class, and position to his unfortunate [219] victim, the peculiar meanness and unfairness of this special section of masculine legislation is the more striking.

Maud Churton Braby, Modern Marriage and How to Bear It, *1908*

[90] [A]fter marriage it is generally the woman who is most discontented. Of late years a spirit of strange unrest has come over married women, and they frequently rebel against conditions which our grandmothers would never have dreamed of murmuring at. There are a variety of causes for this:

49

one that marriage falls short of women's expectations . . . another that they have had no *feminine* wild oats. Please note the qualifying adjective, duly italicised, and do not attempt to misunderstand me. I am no advocate of the licence generally accorded to men being extended to women.

'Wild oats' of this nature, otherwise an ante-hymeneal 'fling,' was certainly not a necessity of our grandmothers, but a certain (fairly numerous) type of modern women seem to make better wives when they have reaped this harvest.

[141] Free love has been called the most dangerous and delusive of all marriage schemes. It is based on a wholly impossible standard of ethics. Theoretically, it is the ideal union between the sexes, but it will only become practical when men and women have morally advanced out of all recognition. When people are all faithful, constant, pure-minded, and utterly unselfish, free marriage may be worth considering. Even then, there would be no chance for the ill-favoured and unattractive.

Under present conditions no couple living openly in free love is known to have made a success of it – a solid, permanent success, that is.

[171] Of all the revolutionary suggestions for improving the present marriage system, the most sensible and feasible seems to me marriage 'on approval' – in other words, a 'preliminary canter.' The procedure would be somewhat as follows: a couple on deciding to marry would go through a legal form of contract, agreeing to take each other as husband and wife for a limited term of years – say three. This period would allow two years for a fair trial, after the abnormal and exceptionally trying first year was over. Any shorter time would be insufficient. At the conclusion of the three years, the contracting parties would have the option of dissolving the marriage – the dissolution not to become absolute for another six months, so [172] as to allow every opportunity of testing the genuineness of the desire to part. If no dissolution were desired, the marriage would then be ratified by a religious or final legal ceremony, and become permanently binding.

In the case of a marriage dissolved, each party would be free to wed again; but the second essay must be final and permanent from the start. This restriction would be absolutely necessary if the preliminary canter plan is not to degenerate into a species of legalised free love.

Christabel Pankhurst, The Great Scourge, *1913*

[130] [W]e detect a tendency in many quarters to preach to women the observance of a looser code of morals than that they have observed hitherto. 'You are asking for political freedom,' women are told. 'More

important to you is sex freedom. Votes for women should be accompanied, if not preceded, by wild oats for women. The thing to be done is not to raise the moral standard of men, but to lower the moral standard of women.' To this proposal the women reply by a firm and unqualified negative. Votes they certainly intend to have, and that quickly, but they know too well what is the harvest of wild oats, and having that knowledge, they refuse to sow any.

When women have the vote, they will be more and not less opposed than now to making a plaything of sex and of entering casually into the sex relationship.

[131] In the opinion of the Suffragettes sex is too big and too sacred a thing to be treated lightly. Moreover, both the physical and spiritual consequences of a sex union are so important, so far-reaching, and so lasting, that intelligent and independent women will enter into such union only after deep consideration, and only when a great love and a great confidence are present.

Lucy Re-Bartlett, Sex and Sanctity, 1914

[57] We allude to those women who wish to make the father of as little account as the mother has sometimes been in the past – to perpetuate the evil of one-sided parentage, making the evil merely maternal, instead of paternal. The sin of man in the past has been that of forcing children upon woman when often there was some good reason why she should not, and did not wish to have them: in this way children have come into the world in a one-sided manner, deprived of the full co-operation of the mother. But parentage does not consist only in the act of creation, and what are we to think of those women of to-day who claim the right to bring children into the world either as the result of a passing passion of their own, or even without passion, simply because they wish to have a child – in either case treating the father as a mere passing phase, and relegating the child deliberately and with forethought to a fatherless and nameless existence?

Mary Scharlieb, What It Means to Marry, 1914

[48] Ellen Key and others urge that free love is essential to perfect realisation of life and self-expression; they suggest that the marriage tie becomes hypocrisy and degradation when the love which should sanctify it has ceased to exist. They say that love is the only valid sanction of union, and that with its disappearance the bond itself should be automatically dissolved. [50] Further, the apostles of free love urge that

unions between men and women would be purer, more sincere, and more dignified were they founded entirely on mutual love.

[. . . .]

[51] Those who advocate free love ignore the position that leasehold marriage would force upon women. Theoretically, the woman would be as free as the man, but practically she would be less likely to tire of him than he of her, and she would be hampered by her children and her mother-love.

Downward Paths, *1916*

[83] It is undoubtedly the case that in many districts, chiefly rural, pre-marital sexual freedom is less the exception than the rule: that it is in these places the custom among honest and self-respecting young people for sexual relations to follow engagement, and for marriage to be delayed until the birth of a child is expected.

[85] [T]he relation of seduction to prostitution varies enormously with local public opinion in regard to the pre- [86] marital chastity of women. The seduced girl who knows that her family, her neighbours, and her class hold unchastity to be a grave sin, feels her disgrace – particularly if she is going to have a child – to be almost as complete as if she were already a prostitute . . . .

Of course it does not follow because a girl gets into trouble through a man that she was heartlessly seduced. Such cases occur, but the sentimental notion that the man is entirely responsible is hardly borne out by enquiry. Young people of both sexes are often deplorably ignorant of the temptations that arise and of the consequences of yielding to them . . . .

This is not to say that in innumerable instances women are not the victims of heartless fraud as well as natural temptation, as in cases of seduction under promise of marriage . . . . Particularly difficult for a woman to understand are the cases where an apparently decent and kindly married man seduces a girl under promise of marriage.

[178] Many employers seem to have no scruple about making advances to their typists . . . . It must be remembered that many men who behave properly to women whom they meet in their own social world have no hesitation in offering familiarities to the women whom they meet at work.

[179] [T]here are girls who go into offices because 'you have so much fun there, get taken to theatres, and generally have a good time.' Sometimes this frivolity becomes something less innocent, and we are told that it is not uncommon for a typist to be her employer's 'left-handed wife.'

Mary Scharlieb, The Hidden Scourge, *1916*

[75] [T]here is unfortunately no reason to doubt that the wave of patriotic feeling and general excitement that passed like a flame over the land during the first months of the war did result in a dangerous heightening of sexual passion.

Both young men and young women were too often swept off their feet by unrestrained emotion, and much wrong-doing was the result.

Mary Scharlieb and Barbara Butts, England's Girls and England's Future, *1917*

[9] [M]ost frequently neither boy nor girl may mean any harm. They begin by a few pleasant words, then they walk together, the boy puts his arm round the girl's neck or waist, then kisses are exchanged, the feelings of the young man and the girl are aroused and the intimacy grows fast. It grows too fast and they lose [10] their heads – they think only of the pleasure of the moment, and if they 'give way' the harm is done and in many cases one or both of the young people may be ruined for live. But as a whole the heaviest share of trouble falls on the girl.

F. W. Stella Browne, Sexual Variety and Variability among Women, *1917*

[7] [W]omen must demand more of life – and give more to it. Let them set their own requirements, and boldly claim a share of life and erotic experience, as perfectly consistent with their own self-respect . . . . Both the experimental love of variety and the permanent preference for one mate are inherent in all human beings. And in women there is a special need for recognising free experiment. First love is generally almost entirely an illusion, and many women have ruined their lives, because an illusion was made permanent and petrified by marriage . . . . Women's erotic experiments will probably be always less numerous than men's, and include more 'amitiés amoureuses'; but they are an integral part of life . . . .

Even the great love, *in women as in men*, by no means always excludes lesser attractions and intimacies, which may run the whole gamut from sentiment and camaraderie to the frankly physical, yet remain totally distinct from the dominant passion. I allude, of course, to genuine, even if transitory, impulses, not to commercial [8] transactions for pearls or cheques or livelihood. Indeed, I think this is the test of the great love, that any minor episode seems to heighten one's desire for, and pleasure in, it.

Same-sex relationships, celibacy, and singleness generally

A number of writers make a case for deliberately chosen celibacy in the face of the corrupt nature of existing male-dominated sexual institutions. The possibility of single women living a fulfilling life is suggested. And a few women suggest that sexual relationships between women are possible, and not necessarily a bad thing, in certain circumstances, and also indicate that attraction to the same sex is often part of normal development.

Frances Swiney, The Awakening of Women, 1908

[93] Woman is a necessity to man; but man is not necessary to woman. Physical science demonstrates this fact more plainly in every research. [94] Woman retains in single life health, strength, and vitality; as a fact, more unmarried women arrive at a good age, and with their functions unimpaired, than the corresponding number of married women who, in the cares and pains of maternity, have weakened and worn out their frames.

Cicely Hamilton, Marriage as a Trade, 1909

[33] In sexual matters it would appear that the whole trend and tendency of man's relations to [34] woman has been to make refusal impossible and to cut off every avenue of escape from the gratification of his desire. His motive in concentrating all her energy upon the trade of marriage was to deny it any other outlet . . . .

The uncompromising and rather brutal attitude which man has consistently adopted towards the spinster is, to my mind, a confirmation of this theory . . . . That active and somewhat savage dislike must have had its origin in the consciousness [35] that the perpetual virgin was a witness, however reluctantly, to the unpalatable fact that sexual intercourse was not for every woman an absolute necessity.

[226] [I]n the recent history of woman nothing is more striking than the enormous improvement that has taken place in the social position of the spinster. In many ranks of life the lack of a husband is no longer a reproach; and some of us are even proud of the fact that we have fought our way in the world without aid from any man's arm. At any rate, we no longer feel it necessary to apologize for our existence; and when we are assured that we have lost the best that life has to offer us, we are not unduly cast down . . . . [227] By sheer force of self-assertion we have lifted ourselves from the dust where we once crawled as worms and no women; we no longer wither on the virgin thorn – we flourish on it.

[240] Under present conditions, it is not easy for self-respecting woman to find a mate with whom she can live on the terms demanded by her self-respect. Hence a distinct tendency on her part to avoid marriage. Those women who look at the matter in this light are those who, while not denying that matrimony may be [241] an excellent thing in itself, realize that there are some excellent things which may be bought too dear. That is the position of a good many of us in these latter days. If we are more or less politely incredulous when we are informed that we are leading an unnatural existence, it is not because we have no passions, but because life to us means a great deal more than one of its possible episodes.

Olive Schreiner, Woman and Labour, 1911

[127] It is this consciousness of great impersonal ends, to be brought, even if slowly and imperceptibly, a little nearer by her action, which gives to many a woman strength for renunciation, when she puts from her the lower type of sexual relationship, even if bound up all the external honour a legal bond can confer, if it offers her only enervation and parasitism; and which enables her often to accept poverty, toil, and sexual isolation.

Lucy Re-Bartlett, The Coming Order, 1911

[64] There is a celibacy which we may call *positive celibacy*, which does not belong to asceticism at all, in so far as it is easy, spontaneous, a natural turning of the energy to the things of the spirit. This is the stage at which spiritual creation is possible, and indeed inevitable, and a life of celibacy at this stage knows nothing of partiality – it is vital, expressive, complete and satisfied in its generation of another kind. But there is also another celibacy, which we may call *negative celibacy*, where the energy is not yet such as to be spiritually productive, and where the single life is lived not so much from a call to the things of the spirit, as through a shrinking from the abuses of the flesh.

Edith Lees Ellis, 'Eugenics and the Mystical Outlook', c. 1911

[47] Wilde's mother . . . prayed continually for a girl . . . . That her prayer was partially granted in that perplexing mixture of artist, man, woman, and egotist the world knows as Oscar Wilde was perhaps one of Nature's satires in order to show what we do when we force, through our limited laws and barbaric persecutions, these peculiar people into becoming menaces

55

to the State through lack of capacity either to understand them or to educate them . . . . Even in abnormality, in its congenital manifestations. Nature may have a meaning as definite in her universal purpose as the discord is in music to the musician.

[48] Often what we count as vicious, or even abnormal or insane, through the very fact of unusual suffering involved in it, or of some new courage born of a rare vision of love on a specialised plane, may be an aid to purity, rather than a degradation.

Edith Lees Ellis, 'Eugenics and Spiritual Parenthood', c. 1911

[56] What is to become of those, however, existing to-day, who have been born and live outside the cold laws of Eugenics . . . . I am not speaking of the imbecile or the feeble-minded, but of those whose mentality is often vigorous and exceptional, and who have original powers of a high order. These 'peculiar people' are often ostracised when recognised, and are often as much bewildered about themselves as specialists are about them. What has a eugenist to say to a class of people definitely in our midst who are, from the point of view of Eugenics, unfit to propagate and [57] who appear to the casual observer mere freaks of nature?

From a eugenist's point of view, persons unfitted to have a child should be encouraged to devote their energies to those ends which indirectly aid the higher development . . . . In this way, through the understanding of their nature and their limitations, and also through comprehension of the varied needs of a complex society, from a eugenist's point of view these persons might doubly bless what, otherwise, they might curse, the future generation . . . . The work of the eugenist is not only to prevent the waste and ruin of lives, but to help and to stimulate existing powers, *however curiously* [58] *manifested*, into channels of service and joy . . . . It is not only the abnormal by any manner of means who need guidance and warning about these subtle dangers. As many sins against great underlying laws of affinity are committed in legal marriage.

[59] Perhaps it is a somewhat daring statement to make when I say that no *true* abnormality exists that [60] cannot be converted into power if conditions and environment give it a chance. I say 'true abnormality' advisedly, for mock abnormality is a great danger to the State, and it is a growing one. By mock abnormality, I mean an attitude towards passional experiments and episodes outside normal lines merely of self-gratification. Indulgence for the sake of indulgence . . . is, in the light of modern ethics, a shame and a disgrace, and it is the nearest approach to sensual sin we

can imagine . . . . Real abnormality is neither a shame nor a disgrace, but a problem to be reckoned with and tested by one fact and one only – its result on the individual and on the whole community . . . .

Science and love have proved that there are, and always have been, men who have the souls of women, and women, who have the souls of men . . . . However much learned or ignorant people call abnormality a disgrace, or a hideous disease, the matter faces us day by day . . . . [61] Condemnation is the attitude of the ignorant or the cowardly. If abnormality is sheerly evil, it is time that Religion and Eugenics took it up and helped to ostracise it. If it is merely a problem . . . this is surely another reason for studying it.

[62] There is surely a place in the great scheme of things even for the abnormal man and the abnormal woman, but it is not an easy place. Possibly it is a very high place: the place of clean living and renunciation. Under the highest laws of both Love and Eugenics I feel its place is one of spiritual parenthood. Neither bromides, loveless marriages, nor asylums will cure congenital inversion. The real [63] invert is an invert from his birth to his death.

[65] The true invert . . . has to face either total renunciation of the physical expression of love, or, if Fate send him a true mate in the form of another alien, for in these things affinity has its own laws and pure love can be traced in strange hiding-places, then the bond shall be as binding, as holy, and as set for splendid social ends as the bond of normal marriage. There [66] is surely no other solution of this vexed question. Any concession, any compromise with seduction, or prostitution, or cheap physical expression, though no worse in many ways in abnormals than normals, but destructive in either, hinders the development of true love, and so the betterment of the human race, which betterment should always be an outcome of personal love.

Christabel Pankhurst, The Great Scourge, *1913*

[131] And here we may, perhaps, deal with the statement made by some men, that women suffer who are not mated with men, and that what they are pleased to term 'the unsatisfied desires' of women are a problem . . . . [N]owadays the [132] unmarried women have a life full of joy and interest. They are not mothers of children of their flesh, but they serve humanity, they can do work that is useful or beautiful. Therefore their life is complete. If they find a man worthy of them, a man fit physically and morally to be their husband, then they are ready to marry, but they will not let desire, apart from love and reason, dominate their life or dictate their action.

It is very often said to women that their ideas of chastity are the result of past subjection. Supposing that were so, then women have the satisfaction of knowing that their subjection has brought them at least one great gain – a gain they will not surrender when the days of their subjection are over. The mastery of self and sex, which either by nature or by training women have, they will not yield up.

Lucy Re-Bartlett, Sex and Sanctity, *1914*

[36] It is our intention therefore to limit ourselves entirely in this essay to the discussion of these latter causes – the causes which we believe will be chiefly responsible for the maintenance and increase of woman's celibacy in the future unless a wider comprehension can be forthcoming.

For many reasons may it be said that the women who to-day decline marriage offer a much greater problem than those to whom the chance of it does not come . . . . [37] [W]e may conclude . . . that the wish of marriage amongst our so-called 'surplus' women is at least no burning desire . . . . And that want of desire is really the principal factor with which we have to deal is still more clearly shown when we consider the ever-increasing number of women to whom the chance does come, and who decline it, or those again to whom no actual proposal perhaps may come, but whose attitude of mind and choice of life constitute what we may call an initial refusal. This last class of women is very numerous, and we may profitably commence our study with them.

[42] [S]o soon as she reaches to any depth of insight, woman recognizes that her chief battle-ground lies here – that laws which have decreed her subjection, and will maintain it, until she is mistress of herself. These large and fundamental facts of life the spiritual woman grasps very early on her spiritual pilgrimage – grasps them very often intuitively, before her mind has been able to present them to her clearly. And this it is which gives us the second class of celibate – the young girl who living in the social world will yet not go beyond friendship with men – who hates sentiment, and draws back from the first touch of love-making. Yet who puzzles people often, because they recognize that she is not the least masculine, nor the least cold, and apparently is not turning aside towards another life, like her more intellectual sisters . . . .

It is the soul struggling for its liberty with that same blind desperation with which man has often struggled for it in the outer world: struggling as a drowning person might struggle to keep his head above the water – struggling almost with the instinct of the animal – that instinct blind, [43] yet so unerring. Is the thing so hard to understand? It is simply the struggle for existence – that struggle which all humanity has waged – lifted to the spiritual plane. It is the soul here which is crying out for room to breathe, but just as all humanity has cried out in the physical world.

When this type of girl marries – and she does sometimes – there is always tragedy.

Norah March, Towards Racial Health, *1915/20*

[32] It is a stage in the life of the normal child during which ardent affection of a more or less passionate type may often be focused upon individuals, regardless of age, regardless of sex. Very often the adored one is considerably older than the child, as in the case of a young pupil forming a passionate attachment for a teacher . . . an attachment that is beyond all ordinary definition of affection, one which embraces all degrees of sentimental feelings and ideas, and even may include jealousy. Particularly in boarding-schools for girls does one meet with instances of this sort: a girl will become infatuated with another girl – it may be younger, but more often older, than herself – or with a mistress in the school. Such infatuations often become the fashion, leading to an unhealthy tone about the school.

Those cases which are simply imitative are easily discouraged and soon forgotten, but there are instances of this undifferentiated stage persisting, particularly if unwisely fostered, and forming a basis for perversion. In the main, though, the stage of undifferentiated sex impulse, though it may extend over a number of years, even to early adolescence, gradually passes away, to be replaced at a later age by normal impulse towards the opposite sex. Moreover, it is by no means a rule that every individual passes through this stage; and very often in those individuals in which it has occurred, it frequently passes away from the memory altogether, [33] as it yields in ordinary normal development to the incoming of the normal differentiated impulse. At the same time, many adults can look back to their younger days and recognise an experience of the type which has been described.

F. W. Stella Browne, Sexual Variety and Variability among Women, *1917*

[10] We are learning to recognise congenital inversion as a vital and very often valuable factor in civilisation, subject of course, to the same restraints as to public order and propriety, freedom of consent, and the protection of the immature, as normal heterosexual desire . . . .

[11] Certain minor and occasional aberrations are part of the complete life. But the system of silence and repression often reacts on women's

organism in a thoroughly abnormal manner, and a completely *artificial* (this is the point) perversion may be established, and if it is established early enough, may be quite unconscious for years. And the most sensitive and diffident and amenable to ideas of modesty the girl is, the more easily may this process be developed . . . .

Artificial or substitute homosexuality – as distinct from true inversion – is very widely diffused among women, as a result of the repression of normal gratification and the segregation of the sexes, which still largely obtains. It appears, I think, later in life than onanism: in the later twenties or thirties rather than in the teens. Sometimes its only direct manifestations are quite non- [12] committal and platonic; but even this incomplete and timid homosexuality can always be distinguished from true affectionate friendship between women, by its jealous, exacting and extravagant tone. Of course, when one of the partners in such an attachment is a real or congenital invert, it is at once much more serious and much more physical. The psychology of homogenic women has been much less studied than that of inverted men. Probably there are many varieties and subtleties of emotional fibre amongst them. Some very great authorities have believed that the inverted woman is more often bisexual – less exclusively attracted to other women – than the inverted man. This view needs very careful confirmation, but if true, it would prove the greater plasticity of women's sex-impulse. It has also been stated that the invert man or woman, is drawn towards the normal types of their own sex . . . . Certainly, the heterosexual woman of passionate but shy and sensitive nature, is often responsive to the inverted woman's advances, especially if she is erotically ignorant and inexperienced. Also many women of quite normally directed (heterosexual) inclinations, realise in mature life, when they have experienced passion, that the devoted admiration and friendship they felt for certain girl friends, had a real, though perfectly unconscious, spark of desire in its exaltation and intensity; an unmistakable indefinable note, which was absolutely lacking in many equally sincere and lasting friendships.

Neither artificial homosexuality nor prolonged auto-erotism, to use Havelock Ellis' masterly phrase, prove *innate* morbidity. Careful observation and many confidences from members of my own sex, have convinced me that our maintenance of outworn traditions is manufacturing habitual auto-erotists and perverts, out of women who would instinctively prefer the love of a man, who would bring them sympathy and comprehension as well as desire. I repudiate all wish to slight or depreciate the love-life of the real homosexual; but it cannot be advisable to force the growth of that habit in heterosexual people.

Prostitution and venereal disease

Prostitution continues to be defined as a problem arising out of male attitudes to their own sexual needs and the necessity to provide gratification for these. Increasing knowledge about the extent of venereal diseases within British society adds further weight to arguments against the existing system of sexual morality.

Annette M. B. Meakin, Woman in Transition, *1907*

[65] During the London season of 1906, English ladies found it made unpleasant for them even to step from the theatre into a cab when unaccompanied by a gentleman, and one lady from the country remarked to me, that after seeing the present state of things she should not feel justified in leaving her chauffeur outside a London theatre [66] while she attended a play. The ordinary well-behaved un-ostentatiously dressed woman can rarely pause for a moment before a shop-window in Oxford Street or Regent Street after five o'clock in the evening without attracting attention that she does not seek.

[67] It has been argued that prostitution cannot be the result of social conditions, for, if it were, outcasts would not return to their bad life when once they had been rescued . . . . The truth is that these poor women return to their evil life because . . . man has taught them that a woman's honour does not depend upon her will, and that it can be taken from her independently of her will. Man has also made it hugely difficult for her to retrieve the first false step, and that is why she too often sinks to the lowest degree of vice.

[70] [S]uppose we take it for granted that those men are right who assert that the morality of English homes is due to such a system. It only comes to this that for every honest wife, mother, sister or daughter, someone else's wife, mother, sister or daughter must be victimised . . . . Why does the pure English lady turn away with such disgust from the gaudy painted woman who now confronts her by daylight [71] in every London street, and who even rides beside in the motor omnibus? English women are at last refusing to believe that man was fashioned lower that the brute, that instincts have been given him by his Creator which he has not the power to control, which must therefore entail the ruin of a fellow-creature before they can be pacified . . . . Prostitution has been supposed to run in the human family, so man has borne with it and countenanced it, and it has prospered hideously, till in these early days of the twentieth century it is a greater menace than ever. The evils which it has brought in its train are undermining marriage, and through marriage, the race.

Frances Swiney, The Awakening of Women, *1908*

[126] Let, then, every woman professing Christianity ask herself, 'Am I my sister's keeper?' Yea! cold, virtuous, untempted, unproven woman, thou art! How hast thou kept thy trust? How does her misery contrast with thy complacency? What action of thine has lessened her wrongs, alleviated her condition, brought hope to her despair? Hast thou unloosed a chain, or broken down a single barrier of sin?

[. . . .]

What duty could be purer and holier than to proclaim to those women, who have fallen in life's pathway, the sublimity of woman's true mission; to plead with men the nobility of their manhood, the divinity of their gift of life; to call forth to active response all that is chivalrous in human nature; to assert that woman is not the slave, but the teacher; not the degraded inferior, but, if worthy of her stewardship, the equal helpmeet of man? Have we, mothers of *Christian* England, hitherto done our duty in this manner? Have we taken our stand firmly, strongly, convincingly, on the side of inflexible *right*?

[. . . .]

[127] Therefore to avert racial degeneration, such as fell upon the ancient civilisation of the world from the same cause, legal supervision, and systematic medical inspection of those of *both sexes*, who, of their own free-will choose a vicious course of life, are necessary and logical measures based upon rational grounds of common sense, justice, and expediency

[. . . .]

Stringent restrictions should be made to apply with *equal* severity to the delinquents of both sexes; more especially are they necessary for the future welfare of the race in the case of the man; and for the following cogent reasons: Statistics conclusively prove that the life of the prostitute is a short one; fallen nature cannot long stand the strain of shame and corruption, and moreover the excesses of a vicious life render a woman childless. Sin, with retributive justice, deprives her of the glory of motherhood.

The future, therefore, of the race has comparatively nothing to fear from the prostitute individually as a race-bearer. She dies out.

Very different are the far-reaching effects of immorality in the case of the man, and in the present sex-biassed inequality of the moral law. He, unrestrained by legal restrictions, unhampered by medical supervision, may at any time, and under any circumstance and condition of disease, contract marriage with a healthy innocent woman; is left free to bring into existence offspring tainted from birth with the worst of human scourges, and may thus vitiate for generations various members of the race. Incontestably, if a woman so far forgets her womanhood, as voluntarily [128] to choose a life of shame, it is meet that she should bear the full measure of its guilt and degradation, still more necessary is the need, from a scientific, hygienic, and practical point of view, to make the way of the male transgressor hard. If the immoral woman is socially ostracised, the like fate should befall the immoral man.

Louisa Martindale, Under the Surface, c. 1908

[11] I suppose there is no subject a woman dislikes so much to dwell upon as Prostitution . . . . And yet surely, so long as thousands of our women have been led through poverty, ignorance, or misfortune, to live a life of shame, the least we can do, is to try to find out what lies at the root of this social evil, so that we may the better help to free women from the slavery it involves. For many centuries attempts have been made not to abolish it, but to make it possible for a man to sin, without contracting diseases which are the natural outcome of such profligacy. No serious attempt has been made by the State to eradicate it from amongst us.

It remains for us women now to take up the question, and to refuse to tolerate houses of ill-fame, and above all to stamp out any State regulation involving the licensing of such houses, and the medical inspection and the registering of the inmates.

If you speak to a prostitute you will find that it is not a question of pleasure or sensual enjoyment.

[70] When we study the life of a so-called common prostitute we find that in the first place she was seduced; then, ashamed to return to her home she finds herself alone without credentials or testimonials and unable to find employment. It is then that she is forced to go on the streets.

With reference to this preliminary seduction, we have to remember that, from her earliest days, she has been imbued with the belief in the superior knowledge of the other sex. She has been taught to be obedient and to be affectionate and charming, and above all to be unselfish . . . . [I]f she falls into the hands of a scoundrel, there is very little chance that she may successfully resist him.

[71] It is men who have made it possible, nay who have demanded that a whole class of women shall be set aside for their momentary pleasure; who have deliberately trained a whole class of women to exercise for gain those functions which Nature has given to them for the propagation of the race only. Even further, it is these men who have instilled into their womenfolk the idea that sexual indulgence is a necessity to their health – one of the greatest fallacies that ever existed.

Cicely Hamilton, Marriage as a Trade, *1909*

[38] This freedom of bargaining to the best advantage, permitted as a matter of course to every other worker, is denied to her. It is, of course, claimed and exercised by the prostitute class – a class which has pushed to its logical conclusion the principle that woman exists by virtue of a wage paid her in return for the possession of her person; but it is interesting to note that the 'unfortunate' enters the open market with the hand of the law extended threateningly above her head. The fact is curious if inquired into: since the theory that woman should live by physical attraction of the opposite sex has never been seriously denied, but rather insisted upon, by men, upon what principle is solicitation, or open offer of such attraction, made a legal offence? (Not because the woman is in danger of the community, since the male sensualist is an equal source of danger.) Only, apparently, because the advance comes from the wrong side. I speak under correction, but cannot, unaided, light upon any other explanation; and mine seems to be borne out by the fact that, in other [39] ranks of life, custom, like the above-mentioned law, strenuously represses any open advance on the part of the woman. So emphatic, indeed, is this unwritten law, that one cannot help suspecting that it was needful it should be emphatic, lest woman, adapting herself to her economic position, should take the initiative in a matter on which her livelihood depended, and deprive her employer not only of the pleasure of the chase, but of the illusion that their common bargain was as much a matter of romance and volition on her part as on his.

[73] [T]he average woman has a perfect right to know what are the results of loose living in so far as those results may affect her and her children. If marriage is a trade we ought to know its risks – concerning which [74] there exists a conspiracy of silence. Is the cause to which I have alluded ever mentioned, except in technical publications, in connection with the infant death-rate?

Those of us who have discovered that there are risks attaching to the profession of marriage other than the natural ones of childbirth, have very often made the discovery by accident – which ought not to be.

Olive Schreiner, Woman and Labour, *1911*

[240] Probably three-fourths of the sexual unions in our modern European societies, whether in the illegal or recognised legal forms, are dominated by or largely influenced by the sex purchasing power of the male. With regard to the large and savage institution of prostitution, which still lies as the cancer embedded in the heart of all our modern civilised societies, this

is obviously and nakedly the case; the wealth of the male as compared to the female being, with hideous obtrusiveness, its foundation and source of life. But the purchasing power of the male as compared with the poverty of the female is not less painfully, if a little less obtrusively, displayed in those layers of society lying nearer the surface.

[242] [T]here is undoubtedly a certain body of females who would lose, or imagine [243] they would lose, heavily by the advance of woman as a whole to a condition of free labour and economic independence. That female, wilfully or organically belonging to the parasite class, having neither the vigour of intellect nor the vitality of body to undertake any form of productive labour, and desiring to be dependent only upon the passive performance of sex function merely, would, whether as prostitute or wife, undoubtedly lose heavily by any social change which demanded of woman increased knowledge and activity.

Frances Swiney, 'The Sons of Belial', c. 1912

[22] Physiology proves that the prostitution of the woman for the pleasure of the man is an unnecessary sacrifice on the altar of humanity. Hygiene goes further and declares that health is found in temperance, continence, and conservation of the sex-energy. Pathology opens her dire records to public view and shocks the whole world with the grim list of transmissible, death-dealing diseases due to sexual excesses and the anomalous, illogical position of the prostitute.
[. . .]
[23] We have to aim at a total reversal of the accepted tenets of sex-morality, and go to the very roots of the Upas tree that has for so many centuries sheltered vice beneath its branches and poisoned the well-springs of humanity with its baneful ramifications of fungus growths. The Upas tree is Injustice. Injustice to women – to the mothers of the race. Injustice bred of sexual perversion.

Frances Swiney, 'State Regulation of Vice', c. 1912

[38] A large majority of persons, ignorant of physiology, still believe in the exploded fallacy of man's necessity for physical sexual expression and the need for its gratification . . . . [I]t must be recognised once and for all time, if the human race is to evolve to its full potentialities, that prostitution of either man or woman of the sex organs and functions is the most serious deflection from the law of life of which any being can be capable . . . . Nature makes no provision for sex-obsession, except through

the righteousness of immutable law governing cause and effect, diseasing, weakening, and ultimately extirpating those who transgress in the way of life.

Christabel Pankhurst, The Great Scourge, *1913*

[4] Women will lay stress upon prevention, because even if cure were possible in the physical sense, it is impossible in the moral sense. A community which tolerates prostitution is a community which is morally diseased. The man prostitute (for why should we give this name only to the woman partner in immorality?) has his soul infected as well as his body.

We repeat that where these terrible diseases are concerned, prevention is better than [5] cure. It is not only better than cure, but it is the only cure, for whether these diseases are curable even in the narrowest sense of the term is very doubtful, and even when cured they can be contracted again.

As the hope of curing venereal diseases is so illusory, prevention is obviously the true policy. No individual can hope to avoid these diseases except by abstaining from immoral sexual intercourse, and similarly a nation cannot remain unaffected so long as prostitution exists.

[6] Therefore prostitution must go! At this shrieks of protest will be raised. We shall hear the usual balderdash about 'human nature' and 'injury to man's health.' Human nature is a very wide term, and it covers a multitude of sins and vices which are not on that account any the more to be tolerated . . . .

Why is human nature to have full scope only in the one direction of sexual vice? The answer to that question is that men have got all the power in the State, and therefore make not only the laws of the State, but also its morality.

According to man-made morality, a woman [7] who is immoral is a 'fallen' woman and is unfit for respectable society, while an immoral man is simply obeying the dictates of his human nature, and is not even to be regarded as immoral. According to man-made law, a wife who is even once unfaithful to her husband has done him an injury which entitles him to divorce her. She can raise no plea of 'human nature' in her defence. On the other hand, a man who consorts with prostitutes, and does this over and over again throughout his married life, has, according to man-made law, been acting only in accordance with human nature, and nobody can punish him for that.

[. . . .]

[8] Men's health can be preserved only at the price of prostitution – such is the ridiculous and wicked theory advanced by many men and some

doctors. The truth is, that prostitution is the greatest of all dangers to the health of men.

[44] [T]o reply to the statement of our critics who say that the reason of sexual vice is an economic one, and that if all men could afford to marry, prostitution would disappear. That this contention is unfounded is proved by these facts. Firstly, that rich men, who can perfectly well afford to marry, are quite as immoral as poorer men. Secondly, that married men as well as unmarried men have intercourse with prostitutes.

The problem of vice is certainly an economic one in this sense, that where women are economically dependent upon men, they more readily become the victims of vice. It should be noticed that the man's instinctive endeavour is to keep the woman in a state [45] of economic dependence. This desire to keep women in economic subjection to themselves – to have women, as it were, at their mercy – is at the root of men's opposition to the industrial and professional employment of women.

[. . . .]

But as we have also said, and say again, sexual vice is not caused by the poverty of [46] men, because the ranks of the vicious are recruited from the ranks of the rich men, the poor men, and the men of moderate means. As we have further said, and now repeat, marriage does not deter men from vicious courses, because married men as well as unmarried men descend to such courses.

The fact is that the sex instinct of these men has become so perverted and corrupted that intercourse with virtuous women does not content them. They crave for intercourse with women whom they feel no obligation to respect. They want to resort to practices which a wife would not tolerate. Lewdness and obscenity is what these men crave, and what they get in houses of ill-fame. Marriage does not 'satisfy' them. They fly to women who will not resent foul words and acts, and will even permit un-natural abuse of the sex function.

[86] The only people who dare face this evil of gonorrhoea and the only people who can overthrow it are women. When women acquire the necessary influence, political and social, they will have it in their power to convince men that to live cleanly or to be cast out from the society of decent women are the alternatives open to them.

[108] Women have a very simple answer . . . and it is: 'You have never tried to abolish prostitution, and so, of course, you have not succeeded.'

Certainly, efforts have been made to cover up all outward trace of the existence of this loathsome thing, but the real cure for it has never been applied. Beneath all the surface appearance of attacking prostitution, men have cherished the belief that prostitution is necessary, and that immorality and incontinence are legitimate for them.

The true cure for prostitution consists in [109] this – the strengthening of women, and the education of men.

Mary Scharlieb, The Hidden Scourge, 1916

[46] [T]he spread of the contagion of these disease is not always the result of illicit intercourse. An enormous number of innocent partners are infected very year, and in the case of married couples the disease is most usually conveyed to the wife by a husband who has had the disease and who has not been properly and adequately treated. Doctors are often asked by men whether they are in a fit state of health to marry – but not all men are prepared to abide by the advice given.

Downward Paths, 1916

[1] Our society and economic conscience prevent us regarding with equanimity the existence within the State of a huge outcast and partly out-lawed class such as prostitution has always made of its servants, and is horrified at the vast sum of money spent in diverting this class from productive labour and maintaining it in parasitic idleness. The advance of medical knowledge and the breakdown of secrecy on the subject have informed us that the prostitute, as well as being heavily stricken herself, spreads about the world a poison which does not discriminate between the guilty and the innocent. And more and more do women feel it is an affront to their pride that large numbers of their sex should live in degraded conditions and be exposed to universal contempt for the convenience of men.

The emancipation of women has indeed contributed to this change of opinion in more than one way. For [2] prostitution is in many matters an active nuisance to the working woman: she will even find that the municipality will refuse to supply her with the decent housing it supplies to the working man, for fear she may be a prostitute, and if she be in a disadvantageous economic position employers may offer her wages calculated on the supposition that being a woman she is inherently ready and willing to supplement them by prostitution. Now that these practical objections to prostitution have been grasped it is not surprising that a great many people are no longer to be overawed by the statement that it is, if not 'the oldest profession' in the world, at least one of the oldest urban problems, and are prepared to revolt against it.

But the most wonderful element in this revolt has been the awakening of the sense of social responsibility among women. Hitherto 'respectable' women have regarded the prostitute as a plague to be avoided, or at least as a lost soul to be saved . . . . She realises that her own immunity from temptation is bought at the price of increased danger for some of the most helpless, wretched and ignorant girls in the community, who are infinitely less well equipped for self-protection than she or her daughters. And now on all sides women are repudiating this bargain, and are even facing deliberately the drastic re-arrangement of cherished social institutions in order to secure the abolition of the prostitute class.

[7] One may see half a dozen wholly dissimilar women in succession going about their similar business. This thin and insignificant girl, quietly dressed, and no longer young, who looks like a teacher on her way home from school until she arouses one's suspicion by hailing a taxi and waiting till a man furtively gets in beside her, seems to have nothing in common with those two pretty girls in evening dress and fantastic hats, who sit together in a restaurant frequented by the *demi-monde*, beating the table with their fists and singing or shouting their loudest when any man approaches their corner, until a final burst of triumph announces the victorious capture of two young men. There seems no link between them and that poor old woman of sixty, stout and motherly and half-drunk, who comes into the women's common lodging-house in a [8] slum quarter at eleven o'clock, with her felt slippers sodden and her skirt bedraggled with the mud of a wet night in January, and, assuming that all present follow the same occupation as herself, confides to each in turn that she has got to go out again as she hasn't got anyone yet, and her poor feet do ache so. She seems to have no relationship to the beautiful young woman wrapped in a rich evening cloak who walks from the underground station in a quiet West End quarter to her flat in the neighbouring square with a step which seems strangely slow for one in the full vigour of womanhood until one sees that it is regulated to suit the decrepitude of the elderly man who is following her at a distance of ten paces. And the brazen and unkempt child of thirteen who importunes passers-by in a slum of ill-repute when no policeman is in sight, is surely unconnected with the apathetic young woman of sixteen, curiously well-dressed for a working-class girl, whose hard-mouthed mother brings her from a tenement in Central London to Tottenham Court Road by motor bus, takes her up a side street, and presently returns alone.

[9] If we have . . . written chiefly of the unsuccessful prostitutes who are described to us rescue workers, our excuse lies in the inaccessibility of the successful prostitute.

This inaccessibility is unfortunately most marked in the case of the most successful women. For, as they are presumably the most intelligent of their profession, it is possible that they might meet an impartial enquirer with ready information and help, and in themselves they would be useful as showing how the character is affected by prostitution when it is unaccompanied by the squalor and disorder which are the concomitants of the lower grades of the profession. But these higher ranks are hidden behind impenetrable walls.

[128] [I]f feeble-minded girls do succeed in getting respectable situations they are very likely to lose them because of their lack of intelligence and general inefficiency . . . .

It is obvious that the mental deficiency which makes such women prostitutes also makes them unsuccessful prostitutes. They are as unfitted for this as for any other profession; more so, indeed, since the successful prostitute needs above all things the attributes of coldness and temperance. Their lack of inhibitory powers makes them liable to try to withstand the nervous exhaustion induced by their life by taking to drink . . . . And feeble-minded women are too witless and too lacking in the sense of self-preservation to take precautions against disease. This inability to look after themselves makes them quick to show the results of their life.

[139] It has been stated again and again by various writers and rescue workers that prostitution is not an economic question. Our enquiry leads us to suppose that this conclusion is based on two misapprehensions. Firstly it arises from the fact that a prostitute rarely gives poverty as the reason for her downfall. This proves nothing, for the class from which she is most likely to come regards poverty as a fish might regard the sea in which it swims; it seems the natural element in which all life is supported. And secondly it arises from a definition . . . of 'economic pressure' as 'low wages.' Yet it is plain that a woman may earn a good wage for nine months in the year and yet be forced into prostitution by economic pressure during the other three months of the year. And she may even earn a good wage all the year round, and yet be forced into prostitution by the [140] conditions under which she must work to get this wage. We must regard as insidious forms of pressure all such industrial risks as dependence on a man in authority for obtaining or keeping a situation: the enforced companionship of persons of low moral standard: conditions which, by exercising an unhealthy influence on mind or body, increase susceptibility to chance temptations: or the publicity of certain occupations, which, by bringing a girl before the notice of men and into their company, afford opportunities alike of marriage, illicit association, or prostitution.

[187] [O]nly in rare instances does natural instinct acting alone lead a woman to adopt a life of promiscuity. Still more rarely does it keep her in it if she is given a reasonable chance to earn a decent living in any other way. The net result of our enquiry is to confirm the experience of other writers, that prostitutes in the vast majority of cases come from regions where economic conditions cramp and deform human beings to such a degree that we can only guess what stature 'nature' intended them to attain.

Maude Royden, **Women and the Sovereign State,** *1917*

[54] It is still frankly admitted that prostitutes are necessary: still urged that they must be harried, punished, kept out of sight. The extremity of the exploitation is even more naked [55] than before, since it is said that the prostitute is necessary for men's health, and it is now known that she herself, in the exercise of her trade, very frequently becomes diseased. Syphilis and gonorrhoea are the industrial diseases of prostitution, but they do not fall within the Employers' Liability Act. On the contrary, it is continually urged that when one of her employers has infected a prostitute, she should be punished for it. It is not suggested that she herself should be protected in the exercise of what is held to be a necessary and known to be a highly dangerous trade. She plies it in the interests of men's health; for this purpose alone is she allowed to exist. How, then, can any penalty be too harsh when she gives to her patron not health but a disease? Should we not, indeed, regard it as an extraordinary exercise of Christian charity – or perhaps a maudlin sentimentality – that she is not at once taken out and shot? What does it matter that she herself was infected by a man? He has a right to infect her, if his health or ease required it. She has no right except the right to be exploited.

The law in this country curiously illustrates the theory of the necessity and wickedness of prostitutes. It is, for instance, a criminal offence in a prostitute to solicit a man to sexual intercourse; [56] it is not an offence for a man to solicit a woman . . . . [N]ot only has the prostitute not been protected from her employer, but the wife has not been protected from her husband. He may infect her with syphilis or gonorrhoea, or both, and goes unpunished . . . . [T]his denial of knowledge to women has again and again rendered vain [57] the nominal protection given them by the law, but this is perhaps the most glaring example of the impotence of ignorance. If a woman has never heard of venereal disease, and even when she has contracted it, is not told what is the matter with her, it is merely a farce to give her the legal right to get a separation from the man who has infected her. It is, indeed, constantly asserted that if women know more the happiness of countless homes would be destroyed, but if a husband is infected by his wife he is not denied the knowledge of his disease. It is only in wives that ignorance is the guarantee of happiness.

The whole position is truly an extraordinary one. One would suppose at the outset that prostitution must be either a legitimate or an illegitimate trade. If it is the former, the seller should not be penalised; if the latter, the buyer should be penalised also. But no; in all nominally Christian States, the seller is penalised, but the buyer is free . . .

There is only one logical explanation of the latter policy: it is that, in fact, women only exist [58] to be of use to men.

[90] It will perhaps be urged that men do not achieve these lamentable results in the attempt to shield their own health only. It is in the interests of their wives and children that prostitution has to be accepted, and the prostitute . . . exists to protect 'the purity of countless homes.'

This view of the matter is difficult to reconcile with certain clamorous facts. Both law and custom in most States, for example, so far from protecting the wife from infection with venereal disease, leave her helplessly exposed to it.

[97] [S]ociety has definitely set aside for the use of men the bodies of a number of women, and – since it is strongly held by the majority that unchastity is an unpardonable offence in a woman – it has also regretfully decided to regard their souls as part of the necessary sacrifice. The process has been complete. No degree of suffering or degradation has been spared to women which was deemed necessary for the health of men.

[103] It does not, therefore, appear that the use of women's bodies, quite apart from all regard for them as human beings, simply as instruments of convenience to society, for the protection of men's health, and through them of their wives and families, has really been successful in achieving the end desired. Neither the health of men, nor of their virtuous wives, nor of their innocent children, has been secured, even at the cost of the complete degradation and damnation of the prostitute. Her body has been sacrificed for the health of men, her soul for the safety of women. Here, surely, is the climax of the exploitation of the individual for the advantage of the State; and here, enshrined in the pages of the Royal Commission on Venereal Diseases, the measure of its success.

Mary Scharlieb, What Mothers Must Tell their Children, 1917

[20] If very unfortunately a boy or a girl has attempted to live a married life before marriage, that is to say, if they have prematurely and wrongly used the sacred powers of their body, it is only too likely that such young people may have injured themselves, and in consequence of their want of care and foolishness they may have acquired certain diseases. These diseases are known as *venereal diseases*.

F. W. Stella Browne, Sexual Variety and Variability among Women, 1917

[4] [T]his class of women is in no State adequately protected, least of all in the States which profess Christianity. It is to be hoped that the whole

question of the status and psychology of the prostitute will be very carefully studied. I will only suggest here, that the experience of Eastern civilisations, frankly and systematically patriarchal for thousands of years, tends to show that polygamy legally recognised, is not itself any remedy against prostitution. That remedy lies deeper.

[6] In a social order where women were not tempted for bread and butter, and any of the 'jam' of life, to exploit the desires of men, it would soon become apparent that the sexual instinct is selective. The most ardent natures, if they are not insane or suffering from prolonged sexual starvation, have their cool quiescent times . . . . Much of the unhealthiness of sexual conditions at present is due to the habit of segregating the sexes in childhood and partly in latter life, and making them into 'alien enemies' to one another.

[9] The existence of prostitution is a great wrong to women and love, in subtle as well as in obvious ways: it not only debases the whole view of sex, but – combined with the abuse of alcohol – it favours a mechanical facility of the sexual process in men, which increases the natural difficulty due to women's slowness in reaching complete gratification, thus causing disappointment and disharmony.

Birth control

The idea of restricting births becomes increasingly a topic for discussion, but for several of these writers sexual abstinence is considered to be the only means which should be used. However, others do allude to the possible use of contraception in an approving, rather than condemnatory, way, though seldom with much explicitness.

Frances Swiney, The Awakening of Women, *1908*

[117] Among the many problems awaiting solution at the hands of science and a deeper moral sensibility, none has greater prominence in the eyes of many earnest thinkers, than the best means to procure the healthy perpetuity of the race under circumscribed limits . . . . It is not the number of children born that tend to the future supremacy of race; but the number of children who, by the law of a natural death selection, survive as the strongest and the fittest for life's work. Two healthy children, born of healthy parents, free from hereditary diseases, will do more for the perpetuity and well being of the race, than seven children born of prolific but delicate parents . . . . Women . . . under an en- [118] forced maternity, prematurely wear out their frames . . . .

No woman can with safety to her own health and that of her child, incur the pains of childbirth year after year. The interval for complete recuperation between the birth of each child should be at least three years: . . . she . . . should run no risk of having any extra strain put upon her most vital functions, which already are either in the course of rehabilitation, or are at their fullest working power for the welfare of her child. In no case should the cares and responsibilities of maternity be undertaken if the mother be in a chronic state of bad health; or suffering from any form of developed disease . . . .

As the lights of knowledge regarding physical science become more diffused, women will undoubtedly take this matter of the rights of maternity exclusively into their own hands; and no self-respecting conscientious woman, fully alive to her own duty as a mother, will permit the grave cares of motherhood to be forced unwillingly upon her . . . .

[119] [I]s it too much to expect the same amount of reasonable consideration from the Anglo-Saxon husband towards his wife, as is shown by many races of so-called savages in their marital relations; where, after the birth of a child, the husband voluntarily separates from the wife for a prescribed period?

Maud Churton Braby, Modern Marriage, and How to Bear It, *1908*

[187] It is not clear to me why a respectable middle-class couple who decide that three children is a more suitable number than twelve or fourteen . . . should be accused of defying God by this exercise of common-sense and self-control . . . . Why are the means of regulating families made known to us if we are not to use them when population-pressure becomes acute?

Cicely Hamilton, Marriage as a Trade, *1909*

[191] I have several times asked women whom I know from the circumstances of their lives to have been exposed to temptation whether the thought that they might some day bear a child had not been a conscious and not merely an instinctive factor in their resistance to temptation and the restraint they had put upon their passions and emotions; and the reply has usually been in the affirmative. [192] I do not know whether such a deliberate attitude towards the responsibilities of motherhood is general, but it seems to me essentially feminine, implying, as it does, the consciousness that it is not enough to bear a child, but that the child must

be born of a clean body and come in contact with a clean mind – that the actual bringing of a new life into the world is only a small part of motherhood . . . .

A good many times in my life I have heard the practice of passing the death sentence for the common crime of infanticide discussed by women . . . . And I have always been struck by the attitude of the women who have discussed it . . . [193] since their sympathies were invariably and unreservedly on the side of the erring mother, and I cannot remember having heard a single woman's voice raised in defence of the right to its life of the unwanted child.

Margaret Stephens, Woman and Marriage, 1910

[67] Although the instinct of reproduction is a natural part of healthy life, it is neither natural nor healthy if uncontrolled, or if choked to death. It needs always to be regulated by the intelligence of those concerned. If they do not possess sufficient intelligence, they should seek or be given enlightenment without loss of time; there is no time to waste; life is too short and the consequences too serious for delay. In some cases the conditions of life are so crippled that it is only right that there should be no children . . . .

That such disease of *mind* occurs is proved by the existence of husbands and wives who dislike the thought of having any children at all – men who will actually not allow their wives to become mothers, [68] or, more commonly and still more deplorably, wives who refuse, even at the wish of their husbands, to be hampered by the responsibilities of mother-hood.

Their reasons are manifold; in rare cases they may be good ones, but pure selfishness is the origin of most of them. Such women affirm that they have not the time to spare nor the strength to stand the physical strain, they have no desire for further worry or trouble, they see no possibility of providing for future expense, and so on. The longing for little children is never allowed to pull at their narrow heart-strings.

[81] Many of the artificial methods of prevention are liable to be as injurious as they are useless. There are various devices on the market, some of which are said to be efficacious and non-injurious. Withdrawal immediately before the ejaculation of the spermatozoa is one method, said to be unreliable and detrimental to health.

Lucy Re-Bartlett, The Coming Order, *1911*

[54] [T]hose artificial means which in the educated classes are so largely resorted to in order to prevent results leave the animality resulting from the undue use of the sexual act the same as in the populace, adding to it a new element of depravation through the violation of physical nature which in the populace rarely, and in the animal never appears.

[57] Applying this principle, the act of union would at once be limited to the interests of creation as being the only use for it into which altruism enters in. And with this limitation would vanish instantly all that slumbering antagonism . . . for never would there be any dragging down, and never would the marriage tie feel too close . . . .

Women would not longer have need to feel indignity or humiliation if in the act of union they knew that they had never given themselves to their husbands only, but always to God and to the race. The husband in this way becomes merely the companion in a great act which remains great whatever he may be . . . .

And her maternity, if nothing else, calls woman to comprehend that this, and this only, is the right use for the sexual act in the human being. For how else can [58] she hope to give to her child the pre-natal conditions to which it is entitled? . . . . And in the case even of relatively happy marriage, can a woman's serenity be complete if she know herself to be bringing an *undesired* child into the world – a child perhaps for some good reason undesired by either her husband or herself? It is not enough that such a situation, when it arises, be accepted with resignation – creation calls for something much more vital than resignation . . . .

Let them think just what it means that a woman should have often the choice only between a motherhood undesired, and so unhallowed, and a resort to those artificial preventatives less hallowed still. That there are many women to whom the use of these preventatives offers no difficulty, we know full well, as also that there are women who require no special inspiration for their maternity – who can take it more or less unthinkingly as they take most things in life. But true it also is that these last do not make the finest mothers. And along with the unthinking and the vicious we have the earnest women – along with those who use preventatives lightly, those who would not use them at any cost, and those who use them only with their souls shrinking, under the pressure of circumstances too strong for them. And is this good?

Christabel Pankhurst, The Great Scourge, *1913*

[98] There can be no mating between the spiritually developed women of this new day and men who in thought or conduct with regard to sex matters are their inferiors.

Therefore the birth-rate will fall lower yet.

[99] For several practical, common-sensible, sanitary reasons women are chary of marriage. When the best-informed and most experienced medical men say that the vast majority of men expose themselves before marriage to sexual disease . . . when these medical authorities further say that sexual disease is difficult, if not impossible, to cure, healthy women naturally hesitate to marry.

Mary Scharlieb, What It Means to Marry, *1914*

[38] Worse even than this failure to marry is the determination too often found in married couples to enjoy [39] the comfort and privileges of the married state without accepting its duties and responsibilities . . . . The women are unwilling to accept the children that should be their greatest joy, sometimes on the plausible ground that they do not wish to overburden their husbands, sometimes because they fear detriment to their own health and personal appearance, and sometimes because the care of their children is incompatible with many social or professional engagements. A Nemesis awaits such selfishness, and not only is the country deprived of the sons and daughters who would make her strong, respected, and glorious, but the childless household, or the home in which [40] there is but one little one, is not in so good a position as those richer in children. The punishment falls all round – perhaps most evidently on the country. But it also falls on the father, who gets less than his share of the discipline and therefore of the real joy of life; on the mother, whose nervous system is too frequently injured by her artificial existence.

Maternity: Letters from Working Mothers, *1915*

[59] *Letter #32* I feel that I must write and explain why I advocate educating women to the idea that they should not bring children into the world without the means to provide for them. I know it is a most delicate subject, and very great care must be used in introducing it, but still, a word spoken sometimes does good. Someone has said that most of the trouble with delicate children were caused by women trying to destroy life in the early days of pregnancy. I do not, of course, recommend that sort of thing. It is absolutely wrong. But it is terrible to see how women suffer, even those that are in better conditions of life.

[73] *Letter #47* I cannot tell you much about myself during pregnancy, as I have only had one child and no miscarriage. Perhaps my husband and myself have taken a different view from most people. You see, we both belong to a large family of brothers and sisters, and both had a drunken father, who did not care for their wife and offspring as much as the beast of the field. [. . . .]

When I got married to the man I loved, and [74] who loves me, he said I should never suffer as our dear mothers had done, and that we would only have what little lives we could make happy, and give a chance in life.

[89] *Letter #62* There is one thing – as to mechanical prevention of family. I know it is a delicate subject, but it is an urgent one, as it is due to low-paid wages and the un-earthly struggle to live respectably. All the beautiful in motherhood is very nice if one has plenty to bring up [90] a family on, but what real mother is going to bring a life into the world to be pushed into the drudgery of the world at the earliest possible moment?

[94] *Letter #69* After this, I said to a friend one day, 'If only I could feel that this was my last, I would be quite happy.' 'Well,' she said, 'why don't you make it your last?' and she gave me advice.

As a result of this knowledge, I had no more babies for four and a half years. In carrying this one, I certainly had the bad legs, which I am likely to keep, but my general health and nerves were much better. My health improved, and people said I looked years younger, and I found life a happy place. I sometimes think that the Great Almighty has heard the poor woman in travail, and shows her a way of rest. I had a fight with my conscience before using a preventative. But I have no qualms now. I feel I have better health to serve my husband and children, and more advantages to give them . . . .

I do think that a great deal of misery is caused by [95] taking drugs. The poor woman feels she will do anything to keep herself 'all right.' If only she and her husband also could be taught how to prevent, much good might be done.

[115] *Letter #91* I may say that I have disgusted some of our Guild members by advocating restrictions. I think that it is better to have a small family and give them good food and everything hygienic.

F. W. *Stella Browne,* Sexual Variety and Variability among Women, *1917*

[13] I think much actual motherhood is unwilling, and this is an irremediable wrong to the Mother and the Child alike. Absolute freedom of

choice on the woman's part, and intense desire both for her mate and her child, are the magic forces that will vitalise and transfigure the race . . . . [14] The underhand opposition to the spread of contraceptive information must be overcome. The ineffably foolish laws penalising abortion must be abolished.

Ignorance and sex education

The dangers of sexual ignorance, the paramount importance of enlightenment, and strategies for undertaking this, form a major theme of this period.

Ellice Hopkins, The Story of Life, 1902

[28] Now, when we take away the corolla and stamens, a central fairy pillar is left which is called the pistil, with its slender column, called the style, crowned with the stigma at the top, and at its rounded base, the seed vessel or ovary, all of which form the mother elements of the flower. The style is only a passage-way for the pollen, and is some- [29] times absent. The ovary is the casket in which the ovules or eggs of the plant are held, waiting for the action of the pollen which forms the father element before they can become seeds. When the pistil is ripe the stigma is moist and sticky, and the pollen from the neighbouring primroses is brought to it by insects, or blown against it by wind. When the tiny pollen grain touches the sticky stigma it is held fast. The pollen grain then throws out little filmy tubes, which work their way down through the style of the stigma to the small pearly ovule or future seed of the plant, and through a tiny gateway in the wall of the ovule pour a fertilising fluid which [30] the pollen grain contains. The ovule or future seed is now fertilised, and capable of producing a future primrose. Covered with many protecting coats, it becomes a perfect seed. The ovary swells, hardens, and is transformed into a rounded seed-vessel opening by valves, or a deftly constructed hinge. One day this seed vessel breaks open, scattering the seeds, which complete the cycle or round of reproduction by sowing themselves in the moist sweet earth, where they become primrose plants in their turn, starring the grass with their lovely blossoms.

Sometimes the male and female elements grow upon different plants, as in the catkins you gather in the spring. You know [31] that some are made up of tiny crimson tufts: these are the little mother catkins. Others are dusty with golden pollen: these are the father catkins, and each are barren unless they unite with one another.

[48] As an egg grows it becomes separated from the other eggs and slides down the tube leading from the ovaries to the outer world, but as yet it has no shell. The father bird then deposits the fertilising sperm in the mother bird's body. Each egg, after fertilisation, begins to grow, and becomes embedded in rich nourishing [49] food for the little chick . . . . [T]he mother bird keeps them warm and safe under her own breast, while the father bird feeds her, sings to her 'in full-throated ease,' and in some cases relieves her by taking her place on the nest.

Frances Swiney, The Awakening of Women, *1908*

[134] It is therefore most essential, that as young people grow towards maturity, they should not be kept in ignorance of the wonderful mechanism of the body with which the Creator has endowed mankind . . . . [N]o man or woman should enter on life's duties ignorant of the great potentialities contained within his or her individual organism.
[. . . .]
I am fully aware that this subject is viewed with the greatest repugnance by many worthy and otherwise intelligent and conscientious parents. They still hold by that fatal dictum, 'Ignorance is innocence.' But I put it to the logical verdict of common sense on an analogous case. Suppose it were imperative upon every parent to send forth his loved son or daughter at a certain age to travel through a desolate and terrible wilderness, where on entering the traveller would be beset by many perils, relentless foes, and fearful privations, would not the parent be considered criminally supine and negligent if, knowing himself of these dangers by practical experience, he did not give the wisest and most intelligible directions to his child how to avoid, repulse, and overcome them? . . . .
[135] How many a frail and innocent girl might have been rescued from taking the first step in the downward path, if a mother had lovingly revealed to her the marvellous mechanism of her own frame, the sanctity of wifehood, and the supreme responsibility of maternity!
[. . . .]
Is it not a burning shame, a glaring anachronism in our vaunted cultured twentieth century educational system, that in the scientific knowledge of the human form divine, our children should remain as profoundly ignorant as a Fiji Islander is of the differential calculus? That . . . . woman, the maker of men, is often permitted, unrestrained, when little removed from childhood, to undertake the fearful responsibility of motherhood without warning, without counsel, without knowledge!
[. . . .]
[136] For more especially has this studied ignorance been prejudicial to women. Ignorance has not been synonymous with bliss in their case. The most important study for women is Woman.

Maud Churton Braby, Modern Marriage, and How to Bear It, *1908*

[101] If girls were more reasonably trained with regard to matters of sex, there would be far fewer miserable wives in the world, and fewer husbands would be driven to seek happiness outside their home circle. If, when girls reach years of discretion, they were systematically taught some rudimentary outline of the fundamental principles of existence, instead of being left in utter ignorance as at present, the extraordinary false notions of sex which they now pick up would cease to obtain, and a great deal of harm would thus be avoided. As it is, maidens are now given tacitly to understand that the subject of sex is a repulsive one, wholly unfit for their consideration, and the functions of sex are loathsome, though necessary. I write tacitly with intention, for little if anything is ever said to a girl on this subject; indeed, it is extraordinary how the ideas are conveyed to her without words, but inculcated somehow they [102] certainly are . . . .

Why cannot girls – and boys too, for that matter – be taught the plain truth (in suitable language of course) that sex is the pivot on which the world turns, that the instincts and emotions of sex are common to humanity, and in themselves not base or degrading, not is there any cause for shame in possession them, although it is necessary that they should be strenuously controlled . . . . [T]he present policy of silence on this subject [103] is far more dangerous, inducing as it does a tendency to brood over the forbidden theme.

[. . . .]

This is the kind of teaching that results in those wretched honeymoons which one occasionally hears of in secret, and which produces unwilling wives whose disdainful coldness is their husbands' despair.

Margaret Stephens, Woman and Marriage, *1910*

[11] [I]f parents or teachers would fearlessly face sex union as the source of creation, without thought of or reference to passion (as can be so easily done in reference to the bees and pollen) it would pave the way to the further teaching which must be faced when the lad has to be told, either directly or in- [12] directly, of desires which need all his forces of control, and the girl of her power to stimulate and so debase, or to regulate and so elevate, the magnetism of her sex attraction (Henrietta Barnett, 'Introduction').

[17] Supposing that it were possible to keep from them all knowledge of sexual matters, to be certain that they would remain innocently ignorant until they reached years of discretion, it still remains doubtful whether

such a course would be the best to pursue. But the chances are so enormous against the possibility of the average child remaining in this condition that, among clean-minded parents who give the matter [18] sufficient thought, there can surely be little doubt of the wisdom of forewarning and forearming their children . . . . And it is the duty of those who are the guardians of child-life to forestall any risk of their wandering or being tempted off the right way of living, by instructing them gradually and lovingly in the wonders of creation.

The atmosphere of prudishness in which many young people are brought up is so thoroughly assimilated by them that they cannot, through their false modesty, force themselves to ask one single natural question of their own parents. They prefer instead either to think such matters over for themselves, keeping their eyes extremely well open for the chance of any stray information, or to gratify their curiosity by threshing out points of interest with convenient friends or dependants, frequently in a most undesirable way.

Because of this shyness in asking them questions, many parents imagine that their children are never troubled by curiosity, that such matters are without interest to them. Not once, but many times, have the children been known to say vaguely but positively, 'We could not possibly talk to Mother about these things, you [19] know. What ever would she say?' While at the same time their parents either bemoan their children's want of frankness and confidence, or else they say unconcernedly – indeed, rather thankfully than otherwise – 'Oh, they never give the matter a thought. There is time enough to tell them when they ask us.' Such a time, however, rarely comes, because the children acquire the knowledge in other ways . . . .

By implanting in children clear and simple thoughts on this great law, and by very gradually causing their minds to distinguish between this natural instinct, mothers are preparing a shield of defence for their children which will do yeoman service in keeping them 'pure and unspotted from the world.'

There can be no comparison between this [20] shield so acquired and the flimsy one of ignorance (by no means always innocent) with which indelicate, or at any rate unintelligent, mothers prefer to surround their children.

[275] This solitary indulgence of amativeness, beginning, like most other bad habits, in a small way, may soon become an actual disease of the generative organs. The shock and loss of power consequent on the nervous orgasm affects the whole system, all the vitality of which is thus drained and wasted at a time when it is more than ever needed for proper physical develop- [276] ment. A long train of organic and nervous diseases may result. Symptoms of this vice are: a morbid condition of mind which

shrinks into itself, and which is manifested by an embarrassed appearance under the gaze of others, and by a desire for solitude; unaccountable pains and bodily languor and weakness; dyspepsia; loss of memory; unhealthy skin and dull eyes, and other unhealthy tendencies. The victim who is initiated into it, or who stumbles across it unwittingly, may be too young to possess reason or to exercise conscience. Even older children at the age of puberty, although surely knowing that it is a shameful and unhealthy practice, can have no idea of its harmfulness unless they are warned against it . . . . But the greatest safeguard of all is to explain to children the nature of the habit and the consequences arising from it. And especially is this duty of parents necessary before children are sent to school, for it is appalling how prevalent this habit is said to be in boys' and even in girls' schools. Yet there is hardly a parent who would not repudiate the idea that a child of his or hers could be guilty of such behaviour. When a victim to the habit is discovered, he or she must receive immediate and kindly attention [277] in the way of moral teaching and hygienic living. Kindness and sympathy are essential.

Mary Scharlieb, Womanhood and Race-Regeneration, 1912

[32] [I]t is surely the mother's duty and privilege to teach her children in good time enough of the mystery of life to guide their feet aright. She ought to be able in reverent and careful language to explain to them, as they are able to bear it, the great mystery of the transmission of life. It is not until this subject has been rescued from its present degraded position, and has been recognised as the very acme of human wisdom, that we shall have the 'sweeter manners, purer laws,' so ardently desired by all great and good men. We have to learn that ignorance is not innocence, and that until the children realise that their bodies are the temples of the Holy Ghost, deserving of all reverent and careful treatment, and to be kept with the utmost jealousy from every contact with evil, we shall not attain to the level of purity and moral dignity that would be the salvation of the race. Delicately minded men and women have shrunk, perhaps naturally, but certainly disastrously, from this duty, and the end of it has been that sexual matters have been considered to be necessarily unfit to enter into the education of the young.

[34] It is the mother who ought to be able to impress on the children and young people of the family the right idea of the nobility of home and the dignity of family life; she herself should recognise, and should teach them, that the home is necessary as the unit of civilised society; she should impress on them its dignity, and point them to the fact that the father and

mother are the earthly representatives of the Great Creator, they are the vicegerents of Him who created all the world out of nothing, and who rules it by the word of His power. To the father and mother He has confided the sacred task of handing on the torch of life, and He has left in their hands the formation of the family, the prototype of the kingdom of God.

Dr Helen Webb, Life and its Beginnings, *1913*

[130] As the seed in a flower is fertilised by the pollen from another flower and made able to grow into a fresh plant, so a cell, which is truly a part of the mother, is fertilised by the father, and so given the power to develop and grow into a human baby.

Just as the little lamb is kept safe and warm inside its mother till it is perfectly formed, so our own mothers carry us and protect us within themselves for nine long months, until we become big and strong enough to breathe and cry, and feed, and live as separate beings. The mother knows about it all the [131] time, and thinks much about her little child. She loves it before she sees it, and gets ready everything it will require to clothe it and make it comfortable.

When the nine months are accomplished a way is opened for it, and the baby is born.

There is a great deal about all this which it is impossible for us to understand until we are quite grown up; it is all, however, such a beautiful and intimate thing that we do not speak about it except to our mothers themselves or to some other very dear friend, who is like a mother to us.

Mary Scharlieb and F. Arthur Sibly, Youth and Sex, *1913*

[40] We are indeed only now beginning to realise that ignorance is not necessarily innocence, and that knowledge of these matters [41] may be sanctified and blessed. It is, however, certain that the conspiracy of silence which lasted so many years has brought forth nothing but evil. If a girl remains ignorant of physiological facts, the shock of the eternal realities of life that come to her on marriage is always pernicious and sometimes disastrous. If, on the other hand, such knowledge is obtained from servants and depraved playfellows, her purity of mind must be smirched and injured.

Even among those who hold that children ought to be instructed, there is a division of opinion as to when this instruction is to begin. Some say at puberty, others a few years later, perhaps on the eve of marriage, and yet others think that the knowledge will come with less shock, with less personal application, and therefore in a more natural and useful manner from the very beginning of conscious life . . . .

The facts of physiology are best taught to little children by a perfectly simple recognition of the phenomena of life around them – the cat with her kittens, the bird with its fledglings, and still more the mother with her infant, are all common facts and beautiful types of motherhood. Instead of inventing silly and untrue stories as to the origin of the kitten and the fledgling, it is better and wiser to answer the child's question by a direct statement of fact, that God has given the power to His creatures to perpetuate themselves, that the gift of Life is one of His good gifts bestowed in mercy on all His creatures. The mother's share in this gift and duty can be observed by and simply explained to the child from its earliest years; it comes then with no shock, no sense of shame, but as a type of joy and glad- [42] ness, an image of the holiest of all relations, the Eternal Mother and the Heavenly Child.

Somewhat later in life . . . the father's share in this mystery may naturally come up for explanation . . . In the case of the girl the question as to fatherhood is more likely to arise out of the reading of the Bible or other literature, or by her realisation that at any rate in the case of human parenthood there is evidently the intermediation of a father. The details of this knowledge need not necessarily be pressed on the adolescent girl, but it is a positive cruelty to allow the young woman to marry without knowing the facts on which her happiness depends.

Another way in which the mystery of parenthood can be simply and comfortably taught is through the study of vegetable physiology. The fertilisation of the ovules by pollen which falls directly from the anthers on to the stigma and can be used as a representation of similar facts in animal physiology . . . .

Viewed from this standpoint there is surely no difficulty to the parent in imparting to the child this necessary knowledge. We have to remember that children have to know the mysteries of life . . . . [43] A child's thirst for the interpretation of this knowledge is imperative and insatiable – not from prurience nor from evil-mindedness, but in obedience to a law of our nature, the child demands this knowledge – and will get it. It is for fathers and mothers to say whether these sublime and beautiful mysteries shall be lovingly and reverently unveiled by themselves or whether the child's mind shall be poisoned and all beauty and reverence destroyed by depraved school-fellows and vulgar companions.

Lucy Re-Bartlett, Sex and Sanctity, 1914

[66] There are those who think this difficulty can be met by teachings on botany and biology, and the advisability [67] of sexual instruction on these

lines in the schools is a subject which to-day is occupying many . . . . At best it appears to us inadequate, for it only amounts to a filling of the head, and it is a filling of the heart which in this great matter is chiefly required. No boy or girl in the impassioned moments of life will be ruled by dry thought alone, but they may be ruled by a strongly cultivated sentiment. If the teaching has begun at the right end – that is to say, if the fundamental meaning of sex as love, and something of love in its almighty grandeur has been driven into them – then, and then only, it seems to us, is there much hope that physical passion will find a sufficient check, and physical action fall into its right place and proportion in the general scheme.

It is *Love* which parents require to teach to their children, and much more definitely than in the vague moral way that it is taught to-day. Something of the subtlety of this great force which binds the world together requires to be imparted – the patience, and the delicacy, and the comprehension needed for its maintenance – the greyness of the life which does not hold it′– the gladness always of the life which does. The mysteries of those parts of love which are sympathy and sacrifice – the wonderful interdependence of human lives – the loneliness of the egoist – the gladness of exchange. All these things can be taught *practically* by parents to their children, and they can be thoroughly imbued, through experience, with their truth. Then from this basis the special exchange involved in the love of man and woman will spring naturally, and the special delicacy it requires can easily be taught. Sex is only an advanced lesson in the life of love, but precisely because it is an advanced lesson, its complications should not be embarked upon before the general principles of love be understood.

Edith Lees Ellis, 'Blossoming Time', c. 1914–1915

[72] The child who has developed in an atmosphere of both knowledge and purity, in spontaneous joy and natural expression, through being initiated by those who are born and trained lovers, has a defence against vulgar school-time episodes or when later, in the streets, garbage is offered as a false value in passion.

In blossoming-time the wise parents will train the human being first and let the differentiation of male or female slowly follow in order of gradual [73] evolution. The mother of fertile imagination will soon find out whether to divulge the mysteries of love and birth to her little ones through fairy tales, science, or mathematics. The evolved woman, however, realises in any case that she must interpret these facts to her child in some form of truth, however fantastic or trite the medium may be. The stork, the doctor's box, and the parsley bed are not only stupid but dangerous fabrications . . . . The naked truth about sex is too beautiful to distort, and the parents of the future . . . will have got rid of the old shames and base fears about processes which are at one with beauty and order.

[74] When a mother sees a child she has borne in the first stage of inquiry as to how he got upon this planet she generally evades the questions he asks . . . . Her own initiation into the mysteries of motherhood and fatherhood makes her hesitate before plunging her child into vague or troubled water about its origin. She cheats herself into the idea that ignorance is safety, forgetting that what she refuses to divulge her nursemaid may vulgarise or misinterpret . . . . To explain to a child the simplicities and intricacies of birth one must be able to dwell in fairy-land and hold a magic wand. Common sense to a child is often sheer nonsense and uncommon nonsense reality . . . The mother must be well trained, scientifically and socially, in order that she can answer in rhymes and pictures the questions she is asked. A symbol is the child's epistle, and the truth in that symbol his little [75] gospel. The link between mother and child makes it possible for her to bare her intimate experiences by turning them into fairy lore . . . . To a true mother natural facts cannot but be lovely. Interpreted in this spirit to her child they spell love.

[76] Botany is a wonder-world of suggestion from which to teach a child of human earthly matters . . . . There is no natural fact told simply and sweetly to a little child which can shock it. It is the unnatural emphasis on a natural process which bewilders and destroys.

Mary Scharlieb, The Seven Ages of Woman, 1915

[54] Moral education should, of course, have begun long before the years of adolescence. In early childhood physical facts can be accepted by children without shock and without undue emphasis. Many parents shrink from imparting moral education, and more especially instruction in sexual physiology, to their children. Some [55] of them think that it is wiser to do nothing in this direction; they believe that a child's mind is like a sheet of fair white paper, unwritten on and absolutely blank; they will not take the responsibility of writing on this virgin surface, they prefer to leave it to chance. Logically, they may fairly expect that the page will become dusty and flyblown, even if no worse defilement happens. As a matter of fact, the child's mind is not a fair, unwritten page; it is a *palimpsest*.
[. . . .]
[56] In the moral and sexual education of children one great principle must be observed: the truth, and nothing but the truth, is safe. Among the earliest problems of childhood are those great questions of 'Whence

came I?' 'What am I?' These questions are forced on the child by the circumstances of life. The advent of the new baby, the arrival of the kittens and puppies, the eggs and the nestlings, are constantly before its eyes. Whence came those new and delightful beings? Woe be to the parent who prevaricates, or, worse still, who lies.

Norah March, Towards Racial Health, 1915/20

[9] [W]e must begin to unfold the story of birth during the years of little-childhood, and after the fact of motherhood has been grasped, gradually and unobtrusively, very beautifully, the story of human parenthood should make its way into the child's mind. The simplest and most reasonable way in which this may be done is by making use of the wonderful array of example and illustration provided by the living plants and animals about us, so that the child becomes familiarised with the processes involved in the transmission of life from one generation to another, and becomes acquainted with the right words and terms in which to clothe the facts, all by study of simpler types than the human. Some children have ready, alert, mental activity, and quickly associate one fact with another, realising the whole story in a quick, vivid flash of insight. Other children have thoughts that come ponderously and slowly and need [10] many more facts and details to help them up to the goal.

If the facts of human parenthood are to establish themselves firmly in the young mind and if, moreover, they are to establish themselves in the right attitude and draw unto themselves the right and not undue proportion of consideration, they must be shown in relation to the whole of organic life . . . . [W]hen details of the human processes are later referred to, in intimate confidence between parent and child, the child may, as it were, say to itself, 'I seem to have known that all along.'

Sex instruction, however, cannot faithfully be regarded as complete if it stops short at this point, for we are only at the beginning. The very object in giving these facts of information on human parenthood is that the child's mind may be prepared to accept further information as time goes on, and may be ready to appreciate the meaning of coming changes – the changes of body and mind which accompany the dawn of adolescence. This is simply the first step to be accomplished in direct education for parenthood.

Side by side with the incoming knowledge of the physical facts concerning birth and parenthood, a grand ethical concept must make its place. This important phase of training is even more important than training in knowledge only, but its full magnitude of possibility and its potential influence for promoting integrity can only be adequately realised and obtained when we have a knowledge of physical facts to go upon.

[60] [I]t is infinitely better that the main facts involved in parenthood should be learnt early rather than late – before ten years of age – very often earlier. Childish curiosity concerning these and other things varies greatly in degree and in rate of development: another reason for drawing attention to the mother's privilege . . . . If she allows these opportunities to pass by, unappreciated, her chance is probably gone; for this curiosity which children show is perfectly natural and healthy, and, moreover, is invincible, and if its claims are not satisfied rapidly, legitimately, and progressively by the one in whom all trust should be reposed, the child will be driven to seek the information from other sources – sources often wholly undesirable, often vulgar and pernicious, at any rate less valuable and wholesome than the mother's loving instruction could provide.

As the years of childhood pass, youthhood draws nigh; the transition from the one epoch to the other is a difficult period, one which, accompanied as it is by evidence of physical change, the boy and girl should not be allowed to meet unprepared.

[73] How far it may be necessary and advisable to warn boys and girls against self-abuse is a question which must necessarily be settled for individual cases. Those children who have been wholesomely and adequately instructed in all matters concerning the care of the body, and who have been taught the facts concerning parenthood, and who lead more or less sheltered lives under the constant care of their parents and teachers, will usually be sufficiently fortified against temptation, because the reserve and reticence which should accrue from such training should render them unlikely subjects for objective temptation; or, at any rate, they should need just the incidental word of caution against unnecessary touching of that part of the body. But boys and girls . . . who may be going away from home to boarding-school, or who may be going out into the world to work, stand in need of more definite caution against possible temptation.

Maternity: Letters from Working Mothers, *1915*

[30] *Letter # 11* I had a stepmother who had had no children of her own, so I was not able to get any knowledge from her; and even if she had known anything I don't suppose she would have dreamt of telling me about these things which were supposed to exist, but must not be talked about. About a month before the baby was born I remember asking my aunt where the baby would come from. She was astounded, and did not make me much wiser.

[64] *Letter # 37* I might say that I was very ignorant when I was married; my mother did not consider it at all proper to talk about such things. There

is too much mock modesty in the world and too little time given to the things that matter.

[72] *Letter # 45* I had no mother to talk to me, or for me to ask questions, and both my husband and myself being of a reserved nature, I suffered, perhaps, more than I need have done.

[95] *Letter # 70* I am so glad the Guild is taking up the question of maternity, and also 'Moral Hygiene,' as I feel sure if only young people were advised, both before and after [96] marriage – a great deal of suffering caused to mother and child might be avoided.

[97] *Letter # 72* I have thought, especially since hearing Mrs. ———'s address on 'Moral Hygiene,' what a comfort and help it would have been to me, had the above subject been taught when we were young by school-teachers, or had our mothers realised the need of explaining nature as a necessary form of education. I do hope that the community will soon realise how necessary it is for boys and girls to have knowledge of this important subject.

Downward Paths, *1916*

[33] [I]t must be borne in mind that these girls have been brought up in an almost complete ignorance of the nature and functions of their own bodies. It may seem absurd to urge ignorance of natural facts as an excuse when dealing with the products of congested towns and villages, but it is common experience that profound ignorance often co-exists with hardened depravity. An unwholesome upbringing usually acts in another unfortunate way by producing a curious prudery and false modesty, which makes such girls very inaccessible to attempts at instruction in hygiene, physiology, etc. Certainly the conventional adult policy of leaving the child to pick up its knowledge of sex and reproduction from casual and usually tainted sources, is responsible for many of the difficulties experienced in discussing adolescence and sex with young persons who might be averted from a vicious life by enlightenment and suggestion.

Mary Scharlieb, The Hidden Scourge, *1916*

[51] For generations those who love the young, and have their welfare most at heart, could find no better method to secure their safety than repressive measures and an earnest endeavour to prevent the young people from obtaining any knowledge of sexual matters. Ignorance was

mistaken for innocence, and especially in the case of girls, warning and instruction on the physical side of the facts of life were deliberately and carefully withheld.

It was hoped that the children would grow up without knowledge, and therefore, so it was expected, without risk of contamination. These expectations were seldom fulfilled . . . .

[52] It is not the knowledge of sex matters that defiles the minds and blunts the consciences of young people; it is the vulgarity and the want of reverence with which knowledge is conveyed. If all parents were able and willing to teach their children the facts of life in a reverent and a religious spirit, if they were able to point to human parenthood as the humble and earthly reflection of the divine fatherhood, if they were able to kindle in the minds of the children reverence for their mothers, and a grateful appreciation of all that she suffered and bore for them, the knowledge gained would prove elevating . . . .

[53] Unfortunately, there are but few parents who are fitted either by education, sentiment, or inclination, to give this knowledge to their children. It is to be remembered that the gift of teaching is chiefly enjoyed by those who have themselves been well taught, and that, therefore, the great majority of parents are not only unwilling but are practically unable to help their children in this way. There are mothers, and a constantly increasing number of mothers, who recognise that this duty lies upon them, and who are anxious to instruct their children, but who find in their own want of knowledge and in their want of teaching power in general almost insuperable obstacles. Such mothers need to teach themselves in the first instance, and already there are certain books and pamphlets written with a view to help them.

F. W. *Stella Browne*, Sexual Variety and Variability among Women, *1917*

[13] The realities of women's sexual life have been greatly obscured by the lack of any sexual vocabulary. While her brother has often learned all the slang of the street before adolescence, the conventionally 'decently brought-up' girl, of the upper and middle classes has no terms to define many of her sensations and experiences. When she marries or meets her first lover, she learns a whole new language, and often this language has been defiled in the mind of the man who teaches it to her, long before they met.

Mary Scharlieb, What Mothers Must Tell their Children, 1917

[10] Now do you not think that it is a great pity for girls to grow up ignorant of the wonderful powers that belong to their own bodies? Is it not hard on a girl that she should not be told in good time of what she has to expect both during the change from childhood into girlhood, and also of the extraordinary dignity and happiness to which she may be called a little later in life? . . . . [11] There is a very natural curiosity among young people about the facts of life, and all little children wonder how these things can be. Little people have eyes to see and brains with which to think, and when they find that the cat has new kittens, that the dog has puppies, and the little birds come out of their egg-shells, they are very eager with their questions of how did these little ones come, and where did they come from? Just in the same way even quite small children of four or five years of age are likely to ask where the mother got her new baby. I am sure that you will agree with me that it is altogether wrong and unfair to snub the child and to tell it not to ask questions, and also you will agree with me that an even worse plan than snubbing is to tell the child something that is not true. Children expect their parents to be everything that is good and wise; [12] they have a strong instinct which enables them to find out when we do not tell them the truth, and any mother who tells her child that the doctor brought the baby in his black bag wounds her little child's love for her and his trust in her. The child knows quite well that the mother's answer was untrue, and his trust in her will never again be as perfect as it was before.

[14] The question is not whether children shall know or shall not know these things, but the question really is in what way they shall know them. Will the mother tell the child herself at the right time, and in the best way, or shall the child be left to the pollution and injury to its purity that is sure to occur if these most sacred subjects are discussed in an improper manner?

Some time or other the father's share in the transmission of life will be asked about.

Nature study is a real help in this matter. Elementary botany is taught in most schools, and children see the beautiful arrangements for the continuance of vegetable life.

Maude Royden, Women and the Sovereign State, *1917*

[118] Generation after generation of young girls have been brought up to believe that for women not to know what life, the world, and their own

bodies are like, is in some mysterious way an inspiration and help to virtuous conduct on the part of men. The training such girls have been able to give, when mothers, to their daughters or their sons, has been on these subjects, therefore, valueless, or worse. A mother observed at a meeting for the discussion of such matters that she had brought up all her sons to believe that all women were good: when about to leave school and enter the world, she had informed them that 'not quite *all* women were good.' This, she affirmed, was all that any young man needed to know. If her sons were able to regard their mother in the cold light of reason, they must have concluded that she was a liar or a fool . . . . [119] Nor can this conscientious refusal to know what life is really like be without its effect on the rest of a woman's being. Here, again, one cannot stultify one's mind or prefer mystery to knowledge and a fool's Paradise to reality, without vitiating one's whole attitude of mind and one's capacity for intellectual honesty. The power of shutting the eyes to one set of facts, and deliberately and conscientiously refusing to know one truth, will not be confined to one department . . . but stupefies reason itself in time.

[126] Men have allowed, even demanded, that women shall enter into the holy estate of matrimony without having even the glimmering of an idea what it involved, [127] though the same men would have shrunk with horror from making a contract with another man who should be in total ignorance of its meaning or its consequences to himself . . . . Even the possibility of disease and death resulting from marriage has often been concealed from the bride, who takes a frightful risk without knowing that there are such risks in the world.

Mary Scharlieb and Barbara Butts, **England's Girls and England's Future,** *1917*

[4] There is a very real danger of all this and it is hardly fair if the people who do know about it keep their knowledge from you.

[5] This danger I am speaking of is a danger not only for yourself, but for others. When you have read the rest of this leaflet you will know to fight against the causes of it, and to help others to fight.

You must do it for the sake of the homes of England and the little helpless babies who have never done any wrong. Remember, it is the babies who will suffer if you are not careful with your life. Remember also that girls may lead boys wrong; and that it is cruel to excite in them feelings and desires that cannot be gratified without injury to their bodies and minds.

Some people think that disease and misery only come to those who are really wicked and who lead what is known as a life of sin. This is not true. The truth is that through one act of folly, once you 'go wrong with a man,' you may be infected with disease. The disease [6] that arises from this infection may cause misery not only from personal suffering, but misery because the disease is easily conveyed to others, and unless it is cured it will be handed on to the sufferer's children.

Some people also say that a girl can keep straight if she tries, but that a man cannot. This also is not true . . . . Girls and women are taught that they must exercise self-control. They know that if they give way to temptation sorrow will come. The man who has shared their sin is likely to turn his back on them, their parents may shut their door on them, and they will be left alone to face the perils of childbirth and to provide for themselves and for their babies.

[. . . .]

[7] Wrongdoing between man and woman does not only lead to all these sorrows and hardships, but it sometimes leads to infection with disease and to the birth of poor little sickly babies.

Chapter Three

ᶾ❧

The Stopes era, 1918–1929

Introduction

Following the concession of the limited suffrage in 1918, and the up-heavals of the Great War, new feminist visions of sexuality appeared. Although censorship was still rife, it was increasingly possible to discuss sexual matters rather more openly.

In her epoch-making *Married Love,* published in 1918, Marie Stopes set out a new agenda of sexual satisfaction within marriage on female terms. In 1921 she and her husband established a birth control clinic in North London, and birth control was becoming much more widely debated, although only Stella Browne was yet demanding legalization of abortion. In 1923 a new Divorce Act was passed making adultery by either party grounds for divorce. Clemence Dane commented: '[T]his slip of paper is one of the most important scraps of paper in the history of women, in the history, at any rate, of English women', because it 'defined, so long as England and the English idea shall endure, the status of women: it concedes for the first time her absolute right as a human being to the same law and the same justice that man enjoys.'[1]

Psychoanalysis was becoming fashionable, and its influence on the discussion of sexual questions is discernible. Mentions began to appear of alternatives to heterosexual marriage besides celibate spinsterhood. The problem of the single woman became even more acute in the aftermath of the Great War and perceptions that many women had lost their potential, if not actual, husbands in the conflict. Issues of both non-sexual

1 Clemence Dane, *The Women's Side,* 1926, pp. 106–107.

and sexual friendships between women were being debated. Campaigns continued for the provision of sexual enlightenment to the young. There was still strong representation from the social purity tradition, by the now very elderly (Dame) Mary Scharlieb among others, but their views were increasingly being contested by a new generation who saw sexual pleasure as a good thing in itself, even while continuing to deplore the exploitation of women, the lack of adequate sexual knowledge, and other issues of concern since the days of Josephine Butler (a heroine to such apparently unlikely figures of the day as Stella Browne).

Women commented on the progress made since the end of the nineteenth century, but also argued that it had still not gone far enough and that many patriarchal and Victorian attitudes still survived: Vera Brittain, in *Halcyon*, deployed the conceit of a historian looking back from the distant future in order to critique contemporary attitudes. The inter-war period has often been characterized as one in which the vigour of feminism rapidly declined once the suffrage had been achieved. The material quoted here contradicts this simplistic analysis of an era in which feminist fervour was taking many different directions. Dorothy Russell remarked in her opening speech to the World Congress for Sexual Reform in London in 1929:

> As a woman I am especially glad to see so many prominent and able women present at this Congress. I think it is not too much to say that the great progress which has been made during the last ten years or so in freedom of thought and action as regards sex matters has been in the last resort due to the emancipation of women and to the courage of emancipated women in tackling these problems. Here I do not need to mention names, for the names of pioneers are well-known to you. I should like rather to stress what has been done in this country, especially on a subject like Birth Control, not by single individuals, but by the united action of organized bodies of women. We are rather proud of the efforts of political Women's Conferences in bringing this subject before the public and persuading them that the women most concerned did not think it too indecent for discussion, but, on the contrary, a matter of national importance. In fact, I think it is true to say that what holds back reform as regards marriage, child care, and sex in general, is rather the conservatism of men than of women, though it used to be pretended that conservative customs were demanded by women for their protection.[2]

2   Mrs Dora Russell's welcome speech to the Sex Reform Congress, in Norman Haire (ed.), *World League for Sexual Reform: Proceedings of the Third Congress, London, 1929* (London: Kegan Paul, Trench, Trubner & Co., 1930).

Other recommended resources

The later reports and evidence received of the (non-official) National Birth-Rate Commission of the National Council of Public Morals. The Report and Evidence of the Street Offences Committee, 1928. Women's magazines: see especially *Modern Woman*, of which Leonora Eyles was agony aunt, and which introduced popular Freudian terms such as 'complex'. *Time and Tide*, an 'equality feminism' periodical edited by Lady Rhondda, which by the late 1920s was increasingly giving space to debates on birth control, and the censorship of Radclyffe Hall's lesbian novel, *The Well of Loneliness*, itself an important source of the period. Another novel of significance was Clemence Dane's *Regiment of Women* (1917, many subsequent editions), frequently cited in discussions of same-sex relationships.

Marriage

There is a new discourse of marriage as a rewarding and erotic relationship, in which companionship, rather than hierarchy, is the dynamic force. However, this vision of transformed heterosexual monogamy is advanced against a background of sexual apathy and boredom, and even resistance to husbandly coercion of marital 'rights'. The perilous passage of the wedding night and its potential to shock unsuspecting brides remain the subject of recurrent warnings.

Marie Stopes, Married Love, *1918*

[xi] To-day, particularly in the middle classes in this country, marriage is far less really happy than its surface appears. Too many who marry expecting joy are bitterly disappointed . . . .

It is never *easy* to make marriage a lovely thing; and it is an achievement beyond the powers of the selfish, or the mentally cowardly. Knowledge is needed and, as things are at present, knowledge is almost unobtainable by those who are most in want of it.

[22] It has become a tradition of our social life that the ignorance of woman about her own body and that of her future husband is a flower-like innocence. And to such an extreme is this sometimes pushed, that not seldom is a girl married unaware that married life will bring her into physical relations with her husband fundamentally different from those with her brother. When she discovers the true nature of his body, and learns the part she has to play as a wife, she may refuse utterly to agree to her husband's wishes . . . . There have been not a few brides whom the

horror of the first night of marriage with a man less considerate has driven to suicide or insanity.

[70] [A]n important piece of advice to wives is: Be always escaping. Escape the lower, the trivial, the sordid. So far as possible . . . ensure that you allow your husband to come upon you only when [71] there is delight in the meeting. Whenever the finances allow, the husband and wife should have separate bedrooms. No soul can grow to its full stature without spells of solitude. A married woman's body and soul should be essentially her own, and that can only be so if she has an inviolable retreat. But at the same time the custom of having separate rooms should not mean, as it often does, that the husband only comes to his wife's room when he has some demand to make upon her.

Marie Stopes, A New Gospel to All Peoples, *1920*

[16] No act of union fulfils the Law of God unless the two not only pulse together to the highest climax but also remain thereafter in a long brooding embrace without severance from each other; by which and through which only can the vital interchange be perfect, and following from which only can the love of the man toward the woman remain undiminished. For then, and then only, does the man receive back from the woman an exchange of vitality, which more than compensates [17] for that which he has given to her. Ignorance of this truth has led the multitudes into a befouling and debasing view of the union in which the man is encouraged, even by the Ministers of the Church, to look upon his own part in this holiest of all sacraments as a mere gratification of his own lust instead of a mutual enrichment for God's service. Through this error multitudes of men have missed the compensating return from the woman, and, therefore, have felt a reaction of dulness [*sic*] or of active dislike against their partners, which reactions have caused untold sorrow, humiliation and weakness to women who would otherwise have been radiant and joyous reflections of God's love on earth.

Arabella Kenealy, Feminism and Sex-Extinction, *1920*

[184] Nothing less binding than a lifelong contract is coercive enough or is sufficiently chastening to bridle woman's native changefulness and curb her instinctive emotionalism. The realisation that there is no way out of a situation is her finest incentive to nobility. She bruises her impulses against the iron of circumstance, and the essences of her intrinsic Woman-soul distill in patience and in sweetness.

H. M. Swanwick, Women in the Socialist State, 1921

[36] [A]nything which tends to weaken personality, to make one of the partners a slave or an appendage of the other, weakens marriage. The economic dependence of a woman on a single man does, as a matter of fact, make her his slave. He may repudiate the state of master in his inner-most heart, but his own economic situation may render it impossible for him to make her free. He may refuse to take any actual advantage of the odious position into which he is forced by no fault of his own, but so long as the present economic system lasts, very large numbers of women will be the economic slaves of individual men.

There is something terrible about the intimate dependence of one person upon the other in the sex-relation. But if that dependence be personal, it may [37] have a terrible beauty; there is nothing but terrible squalor in the dependence that is purely economic.

Lady Barrett, Conception Control, 1922

[17] Where the whole being enters into the union of the sexes, the complete joy of marriage is realised, the characteristic of which is that it does not fade, but becomes ever deeper and more fully realised, a sure indication that the highest pleasure of sex union is only attained when it consummates a love which involves mutual sympathy and consideration. Physical union alone produces dissatisfaction the more quickly in pro-portion as it is physical only; on the other hand, when all parts of the nature find their counterpart in another, the joy of such intercourse pervades the whole life, and frequent repetition of physical intercourse is not essential to its highest development.

This is well known to all true lovers who have for varied reasons exercised some voluntary self-control in regard to the physical side of sex in marriage, either in deference of the one to the desire of the other, or to avoid too frequent child-bearing, or in special seasons such as Lent.

On the other hand it has been observed by most people that many marriages which seem [18] to promise well, quickly lose even to the eye of the outsider all the romance of the days of courtship. Is not too frequent physical indulgence sometimes the cause?

Norah March, Sex Knowledge [1922]

[7] There are remarkably few really happy marriages, marriages, that is to say, in which life-long fidelity of each to each is the joyful, voluntary choice, in which parenthood is welcomed, in which comradeship exists between

husband and wife, in which a wise understanding of the emotional needs of each leads to entirely satisfactory marital relationships; unions in which, through love, strength is given to meet serenely all the many trials which domestic life, for most families, is bound to hold. The number of divorce cases, which seems to have increased so greatly during recent years, represents but a tithe of the unsuccessful marriages which never come to the divorce [8] court for solution. The number of divorces may, in itself, be a sign that men and women realise that there is something deep and significant in love, and that they are questioning whether it is right to prolong such an intimate partnership as marriage without the harmonising influence of love.

Maude Royden, Sex and Common-sense, *1922*

[84] [T]o my mind those who do not admit the concern of the community in their marriage do lack something. But to suppose that those people are immoral, when others who live together, legally licensed to do so, in selfishness, in infidelity, for financial reasons, or for social reasons, are moral is fundamentally dishonest. When a woman sells her body for money, do you think that it makes it moral that she does it in a church or in a registry office? . . . . [85] If you marry for any reason but love – for experience, to 'complete your nature' – without much regard to the man or woman you marry, or to the children you bring into the world, are you not exploiting human nature just as certainly, though not so brutally, as a man who buys a woman in the street?

[106] I cannot help feeling that when through years this conviction that there is no reality in a marriage persists, this is the one really decent and sufficient reason for declaring that that marriage is dissolved. Let us have done with the infamous system now in force, by which a man and woman must commit adultery or perjury before they can get us to admit the patent fact that their marriage no longer exists as a reality . . . . To force a woman to demand the 'restitution of conjugal rights' when such 'rights' have become a horrible wrong; to compel a man to commit, or perjure himself by pretending he has committed, adultery, before he can get the State to face the fact that his marriage is no longer a reality – is this to uphold morality?

[123] I have known marriage after marriage wrecked by the almost unbelievable ignorance that has been present on both sides. I say both sides. First of all, there is the girl. To her, marriage comes sometimes as so great a shock that her whole temperament is warped and embittered by it. Then there is the man, equally ignorant – very often, probably less ignorant

of himself, but equally ignorant of her – not realizing how she should be treated.

[180] [H]usbands have, in genuine ignorance of the cruelty they were committing, raped their wives on their wedding night. Judging by what one knows of wedding-days, it could hardly be supposed that there could be a more unpropitious moment for the consummation of marriage. And when to the fatigue and strain of the day is added – *as is still quite often the case* – blank though uneasy ignorance as to what marriage involves, or the thunderbolt of knowledge launched by the bride's mother the [181] night before, or the morning of the day itself, it would be difficult with the utmost deliberation and skill better to ensure absolute repulsion and horror on the part of the bride . . . . But I wish men could . . . understand that to enforce physical union when a woman's psychical and emotional nature does not desire it, is definitely and physically cruel. Woman is not a passive instrument, and to treat her as such is to injure her.

Perhaps I may be forgiven for labouring this point because, in fact, misunderstanding here is so disastrous. Marriage, after all, is a relation into which the question of physical union enters, and if there is no equality of desire, marriage will be much less than it might be. Women are – idiotically – taught to believe that passion is a characteristic of the depraved woman and of the normal man, who is shown by [182] this fact to be on a lower spiritual level than (normal) woman. This senseless pride in what is merely a defect of temperament where it exists has poisoned the marital relations of many men and women.

Leonora Eyles, The Woman in the Little House, 1922

[129] 'I should'nt [*sic*] mind married life so much if it wasn't for bed-time.' This remark has been made to me on five separate occasions, all of which are very vividly impressed upon my memory, because, before I was married, it puzzled me intensely, and thus 'stuck': afterwards it seemed astonishing to me.

The first time I heard it was when I was about seventeen; it was said by the wife of a carpenter in Staffordshire, where I had a room for a month; they had seven daughters; they were kindly, pleasant folks; in all the month I did not hear a word of unkindness from any of them. Then – that astonishing remark. She grew confidential, did Mrs Smith . . . . She spoke of many struggles, and looking quietly into the fire, finished up in a dull, grey voice:

'But I didn't mind any of them things. I could put up with anything but the going to bed side of it.'

[. . . .]

[131] [I]n London three women said the same thing to me, and from conversations I have overheard, I know that many others think in the same way . . . . One would hear such remarks as this from a woman in the thirties:

[132] 'Oh, well, say what you will, there's a lot to be said in favour of the old Kayser! You do get your money certain of a Monday now, and don't get it subbed back off you all week! And you do get your nights to yourself, and no fear of another blooming kid!'

A young woman, a war bride with perhaps a week's honeymoon as her sole experience of marriage, would protest that she didn't want her nights to herself, and the older woman would say cynically:

'No, my dear, you don't know what you're up agen yet. But you wait till you've been to bed over three thousand nights with the same man like me, and had to put up with everything. Then you'd be blooming glad the old Kayser went potty.'

[140] The prevalent idea among men, from what women tell me, is that continence is wrong; he thinks he is a decent British working man who married and supports a woman for various reasons, and he 'is entitled' to his pound of flesh. The very idea of being 'entitled to' something that should be mutual puts the wrong construction upon it at once; the very moment that people begin to mention their 'rights' over each other, all the mutual joy of loving and giving vanishes automatically.
[. . . .]
The man who, because he knows nothing of control, and has never had it suggested to him that control is desirable, makes the exercise of the sex function a nightly occurrence, is not only submitting his wife to an unendurable nervous strain; he is spoiling his own pleasure also. He is making what should be a feast into a dreary penance.

[147] I am convinced that the sex impulse which brought the two together, is not paralysed in these ten-years-married women. But they have found, by bitter experience, that what was at first charming and exhilarating, has grown, through their husbands' selfishness and carelessness, to be unendurably distressing to nerve and body and mind alike . . . . [148] Men must be taught that what amounts to forcing their wives' imitation love is not going to make for comfortable homes, married harmony, and even lasting physical pleasure, though it does produce unendurable and insupportable numbers of children.

Isabel Hutton, The Hygiene of Marriage, 1923

[1] It is in the first months of marriage that the basis of the happiness, and often of the health, of the whole of married life is made. The years that follow are coloured by those early days, probably the most momentous in the life of a man and certainly so in the life of a woman. Want of knowledge on the part of both partners and want of a proper outlook on all that marriage means on the part of the woman, may cause physical and mental suffering. This may have ill-effects at the time, and recent researches in nervous diseases have shown very clearly that the strain of the early weeks of marriage may cause nervous and mental troubles many years afterwards.

[2] Most of this strain or indeed all of it in normal people, could be entirely avoided if a few simple anatomical and physiological facts were clearly understood. They must, however, be looked at in a thoroughly open and natural way and not through the mist and haze of poetical and romantic language.

[33] They have been brought up in total ignorance of all that relates to the 'mystery of sex.' Its very mystery has made it a subject for introspection and often for very coarse humour. Surely it is time to unveil it of its mystery and deal with it in a perfectly frank and impersonal way. Only when discussed in this way will it lose the unhealthy atmosphere which surrounds it, and men and women ceasing to be morbidly curious about it, will look forward to the consummation of marriage without fear. Women will also learn to regard sex life in marriage, not only as a duty to the man they love, but as something to be joyfully shared between them. They will think of it as a natural, healthy part of married life, and they must be taught that which otherwise they will learn only by bitter experience, that without a normal sex life their marriage will be unhappy, and one or both partners will suffer in health.

Ettie Rout, The Morality of Birth Control, 1925

[128] Conjugal rights are really natural rights, and if they are wilfully withheld by either party to a marriage, and without the consent of the other party, then that withholding constitutes valid grounds for the dissolution of the marriage. The legal way of settling such a difference may not be wise or nice, but that is beside the point. The marriage has been practically annulled and its legal dissolution should follow automatically. Age, temporary absence, illness, and a host of other conditions may lead to the suspension or cessation of intercourse: an open or tacit agreement of both husband and wife as to the permanent cessation of intercourse may occur; but women in particular ought to understand that in marriage they

have no right wilfully to impose total sexual abstinence on their husbands by refusing to have relationship; and if they do so refuse [129] they have no moral or legal ground of complaint if he satisfies his normal sexual needs by extra-marital intercourse. Similarly, if a man, through drunkenness, profligacy, or otherwise, fails to take care of the sexual needs of his wife, he may be cruelly laying waste what does not belong to him – her sexual health and happiness. The basis of the contract made between the husband and the wife is the mutual granting of love-relationship to one another: any variation in this must fairly be by mutual consent: otherwise, clearly there is a breach of contract – a justification for declaring the contract null and void, according to the law of the land.

Mary Scharlieb, 'Courtship and Marriage', 1924

[142] The most intimate relations of married life must [143] always be a matter of deep concern to both husband and wife. The principles upon which matrimonial happiness can be based are well expounded by S[t]. Paul, who tells them to exercise 'due benevolence,' and who admonishes them thus:- 'defraud ye not one the other except it be with consent for a time that ye may give yourselves to fasting and prayers and come together again,' in order that the objects of marriage may be fulfilled, and that they may derive from this intimacy such mutual comfort and support as shall be a real influence for good on every part of their triune nature . . . .

[143] [A]n ideal marriage involves fruition and . . . no domestic happiness is complete without the presence of children.

[146] Another consideration for people who have a difficult married life is that even an erring partner has a very real claim on forbearance and makes a valid demand for help. And after all if there be no remedy, and if no amelioration be possible, it is the wisest part to embrace the sorrow as a means of purgation, to possess one's soul in patience, looking to the end for the reward.

Ettie Rout, Sex and Exercise, 1925

[2] But as to the genital organs and their inter-relationship with the urinary and anal system, woman knows nothing. Thus, the physical basis of marriage is genuinely beyond her comprehension and outside her efficient management and control . . . . Soon after marriage, however, she realises that happiness – and even fidelity – are dependent much more on the personal efficiency of marital intercourse than on the technical control of fertility . . . . [3] This book itself is . . . an effort to explain briefly

the mechanism and functions and development of the lower half of a woman's body, using the simplest language possible and avoiding needlessly technical terms.

Marie Stopes, Enduring Passion, 1928

[2] A generally felt anticipation seems to be: – That the very basis of marriage is thus [3] attacked by the 'inevitable' failure to persist, of the mutual sex attraction. That it gradually fades out altogether as does a child's sandcastle on the shore, eaten away little by little by the advancing tide of indifference the waves of which lap forwards after each act of union in the trough of despondency or indifference which follows it.

[30] A number of married women's lives are rendered unduly difficult . . . because their husbands' demands for union are in excess of what they themselves can give with spontaneous and mutual satisfaction . . . . Such demands, even if made by true love, generally result in the woman becoming the 'slave of man,' as it is rather luridly described by the feminists. On the other hand, her happiness may be threatened by the knowledge that her husband is unfaithful to her, and is impelled to this by mere physical desire. A woman's potential happiness in sex life is deadened or killed outright by demands [31] which are so frequent and so regardless of her own needs and requirements that they crush spontaneity and happiness, and consequently invade the health . . . .

Many women gallantly try to meet it and *act* the daily part which they could, with natural and spontaneous happiness, really feel at less frequent times. Dissimulation, however, is a poor and shifty foundation for so important an edifice as love. Wherever possible something more real should be done to assist in the mutual adjustment.

Vera Brittain, Halcyon, 1929

[27] [I]t is now a commonplace that our present monogamous habits become general only after the complete removal of all restrictions upon the paid work of wives, for this reform not only made possible earlier marriage for the male partner, but allowed the woman wisely to choose a husband whom she loved, instead of being driven by social and economic pressure to take the first comer who could provide her with subsistence.

[88] Human marriage at last appears to have completed its long development away from the total indifference manifested between husbands and wives among primitive peoples, to the point at which life orients itself

round one individual, and sexual intercourse is voluntarily reserved as the supreme and final expression of love for that person. While we regard matrimony as a relationship of which the beauty is not necessarily spoiled [89] by an occasional and frankly-acknowledged extra-marital experience, permissible for some cogent reason such as that of honour to an old obligation, we recognize that this type of adventure should be indulged in only as the outcome of mutual agreement and full confidence between husband and wife if it is not to destroy that loyal attitude of two individuals towards one another which constitutes true monogamy.

Marie Stopes (ed.), Mother England, *1929*

[9] I married knowing practically nothing of what married life would be like – no one ever talked to me and told me things I ought to have known – and I had a rude awakening.

[11] I would like my Husband to satisfy his Desires yet I am terrified at the thought anytime he comes near me and it causes unpleasant scenes in the Home.

[41] [S]ince then we have never let Nature have her full swing (if I may say so), and I feel for his sake. It should not be so, it does not seem right to deprive him thus, but he and I dread it happening again.

[61] [W]e feel we are injuring our health by straining against having any more children . . . . You will no doubt understand that it is only at certain times of the Month when we nearly get beyond control, we have used the preventive yet that does not satisfy the feelings.

[85] I feel frightened to death as soon as something happens between my husband and myself that I shall fall again, I love children very much and my children are fine children but we cannot afford any more . . . . I cannot expect my husband to cease cohabiting with me, for my part I would not mind at all for it's the woman pays each time.

[114] My husband . . . has refrained from any relation whatever since that time, but lately he is beginning to fret under the strain, being the average strong, healthy working man, and although there is no word of reproach, the fits of irritableness and bad temper, are getting worse and more often, and I feel sure will end in a separation soon if nothing can be done. I have [115] a lot of Spanish blood too in my veins which doesn't help any, living as we have to do and is wearing my nerves to pieces.

[120] The two occasions on which our two children were created, was when we both consented. So we dare not 'mutually agree' again, in case something happened, and so often I feel mean in refusing, that which I have a right as a married woman to give, for my husband has been so fine, so patient, kindly and considerate to me, yet there is always the fear, it might happen the very first time I agreed.

Dora Russell, 'Marriage and Freedom', 1929

[27] It is my belief that whereas there is no value whatsoever in a permanent marriage enforced by law, there is for many men and women a rich and abiding happiness in such a marriage maintained by the generous love of both parties, and by the old-fashioned sentimental sanctions of unselfish creative love for the children, the facing of life as a partnership, and the weathering of sorrow and illness side by side. Needless to say, the partners to such a marriage should in my view neither expect nor even persuade each other to grant complete sexual fidelity, but it is essential that they should show each other honesty, and that kind of psychological loyalty which any friend expects of another engaged with him in a difficult enterprise.

Vera Brittain, 'The Failure of Monogamy', 1929

[40] This non-fulfilment of ostensible monogamous ideals is usually attributed to that increase of freedom and sex-knowledge which began in a mild form about 1912 and has since . . . extended to the more sophisticated members of every social class. On the contrary, I believe the non-observance of monogamy to be due, not to a surplus but to an insufficiency of freedom.

[41] I personally believe that . . . there will have to be many forms of marriage in order to suit various types of individual psychology. One type of nature may find stimulus in constant variation, but there is another type that seeks its adventures in intellectual discovery, in creative work, in power, in administration or in politics, that requires a basis in emotional stability and a refuge from change in the security of a personal relation of which the permanence is reasonably certain. In our present state of biological childishness, our still almost complete enslavement to animal instinct, functional change, and physical limitation, there are probably very few married couples for whom monogamy is desirable or by whom it is obtainable. The fact nevertheless remains that when loyal and lasting friendship, arising from highly individualized selection and constantly

cemented by mutual passion, does happen to be embodied in marriage, it constitutes one of the highest and rarest achievements of the human spirit.

Such an achievement, however, is not to be forced upon humanity either by shrill exhortations or by furious prohibitions.

[43] At present the main demands of the woman's movement – that woman shall not be hampered in the struggle for economic independence, and that wifehood and motherhood shall not be penalized by occupational discriminations – are entirely in accordance with the biological needs of the race and the demands of successful monogamy.

Janet Chance, 'A Marriage Education Centre in London', 1929

[38] [T]here is a widespread lack of the experience of orgasm amongst the women. By many it is not even expected that the marriage relationships should be enjoyed by the wife . . . .

This state of affairs, which holds good in all levels of English society, is an extremely serious one. It is responsible for much concealed misery, for the resultant prudery of English women, for their cowardly handling of sex in their nurseries and schoolrooms, and for their grotesque social and political behaviour over the question of Birth Control.

[39] [T]he work of a Marriage Education Centre is needed almost as much by the rich as by the poor of this country.

Desire, pleasure and satisfaction

This post-Great War period sees an articulation of the existence of, and discussions of the nature of, female sexual desire and women's potential to experience sexual pleasure. How this might be achieved is also described with a new explicitness about the mechanisms of female arousal and gratification. The strains lack of sexual gratification might place on the celibate woman are also described.

Marie Stopes, Married Love, 1918

[26] By the majority of 'nice' people woman is supposed to have no spontaneous sex impulses. By this I do not mean a sentimental 'falling in love,' but a physical, a physiological state of simulation which arises spontaneously and quite apart from any particular man. It is in truth the

creative impulse, and is an expression of a high power of vitality. So widespread in our country is the view that it is only depraved women who have such feelings . . . that most women would rather die than own that they *do* at times feel a physical yearning indescribable, but as profound as hunger for food. Yet many, many women have shown me the truth of their natures when I have simply and naturally assumed that of course they feel it.

[. . . .]

[27] [I]n our northern climate women are on the whole naturally less persistently stirred than southerners; and it is further true that with the delaying of maturity, due to our ever-lengthening youth, it often happens that a woman is approaching or even past thirty years before she is awake to the existence of the profoundest calls of her nature. For many years before that, however, the unrealised influence, diffused throughout her very system, has profoundly affected her. It is also true that (partly due to the inhibiting influences of our customs, traditions and social code) women may marry before it wakes, and may remain long after marriage entirely unconscious that it surges subdued within them. For innumerable women, too, the husband's regular habits of intercourse, claiming [28] her both when she would naturally enjoy union and when it is to some degree repugnant to her, have tended to flatten out the billowing curves of the line of her natural desire.

[29] Woman is so sensitive and responsive an instrument, and so liable in our modern civilised world to be influenced by innumerable sets of stimuli, that it is perhaps scarcely surprising that the deep, underlying waves of her primitive sex-tides have been obscured, and entangled so that their regular sequence has been masked in the choppy turmoil of her sea, and their existence has been largely unsuspected, and apparently unstudied.

[47] [W]hen the man tries to enter a woman whom he has *not* wooed to the point of stimulating her natural physical reactions of preparation, he is endeavouring to force his entry through a dry-wall opening too small for it. He may thus cause the woman actual pain, apart from the mental revolt and loathing she is likely to feel for a man who so regardlessly uses her. On the other hand, in the tumescent woman the opening, already naturally prepared, is lubricated by mucus, and all the nerves and muscles are ready to react and easily accept the man's entering organ.

[49] Where the two are perfectly adjusted, the woman simultaneously reaches the crisis of nervous [50] and muscular reactions very similar to his. This mutual orgasm is extremely important . . . but in many cases the man's climax comes so swiftly that the woman's reactions are not nearly

ready, and she is left without it. Though in some instances the woman may have one or more crises before the man achieves his, it is, perhaps, hardly an exaggeration to say that 70 or 80 per cent. of our married women (in the middle classes) are deprived of the full orgasm through the excessive speed of the husband's reactions, or through some mal-adjustment of the relative shapes and positions of the organs . . . . Yet woman has at the surface a small vestigial organ called the clitoris, which corresponds morphologically to the man's penis, and which, like it, is extremely sensitive to touch-sensations. This little crest, which lies anteriorly between the inner lips round the vagina, enlarges when the woman is really tumescent, and by the stimulation of movement it is intensely roused and transmits this stimulus to every nerve in her body. But even after a woman's dormant sex-feeling is aroused and all the complex reactions of her being have been set in motion, it may even take as much as from ten to twenty minutes of actual physical union to consummate her feeling.

Arabella Kenealy, Feminism and Sex-Extinction, *1920*

[167] Physical passion in woman is derived from the Male-traits in her. It is, accordingly, a borrowed, not an inherent instinct. And in all natural women, passion is secondary to love; love belonging to her own intrinsic nature. Because of its heritage, there is, in a true woman's love, always a maternal altruistic element: unselfish, ministering, devoted. Love has come to be intensified in her by fire of passion and by force of personal attraction. It is no longer a mere meek surrender, with fear for spur and maternity for solace. In proportion as she is of high organisation, it has become a complex of mind and emotion and sense; intense and vital. But always, in proportion as she is womanly, her own way of loving – the way of devotion and tenderness – is ascendant over passion.

[170] [S]o potent and subtle is Nature's consistency with regard to this primary and vital function of woman in Life, that whether or not biological issue results, psychological issues do inevitably. Woman's mode and mood of receptiveness in this mysterious union so operate that, in her surrender, she admits to the inmost sanctuary of her being an alien presence – which remains with her till death. Fade as it may from her consciousness, it remains, nevertheless, impressed for ever after on the vibrant records of her sensitive Subconsciousness.

[172] In natural woman who has arrived at womanhood without premature arousing of the senses, soul and sense are at fine poise, and respond in vital unison to love. In girls whose innocence and conduct have not been duly safeguarded, the prematurely-excited senses have become detached from the soul – from the higher emotions, that is.

Helena Swanwick, Woman in the Socialist State, *1921*

[17] It is by no means clear that women are less injured than men by repression. Modern science has shown how much repression has to do with insanity and when we note the high ratio of insanity among women . . . we seem to see a probable connection between repression and degeneration in women . . .
[. . . .]
There are some who, from a perverted sex craving, desire to experience male domination, and others who, from idleness or [18] timidity (natural or acquired), do not care to exert their own will. A true libertarian will say, 'By all means let such a woman find a domestic tyrant and may she have joy of him.' But he will add, 'Do not let our social system deliberately encourage such perversion, idleness and timidity. On the contrary, let us make institutions under which women can grow to their full stature as responsible human beings.'

Maude Royden, Sex and Common-sense, *1922*

[32] Yet how long have women been taught that this divine impulse of creation is something base! Base even in a man, belonging to his lower nature; still more deplorable in a woman, a thing to be [33] ashamed of, a thing to crush down and suppress, a thing you would not confess to your nearest friends, or discuss with your physician. To speak of it even to your own mother would be to be met with the averted look and word of disapproval. If, as a consequence of this, women have inhibited their own nature, so that many women have created in their minds a kind of tone-deafness, a colour-blindness to this side of life, does that not seem to you a tragedy?

[116] I did not say that men and women suffered *in the same way*. I said that they suffered *equally*; and since the question has been raised, I should like just to answer it here . . . . [117] [I]n the case of a woman . . . very often the strain on her is much less dramatic, much less violent, and more persistent. I think of the strain as something like that silent, uninterrupted thrust of an arch against the wall, of a dome on the walls that support it. There is no sign of stress. But it is so difficult to build a dome rightly that Italy, the land of domes, is covered with the ruins of those churches whose domes gradually, slowly, thrust outwards till the walls on which they rested gave way and the church was in ruins. That kind of strain is easily denied by the very people [118] who are enduring it. It is so customary, so much a part of their life, that they are unconscious of it.

Isabel Hutton, **The Hygiene of Marriage,** *1923*

[22] There are women who, up to the time of their marriage, and even throughout the whole of their married life, never experience any sexual feeling. It is probable that those who do not develop it after the first year or so of married [23] life are not normal. It is quite normal, however, for a woman not to experience in any way the feelings of sexual excitement, even towards the man she loves, till some time after marriage has been consummated. In these cases it is apt to be somewhat of a mental shock to her to discover the strong sexual feelings of her husband in the early days of marriage.

Courtship is a gradual preparation for marriage, and during this time the woman, whether she be young or no longer very young, often begins to experience for the first time her sex instincts with her growing love for the man. In women it is probably much less a separate instinct than in a man, and much more coupled with feelings of tenderness and maternity.

After marriage it is altogether different, and most women develop strong sexual instincts; in the cases in which they do not, there is little chance of health or happiness in the union.

There is also the woman who has a well-marked sexual instinct developed before marriage, and if this be added to the love she bears her mate, then she is starting her married life under the very best circumstances.
[. . . .]

[24] Many women who do not actually experience sexual emotions before marriage really have them, but consciously or unconsciously sublimate them into other feelings and activities. This often takes the form of a desire to have children which is unaccompanied by any sexual feeling.

[45] When she is ready for the act to begin, the stimuli to the local nerves cause a flushing of the parts and a dilation of the vaginal aperture. Certain glands are rendered active and pour out a mucous substance which lubricates the parts and makes entrance easy. The male organ is then pressed against the vaginal aperture and the sensitive glans at the point of it receives further stimulation set up by contact, and it enters into the vagina . . . .

[46] As excitation continues, the vagina of the wife becomes congested, and rhythmic muscular movements take place which envelop the erected penis in a soft but firm grip, and so stimulate it, that the act continues involuntarily and without effort on the part of either the man or woman. The two are thus, for the time being, physically as well as mentally one, and a mutually adjusted couple should now proceed simultaneously to the climax of the act. At the height of excitation in a fully aroused woman, the spasmodic contractions of the vaginal walls very slightly draw down the uterus . . . .

After a varying time the climax of local and general pleasurable excitation occurs, and with the completion of the act which is, in the male, the ejaculation of seminal fluid into the vagina, and in both the sensation which is called orgasm. It is this orgasm which is so essential to the health and happiness of the couple, for without it the act is not completed.

Orgasm varies in intensity, but is always an unmistakable sensation which pervades and thrills through every fibre of the being; it is especially concentrated in the organs of generation, and following it there is a general feeling of fitness and well-being.

[68] When the wife becomes sexually mature there may be times when she desires intercourse although her husband may not have suggested it. This is only natural and normal . . . .

[69] It is true that many married women keep from their husbands the knowledge that they enjoy partaking in the act and would feel a certain sense of shame in acknowledging it . . . . Nothing could be more wrong that this point of view, for the normal woman should share equally in all the joys of married life. If she does not do so, many organs in her body will never function, and she cannot reach full maturity or perfect health.

Ettie Rout, The Morality of Birth Control, 1925

[61] [W]omen experience sexual pleasure only when having intercourse with a man who is beloved by them. Hence whenever woman is free, and economically independent, she gives herself only in love; that is, she is naturally chaste. This fastidious loving selection is the foundation of [62] morality . . . . Promiscuous intercourse is not natural to women at all. Women prostitute themselves because of poverty, moral imbecility, and so forth. But normal healthy economically-independent women have no temptation to give themselves excepting in love, and it requires very little effort indeed for a girl to be virtuous in the presence of a temptation which makes no appeal to romance or affection.

Ettie Rout, Sex and Exercise, 1925

[13] Pseudo-frigidity occurs when the slumbering sexual perceptions have not been roused, or perhaps where the woman has been shocked or mis-educated. Falling in love and a wholesome re-education are the obvious remedies, though not always easily applicable. So long as society continues to teach girls that sexual intercourse is something shameful and secretive, and gives brides no knowledge at all of the realities of wedding, naturally

there is grave danger of young women's views being distorted, and of their becoming artificially frigid. It is this artificial frigidity, not the natural warm-heartedness of youth, that brings so many marriages to ruin.

In some cases frigidity is due to masturbation (self-abuse) in early life. Masturbation lowers sexual excitability in women much more than it [14] does in men. It blunts women's sensibility for normal sexual intercourse [. . . .]

In marriage, sexual frigidity may also be due to over-haste, mal-adroitness, or brutality on the part of the husband; intercourse being more of a pain than a pleasure to the wife.
[. . . .]

[15] Absolute permanent frigidity is irremediable; but most of the frigidity in women is not of this nature at all; it is more apparent than real, and temporary and partial rather than permanent and absolute.

Quite frequently the root-cause is *prolonged constipation*.

Science is beginning to teach us that something which all healthy-minded, healthy-bodied adults regard as necessary and desirable – marital intercourse – cannot be happily practised, is not even wished for, if the excretory functions are in disorder. When we suffer from prolonged con-stipation, that is, when the large colon (bowel) is overloaded with waste putrefactive matter, normal sexual desire may be replaced by abnormal sexual disgust.

Marie Stopes, Enduring Passion, 1928

[39] [A] woman making sex demands greater than can be met by her husband, is a creature almost unthought of by the Victorian social code. She is, however, a very real person, known to antiquity, feared throughout the ages, and perhaps now at last, as a result of the recent frank attitude towards sex and its problems, openly recognised once more.
[. . . .]

[40] What of a woman whose sex needs are such that she is left either below par and dissatisfied or really physically unhappy, almost ill, without frequent sex union, if her husband, while being not abnormally under-sexed, yet is unable to meet her demands? Many women suffer frightfully in secret when placed in such a position in a 'civilized' community. I am inclined to think that a large number of those in a 'neurotic' condition, sufferers from sleeplessness, bad temper, indigestion and so on, are the victims of sex-deprivation. The profounder needs of their whole organisms are not being met.

Can anything be done? Of course *self* stimulus, or masturbation is extremely common. It is used by married women whose husbands, having stimulated them, leave them in 'mid-air' with no orgasm, causing nervous irritation. Masturbation is *not* the proper remedy, and a careful husband should secure orgasm for his wife.

[89] In a normal woman, this nervous complex [the clitoris] is extremely responsive and is one of the main avenues leading to complete orgasm, but this may be under-developed in some women and in others may be almost entirely absent. [90] Where it is very much reduced or absent, the chances of the woman being able to experience the full nervous reaction of married union is very materially reduced . . . . Some women on the other hand experience orgasm mainly or solely from the stimulus of the region of the cervix (the neck of the womb, an organ entirely internal), and never experience a clitoris-orgasm at all.

These two quite distinct sensitive areas in women, both of which or either of which without the co-operation of the other may lead to a full and satisfying muscular orgasm in women, give rise to orgasms differing both in quality and result.

[166] [A] very large number of women begin, after the Change of Life, for the first time really to enjoy their sex spontaneously and happily. I even know a woman, aged 60, who *for the first time* at that age began to enjoy sex union . . . .

[167] This woman is not at all abnormal; others are like her although she was a little unfortunate in having to wait so long for the true realisation and enjoyment of the natural physiological process of sex union. There are many who, having enjoyed it but little in their youth and early middle age, after the freedom from anxiety of the menstrual period with its recurrent tendency somewhat to reduce the vitality, benefit when the natural vitality of the system tends to accumulate instead of waste, and they derive more spontaneous gaiety and real benefit from sex union than ever before.

Marie Stopes (ed.), Mother England, 1929

[53] I am very passionate as well as He, and we have been so wonderfully happy and I do so want to make this happiness last.

[136] With the love we bear each other its impossible to put passion entirely out of our lives, for it's the love I bear my dear Husband that makes me yield to him at such times.

[151] I never knew before then the want of my husband as I do now at times it has come over me about three times now in the last six months . . . . I feel so un- [152] happy and so irratable and bad tempered I feel that I am just the cook and housekeeper.

115

[156] [M]y husband tells me to control and hold myself in check, well I can, but we do without kisses, and oh, lots of other little things that help to make life pleasant, then I get depressed, my husband gets ill-tempered, we quarrel, make it up and afterwards I am in torment.

Heterosexual relationships outside marriage

There is increasing mention of consensual, non-commercial, relationships outside the bounds of marriage: however, it is not entirely clear whether the perception that these were happening to a far greater extent is altogether borne out by reality. Some writers clearly take birth control to be much more available and reliable than is the case at this period. Another motif of this period (partly a result of the loss of so many men in the war) is 'free motherhood': the deliberate choice of maternity outside marriage. Opinions about this were mixed. The question of 'anticipation of marriage' also appears.

Marie Stopes, The Truth About Venereal Disease, 1921

[29] All women, from the innocent girl tempted for the first time, who yields from trustful if foolish and immoral love, to the practised woman who has had pretended love affairs with a dozen different men, to the tragic figures of the women paid by hundreds – every such girl, every such woman has taken a great risk on every occasion, for the man who swears that he is clean may yet convey to her those invisible germs. What is she to do?

A woman's bodily organs are of a different shape from those of a man, much less easy to rub and to wash, and offering places where it is more easy for the germs to conceal themselves, as within the soft folds and crinkles of her inner skin. What is she to do? Of course, what she should do is not to allow the touch which may bring its pollution with it, but, if she is overcome by circumstances, or if her soul is [30] not the mistress of her body, she may at least try to cleanse herself.

[35] [W]here for instance the man and woman have something approaching to or have even a real warm and affectionate feeling for each other, and where the woman is not a professional prostitute but a private woman who holds her honour cheaply, or who may perhaps be prevented by circumstances from marrying the man she loves, then the risk of infection and of the transference of disease germs from one to the other is much greater . . . . it is necessary, however repulsive and displeasing it may be, to separate and repeat after each connection the washing and the most careful greasing and disinfection.

Maude Royden, Sex and Common-sense, *1922*

[54] These nomads of the affections give and take so little as they pass from hand to hand that they become cheap and have little left to give at last: nor do they really get what they would take. Men and women claim the right to 'experience,' but experience [55] of what? We do not live by bread alone, and the physical experience is not really all we seek. It is something, however? Yes – certainly something: but by a paradox familiar enough in human affairs, to snatch the lesser is to sacrifice the greater. The experimental lover, the giver whose small and careful gift is for a time, claims in the name of 'experience,' of the 'fulfilment of his nature,' what really belongs only to a greater giving.

[57] Let me say one last word on . . . those who affirm for every woman 'the right to motherhood' . . . . [58] I realize the cruelty of a civilization in which war and its accessories create an artificial excess of women over men, and in consequence deprive hundreds of thousands of women of motherhood. I do not think I underestimate that cruelty or its tragic consequences. I admit the 'right' of women to the exercise of their vocation and the fulfilment of their nature.

But I affirm that those who base upon this claim the right to bring children into the world, where society has made marriage impossible, are not moved to do so by the instinct of motherhood. No, no, for motherhood is more than a physical act; it is a spiritual power. Its first thought is not for the right of the mother but of the child. And what are a child's rights? A home – two parents – all that makes complete the spiritual as well as [59] the material meaning of 'home.'

[168] A girl will sometimes play on a man as a pianist on his instrument, put a strain on him that is intolerable, fray his nerves and destroy his self-control, while she herself, protected not by virtue but frigidity, complacently confirmed that she 'can take care of herself.' The blatant dishonesty of the business [169] never strikes her for a moment. She takes all she wants and gives nothing in return, and honestly believes that this is because she is 'virtuous.' That she is a thief – and one who combines theft with torture – never occurs to her; yet it is true.

[172] I want boys and girls, men and women, to see far more of each other and get to know each other much better than in the past. I believe in co-education, and in *real* co-education – not the sham that is practised in some of our universities and colleges. [173] I see the risks and I want to take them. I know there will be 'disasters,' and I think them much less disastrous than those attending the methods of obscurantism and restraint. I think the idea that a boy and girl may not touch each other introduces a

117

silly atmosphere of unreal 'romance' where commonplace friendship is wanted.

Leonora Eyles, The Woman in the Little House, *1922*

[149] [S]peaking from a fairly deep enquiry into the statistics of the illegitimate children of married women during the war, I am convinced that the sex impulse comes partly from propinquity, partly from monotony – by this I mean the sex impulse to infidelity . . . .

[150] Another man – the lodger, the employer, the casually-met man who speaks nicely to her – can, for a while, bring back some of the thrill of courting days; he is adorably *new*: not being her owner, not being sure of her, he has to 'make love' before he can gain any satisfaction for his desires; he finds it so easy to turn her head, full as it is of little, sordid worries. It is understandable that *any* woman, whose husband only talks to her about mending, money, children, and other worries, will be a little bowled over when some other man tells her, however insincerely, how charming she is! Women are incurably romantic; the weariest, most unattractive of them will grow young for a minute as they catch, in some quite mediocre man, a vision of the Fairy Prince left over from girlhood – and it is only afterwards that they find that he wasn't a Fairy Prince at all, but something of a satyr.

Mary Scharlieb, Straight Talks to Women, *1923*

[73] As an old doctor I am constantly hearing the story of a girl's ruin. It is seldom the one impetuous, inevitable, irrevocable deed – it is usually the gradual breaking down of conventions and restraints, the constantly increasing acts of familiarity, and the final yielding in response to the lover's assurances. It cannot be wrong, he pleads, to forestall our happiness a little, a very little! Surely you trust me! You know that you are everything to me! We are soon to be married! In God's eyes we are already one – only these dull, stupid people would keep us from each other's arms! Come to me! Believe in me! Cheer me, I am thy husband! And then – the girl who yields finds that her lover is no longer so desirous, no longer so keen on the home they were to build. His respect for her has gone, and what she yielded lightly is henceforward claimed as a right. On her falls all the shame and on her the burden of the long and difficult years, the struggle to [74] regain her social status and, still more difficult, her self-respect.

Engaged couples cannot be too careful. In all their innocent happiness there lurks the possibility of mutual dishonour and the threat of a ruined future.

Dora Russell, Hypatia, 1925

[29] I would hazard a guess that, relatively to the population, fewer women retain their virginity till death than in the Victorian period or the Middle Ages. In all probability it is sex, not sexlessness, which makes women cling so tenaciously to the right to earn their living. Marriage brings a jealous intolerant husband, children, prying and impertinent neighbours – degraded and [30] humiliating slavery for the vast majority of women. Thirty shillings a week and typing or working in a shop, a still tongue, or a toss of the head and the assertion that independence is the best; and, in the background a lover with whom somehow evenings are spent – a lover who has no claim and cannot tyrannize . . . . Marriage would change him: Aspasia knows it. Marriage would also rob her of that thirty shillings a week, which alone stands between her and the abyss of primeval submission . . . . There are holidays of delight and secret dread of the scandal which will end the work Aspasia loves – or marriage and the certainty of that end at once.

Marie Stopes, Sex and the Young, 1926

[133][H]ealthy illegitimacy seems to me immeasurably less awful than many other aspects of the foul diseases and perversion into which a base attitude towards sex has led men and women. Certainly, illegitimacy impinges on the vital problems of race in a most serious way . . . . Those who harshly and cruelly visit the sins of the fathers upon the children and make the lives of normal yet illegitimate children unbearable, are cruel and much to be condemned from every point of view. At the same time a racially subversive tendency is at present current on the part of some well-meaning people who desire chivalrously to protect the unmarried mother and her child . . . . *[H]is mother has failed to maintain her self-respect and the respect of the father*. Therefore the illegitimate child does not possess in his mother the creatrix whom he has a right to expect.

[135] Illegitimate children are the offspring of mothers who vary widely . . . .

Women of supreme self-respect and independence of mind. These are not numerous and form only a small minority. They have resented intensely the iniquitous laws giving the sole legal ownership of their children to the legally married husband. They resented also the other unnatural supports given to male sex dominance by our laws relating to marriage. They therefore refused [136] legal marriage but, as a result of deep love and the desire for a child, they bore to their lover a child or children without going through the legal ceremony of marriage.

As regards home influences, children born of such unions are in almost as good a position as the legitimate child; possibly at times better than the children of many legal unions . . . .

The number of such deliberate and self-respecting mothers of illegitimate offspring, however, is not large.

[138] The third type of unmarried mother is she who, having forgotten her own personal honour so far as to trust a man's promises that he would cherish and regard her without wedlock, finds that in practical matters he fails and betrays her by allowing her to become pregnant after assuring her that she would not; and then that he will not or cannot marry her. Yet she does not try to evade her motherhood, and lovingly endeavours to do the best for her child. This girl too merits sympathy, for one feels that her up-bringing and education have grievously failed in not having guarded her with an impenetrable armour of self-respect which would render it impossible for her to permit physical relations before marriage. Were girls instructed (as this whole book is a plea that they should be) in the physiological facts of sex, they could not believe what was told them by a [139] young man desirous of caressing them ephemerally, nor would they trust the various amateur means of controlling conception which are popularly supposed to be within the man's power.

Mrs Cecil Chesterton, In Darkest London, 1926

[26] 'You'll want all the goodness you can get, my girl, and so shall I. This one will be my first, and I'll take care there's not another. Gawd!' she clenched her thin hands in denunciation. 'Men are rotters, aren't they? It's a bleeding shame we should have to pay for their pleasure!'

All the bitterness of woman from the first beginnings was in that voice, all the passionate revolt against the fate which makes the woman pay. It was a dramatic moment. Instinctively I caught my breath. It was the Madonna of the club foot who answered her.

'Ah, yes!' she said, with a wonderful smile, 'they may have the pleasure, but we have the babies. When I knew mine was coming, I felt a bit like you; I couldn't know how I should want it; and then it came, and something grew in me as if my heart would burst, and I don't care what happens, so as he's mine!'

[27] 'But how do you keep him – and you with another coming?' . . . .

I hoped that the discussion would go further. It was a revelation to me to hear these young unmarried mothers handle the vital things of life with such clear-sighted honesty. It was as though I had come to a [28] new and undiscovered country. We are all of us so fond, in literary circles, of discussing whether the modern woman has any use for love; we are most of us agreed that she has very little for sex! In Mare Street, Hackney, they would stare astonished at such arguments. They know exactly what they risk and why they risk it. And they do not grumble when they get hurt. They do not rebel against their fate, nor very much against the men who get them into trouble. They have the babies – that is enough, and, secure in achievement, they go on with their life.

[39] It is often said that a girl who has 'fallen' – most hideous and obscene description – once, will 'fall' again, and that the majority of unmarried mothers find their way to prostitution. This is contradicted alike by figures, facts and experience. My little Madonna of the club foot, about to have her second baby, will remain the same brave, kindly and hard-working woman should she have twenty illegitimate children rather than two.

Charlotte Haldane, **Motherhood and its Enemies,** *1927*

[92] [I]nsistence on the meritorious aspects of virginity began to be lessened. This disdain for a condition which had previously been considered, among the majority of the population of both sexes, one to be preciously cherished until the wedding night, continued to grow . . . .

[93] A baby, even a subsidized baby, certainly lessens a girl's chances of marriage . . . while the absence of a rudimentary membrane is not a similar consequence. So long as books on birth control can be purchased at every railway station, and means to practise it at almost every chemist's, we must as a matter of mere common-sense assume that they will reach those for whom they were not originally intended. We have also to note that since the war the professional prostitute has not only to reckon on a formidable competitor, who generally earns her living at some other occupation, but that there is no longer a single class of women certain to avoid the risk of venereal disease before marriage.
[. . . .]
[94] Amateur prostitution seems to be one of the economic consequences of the peace which have not been sufficiently examined . . . . Their wages do not suffice to buy more than their board and lodging at home and the finery they consider indispensable; if they did, the remnants of a 'chivalrous' point of view teach them to expect attentions from their young men or 'boys' . . . . As far as I can see, the girl, if she is fond of the boy or wishes to obtain more treats from him, can reward him as she chooses and as freely as circumstances permit. It is certainly not for the young man to teach her moral [95] restraint. He will be kept from a professional competitor, but as the figures for the troops prove, he will not necessarily be the better in health for that.

[136] A female type of whom, as far as I know, no authoritative psychological study has been made, must now be considered. She approximates, perhaps as closely as any modern woman can, to the 'Companion' of ancient Greece. The more intelligent women of this class are absorbed by the interpretative arts. In music, the drama, or on the film they are successful and valuable. But others who possess beauty do not need intellectual gifts. They find men willing to support [137] them either in or out of wedlock. All, however, traffic in their appearance, competing with prostitutes for male favours, always on the understanding that they shall not be requested to reproduce . . . . At present it is difficult to explain social tolerance of these female parasites on any other hypothesis than that there is an economic demand for them; but changing economic conditions may alter their position in future . . . .

They are in fact, whether outwardly respectable and married or not, the higher members of the old professional prostitute class. The amateur is distinguished from them by the fact that she earns her living, while unmarried, or when married while unencumbered with children, in factory or office. With her the lure to the streets is not essentially economic but psychological.

Vera Brittain, Halcyon, 1929

[13] In the endeavour to offer their readers sentimental consolations for the alarming increase of illegitimacy, some of the more passionate newspapers of the period gave way to quite hysterical outbursts on the fruitful topic of war-babies. The mothers of these infants were said to have given 'all' . . . for the love of their country and of some noble soldier . . . .

This characteristically British type of toleration proved to be quite ephemeral, for whenever, after the War ended, a woman indulged in a peace-baby with an exactly similar unorthodox origin, her neighbours again considered her conduct to be highly reprehensible.

Mary Scharlieb, The Bachelor Woman and Her Problems, 1929

[61] It may be quite possible for a woman, whether married or unmarried, to covet and earnestly to desire the possession of the love of some man who has already vowed his life to the service of another woman, and consequently she is predisposed to believe that the man of her choice is not happy with his wife. She may come to believe that the wife is neglectful, cold, and unsympathetic; she may, more or less sincerely, think that if she had the management of that man's life she could help him more efficiently

than does his wife, and that her influence on him would be entirely for good.

[63] [I]n considering the question of divorce it is essential to remember the many cases in which it is obtained by means of terrible dishonesty. These are the cases in which a woman, married or unmarried, conceives a great passion for a married man, and without realizing the wrong inflicted upon the man's wife and on their children, [64] uses every influence and employs every means in her power to have a divorce pronounced so that her passion may be satisfied, and she may even hold the wife up to scorn and derision if she objects to part with her husband and to break up their home.

Same-sex relationships, celibacy, and singleness generally

The situation of the unmarried woman becomes a particularly acute one in the aftermath of the Great War and the slaughter of so many actual or potential husbands and fiancés. There is a good deal of sympathy for the plight of these women and suggestions as to how they might best manage their lives. Although some anxieties about the problem of 'inversion' are raised, particularly in the context of adolescent development, affection between women is by no means decried and is even praised, providing that it does not slide into morbid emotional outbursts of jealousy and hysteria. A sound and rational friendship between women is even seen as a legitimate and socially desirable substitute for the marriage denied. The growing influence of psychoanalysis on these debates is apparent, though the new science of 'glands' and their secretions is also deployed.

Constance Long, Collected Papers on the Psychology of Phantasy, *1920*

[138] Women have been obliged willy-nilly to do men's work in engine yards, in munition factories, on the land – in every field in fact of industrial and professional life. Something male in a woman's psychology has been called for, and we have seen there is a latent sex-element which enables her to respond. In fact, the regulation tasks of the sexes have been completely mixed, for in many camps and hospitals the women's work has been done exclusively by men.

If homo-sexuality crops up at such a time . . . its existence is not new. Perhaps the necessity to accept and consider it as one of the problems of our times is new. Franker discussion of all sex problems has made it possible to consider it here to-day.

Homo-sexuality then is love for members of the same sex. It begins at home among brothers and brothers, sisters and sisters, and has always united mothers and daughters, fathers and sons in bonds of friendly love. This useful emotion is emphasised in school and college life, and not excluded from existence and importance by the fact of co-education. It has great value in promoting *esprit de corps* . . . . [139] It is the beginning of lasting friendships. It is a way in which humans find some of their relations with each other and with society . . . .

Personal friendships which are fraught with such fair promises have their dangers too. The erotic element is capable of taking concrete and undesirable forms. Here, too, the heavy hand of conventional morality comes down with excessive tyranny, and boys particularly, and more rarely girls, are sometimes summarily expelled from school for an error they but half understand. Some promising careers have been wrecked this way, and love, which is such a valuable teacher, has been tortured into a demon shape.

[141] It is even a question whether people who are exclusively homo-sexual really exist. I think they do. But the majority so-called are so because the libido which might have gone on to the further hetero-sexual stage becomes fixed in this immature and regressive form, so that the highest type of actual love in an individual case never outgrows this character; and difficulties which are estimated as 'insuperable,' are experienced in loving a member of the opposite sex.

The homo-sexual tendency may become 'fixed,' because in the absence of personal effort and development, it is the easiest sexual expression life offers to a given individual. It arises as we have seen out of unnatural conditions such as the segregation of the sexes, – or out of the economic difficulties in the way of marriage. Among women, whose numbers [142] considerably surpass those of men, there is an arithmetical reason for it in the impossibility of marriage.

Arabella Kenealy, Feminism and Sex-Extinction, *1920*

[259] This misplaced affection for members of the same sex arises from the attraction of traits of the opposite sex unduly developed in them. While indifference to members of the opposite sex results from lack in these of the characteristics of their sex, normally accentuated. Thus a woman is more drawn to one of her own sex possessing virile characteristics, physical or mental, than she is drawn to a weak-brained, emasculate man. Masculine women are attracted likewise by the womanly graces and quality of feminine women . . . .

All is an expression of the law of the Attraction of Opposites, which (normally) causes persons of opposite sex to be strongly drawn to one another.

On the other hand, the development in himself, or in herself, of the characteristics of the opposite sex makes members of either sex independent of and indifferent to members of the other, by supplying them with a spurious counterfeit of qualities it is natural to seek in those others.

Maude Royden, Sex and Common-sense, 1922

[7] I want to emphasize with all my power that the hardness of enforced celibacy presses as cruelly on women as on men. Women, difficult as some people find it to believe, are human beings . . . . The idea that existence is enough for them – that they need not work, and do not suffer if their sex [8] instincts are repressed or starved – is a convenient but most cruel illusion. People often tell me, and nearly always unconsciously *assume*, that women have no sex hunger – no sex needs at all until they marry, and that even then their need is not at all so imperious as men's, or so hard to repress.

[10] [T]he normal – the average – woman sacrifices a great deal if she accepts life-long celibacy. She sacrifices quite as much as a man . . . . I do not say, and I do not believe, that passion in a woman is the same as in a man, or that they suffer in precisely the same way . . . . But I am persuaded that we shall not even begin to reach a wise morality so long as we persist in basing our demands on the imbecile assumption that women suffer nothing or little by the unsatisfaction of the sex side of their nature.

[29] I want then to combat with all my power this ancient but un-Christlike belief that women miss their object in life if they are not wives and mothers. It may seem something of a contradiction that I should . . . have emphasized the need of women for the satisfaction of their sexual nature, and now be arguing that we must not assume that they have no right to exist if they do *not* meet this particular satisfaction; but I think you will realize that it is not a paradox . . . . [30] A woman may and does suffer if she does [31] not fulfil the whole of her nature, and yet . . . it is a monstrous fallacy to affirm that, because of that, she ceases to have any reason for existence; that she is a futile life, a person who does not really 'count.'

[135] People have sometimes discussed with me whether it is right to have as intense and absorbing a love for a friend of one's own sex as exists between lovers. The word 'absorbing' is perhaps the difficulty in their

minds. All love is essentially the same, and it has been pointed out that the great classic instances of great love have been almost as often between friends as between lovers. But the test of love's nobility remains the same. If it is in the strict sense 'absorbing' – if, that is, it is exclusive, if it narrows one's interests instead of enlarging them, if it involves a failure in love or sympathy with other people, it is wrong – it is not in the true sense 'love;' but if it enriches the understanding, widens interest, deepens sympathy – if, in a word, to love one teaches us to love others better, then it is good, it is love indeed.

[139] [T]hose who uphold the Platonic view are not always debauchees but sometimes men and women who, however incomprehensibly, still sincerely believe that they and not we who oppose them are the true idealists. This is why it is worth while to state our reasons for our profound disagreement, and to do so as intelligently and fairly as possible. [140] It is also worth while because no one has suffered more cruelly or more hopelessly than those whose temperament or abnormality has been treated by most of us as though it were *in itself*, and without actual wrong-doing, a crime worthy of denunciation and scorn.

First, then, let it be remembered that the highest types humanity has evolved have been men and women who are really 'human,' that is to say who have not only those qualities which are generally regarded as characteristic of their sex, but have had some share of the other sex's qualities also.

[. . . .]

[141] It is not the absence of the masculine qualities in a man, or of the feminine qualities in a woman which raises above them above the mass; it is the presence in power of both; and no man is truly human who has not something of the woman in him – no woman who has not something of the man.

[. . .]

[142] For harmony of life and temperament the body should be the perfect instrument and expression of the spirit. When you have the temperament of one sex in the body of another, this cannot be. There is at once a disharmony, a dislocation, a disorder – in fact, a less perfect not a more perfect type. Humanity does, I believe, progress towards a fuller element of the woman in the man, the man in the woman, and the best we have produced so far confirm the truth of this. But it is not an advance to produce a type in which the temperament and the body are at odds. This is not progress but perversion.

[144] What then should those do who have this temperament? No one perhaps can wisely counsel them but themselves. They alone can find out the way by which the disharmony of their being can be transcended. That

it can be so I am persuaded. That modern psychology has already made strides in the knowledge of this problem we all know. What is due to arrested development or to repression can be set right or liberated: what is temperamental transmuted. But I appeal to those who know this, but who have suffered and do still suffer under this difficulty, to make it their business to let in the light, to help others, to know themselves, to learn how to win harmony out [145] of disharmony and to transcend their own limitations . . . . It may be that out of a nature so complex and so difficult may come the noblest yet, when the spirit has subdued the warring temperament wholly to itself.

[. . . .]

We are content to condemn in ignorance, boasting that we are too good to understand. In consequence, though a few here and there have preached homosexuality as a kind of gospel, far [146] more have suffered an agony of shame, a self-loathing which makes life a hell.

To be led to believe that one is naturally depraved! – to be condemned as the worst of sinners before one has committed even a single sin! Is that not the height and depth of cruelty? Do you wonder if here and there one of the stronger spirits among these condemned ones reacts in a fierce, unconscious egotism and proclaims himself the true type of humanity, the truly 'civilized' man? How shall they see clearly whom we have clothed in darkness, or judge truly who are so terribly alone?

To have a temperament is not in itself a sin! To find in your nature a disharmony which you must transcend, a dislocation you have to restore to order, is not a sin! . . . .

[148] It is no more 'wicked' to have the temperament of a homosexual than to have the weakness of an invalid. It is difficult for the spirit to dominate and to bring into a healthy harmony a body predisposed to illness and disorder. The greater the glory to those who succeed! Let us confess with shame that in this other and far harder case we have not only ignored the difficulty and despised the struggler, but – God forgive us – have, so far as in us lay, made impossible the victory.

Norah March, Sex Knowledge *[1922]*

[23] It is a stage through which most women have passed as school-girls, when they conceived a more or less violent affection of a sentimental nature for a woman teacher or for a school-girl, frequently older than themselves . . . . [24] Some individuals, grown up to-day, can look back into their lives and identify their passage through this stage of 'homosexual interest,' as it is called. Others are unaware of having passed through it, partly because they happened to pass through it very quickly and proceed to adult development, and partly perhaps because it has been associated

with experiences conceived in themselves or by their consequences, to be so unpleasant that they have been thrust away from the memory, that is, forgotten; while yet others can, looking into their own lives, realise that they are still experiencing homosexual interests. It may be that development has never gone beyond this stage, that, in short, the individual has never properly 'grown up,' or it may be that the stage has, as the auto-erotic stage may do, tended to persist, alongside of the next, the adult stage of development.

[60] In the realm of the mind . . . as well as that of the body, it would seem that the continent life may, while admittedly the incomplete life, be entirely compatible with health and efficiency. But – and here lies the importance of self-knowledge – if control is associated with compulsion, with fears, with anxieties, if, in short, it is not the *voluntary* choice of the individual, it may be achieved at the cost of some mental serenity, efficiency, and of happiness. Yet even at that cost it is worth while, if, by its observance, the well-being of others is assured.

It cannot be too strongly emphasised that the great secret of real happiness in the sexual life lies in self-mastery. The master force of sex must itself be mastered – *mastered*, not extinguished – an important distinction. In mastery the rich promise of sex is reaped. Through mastery, sublimation of sex energy gives greater force to the personality, greater power to the mind. Unbridled and flagrant yielding to passion, whether within or without the bond of matrimony, does not bring joy – only a loss of self-respect.

[61] Through work is the great tide of sex energy directed into other channels than those of bodily sex interest.

Marie Stopes, Sex and the Young, *1926*

[53] [W]here the staff are all unmarried I fear I am not pessimistic in saying there is increasingly the risk that there may be one or other member whose sex manifestations are not natural, and who is partly or completely homosexual. Such a one may have a social conscience well enough developed to restrict the expressions of abnormal feeling to an adult partner, but, on the other hand, it is not unknown (although it is generally completely hushed up) that such an individual may corrupt young pupils under his or her charge. As in all else human, the degrees of variability in this feature range widely. There are those who are merely slightly erotic and almost hysterically affectionate to another member of their own sex: those who develop a passion for one of their own sex without any physical manifestations: those indulging in intense and repeated physical experiences with a member of their own sex. Some form a mutual attachment lasting

faithfully for many years; others are fickle and desirous to corrupt ever fresh young lives.

Such perverts are not so rare as normal wholesome people would like to believe, and now act as though they did believe them to be.

[155] The danger I see in the false hopes which have been raised is that a mother ardently desiring a child of one or the other sex, and thinking she has secured such a conception may be mentally determined that this sex is coming to her, whereas nature may have decreed otherwise, when the normal development of the child may be thwarted and interfered with. Not many cases of perverted sex as a result of the ardent desires of the mother are on record, but there are enough to make one extremely cautious about attempting to interfere with nature in this matter which is still entirely [156] beyond our control.

Clemence Dane, The Women's Side, 1926

[54] [T]he use and abuse of friendship between man and man, and woman and woman, are only [55] indirectly under discussion here. The reader is concerned with this problem as it propounds itself in the schools, and in the schools, perhaps significantly, it has no name, it is only recognised by a slang phrase. In the American girls' schools it is 'a crush'. Over here it is known as a 'G.P.' or as 'being keen on' someone. In Germany they call it *Schwärmerei*, an elastic word that covers 'hysteria, enthusiasm, hero-worship, dreaminess, fanaticism, extravagant devotion, exaltation, visionary raving, bees about to swarm, dissipation and ecstasy.'

The words stand also for the queer fact that girls of thirteen and onward, at day-schools and still more at boarding-schools, not only form normal and wholesome friendships with children of their own age, but that they are easily moved to a sort of hero-worship for an older girl or woman which, not always, but very often develops into a wild, unbalanced passion of affection that directly affects their health and happiness and indirectly their whole future. To put it crudely, a girl, before she is either physically or mentally ripe for it, sometimes falls in love, goes through all the nerve-shattering emotions proper to such a state of mind, and suffers even more than an older woman in the same situation because she has no idea of what is the matter with her, [56] and because there is no possibility of her affection being satisfactorily returned.

[62] [B]y acknowledging that sex is at the root of the trouble we at least clear the ground: we [63] at least admit that all these boys and girls, instead of being 'silly' or 'abnormal' or 'wicked', or whatever we choose to call it, are following as well as civilisation will let them the laws of their being.

They are with Nature, not against her, and if things go wrong they must in common justice be considered, not knaves and fools, but victims . . . .

[T]he present system of education does not render it impossible for a morbid and selfish woman to amuse herself and gratify her love of excitement by playing on this tendency to exaggerated [64] hero-worship in the children and mistresses under her care. Such women do exist. It is to be hoped that they are rare; but they do exist.

[69] [I]t is the normal child whose instincts become temporarily diverted from their proper channels who is the problem. But surely it is as short-sighted as it is cruel to brand as 'morbid' just those fine and sensitive spirits in a school who, because they are more delicate and highly strung, respond more quickly and show more disastrously the effect of an unsuitable environment. For it always seems to be the cleverest and most impressionable of the children who take the longest to shake off the effects of this false dawn of sex.

[73] [T]he uncomprehended impulses that a decade or two ago caused these outbreaks of sentimental measles will not automatically cease because the victims of such impulses have become teachers instead of learners. It is not pleasant to think of what the more imaginative and passionate among such women must suffer. And the fact that they are rare, that with most women, the sex feeling is rather indirect and passive, that their active emotions are more maternal and spiritual than passionate, does not solve the problem either. Women can have an intense longing for attention and affection and comradeship without necessarily or consciously wishing to marry. But what opportunity has a woman to mix freely with men and women alike, so as to understand her own outlook on these matters, to test her feelings, to differentiate between her need of friendship and her need of love? Her sole emotional outlet is her fellow- [74] mistresses and her pupils. Is it a wonder that, as a result, she occasionally behaves unwisely? Surely the system is as bad for her as for the child she teaches.

[127] Here you have the problem, inevitable in a country where monogamy is the custom and where women greatly out-number men, of sex in the unmarried girl. The girl who doesn't marry (except in rare cases usually balanced by equivalent rare cases among men) is in no way different, physically, mentally, emotionally, from the girl who does marry. The law of numbers is against her, nothing else.

Consider her case! She is young, pretty, or at any rate 'pretty enough' as they say, with the charm of youth that even the plainest [128] girls possess for a year or two. She has within her all the wholesome instincts of her age and sex. Whether she analyses the situation for herself or not, she wants to fall in love and make a home with a man and have children by him. If she didn't have these instincts, conscious or unconscious, we should draw away from her, instantly, instinctively, as if we were confronted with something abnormal, perverted, unnatural. Yet when, through living in a country where there are more women than men, she becomes 'odd woman out', what do we expect of her? Nothing less than that she should wipe out of herself all these instincts and wishes and feelings that we so highly approve in her if she marries . . . . [129] But if she proves that she can love, can play, by an intrigue with a man already married, is there any word too bad for her? And that too is necessary; for we have proved by experience that a monogamous marriage is a finer way of living at its best than any other type of marriage. But it's hard on the extra woman.

Geraldine Coster, **Psychoanalysis for Normal People,** *1926*

[183] [I]f a girl wakes up at fifteen or sixteen to a feeling of contempt, dislike, or fear of her father as a personality, there is a strong likelihood that she will refuse to take the step onward from homosexuality towards heterosexuality, and will go through life with a distaste not only for marriage, but for men as a whole. This is a grave disadvantage even to a woman who enters on a career other than that of marriage. A sane and balanced attitude towards men, and a sympathetic understanding of their point of view, are as essential to the professional or business woman as it is to the wife. A very great number of girls become neurotic and difficult during adolescence, and remain nerve-ridden, repressed, and unbalanced throughout life, in consequence of failure to establish healthy relations with their fathers. They remain fixed in the homosexual stage, and go through all the most difficult years of physical development either without any adaptation to sexual reality, or else with a very undesirable bias on the subject. It is open to woman to find her chief interests in life with friends and colleagues of her own sex, and this is a perfectly legitimate and healthy sublimation of instinct so long as she realizes her position [184] and understands her own psychology clearly. But at the present day, when girls' school life has made the homosexual stage so full of happiness and interest, and when three or four years at college give an opportunity of prolonging that stage far beyond its natural term, there are a number of girls who remain homosexual in their mental and spiritual outlook while their physical sex instinct is fully developed and vigorously demanding expression. They do not in the least realize the situation, and in ignorance and innocence may attempt to find physical satisfaction in ways which if discovered would bring them under the ban of the community. In such cases, undesirable practices innocently begun too often lead to situations which wreck a whole life.
[. . . .]

[185] This whole question of the homosexual is one that demands very much greater understanding and more direct treatment than our present-day standards of social behaviour have permitted. There are individuals in whom the homosexual trend has become so deeply fixed that they are unable to adjust to normal heterosexual life. They are not always of a low-grade type either morally or intellectually.

Barbara Low, The Unconscious in Action, 1928

[54] [T]he man or woman with fairly strong homosexual impulses which are quite unrealized may seek unconsciously to fulfil the unconscious desire by becoming a teacher, with possible evil results to the pupils . . . On the other hand, the homosexual tendencies (which we all possess in some degree or other) may be successfully sublimated in those individuals in whom, perhaps, the impulse is less dominant (or has been able to emerge more freely into consciousness and so obtain some normal gratification, such as in a close friendship with one of the same sex), with results unusually [55] favourable to the work of education. Some of the outstanding names among the world's educators . . . have been people of this type . . . . The important thing is that the educator shall know what is going on within himself, otherwise he may be carried away by deep unconscious impulses, to the very great detriment of the pupils to whom he is in a relation of extreme significance and power.

Marie Stopes, Enduring Passion, 1928

[41] Another practical solution which some deprived women find is in Lesbian love with their own sex. The other, and quite correct name for what is now so often euphemistically called Lesbian love is homosexual vice. It is so much practised nowadays, particularly by the 'independent' type of woman that I run a risk of being attacked because I call the thing by its correct name. One of the physical results of such unnatural relations is the gradual accustoming of the system to reactions which are arrived at by a different process from that for which the parts were naturally formed. This tends to unfit women for real union. If a married woman does this unnatural thing she may find a growing disappointment in her husband and he may lose all natural power to play his proper part . . . . No woman who values the peace of her home and the love of her husband should yield to the wiles of the Lesbian whatever the temptation to do so may be.

A very *very* few women have strong inborn tendencies of this type; most of those now indulging in the vice drifted into it lazily or out of curiosity and allowed themselves to be corrupted. This corruption spreads as an underground fire spreads in the peaty soil [42] of a dry moorland . . . . The bedrock objection to it is surely that women can only *play* with each other and *cannot* in the very nature of things have natural union or supply each other with the seminal and prostatic secretions which they ought to have, and crave for unconsciously.

Hence, homosexual excitement does not really meet their need, for the physiological fact . . . that, apart from the kisses, endearment, flattery, and love-making from her husband, a woman's [43] need and *hunger* for nourishment in sex union is a true physiological hunger to be satisfied only by the supplying of the actual molecular substances lacked by her system. Lesbian love, as the alternative, is NOT a real equivalent and merely soothes perhaps and satisfies no more than the surface nervous excitement.

[51] [T]here are those who are unmarried, and who at periodic intervals feel the passionate need of sex union, and yet, having a moral sense well developed and a recognition of the present social code, hesitate to have union outside marriage, and suffer (some of them suffer excessively) at recurrent intervals. Many such women would be definitely helped by taking such capsules for two or three days at the times of such spontaneous sex excitement.

[. . . .]

I think such utilisation of the advances of modern science and the employment of glandular compounds for this purpose is one of the most potentially useful and socially valuable applications of modern research.

[. . . .]

[53] For the first time in history our generation finds it possible to give some practical help to those naturally so strongly sexed that 'self-control' becomes almost a physical impossibility through the frantic urge of physiological starvation. They may by quietly swallowing the glandular compounds they lack, assist themselves to become . . . less the slave of their nature's demands for the enjoyment of the other sex.

Mary Scharlieb, The Bachelor Woman and Her Problems, *1929*

[45] Among the drawbacks in the lot of the unmarried woman must be reckoned the injuries to character and failures of development which may be caused by unfulfilled desires. Powers of mind and body which are not used are liable to atrophy . . . human beings whose powers and gifts are not kept in constant exercise will eventually be as if they had never possessed them.

[49] A somewhat unexpected consequence of the want of natural and desirable outlets for love and all the motherly virtues may be found in what are sometimes called 'absorbing friendships,' or 'obsessive friendships.'

There are people who entirely condemn a great and passionate friendship between two people of the same sex. They say, and no doubt they say truly, that there is a great risk, that such a stirring of emotion without any practical outcome must of necessity be bad both for the lover and the beloved . . . . [50] But surely, as in other cases of friendship and platonic love, each case much be judged on its merits and by the effects that it produces. The two chief tests available for the detection of the healthiness or the unhealthiness of the position would be the selfishness or unselfishness evidenced, and the influence of the passion on conduct and character.

[. . . .]

[51] These master-friendships between members of the same sex appear to be beneficial or disastrous in proportion to the wisdom and unselfishness of the one who receives the adoration . . . . [T]he superior in a *wise* absorbing friendship takes all the incense, flowers, and songs in so motherly, and in a way so superior a manner, that the reaction on the junior is all to the good. Where the outcome of an absorbing friendship is deleterious, and tends to the junior partner becoming as it were a slave or a parasite, it is because the senior is not sufficiently big to carry unmoved and unspoiled all that the junior offers.

[. . . .]

[53] [T]he love of the elder, so much like that of a mother, must be affection as well as passion, calm, deep, and true, without the foam and fury of passion as generally understood. She should be able to receive the caress and the love of the younger without losing her balance, and without feeling any ministration to her self-appreciation and self-value.

In this way possessive, absorbing, obsessive friendships or adorations may be transmuted from sentimental follies, dangerous alike to worshipper and worshipped, into instruments of tremendous uplift and sublimation. Where the choice of friends has been wise, the warmth and depth of the friendship will enable each to supplement the deficiency or weakness of the other, and may provide them both with exactly the object of love, devotion, and appreciation which each nature was craving.

A wise and good friendship between two women may be the consolation and satisfaction that is necessary to secure such a degree of development as may be possible to each. It is to be remarked that many single women, realizing their own incompleteness, are led to special friendships as the best consolation for a contrary tide in their life's ocean which has hitherto involved [54] isolation. It is quite a mistake to think that the majority of single women are ardently desirous of the completion of their nature by marriage.

Prostitution and venereal disease

In spite of perceptions that commercialized sex relationships are being replaced by gratuitous 'promiscuity', prostitution remains a cause for concern, while there are also anxieties about the relationship between the apparent relaxation of moral standards and the spread of venereal diseases.

Marie Stopes, Married Love, *1918*

[23] Many men who enter marriage sincerely and tenderly may yet have some previous experience of bought 'love.' It is then not unlikely that they may fall into the error of explaining their wife's experiences in terms of the reactions of the prostitute. They argue that, because the prostitute showed physical excitement and pleasure in union, if the bride or wife does not do so, then she is 'cold' or 'under-sexed.' They may not realise that often all the bodily movements which the prostitute makes are studied and simulated because her client enjoys his climax best when the woman in his arms simultaneously thrills.

[103] Women feel a so righteous and instinctive horror of prostitution, and regarding it the experience an indignation so intense, that they do not seek to understand the man's attitude.

The prostitute, however, sometimes supplies an [104] element which is not purely physical, and which is often lacking in the wife's relation with her husband, an element of charm and mutual gaiety in pleasure.

If good women realised this . . . they might be in a better position to begin their efforts to free men from the hold that social disease has upon them.

M. K. Bradby, The Logic of the Unconscious Mind, *1920*

[238] *The problem of prostitution* is even more than most social problems involved in the obscurity of unconscious motives . . . .

[239] We have assumed . . . that the desire for sexual intercourse in the normal human being (as in the normal higher animal) goes along with, and is part of, the instinct of 'sexual love' in its narrow sense, and that this includes a more or less permanent relation with a sexually attractive person. In the man who resorts to prostitutes, one factor of sexual love is taken from the total animal instinct and cultivated on its own account, while the remaining factors are habitually repressed.

[. . . .]

If this diagnosis be mistaken, if Man alone among the higher animals has an instinct for passing and unselective sexual intercourse with any attractive individual other than his 'mate' for the time being; then the problem is how to gratify this instinct with the minimum [240] of social injury, instead of, as at present, with almost the maximum, through the spread of venereal disease. If, however, the view here is taken to be correct, the problem is chiefly how to cure a neurotic habit, and above all how to prevent its manufacture in childhood and youth.

The whole question needs to be raised from the region of 'repression' appropriate to a stage of mental development which Man is outgrowing . . . .

To-day there are signs that a saner, more humane, and more developed treatment of the problem is taking the place of that mixture of silence, pretence and regularisation of crime within limits, which the English gentleman has found so personally helpful.

Arabella Kenealy, Feminism and Sex-Extinction, 1920

[180] Among other Feminist fallacies, the *demi-mondaine* has come to be regarded as victim merely, on the one hand, of an unjust, man-administered economic system, on the other, of masculine libertinism. The truth is that the vast majority of immoral women are under no compulsion, but voluntarily adopt this mode of life, either to escape work, or because of a natural vicious proclivity. A number are mental defectives; some actually feeble-minded, others only morally deficient.

[. . . .]

And although this is not, of course, the calculated purpose of this lamentable under-world, the rough division of the sex thereby into two main classes has been of service, by supplying a sociological backwater wherein the worst of our racial derelicts – mental and moral defectives – are segregated; and are precluded, for the most part, from perpetuating their mental and moral defectiveness . . .

[181] The Feminist fallacy that prostitution is almost entirely a product of male economics has been strikingly refuted, too, by War-conditions, which opened numerous well-remunerated employments for the sex. Yet, coincident with a sad deficit of women to fill these, prostitution has waxed rampant.

Wise and discreet were those early Victorians, with their uncompromising ostracism of loose women.

Marie Stopes, The Truth About Venereal Disease, 1921

[11] What audacity then for men to blame wives who have only one child, what heartless ignorance for other women who have been spared this horror to sneer at and condemn those who may be the innocent victims of a husband's cruel wrong-doing! And, on the other hand, what incredible racial neglect that girls should be allowed to injure themselves through immoral acts (ignorant of what the evil result will be), which may sweep out of the realm of possible existence the little children they may later long for.

H. M. Swanwick, Women in the Socialist State, 1921

[39] The dividing line between promiscuity and prostitution is not a sharp one, and there must be many prostitutes who began by liking best the men who had money to spend and who went with them because it was easy and pleasant, with no intention of being actually paid for what they gave in return; mostly with no foresight at all as to what their own share of the transaction would eventually be. It appears to be fairly well established by investigation recently carried out in this country that shortage of the first necessities of life has been [40] responsible for only a small proportion of the prostitution of women. On the other hand, very large numbers of girls are so poor that their lives are more dull and grey than they can endure with patience, and if easy pleasures offer, they will be snatched by a considerable proportion of such girls, especially when these pleasures are offered, not against the natural urge of youthful appetite, but in conjunction with it . . . . Under Socialism, all women would be given the means to earn a human existence filled with natural pleasures; under Socialism there would be a very much more even distribution of the wealth which, concentrated in the hands of men, enables them to buy up women and induces profiteers to make a lucrative traffic in vice. One would not venture to predict that prostitution would cease, but it would quite certainly be immensely reduced.

Ettie Rout, Safe Marriage, 1922

[20] [E]xtra-marital relationship is never ever safe, because of its promiscuity and impermanence, except in properly conducted and effectively supervised tolerated houses. The tolerated house is absolutely necessary at present to protect women from disease and immorality, by confining this kind of intercourse as far as possible in certain definite channels . . . . Separated from their toilet equipment the women cannot make and keep

themselves clean; on the streets they are not taught to refuse intercourse with diseased men; thus their occupation becomes more and more dangerous as medical supervision is removed. They inevitably become diseased; sometimes contract mixed infections, which they pass on to their clients – the future husbands and fathers of the nation . . . . All this would be impossible if women generally would recognise the primary fact that because a man is immoral that it is no reason why he should become syphilitic . . . .

[21] Similarly every effort should be made to prevent women becoming diseased, no matter how immoral they may be. The prostitute is very often a woman of peculiar mentality or over-developed animal instincts; and many women are driven to prostitution by drink and poverty. The prostitute class is largely recruited from mentally and morally deficient girls, who are themselves the offspring of syphilitic or alcoholic parents. Prostitution is the effect – not the cause – of anti-social acts and conditions. We must remedy the causes of these before we can hope to remove the effects. Under present social conditions, attempting to abolish prostitution by shutting up tolerated houses is just as idle as attempting to lower the temperature of a room by smashing the thermometer. All we can do is to make and keep these women clean.

[27] Every well-informed woman knows that there is far more venereal disease in the world to-day, among men and among women, than there was before the war, and she should train all the members of her household in habits of strict cleanliness. Instinctively they will then avoid risking their health by contact with a possible source of defilement, or if the risk has most unfortunately been taken, they will instantly and instinctively remove and destroy the possible infection . . . . [28] By all means let the mothers continue to inculcate virtue, but they should also teach sexual cleanliness directly and indirectly, themselves setting the example. After all, the microbes of venereal disease grow almost exclusively in the genital passages, and if these were kept sweet and clean there would soon be an end to venereal disease. It is . . . a matter of restoring and maintaining physical health, family and national, and above all, of protecting innocent women and children.

[63] All women should be in favour of reasonable measures for ensuring the voluntary, and failing that the compulsory, treatment of venereal disease among men and women. It is troublesome to prevent a man getting disease if he is running into a pool of infection, and such cesspools should be cleaned up or cleared out of the community – *i.e.*, cured or quarantined. Similarly, it is even more troublesome to prevent a woman becoming infected if she is having relationship with an active gonorrhoeic or syphilitic man, and such men should be treated voluntarily, or

compulsorily if they refuse or neglect voluntary treatment . . . . This pre-supposes that the teaching of self-disinfection has been done confidently and authoritatively. When prevention has been properly taught then it is fair to penalise those who wilfully neglect to take precautions. It was a great misfortune to the Anglo-Saxons when the Contagious Diseases Acts were abolished; instead they should have been improved [64] and extended to both sexes.

Ettie Rout, The Morality of Birth Control, *1924*

[64] Under civilization, a woman who is abjectly poor, without money, out of employment, lacking in food and shelter and clothing, must obtain work for wages – or sell herself . . . . All women are not free to leave this life suddenly: they may have others to provide for: so women [65] force themselves to be immoral. Yet they may be naturally good women. It is society, not they, who must be blamed.

Sometimes I think there are no bad women. There are just sick and poor and abnormal women: women whom society should not reproduce; and then there are the women who are lucky enough to be born normal and healthy. If, therefore, we would only re-build society so that no woman could possibly be left stranded without the necessaries of life, women would not be driven by poverty to prostitute themselves. The morons and imbeciles should not be produced at all, and certainly should not be permitted to reproduce. Thus Birth Control instead of fostering immorality would help to drain the swamp of prostitution. But so long as we go on manufacturing prostitutes, and insist upon retaining hygienic and social and economic conditions which inevitably force women into prostitution, the problem of immorality is insoluble.

Mrs Cecil Chesterton, In Darkest London, *1926*

[63] 'I've had awful bad luck to-day,' she said. 'But I'm going another shot before I turn in. There'll be time before the pubs close to go up to the park, and maybe, I'll get a man to buy me a drink.'

A dark faced, bobbed haired girl said she would go too, though, as she explained, she was rather tired, and had already walked from Hendon, where, among other things, she had been shying for cocoanuts . . . . [64] The two went off together to try their luck, I hoped sincerely they already had the price of their beds. There was something inexpressibly tragic in the thought that these two young things had to go to the park, not for a drink alone, but to earn a pitifully small sum for the hire of their bodies.

Several girls came in to 'arrange their faces,' and one, a very slender, piquant creature, took out of her Dorothy bag an entire set of silk underclothing, which she had washed at the public baths and brought into the kitchen to dry. She held them before the coke fire, chatting the while of her experiences.

'Any luck, dearie?' said a soft-voiced Irishwoman.

'No, luck's right out,' said the slim one. 'I tell you I'm getting fed up with bits and scraps of things. I haven't had a whole night with a man for six weeks.' She made the statement with a complete frankness that had not the least touch of obscenity, and her sentiment was generally applauded. You must understand that the attitude of these young people towards sex cannot be described as immoral; nor is it immoral. It is the result of the will to live; they are unable to keep themselves in any other manner. They have their own code of ethics, a rigid one, which demands an irrevocable [65] decision not to let a pal down, and never in any circumstances whatsoever to interfere with other people's business or give away their affairs.

[79] The young, pretty prostitute of the humbler walks of harlotry is a growing problem. The older women, who have long graduated in the profession, are of a different category; with these I did not come into contact, except in one or two instances where circumstances had pushed them from comparative prosperity into destitution. The type of girl I encountered in the public lodging houses is, as a rule, fresh, amusing and very friendly.

How do they find themselves members of this calling? The reasons are various; but sheer vice is not one of them. Viciousness is generally accompanied by a peculiarly commercial sense, which very speedily increases a woman's earning capacity in this particular walk of life. The majority of girls are victims of circumstance . . . . A number of them have been domestic servants who have stayed out late on their evening off, and been too apprehensive to return after the appointed hour . . . . [80] It is not difficult for an attractive young thing to form an acquaintance, and in sheer high spirits and love of fun she will go to lengths she had never contemplated, and wake up the next morning in a man's bed.

Once this has happened, it is very difficult for a girl to get back to routine work.

Marie Stopes, Sex and the Young, *1926*

[130] The older pupils should have the above explicit information about the life history of the *Spirochaeta pallida* given to them in their general Biology class. Its life history is far more important than that of the rotifers

or the foraminifera whose lives are often minutely studied. If the life history of the germ is given as a class subject and an illustration of a microscopic species, I think the mental shock is likely to be less than if it were only spoken of in connection with sex disease. Yet, the warning should be quite as effective.

Boys are liable in the vacations or as a secret 'lark' to go to some prostitute house out of bravado, or to play in some illicit fashion with a girl companion. Although fortunately rare, it is not unknown that a girl of only fourteen or fifteen makes a boast of the number of boys with whose sex organs her own have come in contact. One such girl in a district is enough to initiate more venereal disease than a professional prostitute, and far more than doctors and school teachers [131] can overtake after the deeds have been accomplished . . .

It is most unfortunate, indeed deplorable, that the bright and beautiful trustfulness and unconsciousness of healthy youth should be soiled by learning of such facts. I sincerely hope that a generation hence there will be no need for such instruction. By that time the germs of sex diseases might be non-existent in this country if active steps were now taken to stamp them out.

Charlotte Haldane, Motherhood and its Enemies, 1927

[89] The war, however, did more than demonstrate the ability of military organization to grapple with the problem in essence civilian.

Until its outbreak prostitution had remained very largely professional. Although a certain number of 'fallen' girls were forced into it because in those days the first step was considered the most unforgivable, we have a record of other important bearings on the matter besides the purely moral pressure . . . .

[91] [T]he wages and surroundings of working women have been immeasurably improved within recent years and especially since the war, both in public and domestic service . . . . [T]he minority of prostitutes now earn little more than can be gained by an honest hard-working woman; the majority probably less than an energetic girl with initiative and ability. And the first lapse from virtue is now generally condoned, as we have seen. In consequence the economic incentive to a career of prostitution is growing steadily weaker.

Birth control

With Marie Stopes in the articulate forefront of the campaign, this is the period when birth control comes out of the shadows and in from the fringes and is widely debated and advocated. The new erotic vision of marriage requires contraception to be a workable proposition. There are still voices condemning the use of artificial contraception as immoral and deleterious, and others who clearly wish some other means could be found, but by the end of the 1920s birth control has become largely acceptable. Abortion is mentioned, usually as a concomitant of the lack of birth control knowledge, but throughout this period Stella Browne argues that safe legal abortion is an essential part of any realistic provision of birth control.

Marie Stopes, Married Love, 1918

[79] If the theologians really mean what they say, and demand the voluntary effort of complete celibacy from all men, save for the purpose of procreation, this will *not* achieve their end of preventing the destruction of all potential life; and the monthly loss of unfertilised eggcell by women is beyond all the efforts of the will to curb. Nature, not man, arranged the destruction of potential life against which ascetic Bishops rage.

If, then, throughout the greater part of their lives the germinal cells of both sexes inevitably disintegrate without creating an embryo, there can be nothing wrong in selecting the most favourable moment possible for the conception of the first of these germinal cells to be endowed with the supreme privilege of creating a new life.

Marie Stopes, Wise Parenthood, 1918

[1] A family of healthy, happy children should be the joy of every pair of married lovers. If, however, the course of 'nature' is allowed to run, unguided babies come in general too quickly for the parents' resources, and the parents as well as the children consequently suffer. Wise parents therefore guide nature, and control the birth of the desired children so as to space them in the way best adjusted to what health, wealth, and happiness they have to give.

[. . . .]

The question before us . . . is not whether or no birth control should be allowed. It is in daily use by the great majority of the more intelligent married people.

General dissatisfaction with most of the methods used is prevalent; and it is not being alleviated, because there is also a widespread ignorance of satisfactory methods even on the part of medical practitioners. Numbers of people who are practising and have been practising birth control by various means for years are in urgent need of a better method than any known to them . . . .

What we are here concerned with is the fact that birth control methods of all sorts are now so widely used that it is high time serious attention should be devoted to the subject. People should not be employing anything less satisfactory than the best now obtainable; but, unless they are given the best, they will assuredly use some less desirable means.

[6] Churchmen recommend (though I wonder if they practise) 'absolute continence.' Where the mated pair are young, normal, and in love, such advice is not only impracticable, it is detrimental. A rigid and enforced abstinence can be as destructive of health as incontinence.

Destructive of the health both of mother and child are the frantic efforts of women 'caught' prematurely after a birth, or too frequently in their lives, by undesired motherhood. The desolating effects of attempted abortion can only be exterminated by a sound knowledge of the control of conception.

[9](a) It is advisable not to have a child in the very early days of marriage, because in the first few months at any rate the woman's system should be adjusting itself to new conditions, benefiting from the change in her life, and gaining poise and strength for the burden which she will have to bear . . . .

(b) After the birth of a child it is essential that there should be no hurried beginning of a second.

[24] The method perhaps most widely in use of all, and which appeals to many people because it requires no special appliance or chemicals, is *withdrawal*, or *coitus interruptus*. Many who are inclined . . . to condemn other methods, consider that this must be entirely harmless, because nothing is involved which they consider 'unnatural.' Nevertheless, this method has without doubt done an incredible amount of harm, not directly, but through its reactions on the nervous systems of both man and woman . . . .

The great majority of women whose husbands practise this method suffer very fundamentally as a result of the reiterated stirring-up of local nervous excitement which is deprived of its natural physiological [25] resolution.

Marie Stopes, Letter to Working Mothers, *1919*

[3] I expect your first child was a great joy to you and your husband, but you went on having children so rapidly that you got very tired and worn out by the third or fourth child, or miscarriage. Also, if they came about every year, you had not time properly to nurse one before another was on the way, and you noticed that they seemed not to be so strong as you would like. You wanted a good family, but you did so want time to rest and get strong yourself between their coming, and you so wanted that every child you bore should be strong enough to live and grow up . . . .

[4] [Y]ou are still young, and you are living with your husband, and there is always the shadow of fear hiding in the corner of your bedroom that, if you let him have his way, there will be more babies, and that will stop you working and will bring another child to feed, and you feel you cannot face it . . . .

So you begin to dread what used to be your chief joy, that is to have your husband with you. On the other hand, if you are a strong-minded woman and you rule your husband and prevent him having his way, there is another fear, however much you may hide it deep in the bottom of your heart, and that is that you will not keep him, and that some bad girl will get him . . . .

This makes things very difficult for you, and very often it happens that you get 'caught,' and you know that the baby that you feared might come has already begun . . . . [5] So you do, or you try to do, a desperate thing: you try to get rid of that baby before it has 'gone too far'.
[. . . .]

I am going to begin by telling you of one or two things which many of you do, and which you ought *not* to do. But the reason I am speaking of these 'ought nots' is only in order to show you a much better and healthier way to get just the results which you have been [6] trying to get in the wrong way.

Norah March, Sex Knowledge *[1922]*

[48 [T]he effort of bringing a child into the world is a great strain upon a woman, and . . . after each child is born there should be a reasonable time elapsing, to allow of complete restoration of the mother, before another child is born unto her. Too frequent pregnancies make life an intolerable burden to a woman, and unwanted motherhood brings sorrow and trouble in its train, while voluntary motherhood is naught but a joy. The husband who truly loves his wife does not wish her to be exhausted with repeated childbearing.

144

At the same time, of course the matter must be looked at from the national point of view. It is obvious that whatever the pros and cons of increase, the population should not be allowed to decrease in numbers.

[50] The daily and nightly companionship which married life implies, to the loving and emotional nature provides, naturally, many a stimulus to sex love far and away beyond the strain which ordinary companionship of men and women imposes. Sex intercourse is in itself an expression of love itself, apart altogether from the possibilities of parenthood following: the normal emotional reactions attendant upon it are beneficial to man and to woman alike. To limit this expression of love to accord with the number desired is, for most happily married couples, an impossibility, and by most held to be entirely undesirable, though there are others who hold that marital relations should be ruled by this dictum . . . . [L]imitation of the size of the family would seem, if one is to go by public and private utterances, of those who are competent to judge, to be developing as a regular custom, at any rate among those who are educated enough to tackle the personal problem intelligently. From the racial point of view, it is regrettable that just those sections of the community who add to the derelicts are reproducing their kind without restraint . . . .

[51] There are those who fear for the morals of society as birth control methods become increasingly widely known. They fear that such knowledge may provide an easy pathway to immorality. Whether these fears are justified or not, it is obvious that it is not knowledge which may do harm, but the use which is made of knowledge.

Ettie Rout, Safe Marriage, 1922

[47] *Before Intercourse, Wash and be Clean.* –

Insert soluble suppository, and then place rubber pessary in position, concave side downwards. This will slip up more easily if slightly soaped. No harm can possibly come either to husband or wife from these appliances, and neither party will be conscious of the presence of the occlusive rubber pessary . . . The pessary can be inserted some hours before intercourse, and need not be removed till some hours afterwards. *The rubber pessary should not be worn continuously*. If you have mislaid the rubber pessary, a small sponge, a piece of clean cotton-wool, or even a piece of soft tissue paper can be used . . . . If sponge or cotton-wool is used, it [48] should be saturated in contraceptive lotion or smeared with contraceptive ointment before insertion. But always remember – the rubber pessary is cleanest and safest.

145

Maude Royden, Sex and Common-sense, *1922*

[191] [I]t seems to me of supreme importance (1) that every child that is born should be *desired*, and (2) that no mother's time and strength should be so far overtaxed as to prevent her giving to each child all the love and individual care that it requires.

This necessitates control of the birth rate, for a baby every year means a too-hurried emptying of the mother's arms. But I disagree – very diffidently – with the majority of my friends and acquaintances who hold that the right and best method is the use of contraceptives. I do not think it the best; I do not think it ideal. Unlike some authorities who must be heard with respect, I can say with confidence that some of the noblest, happiest and most romantic marriages I know base their control of conception not on contraceptives but on abstinence. They [192] are not prigs, they are not asexual, they do not drift apart, and they have no harsh criticism to make on those who have decided otherwise. These are facts, and it is useless to ignore them.

On the other hand, it is equally true that sometimes such an attempt at self-control leads to nervous strain, irritability and alienation. These also are facts.

Lady Barrett, Conception Control, *1922*

[14] [T]he claim is made that marriage exists at least as much for the fulfilment of happiness in union with the beloved as for the procreation of children; and that it should be possible for a married pair to have the fullest gratification without fear of children unless they desire them.
[. . . .]
[15] At first sight it might seem a comparatively simple thing, in view of the knowledge which already exists of the physiological processes involved in conception, to advise a method which shall prevent conception at will without harmful effect upon man or woman and yet leave intercourse unimpaired. But even at first sight it is obvious that whatever knowledge may be available, and whatever methods may be devised, it would not be easy to convey this knowledge rightly to the individual it is hoped to benefit without doing harm to others. Further thought shows that the national problems involved are so important and far reaching in effects that they might well arrest the attention of the most careless advocate of indiscriminate conception control.

This is a subject, therefore, which requires careful consideration from the point of view of the individual, of public morality, and of [16] national welfare – and the more closely it is studied the more apparent are the far reaching issues involved. It is improbable that the practice of using contraceptives will continue for even a generation without revealing the harmful effects which must to some extent ensue.

[40] Those who after careful consideration choose to use artificial means to prevent child-bearing will be wise if they consult their medical attendant as to those methods which are least harmful for their individual case, and ask for careful instruction in their use.

[. . . .]

[41] All these artificial preparations for intercourse demand from the woman an investigation of and interference with her own internal organs, which is revolting to all decent women, and such teaching is directly opposed to the advocacy of cleanliness and non-interference with the genital organs, which is the natural habit of healthy-minded women.

Leonora Eyles, The Woman in the Little House, 1922

[159] Quite often a woman who has had several children determines not to have any more. Her husband will do nothing in the matter; even if he were willing to, preventives are expensive, and are only on general sale in certain districts. So she begins to take quack drugs, poisons of various sorts, gin and washing soda, draughts of turpentine and various almost incredibly foolish things to procure abortion. She hears of other – mechanical – means . . . and, as recent inquests are proving with rather alarming frequency, adopts them at the cost of her life.

Isabel Hutton, The Hygiene of Marriage, 1923

[95] It has often been said in argument that continence should be the only method of birth control, and therefore ought to be observed. Continence is, however, now known to be definitely harmful to normal husbands and wives if they are living together. The continual sexual emotion which is stimulated, and the consequent sex repression if intercourse does not take place, is utterly devastating for both. Continence, therefore, frequently results in nervousness and general ill-health, and sometimes in nervous breakdown and neurasthenia. It has also been shown that without a healthy sex life in marriage there cannot be happiness or complete understanding and love: this method is, therefore, impracticable.

The question is often asked whether more harm than good will result from giving people the means and knowledge necessary for the control of pregnancy. The possible ill-effects can be summed up under three headings: sexual excess, unchastity in those who are not married, and an increase in the number of childless marriages.

It may fairly be said that in the country at least sexual excess is not common. It is obviously difficult to obtain the true facts, but, at any rate, doctors see few married people who are suffering from the effects of sexual excess while they see a good many who are suffering from the effects of continence . . . .

[96] If this knowledge is likely to cause more illicit intercourse among unmarried men and women, and if it is only because of the risk of having a child that the modern woman remains pure, the standard of to-day is indeed a low one.

Mary Scharlieb, Straight Talks to Women, 1923

[122] The advocates of the control of conception have many reasons to urge in defence of this practice, but none of them carries conviction to my mind. They are based on materialistic considerations, and although every one will agree with those who urge them in desiring the welfare and happiness of the race, many of us cannot but disagree with the methods whereby such advantages are sought.

[130] The rule should be nine months pregnancy, nine months lactation, six months sexual holiday. Some women say, 'oh my husband would never agree to such a plan,' but if this were true it would mean that human beings with their reason, their chivalry, and their boasted superiority were incapable of true unselfish love and of self-control. It is not thinkable that men brought up to subdue their bodies and to keep them under could not, and would not, deny themselves so as to permit their beloved a time for recuperation.

Another natural method of avoiding conception and of spacing the family, consists in avoiding intercourse just before and for some time after a period.

[165] Artificial limitation of conception is in competent medical opinion doubtful in principle, and injurious in its methods. Therefore men and women who value their health will agree that it is a wrong to their bodies, and men and women who wish to live together according to God's ordinance will seek some other way out of their difficulties.

Ettie Rout, The Morality of Birth Control, 1924

[191] Nothing will ever make women content to bear or rear children by men whom they do not wish to be fathers to their children. Efforts to impose such obligations on women have always failed: women invariably

take the law into their own hands. They do this instinctively – not to save themselves, but to save the race. Under civilization women have advanced sufficiently to abhor infanticide. They still practise abortion very largely, but regard it as highly undesirable, if not immoral – admissible only to save worse ill. The advancement of the civilized woman is shown by her preference for contraceptive measures – measures which have been known in essence and practised imperfectly for many thousands of years, but which even now are [192] only partially developed by medical science. The civilized woman and the primitive woman meet on level terms in their unchanging unswerving desire and endeavour – first, to prevent the temple of their bodies being profaned by men whom they do not love and upon whom they do not wish to confer fatherhood; and, second, to give themselves freely and voluntarily to the men they love, and to secure fertilization by the finest possible fathers for the children they wish to conceive in love, and bear and rear for the welfare of society and the evolution of the race.

Dora Russell, Hypatia, 1925

[41] [M]any considerations . . . forbid a yearly child. I read recently in an article by G. K. Chesterton, that sex without gestation and parturition is like blowing the trumpets and waving the flags without doing any of the [42] fighting. From a woman such words, though displaying in-experience, might come with dignity; from a man they are an unforgivable, intolerable insult. What is man's part in sex but a perpetual waving of flags and blowing of trumpets and avoidance of the fighting? The vast majority of men are not even tender or kindly to their pregnant or nursing wives, nor will they give help or consideration to the care of their young children.

A revolt against motherhood under present conditions is not surprising, nor is it entirely regrettable. There are quite a number of women whose minds and bodies are not fitted or have not been fitted by their upbringing and education to produce and care for children.

Mary Scharlieb, 'The Medical Aspect of Conception Control', 1926

[59] Not unfrequently a married couple misinterpret something said by their doctor and come to believe that . . . 'The doctor told me I must have no more children, and therefore either my husband or I must do something to prevent the arrival of another baby.' In the great majority of such instances the doctor's veto has been for a time only, and probably

referred as much to coïtion as to childbearing. There are states of health in which a woman would profit greatly by physiological rest, a condition which cannot be attained so long as she is living an ordinary married life. No doubt married couples should live together according to God's ordinance and in obedience to their right and natural instincts, but . . . the organs of reproduction may require a limited period of rest.

[62] [W]here deterioration of health, serious financial strain or other unselfish reasons exist, the couple should practise a certain amount of self-denial, and should restrict the act of marriage to that portion of the menstrual cycle which recent experience assures us is infertile, or at any rate practically infertile . . . .

[63] Patients seeking advice should be told of these observations, and they should also be informed that intercourse during this period alone, although probably not securing all that might be wished, is yet sufficient to gratify the really deep desires of a married couple. This medical advice ought to be combined with the admonition that although it entails a certain amount of self-control and self-denial, it admits of the desired spacing of the family without the use of an artificial contraceptive which might injure the health of either the husband or the wife, and which in some cases might entail future sterility.

Letitia D. Fairfield, 'The State and Birth Control', 1926

[124] It is said that the teaching of contraception at municipal clinics will destroy the unsavoury atmosphere with which it is admittedly surrounded and will make Birth Control respectable . . . . Rather would it appear that by the seal of official approval, lingering scruples against mutilated intercourse will be diminished. Already it is notorious that many women, who would otherwise have remained continent, are led into illicit unions by the knowledge – or the hope – that no child will result. A community may well pause before it scatters more widely the knowledge of a practice that has already proved itself a two-edged sword.

Leonora Eyles, Women's Problems of To-day, 1926

[15] When men and women are no longer dispossessed the problem of Birth Control will cease to exist. The knowledge will be there for all to use, and because their souls are alive and functioning they will not let their bodies be guilty of licence. I make this remark because this is a subject that bids fair to split our women's sections grievously; there is a way out of the difficulty without offending the ideas of religion or freedom. But this

is not the place to discuss it, beyond saying that when men's and women's souls are freed, their bodies will not offend against natural law.

Charlotte Haldane, Motherhood and its Enemies, 1927

[206] The invention of a biological instrument of contraception which could be [207] used without fear of dangerous consequences, at first released wealthier and more intelligent women from the necessity of undergoing abortions. It provided them with a weapon, and hence with free choice in the matter of child-bearing. At present various private organizations are trying, in countries where hostile influence is not too strong for them, to pass this weapon on to poorer mothers. Obviously the importance of this cannot be exaggerated. Political emancipation by itself, though advantageous in some ways, could hardly suffice to secure a higher standard of living for mothers. I have tried to show that in many instances the vote, shared by mothers and spinsters alike, operates to some extent in favour of the unmarried as against the married woman. But the ability to limit the number of citizens they choose to contribute to the State for the first time confers political importance on mothers.

Marie Stopes (ed.), Mother England, 1929

[36] [M]y husband has always been very good to me and yet I have fallen and not known how it has happened & I feel I am making my husband's life a burden because I have got so nervous that I feel I would forfeit our happiness than have another child . . . . [37] the Matron in the Maternity Home said I must *not* have any more but she never told me how to avoid it . . . .

I do not believe in taking stuff to bring on a miscarriage. I have told People I would rather die in Child Birth than take stuff to do away with it. I think it is very good of you to offer to help us poorer mothers and to give us of your knowledge and I shall look forward to your reply hoping it will bring comfort and happiness to me and to my husband as well. I should like to ask one Question:

A Nurse told me it was perfectly safe to Co-habit within 10 days before courses and 10 days after my husband would be quite willing to wait [38] that time but I dare not *trust* it, it makes me all nerves to think of it.

[59] I have three living, well grown loving daughters and have always had a reasonable rest between, thanks due entirely to my husband who never dreams of worrying me more than once or perhaps twice in a month.

[145] My Nurse on this last Baby told me to douche myself in the morning after connection with my husband and that would be as good a prevention as anything but I thought it a bit risky to trust to it until the morning as the germ may act overnight if I did nothing else to prevent them and I don't believe in drugs of any sort so between everything I simply dread to see night time coming however tired I am because I am always dreading my husband wanting his wishes fulfilled and I am powerless to prevent him and above all things I don't want to drive him to go after other women.

F. W. Stella Browne, 'The Right to Abortion', 1929

[179] [F]or every one case of poor women demanding contraceptive knowledge and help, there are at least three (some say eight or ten) who swallow poisons or fatally injure themselves with hatpins, knitting needles and even meat-skewers (!!) in the effort to procure miscarriage. Or they achieve an incomplete operation, which by their very ignorance and its [180] incompleteness, becomes septic. Every hospital, every nurse, every doctor knows of such cases.
[. . . .]
Let this be cried from the house-tops. The sacrifice of women is unnecessary. A miscarriage is not necessarily fatal or permanently injurious. The statistics of the great Russian experiment prove that very clearly, even apart from the possible extension of methods by endocrine injections . . . .

An apparently plausible case may be made for restricting the right to an abortion in the early months to cases where the mother is unmarried, or to cases of rape . . . . But I think that it would be an equal mistake to ask for relief to unwilling motherhood in the case of rape only . . . . Moreover, it is probable that the vast majority of unwilling and enforced conceptions take place within the marriage tie.

[181] [I]n many cases all known forms of contraception are inadequate and unsatisfactory, in that they destroy or impair pleasure. This is largely a matter of individual constitution, and is of course an added reason for further research in contraceptive methods. But it is also a reason for *extending the area of living*, and the *art of living*, and for making it possible for e.g. women in whom the portio vaginalis and the cervix are as nervously sensitive and active as the clitoris . . . to enjoy and benefit by normal intercourse, without enforced motherhood.

Ignorance and sex education

In spite of several decades during which the need for the enlightenment of the young about the 'facts of life' had been vigorously asserted, the same arguments and the same points are still being made throughout this period as well. A couple of writers even argue against intruding upon the natural innocence of the girlish mind. One new factor is the increasingly awareness and deployment of psychoanalytical concepts and understandings of childhood and sexuality.

Constance Long, Collected Papers on the Psychology of Phantasy, *1920*

[144] [I]n the unconscious mind of the pupil we have a factor that falsifies a great deal of sex instruction. It is on account of the unconscious mind that class instruction on matters of sex is often useless, or even pernicious. [. . . .]

[T]he only side that can be taught with advantage in classes of young children deals with the facts of sex, and even here the facts are best approached through study of the development and fertilisation of plants and animals. Human physiology should be left to the senior classes. When the time is ripe the children will effect a junction of ideas themselves, intuitively.

It is better that the facts should be dealt out to them impersonally. I object to implanting in the minds of children the idea of the 'sacredness of sex.' It would be better to emphasise what is *human* in sex. The generative organs are no more or less sacred than the brain or stomach.

[157] We must note what the child does, and how he interprets our words. Where we find fear associated with the subject we should seek to remove it, but we need not trouble if the child's idea is inexact as long as it serves him as a working hypothesis which allows him to make progress in his human relations. We should not laugh at his mistakes or his phantasies, but try to get into direct contact with his emotional processes, and keep a critical eye upon our own accustomed formulas of sex.

Barbara Low, Psycho-Analysis, *1920*

[173] A willingness on the part of the adults to answer all questions truthfully, to face the references and implications which will emerge, to make their own knowledge as adequate as possible – this will help to get rid of some of the shames, furtiveness, illu- [174] sions connected with sex-ideas. At the same time we realize through Psycho-analysis that in this

direction, above all others, no easy solution is to be found. To suppose . . . that by telling the child 'all about' sex-matters, answering his questions, behaving sensibly and intelligently over sex-affairs, the problem thereby will be solved, is to be in the greatest error . . . . Such an idea assumes that there is only the conscious mind to be considered, rational and logical, whereas the profundities of sex and sex-emotions appertain primarily to the Unconscious. But knowledge can do something, perhaps much, in such directions as the prevention of premature sexual excitation; the making of physical functions as much as possible an ordinary recognized affair, not wrapt in mystery and shame; less setting up of fixed standards of conduct, irrespective of the child's own nature.

Arabella Kenealy, Feminism and Sex-Extinction, *1920*

[234] [T]he immature, susceptible mind of a girl, incapable of apprehending the sex-factor in its true perspective with the other factors of life, becomes unduly dominated by consideration thereof when too early instructed. She is far better left, for so long as is practicable, ignorant or hazy concerning this vital phenomenon, in place of being fully informed, as girls are now-a-days. So that they know all that there is to be known about sex – except its seriousness and sacredness of Love and Birth – which mere knowledge of biological fact is wholly inadequate to impart – such knowledge of fact presents a crude and bald distortion of the truth; only too often imparting an ugly and demoralising warp to mind and conduct. Ignorance is not Innocence, 'tis true, but it serves the same purpose in safeguarding innocence that clothes do in safeguarding modesty. And for one girl who falls in consequence of innocence, twenty fall from sophistication.

Marie Stopes, The Truth About Venereal Disease, *1921*

[46] The sex diseases would never have saddled themselves upon humanity had not all sex knowledge been befouled by prudery. For with a pure knowledge of sex no one could have endured foul unions, and no one could have tolerated any infectious disease as the associate of love. But through centuries children have learnt from dirty-minded servants, other children and school-fellows, such filthy nonsense about sex that their attitude towards the supreme act of life has been so debased that they do not feel the full sacredness of the marriage union.

Norah March, Sex Knowledge *[1922]*

[52] There is a very strong feeling abroad to-day that our policy of neglecting to instruct children on the facts of sex is no longer justifiable . . . . [E]ducation . . . has altogether left out of account one great eventuality, the eventuality of sex and parenthood. Little or nothing has been done to prepare the individual to meet the eventualities of sex and parenthood nobly and efficiently. It is unreasonable, though many sufferers through ignorance have been inclined to do it, to turn round and blame our parents for this neglect, for they themselves were not taught.

[54] It is a reasonable thing to follow a child's own indications as to what it requires. When its mental development has reached that stage in which it is anxious to understand some of the mysteries of life, it will ask questions pertaining to sex. These should be answered simply and truthfully . . . . The inquirers should be told just what they want to know, but no more. Yet that little should be given in such a fashion as would lead the child to come to the same source for further information. Simple devices can safeguard against the possibility of chattering to playmates and others on these matters. The child's curiosity in regard to questions of sex is an invincible one, and if satisfaction does not come at first from those in whom the child has confidence, usually its parents, the child seeks the information elsewhere, often gathering that information from undesirable channels . . . .

[T]he majority of early questions come somewhere between the ages of three-and-a-half and seven years, occasionally earlier and occasionally later. As time goes on further questions arise. These should be answered satisfactorily to the child's intelligence. An impersonal method of treat- [55] ment is more satisfactory than a personal. Much illustration can be culled from and much explanation can be given by the use of flowers and the facts of animal life. When the main facts of human motherhood have been told, the fact of fatherhood can also be given at a suitable time, and the note already sounded – two specks of life to make a new life – is the one to follow . . . .

Young girls and young boys, exposed as the majority of them are nowadays to temptation in social life, should know of the nature of the relationships of the sexes in marriage in order that they may not, through ignorance, be victims of evil suggestion.

Leonora Eyles, The Woman in the Little House, *1922*

[133] There is a conspiracy of silence on the subject of sex that makes for unhealthiness, and either (according to temperament and environment)

inhibition or risky experiment. Girls and boys grow up to the age of fourteen and leave school without the vaguest idea of physiology . . . . [134] They understand pregnancy in its effect, and very vaguely in its cause. Usually they snigger at it. Children – as recent psychological research has proved – are not born entirely lacking the sex instinct; in fact, they are born with it quite normally keen, and it is only repressed by foolish, wrong-headed education. Many children, as I have shewn, sleep with their parents or in the parents' room; they see or overhear things; mentioning them innocently, they are punished for being so 'saucy'; the next time they pretend to be asleep, and say nothing about what they overhear to their parents; quite often they experiment with other children, and are punished when they get found out. They get the idea, from things overheard, that the father hurts the mother at these times. *This starts a boy or a girl with entirely the wrong idea about the sex question.*

[136] Singularly few girls in their early teens receive instructions from their mothers . . . . Mothers are so terrified to mention the tabooed subject, babies, to their daughters . . . . Several girls have told me that their 'boys' have explained the whole subject to them; some boys do it delicately and nicely; others in a lewd, ugly fashion.
[. . . .]
    [137] [M]others think such subjects disgraceful – and mothers are very ignorant, even after they have had children, of the scientific side of the question . . . . Sex instruction will simply have to form a part of the school curriculum, without any possibility of interference from ignorant parents; in this way the muddles that may spoil the next generation can be obviated . . . .
    [138] If physiology could be taught in schools so that light could take the place of darkness, sex problems would cease to exist . . . . It is just as silly to let each girl and boy, or each man or woman, find out the mysteries of sex for themselves, as it would be to instal [*sic*] chemical apparatus in every home for the making of common salt.

Maude Royden, Sex and Common-sense, *1922*

[114] At some point in our lives we begin to be curious: we ask a question; we are met with a jest or a lie, or with a rebuke, or with some evasion that conveys to us, quite successfully, that we ought not to have asked the question. The question generally has to do with the matter of birth – the birth of babies, or kittens, or chickens; some point of curiosity connected with the birth of young creatures is generally the first thing that awakens our interest. [115] When we meet with evasion, lies, or reproof, we naturally conclude that there is something about the birth of life into

the world that we ought not to know, and since it is apparently wrong of us even to wish to know it, it is presumably disgusting. We seek to learn from other and more grimy sources what our parents might have told us, and learning, arrive at the conclusion that in the relations of men and women there is also something that is repulsive . . . .

It means that almost at once those of us who persist in our desire to know are in danger of losing our self-respect. We learn that there is something in sex that is base – so base that even our own parents will not speak to us about it.

Mary Scharlieb, Straight Talks to Women, *1923*

[16] What are known as 'bad habits' are easily formed, and in the majority of cases they are due in the first instance to some slight but persistent irritation. The drawers or knickers may be too tight in the fork, the child may suffer from worms, it may be allowed to go to bed without emptying the bladder, it may be constipated. Any one of these conditions leads to discomfort or to an uneasy sensation. To relieve this discomfort the child innocently rubs, pulls or scratches. In this way a pleasurable sensation is produced of which the little one understands nothing but which he may wish to reproduce, and so the habit of masturbation is acquired. The habit is injurious in two ways. It gradually, as the child grows into adolescence, develops into premature sexual impulse which is extremely injurious, physically and morally. The bad [17] habit is also injurious because, instinctively, it is felt to be wrong and yet there is neither the knowledge nor the strength that would lead to its correction . . . .

No child should be punished for bad habits. They are seldom his own fault although they may have been learnt from some other person. The father or mother should tell the child that the habit is bad for him, that unless the body is respected and kept pure, trouble will surely come. The child should never be frightened.

[46] Soon the time comes when [the mother] must tell the child the wonderful story. How God gave her the baby when it was too small and too weak to live in the outer world – and so God gave it to her in her own body, near her heart – so that she could keep it warm and safe from all harm. That there, as in a [47] soft warm nest, the tiny helpless thing lay safe and was nourished and grew so that it became the fine big baby lying on her knees able to move, to cry, to suck and to do all the wonderful things the child sees him do. 'Where was the baby before God gave him to you?' 'Why! Of course he was with God, but not such as you see him now.'

The father's part in the wonderful drama seldom comes under the child's consideration until he is older, and ought to have had the help of

knowing a little vegetable physiology. There are some plants the reproductive organs of which demonstrate the process of fertilization in a most
helpful manner. Take for instance, the lovely Madonna lily. Any mother can
show her child the delicate hair-like stamens each bearing a little box
(anther) filled with golden-brown dust. With the help of a pocket lens this
dust is seen to be tiny globules or seeds. Deeper in the flower there is a
green sticky cushion, the stigma, which represents the mother part of
the plant. When the seeds are ripe the anthers open and let them fall
on the stigma. Immediately fine tubes grow down through the stigma and
penetrate the ovary. Within the ovary any small green seeds are beautifully
arranged. By [48] themselves these seeds could do nothing, but when
the life-giving pollen tubes bring the father's contribution, each seed
receives new life which enables it to become an independent plant. Just
so the human father contributes a minute life-giving seed which is
conveyed into the mother's body and there unites with her seed, egg or
ovule, and from this union, if blessed by the Holy Spirit, a new human life
will develop.

[64] It is . . . of great importance not to isolate or to over-accentuate the
teaching of sex hygiene. To do this would be to bring it too prominently
before the child's mind, and would probably defeat our object by leading
him to consider sexual matters as the very central point of life . . . . The
wisest plan is to teach children elementary anatomy, physiology and
hygiene of the whole body and neither to neglect nor to over-accentuate
any portion of it.

Helena Powell, 'The Problem of the Adolescent Girl', 1924

[110] There exists to-day a widespread theory that all the troubles
of adolescence arise from sex-consciousness, and that what is needed
is frank and full explanations of the meaning and implications of sex . . . .
It is doubtless true that many mothers . . . err in not giving quite simply
and reverently, the teaching as to the beginnings of life which can be given
to a child . . . without shocking or disturbing her; so as to prevent a
natural curiosity being satisfied by illicit enquiries. But I believe that an
error even more serious in its consequences is being committed by those
who go the opposite extreme. They urge that it is useless to 'make a
mystery' about the beginning of life; but there is no question of *making* a
mystery; it is there, as those know well who have most understanding
of it, and the mistake lies in ignoring the fact of mystery and violating
the natural instinct of reserve with regard to it . . . . [111] It is better to tell
a little girl that certain ways of behaviour are to be avoided because they

are 'in bad taste' . . . than to explain in detail the underlying reasons for the prohibition . . . .

To call attention to the physical facts of life more than is absolutely necessary is always a mistake. We are constantly told that the process of generation are 'so beautiful.' Beautiful in the sense of adaptation of means to end they [112] may be; so also are the processes of digestion, but few persons would be ready to speak of these as beautiful in the aesthetic sense, or to question the fact that attention to the digestive process is in the last degree harmful to health . . . . [T]he danger of letting the mind linger on the lower level is that sex impulses may be aroused which otherwise would lie dormant . . . .

Well intentioned efforts to acquaint girls with the horrors of vice and its disastrous physical consequences have resulted in not a few cases in producing in a girl the sense of having been outraged in her inner-most feelings, and in some, of inducing a repulsion against everything connected with marriage and the bearing of children.

Dora Russell, Hypatia, 1925

[42] We are always told that boys and girls of all classes nowadays acquire this knowledge easily for themselves, but the mere knowledge is not the only thing to the adolescent mind. Things not spoken of by parents or teachers, things dealt with in hushed voices by moral and spiritual leaders, surrounded by cant and humbug and false sentiment, are bound to be thought nasty by mild young people and to provide ribald laughter for the obstreperous.

This is not to say that sex-information should be given in a spirit of evangelical solemnity and exhortation, nor even of soft sentimentality. All that is needed is lessons in physiology, taught as a matter of course, as botany or nature-study are often taught; and then explanations to boys of the working of their bodies . . . .

[44] Further, they should be told that woman is neither a chattel nor a servant, nor even an inferior . . . . To girls in the same way could be explained the physical changes of puberty, marriage, and maternity . . . . There is nothing in this too difficult or shocking to young or adolescent minds. So many of us can remember the secret conclaves with our friends when we puzzled out and pieced together what scraps of information we could glean, awakening instinct darkly supplementing this knowledge . . . . [45] One straightforward lecture of concise information could have dispelled the lurking mystery once and for all and imparted a sense of magic and wonder and ambition.

Marie Stopes, Sex and the Young, *1926*

[11] One of the dangers in connection with sex . . . is that scraps of information or misinformation are liable to be whispered in a lewd and vulgar manner from one to the other among young people . . . . [12] The fact that such vulgar misrepresentation is possible has, in the past, formed an argument freely used by those who desired to keep all knowledge on leash.

While that attitude deserves consideration, it is immediately counter-balanced and more than counter-balanced by the much weightier arguments in favour of the wise dissemination of the truth. Almost every healthy child has a mind specially adapted to *enquiry* . . . .

It is logical, therefore, to supply correct information in answer to the earliest enquiries, for if first impressions are important in ordinary life, they are still more important in the formation of a special attitude of mind in the child toward the race . . . . [13] *Truth* untampered with, but not necessarily complete, should be supplied to a young mind in answer to every enquiry on any subject whatever, but one must not forget that to an immature mind, unprepared for certain stages of truth, a false impression is conveyed by too large a dose of undiluted fact.

[16] Not very long ago an elderly medical woman,[3] feeling intensely the need of right sex instruction in schools, gathered round her a number of influential persons prepared to push through the reform. Her further advance was impossible because she could find to carry on the work a sufficiency neither of men nor women teachers themselves both instructed and intellectually dowered with the necessary facts, delicacy and sensibility. Nor could she even find books to supply all that was wanted in place of direct instruction.

That this should be so is not surprising when one realises how fundamental in our social life is that attitude of mind towards sex . . . which causes us nationally to look upon it as a subject to be entirely veiled and passed over in silence by those who treat it seriously and reverently, and at the same time to be joked about and sniggered at indecently in [17] the music halls and the gutter . . . . School teachers naturally have the ordinarily acquired human bias in favour of corporate silence about sex, common to almost every adult of British birth.

[18] I oppose *special* sex instruction . . . but because I feel that young people in whom sex surges so strongly, with all the intense potentialities

3   Very probably Mary Scharlieb and the British Social Hygiene Council are being alluded to here.

of youth hovering and not yet balanced and equably established, are liable to be greatly injured rather than benefited by anything specially emphasising sex and setting it apart from the stabilising material facts with which it is linked in everyday life. Emphasis of sex entails distortion.

Every child from the age of about twelve onwards ought to become unobtrusively possessed of a reasonable elementary, and well-balanced, knowledge of the external features, the internal structure, and the racial possibilities of the whole body. This knowledge should not come to them as special sex instruction but as part of the general instruction in human physiology which everyone ought to receive.

[116] It may be partly true that a detailed scientific knowledge of sex and all it entails may make it possible for young people to avoid some of the 'consequences' (in illegitimacy and disease) which their parents' generation incurred. From the point of view of purely personal morals, they have gained nothing by the knowledge, but society has gained enormously.

[122] Many who desire to see the venereal diseases stamped out (as they could be within a generation in this country), are eager to instruct all young people in the dangers thereof and to emphasise with much detail the risks that are run in this connection. I think, however, that such a course is often upsetting and positively harmful to clean and wholesome young people. They should merely be instructed in general about germs, their prevalence, and the constant need for scrupulous cleanli- [123] ness.

[166] *The child's first instruction in its attitude towards its sex organs, its first account of the generation of human beings, should be given when it is two or three years old*; given with other instruction, of which it is still too young to comprehend more than part, but which it is nevertheless old enough to comprehend in part. Very simple instruction given reverently at suitable opportunities at that early age will impress itself upon the very *texture* of the child's mind, before the time of actual memories, so that from the very first possible beginnings its tendencies are in the direction of truth and reverent understanding.

Leonora Eyles, Women's Problems of To-day, *1926*

[62] The instinct for reproduction is the deepest instinct in human nature, deeper even, I think, than the instinct for self-preservation . . . . [63] It arouses questions in the child as soon as it begins to think, and if, on this fundamental question, a child is lied to, or if it hears suggestive, ugly, half-whispered conversations about it, the stream of life is dirtied at the source.

161

[M]any mothers are hopelessly muddled about it themselves . . . . [T]hey confess that they cannot tackle the problem of telling their children the facts of life, giving the impression that to them these facts are too ugly to be mentioned. How terrible to think that these very children must have been conceived in a spirit of disgrace . . . . It is these 'hidden parts' of our lives that make all the neurotic troubles of this most neurotic of all ages. It is, I know, extremely difficult when you reach the age, say, of thirty, to begin to clean your mind of false shames and false ideas, but if you are going to save your children from them you will have to do it . . . .

If you bring up a child to understand the processes of its body, and all that goes on within it, from babyhood, it will never have foul ideas. And if you shirk this duty yourself, he will learn in an ugly way from school-fellows and go on handing on the torch of life with fingers soiled by mud and slime.

[64] [E]nlightenment of our children about sex is a deeply social question . . . . As long as human beings have this ingrained feeling that they were conceived through some mysteriously shameful act, they will go on being subject and humble. Our psychological attitude towards life determines our political and social behaviour. A psychological slave is a social slave. This question is not merely a question of health and domestic happiness, it is a political question. Free people's minds of their sense of guilt about bodily love, and you free them of subservience. What is more, you would stop all desire for illicit love, except in the case of morbid and mentally sick people.

Geraldine Coster, Psychoanalysis for Normal People, 1926

[173] At the present day it is the fashion to endeavour to give sex-instruction to children of all ages, and the practice is of course fundamentally healthy and desirable. But too few people realize how impossible it is to tell a child what it does not at the moment care to know. It is assumed that sex-curiosity is universal among children, but this, so far as my own experience goes, is by no means the case. To a child who is not at the moment curious, the most carefully administered instruction may seem unintelligible and tedious, and while it reaches the hearing may fail completely to reach the comprehension. As a result, all trace of knowledge will have faded from the mind in a very short time . . . On the other hand, to withhold information from the curious is to court disaster. To a great number of children it is essential, as a condition of mental and physical health, that the fullest possible explanation of the sexual functions be given at an early stage. It is not enough for them to know in a vague and general way 'where babies come from'. They [174] must also understand as exactly

as possible both the function of the father and also the way in which birth takes place.

[. . . .]

[175] Nevertheless it is unwise to ask direct questions or offer unsolicited information. Both these methods may cause a child to retreat into an impenetrable reserve. There are many indirect ways of letting a child feel that such subjects are not taboo, and once he knows this he will ask for the information he requires.

Barbara Low, The Unconscious in Action, *1928*

[174] It is probably impossible, even if it were desirable, to give instruction in the school concerning sex-matters, beyond a knowledge of the physiological and biological facts which can best be conveyed by sensible text-books, and so much instruction should be a part of every school curriculum for the adolescent: in addition there should be a readiness on the part of the teacher to answer all individual questions which arise.

Nevertheless, this is the stage which can afford opportunities for freer and more open treatment of sex-matters, provided that the more oppressive inhibitions of the adolescent have been escaped.

Marie Stopes (ed.), Mother England, *1929*

[97] I wish some times there were clinics for men and women, to learn about the Human Body. The majority of people will tell us a lot of filth but when it comes to anything pure and good to help us, they stop – I cannot afford one of your books just now but hope to do so soon.

[119] I was brought up without any knowledge of Sex, my parents' method of bringing up my sisters and myself 'in innocence' – and so – often having made a fool of myself on more than one occasion.

Vera Brittain, Halcyon, *1929*

[11] In those days 'preparation' for marriage consisted, for a girl, in the teaching of cooking and domestic technique . . . . This . . . provided society with a convenient excuse for completely omitting any instruction in the technique of sex intercourse, the knowledge of which, as we ourselves have long been aware, is something quite other than domestic proficiency, and is far more necessary to marital happiness than the most expert culinary skill.

163

[17] The superstitious identification of virtue with ignorance obscured the fact, now familiar to all of us, that adequate pre-marital sex-education is able, with many young men and women, to take the place of cloying pre-marital experience. Few dared to admit, though nearly everyone secretly knew, that the vast majority of nineteenth and twentieth century divorces [18] were caused by avoidable sex-maladjustments. Though successful monogamy can obviously be founded only upon a thorough knowledge of sex-technique and therefore of the workings of the body and its entire range of peculiarities, insuperable obstacles were placed in the way of almost all attempts to give popular instruction in normal or abnormal physiology.

Janet Chance, 'A Marriage Education Centre in London', 1929

[38] You find a neglect of proper education of their children in sex matters by even the most enlightened of these women. It is quite common to hear mothers, who are ready to discuss sex themselves, state that they cannot speak to their children, while there are many more whose minds are on a level with that of the mother who stated that of course she could not have a cat in the house, it led to such awkward questions.

[39] [T]he work of a Marriage Education Centre is needed almost as much by the rich as by the poor of this country, certainly so where the education of children . . . [is] concerned.

Barbara Low, 'Sexual Education: Some Psycho-Analytical Considerations', 1929

[368] [T]he provision of adequate text-books to put into the hands of the young, has hardly yet been touched, at any rate not by the people most fitted to deal with it, and though there is poured out a steady stream of books purporting to give sexual information to the young, it is rare to find one which will supply the real need of those for whom it is designed. Similarly, we have not solved the problem of which persons are best suited to give such instruction, nor under what conditions nor at what stage of development it shall be conveyed . . . . [369] It is an astonishing reflection that in England at any rate . . . the future teacher can go through his whole pedagogical course of two, three or even four years' duration without even touching the question of his own sexual nature and development nor that of his pupils! This fact alone speaks volumes in respect to the prevailing attitude towards sex, an attitude which first denies knowledge to the

teacher, and then proceeds to make use of the teachers' ignorance to support the contention that the pupils manifest no sexuality.

Ethel Mannin, 'Sex and the Child', 1929

[374] Over and over again I have come across mothers who imagine that they are tremendously modern and rational because they have explained to their children what they like to refer to as 'the facts about life' by describing the pollination of flowers . . . . They have the pathetic idea that this explanation of conception and birth makes everything seem 'nice' and acceptable to the child-mind. The fact that they are so anxious to make it all seem nice as explained to their children betrays their sexual self-consciousness and indicates their own attitude towards sex – that it is not quite nice and must somehow be purified before being presented to the child.

They do not realize that these elaborate and solemn explanations are as pernicious as any old-fashioned conspiracy of silence . . . .

[375] Answer a child's questions honestly and simply, but don't let it seem important. Give it simply and precisely the information it seeks – as casually and without fuss as you would give it any other information . . . . Once fall away from an elaborate casualness and the child suspects that you are secretly ashamed of the whole thing and its interest is morbidly quickened and it gets everything out of perspective . . . .

My child knew where babies came from when she was three . . . [376] When she was six I recall that she announced one day when we were having lunch together that she understood where baby things came from but she didn't see *why* they did. What *started* them growing? I replied that there were seeds in the fathers as well as in the mothers; and that the seeds from the fathers could be put into the mothers to make the mother-seeds grow into baby-seeds. She said, 'But *how*?' So we talked comparative physiology for a bit.

[377] [S]ex education *must* be practical and not theoretic; it *must* be casually imparted, not solemnly taught, and the facts must not be confused by any ethical trimmings. It is disastrous to try and drag love into sexual relationships when you are discussing them with a child; the relationship of love to sexual issues is simply not comprehensible by the child; not until it is adolescent and its own emotions are stirred sexually can it comprehend the relationship of human emotions with the sexual act . . . . It is a mistake to give the child more information that it asks for, for it only asks for as much as it can mentally digest – over-feed it and you give it mental indigestion – which is cured less easily than physical indigestion. Obviously one should never shirk giving the child every scrap of information it seeks

165

– but also one should never sentimentalize or idealize or attempt to romanticize the simple biological facts . . . .

[E]ven parents who have been sensible in the manner of their imparting sex information almost always come a cropper over the business of masturbation. They imagine that they are so much more sensible than their own parents were because they do not attempt to put the fear of God into a child for masturbating, and that it is rational to reason with a child that he must not do this because it is a self-abuse which will do him harm – that it will make him stupid is the favourite line of reasoning. They do not, it is true, make the child terrified or ashamed, as our grandparents and parents did, but they succeed in worrying him into the very state of stupidity against which they had warned him.

Chapter Four

ॐ

The Depression and war, 1930–1945

Introduction

The 1930s are often perceived as a period during which feminism was in abeyance. However, the texts represented here suggest that economic depression, the rise of fascism with its strong anti-feminist message, the debates on population decline and their associated pro-natalist rhetoric, provided a background against which a feminist discourse on sexual issues seemed very far from obsolete.

1930 does not, perhaps, look like an obvious breakpoint for the inter-war years. However, that year saw an enormously significant development: the Minister of Health in the Labour government conceded, though in a very low-key fashion, that birth control advice might (at the discretion of the local Medical Officer of Health) be given in local authority welfare centres, though only if the woman's health was severely endangered by further pregnancy. This had been what the birth control movement had been fighting for since 1923, and although the concession was some-what meagre, the message it gave about the legitimacy of birth control was considerable. That birth control was increasingly acceptable was also confirmed by the Lambeth Conference of the Church of England in the same year, which gave its approval to the responsible use of contraception within marriage. (Even though the Roman Catholic position was hardened by the definite anti-contraception statement of the Pope's Encyclical *Casti Connubii*.) A variety of existing birth control organizations joined together to form the National Birth Control Association, which was involved in setting up clinics, campaigning for local authorities to take advantage of the new permissive legislation, lobbying for extension of the conditions under which advice might be given free, establishing standards for the various contraceptive appliances currently available and undertaking research into improved methods. With this important bridgehead won, the more radical vanguard of the movement moved on to join Stella Browne in her previously solitary campaign for abortion law reform, resulting in the establishments of an Abortion Law Reform Association in 1936. The Bourne case of 1938, which Joan Malleson was a key actor in bringing about, created an important case-law precedent for doctors' clinical judgement in performing abortion.

There was continued agitation for the increased reform to the divorce laws, achieved in a limited sense by A. P. Herbert's Private Member's Act of 1937: this extended the grounds beyond adultery to include cruelty, prolonged desertion and insanity, but retained the adversarial, guilty/ innocent dynamic.

The significance of female desire and the importance of women's sexual pleasure continued to be a central motif in much of this writing. It is also noticeable that there was an increased emphasis on women's potential for sexual enjoyment well into later life and the post-menopausal years.

The material from this period shows a growing assumption that birth control was a won cause, not needing defence (although practicalities of provision and method remained), and was a major factor in liberating women from their biology. It also enabled considerations of heterosexual relationships outside marriage which were not about shame or exploitation, and even the possibility of what would later be called 'open marriages'. The single woman continued to be an object of concern, but had several defenders against charges of withered and frustrated spinsterhood.

Other recommended resources

There were a number of inquiries into abortion during the 1930s, unfortunately none of them include full reports of the evidence given to them. *Plan: The Journal of the Federation of Progressive Societies and Individuals* published articles by Stella Browne, Janet Chance and others on issues of sex reform, and *The New Generation* continued to cover more than birth control questions. The supposed autobiography of a prostitute of this period, 'Sheila Cousins', *To Beg I Am Ashamed*, was, unfortunately, actually written by two male authors.

Marriage

Persisting themes can be discerned: problems of the existing state of marriage, as well as its potential to be a mutually rewarding relationship, the dangerous wedding night. The notion of non-monogamy, in the context of open marriages, is also mooted by a number of writers. However, the survey undertaken by Eliot Slater and Moya Woodside from 1943 to 1946 reveals the extremely negative attitudes towards marital sexuality still prevalent among many women.

Naomi Mitchison, Comments on Birth Control, 1930

[13] [T]here are many kinds of mutual caresses and pleasures. It seems probable that it is better for the young couple, both as a matter of health and enjoyment – may I perhaps even say morals? – that they should not have more actual copulation than they both really want to the bottom of their hearts, for it is a thing which develops fantastically easily into a mere pleasant habit of marriage.

[14] Very few normal couples . . . keep up a devouring passion for one another all their lives. Love is not static, however much one might like it to be; it must almost necessarily move away from, as well as towards, passion. Why then, one might ask, do the hypothetical couple want to go on copulating? Because, if it was discovered that after all they did not really want it, then they had better stop . . . . But there seem to be a good many reasons why they should both want and need it.
[. . . .]
   [15] There is kindness, friendliness, some mutual excitement, partly spontaneous, partly worked up by both to put a [16] little brightness and gaiety into plain ordinary life. There is force of habit, the knowledge that nerves will be soothed and pleasant sleep come, the marking of actual possession, if not of one another at least of a relationship, a little world, a certainty among much chaos. There is tenderness and gratitude towards the other parent of present and future babies. All this is real and most likely good, and makes an adequate joy and fire for both, though they may no longer be passionately in love.

Helena Wright, The Sex Factor in Marriage, 1930

[30] The wife who means to have a happy sex [31] life must realise that her mind has a great deal to do with it. She must decide with all her strength that she *wants* her body to feel all the sensations of sex with the greatest possible vividness. A wife who allows her mind to keep any unworthy ideas about sex lurking in its corners, is her own worst enemy. Her body will only yield its fullest joy, will only allow her to know the experience of physical ecstasy, if her mind and her soul are in active sympathy with it.
[. . . .]

Generally speaking, pleasure in the sex-act is easy and instantaneous to normal men. The husband's part is, therefore, to put himself imaginatively into his wife's personality, to determine that he will learn how to arouse in her the most intense and delicate sensations of pleasure of which she is capable. At the beginning of marriage, he more often than not has the role of initiator; his is the magic [32] touch that will awaken his wife's physical nature; her future sex happiness will depend to a very large extent on his knowledge, delicacy, imagination, and sympathy . . . .

There is no human joy possible to man greater than sharing the supreme experience of sex with a wife who is responsive to his every touch, whose whole being flames in ecstasy, whose soul and body become united to his in a bond stronger than any other we know in life.

[56] In our day it is more or less taken for granted that the sex-act shall be completed on the first night after marriage. But why should it be? A number of women date their sexual unhappiness [57] from the fact that their husbands had no patience, and penetrated the vagina before they were emotionally or physically prepared for it. Time and gentleness in this matter bring a golden reward.

Janet Chance, The Cost of English Morals, *1931*

[34] [T]he English married woman is often ignorant of normal sex life. Often she only knows sex on sufferance, and knows nothing of passion; she suffers the passion of another.
[. . . .]
[35] The subject of physical happiness in marriage raises a pathetically eager response in working-women's meetings and invariably calls forth personal corroborations of that truth while the embarrassed silence of the remainder does not suggest a great contentment with their own marital routine . . . . It is often news to them that they might at all share the sex enjoyment of their husbands.

[36] [M]arriage failed and became intolerable because its physical side proved distasteful to one of the partners . . . . It is possible that if this factor, which in the view of so many was mainly responsible for the failure of their marriage, and which is often remediable, were faced and remedied, we should find marriage after all not so unsatisfactory an institution, and find it give our women the sanity in sex they lack to-day.

[37] Too often the moment which for the man is the culmination of ecstasy and romance is for the woman an intimate, too intimate, assistance at a distasteful business.

If this happens even once – and it is unfortunately frequently the first experience of passion – the effects are likely to cast a shade of uncertainty, if not of disgust, over future times of intimacy. And if it happens often, it will require considerable mental control on the part of the woman, if she is to tolerate her partial success and not become permanently emotionally and mentally warped.

Such women have often lain awake, saying to themselves that marriage is the real prostitution because in it something finer than the hopes of a prostitute are continually destroyed.

Helena Normanton, Everyday Law for Women, *1932*

[110] Sexual intercourse during the whole period of the marriage until a separation is decreed by Order of Court seems to be the one outstanding right of the husband . . . .

A husband has also a kind of right to his wife's society and presence in the marital home, but this is a somewhat qualified affair. A husband cannot confine his wife bodily in his home, and she may absent herself from it at her pleasure. If any forcible attempt is made to keep her there she can sue for her liberty by means of a Writ of *Habeas Corpus*.

[124] Divorce is granted to wives upon strict proof, i.e. to the satisfaction of the Court, of one or more acts of adultery by the husband, or upon strict proof of the commission by him of one or more acts of homosexual vice; or upon strict proof that a husband has forced his wife to unnatural connection with himself. (She must not have been a consenting party.)

It is granted to a husband upon strict proof of one or more acts of adultery by the wife; but no relief is given to a husband on account of his wife's addiction to unnatural sexual practices with other women.

[130] Refusal of Intercourse Subsequent to Consummation. This is an all too frequent course in English marriages; indeed English women have a reputation for sexual frigidity which seems to be in many instances well founded.

A certain proportion of men also turn out to be practically inert in marriage. This course of conduct on either side in a marriage inflicts often real hardship, leading sometimes to bad physical effects upon the other partner. English law grants no remedy for non-fulfilment to the normally physical spouse if the marriage has ever been consummated, even if upon only a solitary occasion.

[. . . .]

If a husband continues to dwell in a house with his wife and ceases to have intercourse with her, after once having had it, she has apparently no legal remedy.

Margaret Kornitzer, The Modern Woman and Herself, 1932

[139] Sex-relationships without marriage are not immoral, simply because morality does not lie in the formal tie of marriage. But we do know, deep within us, that stable monogamy is the real aim towards which we are moving, and that, so far, the formal contract is our only safeguard against ourselves. We are, however, coming to a slow [140] recognition that love and not marriage is the true sanctification – the humanising – of sex. We realise that marriage is a safeguard, but we can now also conceive of a morality that transcends safety.

We would achieve a great advance in understanding if only we could stop thinking of monogamy and monogamous marriage as a form of relationship that has been tested through and through and is now worn out, fit to be discarded.

Mary Borden, The Technique of Marriage, 1933

[6] [T]he need of a normal sex-life is not, I maintain, the reason for marriage. The demands of sex can be satisfied quite well without it and outside it, and are. No; sex isn't the answer. It is not the answer to anything. It is merely an element of life, a condition of being alive . . . an urgent, powerful, undeniable condition that comes into everything, complicates all our civilised arrangements and is a constant, threatening menace to marriage. An exaggerated menace perhaps, and a thing in itself of vastly exaggerated importance. There's a deal to be said about the danger of paying too much attention to sex in marriage . . . . [I]t is a serious mistake, and one that leads to endless unnecessary trouble, to think that sexual need is the reason for marriage.

[47] It is very pleasant to us to feel that the bride doesn't know what is going to be done to her. Her helpless innocence is her charm.

She ought to know exactly. It should all have been explained to her long ago, in cold, accurate, scientific language that carried no suggestion of mystery or ugliness. That part of her education should have been begun when she began arithmetic and should have been taught in the same manner.

[51] [M]any marriages that might have begun and continued quite happily start wrong because of the honeymoon. For I believe that this holiday, whose only reason for existence is pleasure, is very often not pleasant at all, but is a painful, difficult, disappointing, nerve-racking experience, both to the man and the woman, and, therefore, an utterly useless, abnormal, unfair test of their love for each other.

This is especially true in those countries and among those people where sex repression is a fundamental part of the moral code.

[61] I wonder to how many newly-married couples the idea has occurred that perhaps they would enjoy being married quite as much or more if they didn't go away . . . with the express purpose of making love to each other all day and all night for a month or so in a solitude of two, but walked straight from church into the normal life they meant to live together, with the wonderful stimulant of their new exciting love.

[120] The whole subject of marital rights needs overhauling . . . . A man's vanity is either too great or too slight to make the delicacies he will employ in an illicit love-affair seem worth while in marriage, and that old, old feeling of possession urges him to take liberties with his wife. The temptation is to prove to himself that she is his property, that he can do what he likes with her; and so he neglects . . . certain courtesies that he would show a stranger, a [121] mistress, or any other woman friend.

[146] [T]he temperature of the blood and the rapidity of the pulse are not reliable symptoms of a heart's condition. It takes a deal of character to face the fact that a peculiarly delicious element in one's life, once uniquely and inseparably associated with one's most intimate companion, has suddenly [147] vanished, but that the companion . . . who can no longer provide it, is nevertheless the same person, just as lovable and just as worth loving as before. If you have been led to believe that sensual delight and passionate rapture are immortal elements in love, it will be very difficult for you to discern this truth and refuse to admit that the end of your desire is a catastrophe.

[150] I am a normal woman and I do not want to be told [151] how to kiss my love by a weighty scientist who knows all about my sexual organs and is convinced that they control my imagination . . . . I saw myriads of husbands and wives kissing as he instructed them, going on with it religiously, keeping it up determinedly, desperately, even when they didn't really want to; and I was a little frightened by the idea that I, like every other married man and woman, must keep on with this forever if my marriage was to survive . . . . I knew in my heart that the Herr Professor was wrong in thinking that the happiness of married life consists in a set of sexual antics endlessly repeated.

[153] [T]here are thousands of women who experience nothing but pain and annoyance during this stormy business, who remain completely unmoved and dreadfully calm, and whose horror, when the men they love are changed suddenly into blind brutes, is commensurate with their sensitiveness and their tenderness.

[155] [E]ven if . . . men and women could somehow contrive to defeat nature and keep their natural physical desire alive for thirty, forty or fifty years, I see nothing very much to be proud of in the achievement. On the contrary, sexual desire in the old is at best a pitiful fact. Lust, divorced from passionate ardour, is, even in a single lonely individual, a painful disgusting spectacle. But the organised, stale and monstrous lust of long habit, carefully and artificially nurtured for their mutual sensual satisfaction by two people in whom youth and passion and physical beauty are long since gone, this, surely, is a monstrous, unnatural and ugly thing.

[157] Sometimes gradually, but sometimes quite suddenly, the wonderful healing and refreshing springs of sex-love dry up . . . . They may long desperately to go on wanting each other, they cannot by any effort or act of will recapture the lovely emotion that is gone, or force themselves to want what they want no longer. Passion has a life of its own.

Leonora Eyles, Commonsense about Sex, 1933

[48] Many a marriage has been wrecked on the marriage night by the girl's unpreparedness and the man's eagerness, and by that convention which demands that the first night shall be an orgy. When one or both of a married couple are ignorant of sex and have been brought up in an atmosphere of prohibition, it is much wiser to go home together after the wedding and get used to each other's bodies by sleeping together for a few nights. This is not easy on the man, I know, but it is worth some amount of self-sacrifice to avoid giving the wife a shock from which she may never recover, and which may make her a frigid and repellent partner for life . . . . It is wise, too, for a man to explore his wife's body as much as possible before connection; the boy who has had contact with prostitutes, or who has had those two-minute affairs in the dark by which our unhappy boys today get their initiation into sex, knows nothing of a woman's [49] body and often carries the two-minute technique into married life, to his own ultimate disappointment and his wife's nervous ruination.

[58] What is so dreadful to realise is the fact that, after marriage, the average man entirely forgets to make love at all. He seems to think that his wife is always ready for his embraces and for sexual intercourse. I know of hundreds of cases, told me in correspondence and in actual words, where there is not even a kiss as a preliminary to intercourse, and where the man, having deposited semen in his wife's vagina after about two minutes' connection, is perfectly satisfied. Then later he wonders why his wife makes excuses to avoid the boredom or the actual disgust of the proceeding.

Gladys Hall, Prostitution: A Survey and a Challenge, *1933*

[100] One of the important facts about the male patronage of prostitutes is the number of married men to be found among prostitutes' customers .... There appear to be several reasons for this, one being the attitude towards sex intercourse adopted by some husbands, to whom it is merely a form of indulgence and whose excessive and growing demands exceed all bounds. Such husbands are a severe problem ... by reason of the wreckage of womanhood they achieve in the persons of their wives .... All social workers ... know of the countless cases where wives, even when near the birth of a child, will do anything to preserve their men from turning to the streets for the intercourse they cannot or will not forgo. On the other hand a precisely opposite cause may be found in the attitude adopted by some wives to the intimate relationships of marriage .... [A] wife will maintain a cold frigidity towards an affectionate [101] husband which has an incalculably bad effect on his whole life. The effect of such an attitude in some cases is found in the patronage of prostitutes, in a vain attempt to assuage the feeling of frustration and loneliness for which the wife is responsible.

Arabella Kenealy, The Human Gyroscope, *1934*

[259] In the degree to which the sexes have evolved their attributes of Individualism, in terms of complex characters of oppositeness on every plane of faculty, their reciprocal attraction has evolved to complex modes of thought and feeling and intensity, as the emotional, devotional and spiritual exaltation of the human love-passion. The herd-instinct of general sex-attraction and sexual promiscuity, found in the lower sub-human creatures, has evolved, accordingly, through higher and progressive monogamous species to this intensely individualised love-passion of the highest creature, Man .... [B]y Nature's ordinance and his own truest instinct Man is an intrinsically monogamous species, being correspondingly sexually selective.

Naomi Mitchison, The Home, *1934*

[93] What is the cause of the terrible attitude of weary toleration shown by so many working-class and lower middle-class women towards their husbands' sexual activities? Is it simply due to the men's lack of sexual education or willingness to take trouble with their wives, or has it to do with the women's fear, overwork, underfeeding or intolerable

discouragement? Or can it possible be that men who are themselves oppressed take pleasure in oppressing others? . . . .

[143] Socially, possession is a terrible evil, leading to every kind of hatred, cruelty, insecurity and despair. But personally it is all right. It is the necessary assuagement of our inherited instincts from the social apes. Everybody minds being owned economically, even when they acquiesce; nobody minds being owned in love. (Or, more accurately, everybody wants to be owned in love.) But when the two things are mixed there is the devil to pay . . . . [W]e have all got them a bit mixed, and that is why the devil is in our sexual relationships. For either women do not want to be owned socially and have got it [144] so mixed up that they will not be owned personally (especially as being owned personally is dreadfully apt to involved being owned socially) even though it hurts them not to be – those are the intelligent women. Or else they do not really want to be owned, but because they like being owned personally, they acquiesce in being owned socially and either try and get round it by grabbing back in some way – being actually owners themselves – or else by pretending to be very proud of it and trying to be as much owned as possible . . . .

[145] As a matter of fact, over this matter of owning and being owned, and wanting and not wanting, actively and passively, personally and socially, there are a very large number of possible permutations and combinations . . . . So no wonder people are in a muddle. But some of these combinations are rare, perhaps even as perversions, and some of them are certainly unhappy-making. It seems to me that there is only one really happy-making combination out of the lot, which applies to both men and women.

The happy-making combination is one of the simplest ones. Here, both man and woman are not owned socially (and do not want to be), and do not own socially (and do not want to) but they are owned personally by one another (and want to be) and they do own one another personally (and want to). That is to say, there are no real conflicts, and the only possible source of conflict is that the overlap between personal and social may not be completely obvious.

Sybil Neville-Rolfe, Why Marry?, 1935

[65] [T]he key in which the music of married life is to be composed is settled on the honeymoon, therefore careful preparation, in thought and in self-education, should precede it.

The woman should hold the tuning fork, as hers is the more complex adjustment. In other words, experiments in physical adjustment should only be made when she is fully willing. Many women have been brought up in the tradition that they play no active part and that it is, therefore, their duty to accede to their husband's request, whenever it is made. The husband must realise that frequent demands, which his partner acquiesces in from a sense of duty, will also result in fixing the relationship on a purely physical basis, unattached to the higher centres of personality. Even if both learn later that a far more complete form of adjustment is attainable, it will take much longer [66] and be more difficult to reach because the old habits of feeling will have to be broken and new ones created.

The reason many are unhappy today is that so few men and women understand the technique or the art of marriage.

[. . . .]

It must not be anticipated that complete unity will be attained without considerable practice. The need for practice, however, does not imply that the physical act should be undertaken with undue frequency.

Miss E. V. Pemberton, Simple Advice to Those About to Marry, 1936

[22] A great many people take it for granted that their marriage must be consummated on their wedding night, but it is a mistake to assume that this is NECESSARILY the best time.

[. . . .]

At the time of his marriage, desire for physical union with the woman of his choice is something of which a man is nearly always fully aware.

It is, however, very important that he should understand that, although in this way her own feelings may already be similar to his, it is not at all unusual for a woman to be deeply and sincerely attached to the man she is about to marry, without having experienced any conscious desire for intimacy.

When this is the case it makes all the difference in the world if he realises that it is quite natural and is content to lead her on gently, step by step, until she shares his own yearning.

When, as sometimes happens, intercourse takes place before the wife feels really ready for it, it is never the satisfying experience it should be for either partner.

[23] Desire can and ought to be just as strong in a woman as it is in a man, but in her case it usually comes to life more slowly.

The privilege of awakening it is her husband's but much will depend on the extent to which she is ready to co-operate.

If she does all she can to help him, and if he is careful to give her time, then in ways which his love for her will teach him, he will be able to arouse in her those feelings which will make her a willing partner and lead her to give herself to him gladly and unreservedly.

Such consideration on his part is always amply repaid, for the final consummation of their marriage is then an infinitely more wonderful experience for both of them.

[26] Intimate times should always be special times, and it is very necessary to guard against their becoming ordinary and commonplace occasions.

It should also be borne in mind that over-frequent intercourse can be physically, as well as mentally and morally, harmful.

Margaret Cole, Marriage: Past and Present, *1938*

[137] It is not true that husbands and wives only divorce, or desire to divorce, one another out of hatred, ridicule, and contempt. Even it if were ever true, it is not true today. It is not true that people as a whole regard a divorced person as a criminal. They may . . . regard those who get into the divorce courts as silly, or uncontrolled, or merely as unfortunate. They may resolve . . . that they personally will not get mixed up in the disgusting moral atmosphere of the said courts . . . . But they do not regard those who do enter the courts as criminals; they are mentioned and even met, not merely in polite society, but in society distinctly verging upon the impolite.

Dorothy Thurtle, Abortion, Right or Wrong?, *1940*

[31] Modern women are learning that their sex life is as important to them as to their husbands, and is not something about which to be furtive or ashamed. They know, further, that it need not be synonymous with child-bearing, and in consequence many married lives are enriched, and are fuller than those of earlier generations. Knowledge of modern scientific methods of birth control has made a significant contribution to marital happiness and mutual understanding. There are still too many women, however, who are unable to protect themselves against unwanted pregnancies, and who consequently feel bitterly at times towards their husbands.

Eliot Slater and Moya Woodside, Patterns of Marriage, *1951*

[167] Sex is duty, and women are not trained to expect any particular pleasure . . . . Several times the phrase recurred, 'I've never refused him', often said with pride. Compliance is seen as an anchor for the husband,

keeping his affection at home. Passive endurance is shown in such phrases as 'he's happy', 'I try to be accommodating', 'it's a satisfaction for him'.

This negative attitude quite often reaches a low point in one of boredom, even dislike, and a desire to get it over: 'I'm not keen', 'I don't think there's anything in it' . . . [168] 'my heart's not in it', 'it's the one part of marriage I could do without'. Husbands are valued in an inverse relation to sexuality: 'he's very good, he doesn't bother me much', 'he's not lustful', 'he wouldn't trouble you at all', 'he's pretty good that way; if I say no, he doesn't go on'.

Desire, pleasure and satisfaction

The existence of sexual desire in women continues to be recognized and defended, its complexities explored, even as a number of voices point out that it is not exactly the same as that in men, and that it could, perhaps, be possible to exaggerate its place in women's lives. It is noticeable during the 1930s that the persistence of and even increase of desire after the menopause form a recurrent theme. The extent of avoidable frigidity is deplored, and advice produced on how to achieve sexual gratification.

Naomi Mitchison, Comments on Birth Control, *1930*

[17] The mere fact that contraceptives are within reach makes the longing less urgent. This probably applies only to some people, but surely to a very large number, and particularly to the woman, if it is she who takes the precautions . . . . Besides she is naturally, perhaps not the passive, but on the whole the courted party, and when she gets herself ready without being specifically asked she feels there is something wrong, she has become the more active and forward of the two . . . .

On the other hand if it is the man who prepares, the woman feels that he has made up his mind, his courting and her acceptance are purely formal and she may be excused if she is rather chilly.

[24] [L]amentably often the woman's sexual experience is anyway incomplete. An astonishingly large percentage of women of all classes have never experienced the final and satisfying crisis, this partly through our fantastic religious and social education, and partly through the incompetence of their husbands. That is to say their sexual cycle is anyhow incomplete, and this incompleteness is far more important than that due to contraception, because there can be no emotional substitute for it.

Helena Wright, The Sex Factor in Marriage, *1930*

[48] The sensation-providing parts in a woman are partly on the outside, and partly hidden. . . . . [A]cuteness of sensation varies: least sensitive are the two large folds covered with ordinary skin and hair, which [50] run from back to front, between the thighs. Protected by them, in the centre in front, is a small round body, about the size of a pea, movable to a slight extent, and coated with delicate membrane, which is always more or less moist. Its anatomical name is the clitoris. This little organ is capable of giving the most acute sensations; the tissue of which it is made is similar to that of the penis, and during sex stimulation it has the same power of filling with blood, and thereby becoming larger and harder than it is in an inactive state. The only purpose of the clitoris is to provide sensation; a full understanding of its capabilities and place in the sex-act is therefore of supreme importance. Running from back to front, inside the large folds or lips, are two smaller and more delicate folds, the inner lips. These join in front of the clitoris in a narrow fold which makes a hood for the further protection of the clitoris. The membrane covering the inner lips is sensitive, less sensitive than the clitoris, more sensitive than the outer lips.

[67] [T]aking everything into consideration, it remains true that women need more time for full stimulation than do men.

It may be that women take longer because their responses are more complex than those of men . . . . In a perfectly balanced married life the husband and wife are free to vary their modes of expression according to mood or circumstance. The description which follows must therefore not be taken too rigidly. Usually at the beginning the man is the initiator, the woman the willing recipient; the husband understanding his wife's nature, has the joy of rousing her gradually, of creating in her an ardour equal to his own.

[70] Sensation in the clitoris and the immediately surrounding mucous membrane can only be aroused by the application of constantly changing pressure. Continuous pressure very soon becomes painful. Fingers are by far the most delicate instruments for arousing definite local sex-sensations. There is an infinite variety in the number of possible movements, and every husband should discover the kinds of pressure and the rhythms of moving which give his wife most pleasure . . . .

During this stage of the sex-act comes the moment which shows that the wife is ready for full reception of her husband. In describing [71] the anatomy of the genital region we mentioned two little glands, called Bartholin's glands, and we said that their purpose is to supply a slippery fluid. As soon as the clitoris is sufficiently excited, these glands work, and pour out their fluid over the walls of the vagina. This appearance of moisture is the sign that the vagina is prepared for the penis.

[72] Nearly all women find vaginal sensation through, as it were, the gateway of clitoris sensation. When they have fully experienced both, they will vary their sex-life according to mood and temperament. For the full experience of the orgasm or sexual climax, intense feeling must generally be present in both places.

The last part of the act, after penetration [73] has taken place, is usually, though not necessarily, the shortest. The wife is now in full co-operation; by the movements of her hips, and consequently of the vagina, she helps to add to her husband's pleasure, at the same time she ensures that at each downward movement of her husband's the clitoris shall be adequately stimulated. This last matter is very important; many wives are unable to reach the climax because their husbands fail to realise that rhythmic friction of the clitoris is necessary right up to the end of the act. If it has not occurred, it can easily be produced if stimulation of the clitoris is continued.

[95] [I]n cases where the bride has had absolutely no experience of sexual stimulation beforehand, an orgasm induced by the husband's hand, [96] and entirely by way of clitoris sensation, may be a kind and gentle way of introducing a timid and perhaps frightened girl to a happy sex-life. Anything is better than the rude shock and pain of complete penetration without the necessary preparation of awakened desire and preliminary sensation

[123] Many women fear that the whole of their sex life must necessarily disappear when their periods stop. Luckily there is no physiological foundation for this unhappy idea. Sexual desire during the menopause has nothing to do with the functioning of the ovaries or the womb. Proof is abundant in the history of the thousands of wives who produce any number of children without ever having experienced sexual satisfaction. If, therefore, reproduction is possible in the absence of sexual sensation, why should the stopping of reproduction have any effect on the presence of the sexual desire?
[. . . .]
[124] [S]exual desire in women is largely governed by psychological considerations, and if a successful sex life has been established during the early years of marriage it is more likely to be strengthened than weakened when menstruation ceases . . . .

[I]n the case of [125] thousands of mothers whose sex experiences have been overshadowed by the fear of unwanted pregnancies because of the absence of adequate contraceptive technique, the years after the meno- pause are the first ones in which they can enjoy peace of mind, and many of these women only wake up to their own sexual possibilities when their reproductive life is over.

Ettie Hornibrook, Practical Birth Control, 1931

[42] Passionate love may certainly be experienced by middle-aged and elderly men and women. The capacity for love is co-existent with life; and the ability certainly continues in old age in normal men and women.

Janet Chance, The Cost of English Morals, 1931

[36] This frigidity itself is often due to the very moral standards which it in turn supports. In . . . a large number of cases a powerful inhibition is exercised by the upbringing which has been based on the conventional moral standards. The wife feels that in some way it would not be right to experiment with or give way to sex feelings.

In spite of all the talk about sex experience, in spite of all the apparent equality of outlook amongst the younger generation, passion in England remains a lopsided affair. The men, more or less, for their part, know what can be. The women, for their part, often do not.

Isabel Hutton, The Hygiene of Marriage, 4th edn, 1931

[101] There is a prevalent idea that, during and after the menopause there should be no intercourse whatever. It is curious that this should be so deeply rooted and so common, in spite of the fact that sexual desire continues for many years after the 'change of life' and, in fact, may continue as long as life lasts. It is undoubtedly this mistaken idea that is responsible for the great majority of domestic tragedies which take place about this time. The wife, suffering from sexual starvation, and in consequence irritable and out-of-sorts, puts down the symptoms to the 'change of life.' She is under the impression, as so many women are, that intercourse will be actually harmful to her at this time, and there is no doubt that a great number of nervous ills which occur at the menopause are due solely to the cessation of marital life. The husband, in his turn, deprived of conjugal intercourse, may make other arrangements for [102] carrying on his sex life, or indeed the couple may separate altogether.

Marital life should proceed at the menopause much as it has done in the past, though naturally unions will take place less frequently than in the early years of marriage.
[. . . .]

After the 'change of life' is over, conjugal life should continue through-out the years, and should vary in frequency according to the state of health of the individuals. There is little or no strain involved on the part of the wife even though she may not be exceedingly strong

Margaret Kornitzer, The Modern Woman and Herself, *1932*

[149] That sex ferment, in women, is far more likely to be introspective and morbid, when denied legitimate utterance, than a straightforward appetite for the unlawful. It is the unique tempting by one man that marks the beginning of her course rather than just the hunger for a man, any man. In that respect a woman is likely to be naturally 'better' than a man in ordinary circumstances, and does not need the same latitude of tolerance for her conduct.

[204] [T]he sooner the mind becomes aware of the precise nature of the messages received from these sex-differentiated organs through the brain, the better will it be for the mental health of the individual. If the mind is not first prepared for the impacts of the physical impulses hot and intimate upon it, there can be nothing but self-terror, and fear and a fervent disparagement of all the processes of the horribly unknown body.

Leonora Eyles, Commonsense about Sex, *1933*

[56] Most girls will have noticed, when washing themselves and so on, that the clitoris changes; sometimes it is quite small and soft, but if it is stimulated by touch, or if the girl is excited by thoughts of sex, or by love-making, it becomes hard and much more sensitive. This is because when people kiss or make love, Nature, who doesn't bother about convention or convenience or anything but love-making and baby-making, sends a message from the brain to the heart which begins to pump blood about the body much more quickly than usual. Some of it rushes to the cheeks, but most of it goes to the sexual organs which, in a woman, include not only the parts I have already described, but also the lips and the breasts, making the lips redder and causing the nipples to harden and become very sensitive to the touch, while the clitoris hardens.

Naomi Mitchison, The Home, *1934*

[49] This moral superiority business is often accompanied by sexual frigidity, a thing which may naturally be [50] expected of women who are chattels and without rights and which has persisted as a result of bad or non-existent sexual education among a generation of women who ought to know better. But even intelligent and reasonable women, married to intelligent and sensitive men with sufficient historical and social sense to understand the position, will sometimes find the mere shadow of ownership lie so painfully upon them that they react in violence against a man who is trying his best to help them.

[146] [P]hysically the maximum fun and heightening of consciousness, toppling over the edge of known feelings into hyperaesthesia that directly affects the mind, is to be had when the woman is overwhelmed and 'possessed' by the man. But this very rarely comes off and when it does it is often followed by a reaction and feeling of guilt. Why? Because this 'possession' has become mixed up with the other kind of possession: the very word makes one react against it. One's historical mind gets at one, pointing out that one is the 'weaker sex', for this reason oppressed and exploited, and one mixes that up with what ought to be the very pleasant feeling of being gripped by muscles of a different strength and texture to one's own, and, hating the one, one's hatred is transferred to the other. One wants, passionately, *not* to be the weaker, and this is understandable considering the history of the last several thousand years, but why on earth should one [147] bother? Men are weaker than elephants and less able to do lots of things: but elephants do not oppress them. Again, one cannot help realising how much of a man's traditional courtship is really a crafty way of getting round one so that one should forget that he is really the master, the patriarch, and so, even when the courtship is now done without any economic content at all, one may still find it annoying. And all these irrational angers and reactions are below the surface of consciousness, so one never knows when they are not going to jump out at one.
[. . . .]
[148] Then again, we are up against the old point of view that a man's 'possession' of a woman should be violent. Why? Because it is taken for granted that no one likes to be possessed, to have something *taken from them*: so it must be by violence . . . . A certain amount of violence is all to the good; it quickens the circulation and makes one more alive. Yet complete 'possession' may be as gentle as you like, and yet give the same feeling.

But, with all this, the thing does not work properly. The well-known phenomenon of the difference of timing in women, especially conscious women, is probably due to the same complex, the [149] same holding back from being owned. I should very much like to know whether it would happen in a society where social and economic owning did not happen.

Irene Clephane, Towards Sex Freedom, *1935*

[230] To-day, when a deepening understanding of the havoc wrought by the suppression of normal sexual instincts is accompanied by a growing appreciation of the comparative unimportance of physical fidelity now that birth-control is possible, men and women alike are experiencing a revivifying of their emotional life and their physical vitality at an age when their grand-parents were settled into the boredom of middle-age.

[237] The realisation by women of their capacity for spontaneous sexual desire has brought with it, as well as greater understanding of life and its possibilities, a knowledge of unhappiness they did not possess before – or sensed but dimly. This desire towards the individual, mixed up as it is with the woman's need to choose a father for her children, would seem in nature to be more deep-seated in women than in men. It is even possible that, if women were untrammelled both economically and sexually, they would allow themselves to feel such marked preferences more freely than they dare in present circumstances. Nevertheless, many, perhaps most, lives would be serener if desire towards particular individuals could be eliminated, and a general satisfaction in sexual intercourse with any reasonably likeable and attractive person could be substituted.

Gladys M. Cox, Youth, Sex and Life, *1935*

[156] The sex impulse may be aroused by the mental effect of erotic books, films, and plays; or by the physical stimulus of kissing and other contact with the opposite sex in flirtation; or by deliberate handling of the genital region (masturbation); and certain normal results are produced. There is an increased blood supply to the genital organs – including the womb – and this leads to a feeling of tension and awareness of this part of the body; and a pouring out of secretion from certain glands in the genital canal, causing a sensation of moistness and possibly the excretion from the vagina of a clear, thin fluid. The feeling of tension may gradually subside when the stimulus is removed, or it may culminate in an emotional climax, a moment of intense sex feeling known as an orgasm, after which there is a more rapid return to normal. Many quite normal girls never experience this intensity of sex feeling until normal sexual intercourse takes place after marriage. Others who are more strongly sexed, or who unwisely stimulate

the sex urge in one of the ways I have mentioned, [157] are tormented by sex desire and may attempt satisfaction by resuming the infantile habit of masturbation . . . at the cost of much mental conflict and expenditure of energy. A wiser solution of their difficulties I shall suggest in the section on SUBLIMATION OF SEX.

Laura Hutton, The Single Woman and Her Emotional Problems, *1935*

[68] So far we have considered only the *physical* aspect of masturbation or self-stimulation. In regard to its psychical significance the matter is a good deal more complicated. Obviously, from this point of view masturbation is not an ideal solution of the unmarried woman's sexual problem, although it may at times and for some women be the only possible one.
[. . . .]
[69] Considered from the point of view that masturbation means using, as it were, part of the language of love for a purpose that has nothing to do with real love, it can never be anything but a very poor substitute for the sexual satisfaction which every normal woman feels the need of from time to time. It may, however, be for some women the best possible occasional solution [70] for the problem of the relief of psycho-sexual tension.

But masturbation is for most women, owing to early training and prohibitions, and to the tacit condemnation of all things sexual under which they have grown up, almost inevitably associated with anxiety and a sense of guilt. It is this anxiety and sense of guilt which have such damaging effect . . . . There is no necessity for these symptoms to follow, provided self-stimulation is practised in moderation, in response to a definite sense of physical need, and without anxiety and a sense of guilt, failure and self-disgust . . . .

[71] In my experience this attitude . . . has the effect of so reducing the conscious guilt and anxiety associated with masturbation that the need almost immediately becomes less compulsive.

[74] It is natural that a fantasy should accompany an act which is a manifestation of the sexual life of the individual, since no part of our sexual nature more intimately combines the physical with the psychical. The trouble is that the fantasies often remain, for the woman without actual sexual experience (and sometimes even when she has had the experience), on a very childish, sometimes almost grotesque level. These are things which are very secret to the person con- [75] cerned, and there is no need to drag them to the light of day unless either they or other manifestations

of the Unconscious become so troublesome as to require the aid of psychotherapy . . . . Otherwise they should be treated, as we suggest the physical impulses to self-stimulation should be treated – that is, they may be regarded as unimportant, to be made deliberate use of, perhaps occasionally, to bring a speedier termination to sexual excitement, but as far as possible not to be allowed to absorb time and attention.

Miss E. V. Pemberton, Simple Advice to Those About to Marry, *1936*

[26] A woman very often finds that in the course of that series of monthly happenings referred to elsewhere, an increased desire for intimacy occurs at more or less regular times.

It makes things very much easier for both of them if her husband understands this and knows that it is something over which she herself has comparatively little control.

Marie Stopes, Change of Life, *1936*

[178] The perfectly healthy and happy woman who is natural enough to feel no 'crisis' in the gradual cessation of the monthly flow, is fortunate also in being free from problems and debates whether she is to love or not to love: she loves. Her love is reciprocated and fulfilled in unions and she both gives and receives benefit to both body and mind . . . .

In some quite healthy women, however, there is a phase . . . . [179] of satiety with love, a time during which sex expression is dormant and the physical unions of wifehood are not desired . . . . [W]here health and normality reign it should be a temporary phase lasting only a few months or a year or two at most.

A good many women during the changes of the menopause pass through a phase when sex union becomes merely uninteresting . . . . [S]o many have maintained their interest throughout the climacteric and after it, and so many are conscious of an increase in pleasure and benefit from sex union after the conclusion of the menopause, that there is no doubt that it is quite natural for the potentiality for sex enjoyment to return.

If this phase of temporary revulsion comes upon one partner in a marriage at a time when the other is in fully-sexed normality, it necessitates much self-restraint and consideration in the more vital partner . . . .

[180] [W]hen . . . . the wife is still fully-sexed when the husband's climacteric impotence comes upon him, she is the one to suffer. She must bear the deprivation with a stout heart and generous care for her temporarily incapacitated husband.

A false social attitude has created the pretence that a 'nice' married woman has herself no sex-hunger, and only out of her graciousness meets her husband's needs. Hence, it is not generally even recognised that a woman at the time of her husband's climacteric may be in a very difficult and thankless position, the deprivation she suffers may place a great strain upon her health.

[183] [A] couple of years later the problem begins to be even more difficult for the woman herself, for she may find that now no longer does she feel sex union entirely repugnant, but with the stabilising of her own health, and the accumulation of her own vitality, she has become sexually potent once more. She may be eagerly desirous of renewing the happy physical relations she had formerly with her husband. But after her emphatic, perhaps even bitter refusal of a year or so ago, how can she intimate to him now that she desires him to return to her bed?
[. . . .]
[184] Not only have countless lives been rendered miserable by the false idea that sex desire and the power to experience sex union fade with the climacteric, but advisors wise and helpful in other matters perpetuate the foolish and cruel mis-statement that the desire for sex union after the [185] climacteric is an indication of disease.

[191] Sometimes, far from the 'sex life being over' at the menopause, it happens that women who have not enjoyed sex-life, and who have been frigid, become very passionate after the change has occurred . . . .

Fear of pregnancy, the terror of unwanted children, caused by the lack of knowledge of means to control conception; and this coupled with belief in the old, but mistaken myth that if the woman did not 'let herself go' and did not respond to ardour in coitus, she would not conceive; these all together have caused a pseudo-frigidity in many women. They have *pretended* to be frigid in order to save themselves from the dangers of pregnancy; or the deep-seated fear affects their attitude towards sex-union and imposes a false frigidity upon them. When the menopause is complete, however, they no longer fear, for they know they cannot become pregnant, and so at last they can 'let themselves go' with an easy mind.

[199] *Dreams of Sex-Union.* These may arise during the change of life in men or women who are not enjoying the natural benefits of normal coitus. They sometimes lead to orgasms, and a reduction of nervous tension . . . . They are sometimes consoling, and if the orgasm is complete they may be soothing and act as a partial substitute for ordinary sex-life.

Ellen Dorothy Abb, **What Fools We Women Be!**, *1937*

[108] Yet one feels convinced that this pseudo-scientific over-emphasis on sex must be deflated to its true proportions if women are not to add another handicap to all those already burdening them. And this is another of the things women must do for themselves, looking at it in the clear light of reason. We listen too deferentially to man. We acquiesced obediently when he told us we were cold, that sex meant little to us; we swallow it with equal docility when he tells us that sex means everything to us. It is time we investigated for ourselves his comforting doctrine – or discomforting, according to whether you are a virgin or rake – that without sexual experience women are unfulfilled, thwarted, liable to all kinds of unpleasant consequences sooner or later.

If it is true, let us accept it and get on with it: . . . If it is not true – or if, as one suspects, it is the half truth that is more dangerous than a lie – then we need no longer exchange our semi-emancipation from the dominance of men for the autocracy of one man . . . .

And as soon as you begin to question the doctrine of the supreme importance of sexual experience, a doubt jumps into your mind. Are those who preach it entirely disinterested?

Margaret Cole, **Marriage: Past and Present**, *1938*

[229] It used to be assumed that women were naturally colder; that theory has gone by the board, and been replaced by one certainly nearer to the facts, namely that women tend to run to extremes more than men, and that whereas there are some women who are colder than almost any man, there are also others whose sexuality runs so high that no ordinary man is likely to satisfy it. It is fairly certain, also, that women are more liable to experience fluctuations in sexual desire, [230] sometimes amounting to a definite periodicity, than men, and that these fluctuations sometimes affect their whole behaviour . . . . Further, there is a good deal of evidence that the pleasure of women in being made love to is more diffused over the whole process and less concentrated in a single moment than that of men. This, like the preceding difference, is clearly related to physical differences between the sexes. Not nearly enough is known about it as yet, partly because so many persons find it too indelicate to discuss. But one can at least plead that people, when they come to make love, should [231] realise that there *are* differences, and try to act accordingly.

Eliot Slater and Moya Woodside, Patterns of Marriage, 1951

[168] Mrs P., twenty-six (27c), says sex is 'perfect'. They have been married nearly five years, but intercourse is most nights, and sometimes in the day as well. She has orgasm every time. He is a perfect lover. She is highly sexed, and finds the enforced abstinence 'terrible'. Sex is 'the only thing in life sometimes'. 'He need only hold my hand, and I want him'.

Heterosexual relationships outside marriage

While many authorities continue to warn against pre-marital experimentation (though Registrar-General's statistics, not published until after the War, were to indicate that nearly a third of brides were pregnant on the wedding day) or diverging from marriage vows, others advanced a different view, influenced by the availability of contraception. If few venture as far as Doris Langley Moore in her clear-eyed and sophisticated recommendations about conducting a love affair, many suggest that experimental relationships between social equals are an improvement over the previous atmosphere of fear and shame. The possibility of 'open marriage' is also mooted.

Naomi Mitchison, Comments on Birth Control, 1930

[10] At present there is a good deal of discussion going on about the advisability of pre-marital sexual experience, of course with the use of contraceptives. There is much to be said both for and against this. Especially with a girl, the first serious love affair is bound to have rather devastating psychological and physiological effects, and [11] it is no use allowing her to believe that she can hop in and out of these troubled waters without any kind of difficulty . . . .

I am inclined to think also that it is possible to overdo the business of casual affairs . . . . It seems to show a certain poverty of imagination to have to plunge at once into the final expression of emotion. No wonder they write so little good poetry. The honest lover, whether or not she marries, is one thing, the amateur prostitute is another, and the girl who considers marriage the only respectable profession and uses her hard virginity as a carrot for donkeys, is another still.

Helena Normanton, **Everyday Law for Women,** *1932*

[96] [S]trictly speaking, from the point of view of law, seduction is part of the law of Master and Servant!

It is also at first sight a surprising fact that a woman herself has no legal right of action against her seducer. If a woman is raped, a crime has been committed, because some man has had connection with her against her wish, and the Law will take criminal proceedings against him. But a woman cannot:-

1. Be of an age to give a legal consent to intercourse;
2. Join in having intercourse; and then
3. Have a right to recover damages for that intercourse to which she has been a consenting party.

It, however, does sometimes happen that a woman is, morally speaking, more or less trapped into having intercourse, and although she may never have been promised marriage [197] and so have no right to bring an action for Breach of Promise to marry, she may have been very prejudicially affected by her seduction and suffer consequences far more grave than any the seducer may ever have to bear. The law therefore has suffered a curious legal fiction to grow up by which the seducer may be sued for damages by any person who can maintain a real, or even a shadowy claim to the companionship or services of the woman seduced.

Margaret Kornitzer, **The Modern Woman and Herself,** *1932*

[77] The fluffy-headed are persuaded that having a good time is not merely risky amusement, but is, in fact, the way to get the most out of life. The sensual have an excuse that is also an encouragement. The serious are intellectually assured that self-gratification is a kind of sacred mission connected with their rights.

Not that, by any means, the majority of young women are fluffy-headedly, sensually or by conviction immoral. This is no more an unmoral age, in the sense of physically unrestrained, than any other. The cause of most of what is loosely called 'immorality' occurs, as always since Adam and Eve, through the force of circumstance.

[121] There is a great danger . . . in a kind of sex-anarchy, in a crusade decked out with almost religious dogmatism against permanent relationships . . . . [I]n such a general mental flux women, torn adrift, in conviction

if not in deed, from their adherence to a single man and a snug-smug home, will feel themselves lost in voids of un-becoming as forsaken as some Outer Hell. For women are not experimental in such matters. They respond more reluctantly but more certainly than men. This is a broad sweep; though there are a million variations on that theme, generalisation is necessary for the picture. For the truth is steadfast. Women would be lost in a series of temporary relationships which [122] proposed themselves a remedy for social ills. The whole meaning of their womanhood would be submerged, damned.

Gladys Hall, Prostitution: A Survey and a Challenge, *1933*

[27] Simple promiscuity often occurs earlier than the first beginnings of commercial prostitution; for although in the case of seduction a child's introduction to commercial possibilities may coincide with her first sex experience, it probably takes some little time to discover that payment may be extracted. School teachers and health visitors are among those who tell of the prevalence of early attempts at promiscuity, not only [28] when, playing at 'fathers and mothers,' the young denizens of overcrowded bedrooms seek to reproduce all that comes to their knowledge, but when actual sexual precocity, having neither guidance nor outlet in other directions, manifests itself in only one way.

[30] There is undoubtedly a reduced male demand for the services of professional prostitutes . . . . [T]he chief explanation of the decreased demand for professional prostitutes is the intrusion into the prostitute's sphere of the amateur, or, as the professional describes her, 'the straight girl.' In other words, a man may, at the present time, have opportunities for promiscuous sex relations with girls from among his own social group whom he knows, or whose acquaintance he may readily make; and there are methods whereby, in the course of conversation, this fact is conveyed to him. Although he usually pays for his satisfaction, the payment takes the form of a gift, or a dinner, or a motor run; the episode appears less commercial and suggests more of passion and spontaneity than a similar episode with a professional prostitute, and for this reason is usually infinitely more attractive . . . . [T]here may be no payment whatever, and the whole episode may be mutually desired and mutually satisfactory. This readiness for sexual experience is, very constantly, regarded as the natural corollary to any degree of affection, or even of friendship, between opposite sexes . . . .

[31] It is undesirable to stress unduly the novelty of this attitude. . . . . Nor is it sought to produce the impression that amateur promiscuity is so universal that professional prostitution is being entirely supplanted.

But the facts are that there is definite acceptance, by a growing number of people extending through all social strata, of the idea, and of the desirability, of complete freedom in extra-marital intercourse; and that there is a decrease in professional prostitution . . . for which the increased amateur practice is largely responsible.

[36] A man will drive his car very slowly alongside the pavement, and by word, or gesture, invite girls to enter . . . . Refusals, or a silent ignoring of the invitations, are usually only accepted after persistent extension of the invitation and by a suggestive and pointed wait in the car near to where the girl is standing. A girl who accepts may or may not know that there is usually one form of return to be made for the 'joy ride' she has accepted. There are occasions when companionship is the only object, but most evidence shows that promiscuous intercourse is usually the ulterior motive and the sequel.

[89] Invitations . . . may come to the girl industrial worker where unscrupulous male superiors in the office may use their powers to force them to comply with sexual demands . . . . It is an event which may and does happen to girl workers controlled by male officials of a certain type, and is one which is often a first step towards promiscuity which was not taken by the girl's wish.

[177] [S]ince sex intimacy into which passion enters does, by its very nature, profoundly affect the whole personality, it seems likely that a series of 'love' episodes, in each of which it is to be supposed that an element of passion is involved, with different people, must result in disturbance of the emotional system in those who experience them. Nor can anyone who awakens the passion of sex love escape responsibility if, retreating from such experiment to seek fresh experience, he or she leaves behind them a tragedy of emotional or physical desolation which the sufferer knows not how to meet or assuage.

But there are certain extra-marital sex relationships favoured by the 'new morality' to which these arguments do not necessarily apply, and which – though neither promiscuous nor in the nature of 'trial marriage', may yet be said to supplement the need for prostitution and must therefore be included in this survey. Concerning these relations, which occur between couples who are entirely faithful to one another without being married, the question is asked, 'Why not?'

Leonora Eyles, Commonsense about Sex, 1933

[20] Sometimes the experimenting in thrills arouses them both so much that they get irritable with each other, not realising that the natural end of

love-making is copulation and that the nerves, stretched to breaking-point by this abortive love-making, are unendurably irritated. If they go on like this, wrangling about chastity is sure to result; the boy, usually more uncontrollable than the girl, pleads for the natural outcome of his ardour, she, more cautious and full of vague ideas about 'keeping herself pure,' 'getting into trouble,' and the like, refuses, until, worn down by his pleading and terrified of losing him to a more accommodating girl, she 'gives way,' and what should have been a joyous coming together becomes an act of terrified [21] submission on her part, an act of cruelty followed by remorse on his.

[22] [W]hile sexual connection in unmarried people is still fraught with possible social consequences in the birth of children who may be a burden on the community, and while young men still lose respect for the girl who gives them what they demand; while, too, sexual connection is still regarded as a very serious matter, pre-marital intercourse can as a rule cause nothing but pain and confusion.

[30] If two young people find each other unsatisfactory as sexual mates it is surely better to do so on the untied side of the marriage ceremony. I would never advise young people to make a habit of sexual intimacy, but then, if they looked upon sex as the ultimate expression of friendship and [31] happiness aroused only by exceptionally deep feelings, they would not run the risk of becoming promiscuous; such deep feelings are not easily aroused either before marriage or after.

Supposing, however, a girl has decided that such 'modern' behaviour is not for her and her lover, the question she so often is faced with is: What is wise and fair and what is not? I think an immense amount of suffering is inflicted on young men by the ignorance or innocence of their girls, and it is only fair to a boy for a girl to inform herself of the possible effects of her behaviour.

[116] I don't advise any young wife to find a lover when she is neglected by her husband. A lover should not be made use of in that way; it is not good enough for any human being to become merely a stop gap or a soothing syrup. I don't say you should not have a lover, any more than I think a man should not; but you should have one only if something vital in you is awakened by him and awakens something vital in him. To have a love affair just because you are bored or miserable, or just because you want to make your husband jealous, or to show him that 'two can play at that game,' is disgusting. A love affair should come from the abundance of vitality and life which flowers when two personalities come in contact. It may be friendship, or it may demand physical expression, but it should never be sought for or fallen into sloppily.

Arabella Kenealy, The Human Gyroscope, 1934

[259] [M]en and women should normally so have emancipated themselves from subjection by the herd-instinct of general sex-appeal as to be unresponsive to it . . . and to select and to mate only with one particular member of the other sex, as specifically individualised as themselves in complementary qualities.

Subhuman habits of sexual promiscuity – polygamy, polyandry, are regressive and de-humanising, and, as practised to-day in the hideous promiscuousness of prostitution, are holding up the further progress of Mankind.

Sybil Neville-Rolfe, Why Marry?, 1935

[28] 'Companionate marriages' differ from trial marriages in that they are not undertaken as a prelude to marriage. Those people, who thus agree to live together for a time, neither of them contemplating marriage, fall into two groups; in one of which they are mutually attracted only physically, while in the other, social or economic conditions are unpropitious to their marriage, and likely to remain so.

The emotional relationship appears to be almost always unequal. The man is usually strongly attracted physically to the girl; the girl, maternally affectionate towards the man, is anxious to supply this need and is stimulated by his desire. The girl herself, on the other hand, may be physically attracted, the man merely [29] lonely and welcoming companionship and yet ready for experiment on the physical side.

Or again, both may be in the romantic stage of development and believe that in full companionship they can test sex life at its best . . . . With the vaunted objective outlook of the modern, they agree that sentiments are likely to change, and that therefore it is to be but a delightful care-free episode in their life's experience. Also there are those companionate marriages entered into at the instigation of the man, who wants the privileges of marriage without its responsibilities – the woman accepting the temporary arrangement in the hope that it will possibly prove to be a stepping stone to marriage.

'Trial Marriage' is undertaken by those who want to satisfy themselves that they are suited to each other by living together for a time, as partners in marriage, on the understanding that they do not have children during the period of probation. This would not be a trial of real marriage, as the essential conditions of real marriage are absent. It would be an open liaison, and we must recognise it as such – better at least than a clandestine relationship and far better than prostitution – but not marriage. Why? Because marriage is entered into in the belief that it will be permanent, and that attitude of mind carries with it an entirely different perspective.

[30] Without the feeling of permanence, all the values of the relationship are altered. Each will feel conscious of being under observation, weighed up and criticised, and therefore a sense of effort and strain will be always just under the surface. This soon frays nerves and brings emotional tension.

[92] Every man and every woman throughout life, whether happily married or single, will experience a physical thrill from members of the opposite sex who are physically attractive to them. Each will, after some years of experience, know the type most likely to prove attractive . . . . It all adds to the zest and interest of life, provided the conscious personality will not thereby become unbalanced! However, when there is strong physical attraction, knowing themselves, husband and wife will not in either case knowingly place themselves under conditions that will strain their capacity to maintain conscious self-control.

[151] Certainly we want conventions that provide for the exercise of the play instinct in sex, but we are far too uncertain still as to the permanent damage that may be done to the individual in checking the balanced development of personality, if in early years the whole physical and emotional sex equipment is engaged while yet un-integrated, and in the lower levels of personality, to give such behaviour general social approval. So far it appears probable that control of the physical sex equipment in youth is essential to full intellectual development; and before the physical act of sex stimulates the emotions, the subconscious emotional energy needs to be related to conscious emotion and brought under the dominion of the reason and the intellect. To place the [152] barrier of experience, based on physical stimulus alone, across the three streams that should flow together in one mature personality would be a short-sighted action.

The second type of promiscuity – that which comes from ignorance and therefore an inability to direct behaviour in ways that allow of conscious control being maintained, are fraught with disaster both for the individuals concerned and for the possible offspring, but it is the community and not the individual that is blameworthy when this occurs.

Gladys M. Cox, Youth, Sex and Life, *1935*

[viii] The following was written by a girl of twenty:

Two years ago, I met a considerably older man who told me that my ideas of sex were prudish and old-fashioned, and that all sensible people had 'affairs' before marriage. He used to take me out to dinner and give me wine, which excited me very much as I was not used to it.

Finally, I allowed myself to be persuaded, and we had sex relations from time to time, until at last he tired of it and started an affair with another girl. Now I have met a man I love and who loves me and has asked me to marry him. I am terribly unhappy about this other affair – I feel somehow besmirched, and the memories are torture to me. I feel that if my fiancé knew it would spoil things utterly for us; I dare not tell him, and yet I feel such a cheat. I feel that this other man has taken what should belong entirely to my husband.

[191] There are those . . . to whom marriage is economically impossible at the age when the sex instinct is strongest, who question why they should not arrange an alternative form of sex association with partners who are willing to join them in temporary 'trial marriage' of some sort. So long as they agree to prevent the birth of children, they argue, the matter concerns themselves alone – they are harming nobody. Sometimes these young people have been misled by the pseudo-psychologists who . . . maintain that sexual continence is *necessarily* harmful, and that 'repression' of the powerful sex urge inevitably leads to all sorts of nervous disease and other forms of ill-health and to a general lack of efficiency. One way or another they may convince themselves and others that the institution of marriage in its present form has had its day, and is no longer suited to the economic and social conditions of modern times.

Now the argument that continence is necessarily harmful because it involves the repression of an impulse is an example of the error and confusion of thought that arises from the assumption that repression in any sense or form is necessarily harmful . . . .

[192] When an irregular sex association is being contemplated, it is well to bear in mind that, besides the loss of caste resulting from the inevitable furtiveness, there is the serious danger of producing an unwanted child; for *there is no absolutely reliable method of contraception* . . . .

In practice, these relationships rarely turn out satisfactorily. The insecurity and lack of permanence often lead to unreasonable jealousy and irksome possessiveness. More often than not, one (generally the man) tires first; and although the two people concerned may have agreed in the first place that their relationship shall be temporary, and that it shall cease when either of them finds it no longer satisfying and helpful, the break is almost always distressing and hurtful.

Marie Stopes, Marriage in My Time, *1935*

[81] Whenever one considers this subject of virginity at marriage, one is confronted with the oft-repeated story of the girl who, trusting a man's promises, allows him the full physical [82] privilege of marriage only to

197

find that he refuses to complete the ceremony and she is deserted . . . .
Nowadays my sympathies incline to the young man. The legal responsibilities of marriage are very considerable, and he is entitled to test the
strength and durability of character of the girl whom he proposes to
maintain for the rest of her life, with whom he plans to create children
to carry on the race and enrich the State, the woman to whom he will give
the keys of his home and his heart. If without marriage she will yield to
him he is entitled to deduce that she would yield to another. It is not
beyond the power of a virtuous and loving woman to avoid any appearance
of mercenariness or hardness and yet to convince the man who loves her
that though she is his in heart and soul she proposes to honour him by
maintaining for him her virginity as a gift for their wedding [83] day . . . .
Inextricable confusion is created nowadays by laxity which tries to dignify
and justify itself as 'advanced.'

Irene Clephane, Towards Sex Freedom, 1935

[220] [V]irginity is no longer the dowry a bride is expected to bring
with her. Rather is the tendency in the contrary direction. The bride who
has had no experience of sex, at least with her bridegroom, if not yet the
exception, is far from being the rule . . . . [T]he woman who has attained,
say, the age of thirty and remained a virgin is rightly regarded as a poor
specimen of womanhood, as something almost unclean. Changed conceptions of the values of life, of love, and of sex hitherto current among
the few are spreading to the many, with a steady gain of psychological
and physiological health. Knowledge of contraception has placed the
woman on an equality with the man: the sex act, which has rarely been of
paramount importance to the man, has ceased to have more importance
to the woman than she cares to give it. She no longer allows herself to
respond to the urgency of her physical sex needs with fear in her heart
– married or unmarried, she can choose the moment of maternity, and
becomes, indeed, a free agent. For it is her justified dread of unwanted
motherhood that has held her in servitude through the centuries. She can
take sex more lightly because it no longer has fears; she can take it more
deeply [221] because she can give herself freely without thought. Whole
realms of dark fears and obsessions have been banished from her spirit by
knowledge of the means of contraception.

[222] A new love gives new colour to life, but, if the basic relationship is
sound, it will appear that more valuable in its serene familiarity by contrast
with the fire of the unfamiliar. Once men and women accept, in themselves and each other, the fact of this elemental longing, and its natural
consequences, they learn that true love and understanding need not be

lessened, but can be increased by new experience. The English divorce system, however, remains a relic of a period of sexual manners which assumed that infidelity necessarily meant a change of loyalties. Divorce will always be the only remedy for incurable marital unhappiness: but much marital unhappiness to-day is due to the survival of outworn ideas on sexual relations, and will disappear with a saner approach to the realities of sexual life.

Laura Hutton, The Single Woman and Her Emotional Problems, 1935

[78] These irregular relationships may, and occasionally do, give very valuable experience, but they may also be deeply upsetting to emotional balance. There is no doubt that the experience of being loved by a man, and having this love consummated in full sexual union can . . . be most beneficial physically and emotionally to an, at any rate, potentially psycho-sexually mature woman, even though social sympathy and support, and the security of marriage are precluded. But . . . such relationships are rarely free from anxiety and conflicts, and . . . these are the factors which always make for unhappiness and emotional [79] instability. In the first place, the woman of the type we are considering has her reputation to consider; it is, from an economic point of view, usually essential for her to consider it, quite apart from any social or conventional point of view. This alone makes the situation an uneasy one. Again, she can never have any real sense of security in her relationship with a man who probably has primary obligations elsewhere. Secrecy and deceit on both these counts are almost inevitably involved. And some other fellow-woman may be suffering as a result of the relationship. The *home*, moreover, and the children instinctively desired by the woman who loves and is loved by a man cannot be hoped for. The risk of pregnancy is indeed likely to be a constant source of anxiety, and leads very often to deviations from normal sexual intercourse which belittle the relationship. Moreover, all the satisfactions of a day-in, day-out living together – real companionship in respon- [80] sibilities as well as in pleasures – are almost never attainable, and this fact alone marks off the 'affair' as something on quite a different level from marriage, in so far as its value in solving the problem of emotional adjustment in personal contacts is concerned.
[. . . .]
[81] [U]nmarried women, lonely and unaware of their deprivations, may be tempted sometimes to enter upon casual affairs with men just for the [82] sake of the experience, of the excitement, or because they feel flattered by the suggestion. Such transitory, loveless affairs are never likely to meet the deep emotional needs of a woman. They are much more

likely to induce psychical deterioration by an all-round lowering of values, including the value a woman sets on herself. Here we have all the disturbing effects of a violation of deeply-rooted standards, and no compensating sense of being loved or respected to rehabilitate the shattered self-esteem. . . .

As regards sexual satisfaction, even is this be found temporarily in this type of relation- [83] ship, it is not likely to contribute much, if anything at all, to the complicated emotional problem of the unmarried woman's existence.

Doris Langley Moore, The Technique of the Love Affair, *1936*

[11] No woman is happy in love unless she sees the possibility of bestowing happiness on her lover . . . . We are innately liberal and yielding, and it is not easy for us to appear otherwise. Yet we dare not give rein to our generosity, for men, like children, soon weary of what is soon obtained.

[21] The love affair handled artistically, as a means to a highly creditable end, is in no sense an immoral practice. I will go further and suggest that so handled it need not be immoral even as an end in itself. Here I know I am treading on delicate ground, and I must go warily . . . .

The love affair need not be unhappy, deep, and ponderous. Skilfully handled, it constitutes an art, a delicate and genial art, and one that inspires other arts. It is capable of yielding nothing but delight; or at least there need be no more heartache in it than there is in anything else that is lovely but ephemeral. For it will, [22] perhaps, always carry with it that sense of incompleteness, that undercurrent of hunger, from which only real and long-proved lovers escape. But if you have skill, or will learn it, there is no reason to believe that in encouraging a love affair you are inevitably producing unhappiness.

[. . . .]

The only justification for an otherwise purposeless love affair lies in its being a work of art and therefore capable of giving pleasure and raising the standard of pleasant things. If it be not a work of art, it is worthless, even pernicious, and rather than meddle with it you had better retire to a convent at once.

[146] [A] yielding, either physical or spiritual, should rarely be spontaneous. Impromptus are seldom perfect: only a great artist can make them memorable. Besides, you should not deprive a fellow creature of the pleasures of anticipation . . . .

[147] She who never gives herself until she can do so in the correct setting, the perfect atmosphere, and at the zenith of her power; who never seeks to excite passion in a man who is tired or disturbed in mind, or asks him if he loves her save when she knows that he is longing for the opportunity of saying so; she who realises exactly when to call for a sacrifice, inflict a punishment, confess a wrongdoing, express a misgiving – why it is an anticlimax to say that such a woman, once having obtained her admirer, will be invincible.

[. . . .]

Your fortress, whatever it guards – your virtue, your freedom, your passion, or your love – should crumble very slowly and reluctantly. But when [148] at last you do grant him a victory, let it be a pleasant one. Let your surrender be thrilling or even amusing, but do not let it be pathetic.

[187] When you have finally decided to be married, it is essential, I think, to enlighten your prospective husband upon any incidents in your past life which he might resent if he heard them from other lips than your own. I need not put this . . . . in its ethical aspect; I mention it simply as a matter of technique. You see, an incident of this nature which had been concealed would look far more serious when found out than it need have done; and moreover, to make a confession is to make a bond. I really pity you if you have nothing of any gravity to confess: a man in love will be so delighted by your daring confidence, and by the high-minded scruple which prompts you to pour it into his ear . . . that his devotion will increase perceptibly in the most charming manner.

[. . . .]

[188] Life is immeasurably more hazardous and complex for an unmarried woman who has flung down the barrier of maidenhood. But though by doing so she discards a powerful protection, her experience, if she is discriminating, will increase her skill and furnish her with new blandishments.

[189] It is not advisable . . . to take more than a small part of that experience with the man whom you wish to marry, until your mating has been duly sanctioned and solemnised – not because he will necessarily respect you less afterwards, but simply because he will desire you less, and will, therefore, feel less inducement to bind himself to you.

[215] A sensible love affair is one which may finish without leaving humiliation or disgust on either side – one which may be contemplated from the distance with entire satisfaction . . . . There must be no false idealism, with its harvest of angry disillusionments, and no mere selfish

carnality to bring about an aftermath of revulsion. And a sensible love affair . . . cannot be otherwise than mutual – with a slight bias in favour of the woman.

Alison Neilans, 'Changes in Sex Morality', 1936

[207] Public opinion in the old days used to concentrate on the sin, disgrace and social offence of the woman and carried the odium over to the child; now it is more concerned to protect the life, health and happiness of the child and to give the mother a chance to get through her difficulties and come back, as quickly as possible, to normal good citizenship. In particular, efforts are made to avoid the separation of mother and child. From the point of view of social ethics public opinion still reprobates illegitimate parenthood, but it no longer downs the woman by persistent persecution when she is trying to make good. There are exceptions to this more human outlook, and the unmarried mother does in some quarters have to face a certain amount of social ostracism, but a kinder, more helpful and less censorious attitude is now the general rule towards her.

[221] [A] new factor . . . which has come into the scene within the last twenty years or so, cuts right across the older theories of equality in sex matters, and is bringing the women's movement to a parting of the ways. The original objective of the movement was not only an equal standard of morals but a high standard . . . the general idea was always that the men's standard should come [222] into line with that accepted as right and desirable for women . . . . But that situation has now been changed; the advent of birth control has placed the woman, if she chooses, in almost the same position of irresponsibility as the man. She can do as she pleases in regard to keeping her chastity, or at least she has reason to believe that, provided necessary and easily obtainable methods of contraception are used, she can avoid the possible consequences of irregular relations. Thus the end of the double standard is definitely in sight, but it is not ending in the way anticipated by the pioneers who fought for it . . . . [223] It would be a mistake to assume that to-day a majority of women enter into irregular relations with men, but it is probably true that in certain strata or groups in the community it is fairly common, while in others it is still the exception. Ethically it is better than prostitution, because such relations, though they may be temporary, are not necessarily promiscuous on [224] either side, and are often based on some friendship and liking and on mutual interests. To some intelligent feminists this new approach to a single standard of morals represents the final triumph of the equality movement; to them this is, at last, freedom.

And when we remember the appalling price which young girls and women have paid in the past for leaving the conventional path of female virtue, it is easy to understand and to sympathize with the feeling of escape which has come to a number of women through the knowledge of conception prevention.

Mary Agnes Hamilton, 'Changes in Social Life', 1936

[267] It is ... easy to exaggerate the number who have adopted the masculine side of the old dual system. They talk about it a great deal: but that talk is part of the regime of frankness, which prescribes that everything once not thought proper for mention should now be shouted ... from the house-tops, in words of Anglo-Saxon plainness.

[268] [I]t is probably the case that the young man who used, in pre-war days, to have obscure and rather dirty affairs with girls of a lower social class than his own ... now goes off for a week-end or longer with a girl of his own sort, whom he may or may not ultimately marry. She will probably decide that question; decision and action have, in fact, very largely passed to her. Once the passive recipient of his 'advances,' she is now more than likely to take the first steps herself and to settle herself the form and scope of the resultant relationship. As to marriage she no more feels committed to marrying him, because of a trial trip, than he to marrying her; both she and he know better, as a rule, than to permit any 'accident' to happen which takes decision out of their hands: and she no more thinks now than he thought in the past, that intimacy of itself involves marriage.

Dorothy Manchée, Social Service in the Clinic for Venereal Diseases, 1938

[40] To the Almoner's door is often brought the difficult problem of whether or not the young couple should marry before baby's arrival. There are, as a rule, strong arguments put forward by the girl's parents in favour of this course to cover 'the disgrace'; sometimes swayed by their influence, sometimes by the fear of her friends' criticism, and sometimes by the desire to make her baby legitimate, but against her better judgement, she marries the man. Indeed, in some instances pressure is brought to bear by the parents of both and two lives are often wrecked in consequence .... It is for the young couple them- [41] selves to make the decision, since they will have to abide by it, and the Almoner's task is to put squarely before them the possibilities open. If they should have desired marriage without the baby, there are chances of happiness if both are courageous and mean to make equal sacrifices. If not, better then for the girl to remain single,

when she can be helped in so many ways with the baby, than married to a man for whom she has no regard and who has made her wife in name for the sake of his or her parents' respectability.

Mrs Cecil Chesterton, Women of the London Underworld, *1938*

[38] It was not a case of uncontrollable passion that drove the girl into the young man's arms, it was a sense of human desolation that made her seek his companionship . . . .

Hyde Park is one of the forcing grounds of prostitution. The in-and-out girl I have mentioned always finds the chance of making a few shillings in a pleasurable fashion . . . . [Y]oung motorists out for a lark slacken their pace, keeping a sharp look-out for a pretty face or figure on the side-walk responsive to the [39] suggestion of a joy ride. A soft whistle, a move in to the kerb, fetches to the car a young thing who, giggling with delight, gets in.

The formula goes to plan. The car drives off to a roadhouse, the girls – sometimes there are two – are given drinks and food, and maybe a dance or a moonlight dive in a bathing pool. In return a variety of 'cuddling' is permitted, but generally it stops short of full intimacy. Half-a-crown, at the most five shillings, is handed over in the small hours of the morning, when the girl is set down, with sometimes an appointment for the next evening. Usually this is forgotten – there is always a new car to choose, a fresh cuddler, and the excitement of strange encounters and vagrant kisses makes normality less and less desirable.

Such a state of mind sounds deplorable. But remember that for this type of girl the alternative to this sort of evening is the sitting-room at a public lodging-house or a stuffy lodging in a slum street . . . .

[40] The little joy-riders in the park do not always get off with kisses. There is a darker side to these excursions.

Margaret Cole, Marriage: Past and Present, *1938*

[248] Such experiment cannot be restricted . . . to a single trial per person . . . . [Y]ou cannot today effectively say to people, 'you may make one mistake; but if you make another you have got to put up with it' – even if you think that people who are always changing their minds and partners are a social nuisance. No modern State that I know of, which has legalised divorce at all, has limited the number of divorces per head. If people have knowledge – and however faulty and wilfully limited modern training is, we may be sure that a good number will get the knowledge from

somewhere – [249] we may also be sure that some, at any rate, will experiment fairly widely. Some will experiment less, and some not at all. I do not think that we can tell for certain, any more than we can tell . . . how far experimentation has gone today . . . .

For myself, I think that much promiscuity is good for very few; I think that it is generally better if the first introduction to sex is serious and charged with some emotional feeling; but I cannot be absolutely dogmatic upon either of these points. I think that continual concern with sex affairs is unfortunate, mainly for the common-sense reason that there are plenty of other important things wherewith to occupy one's time and attention.

[252] [I]f jealousy is to be lessened . . . we shall have to work out a better and more reasonable code of behaviour – 'manners', if you like – as between men and women. Or, rather, a code will have to be found, for there is none which serves at present. By a code of behaviour I do not, of course, [253] mean a law in the formal sense, but a tradition which may be only partly formulated in rules of any kind, but which is understood, can be taught, and, what is more important, can be acted upon at need by people at a loss how to behave, without their having to think out, painfully and from scratch, exactly what a Good Young Person would do in any particular difficult situation . . . . Anarchy in sex behaviour is as impracticable as anarchy in anything else, until we become archangels; and it is simply asking for trouble to let girls go about freely with, and work alongside of, boys, when neither party knows what the rules are, if there are any rules at all, or whether if there are the other party is acquainted with or subscribes to them . . . .

[259] [B]astardy is now much less probable . . . therefore one of the age-old arguments for the fidelity of wives is slowly losing its real force, though it may be a long time before its emotional force fades; the recognition of differences in sexual desire may in time make people realise that it is neither in itself insulting nor disloyal if one partner seeks from outside the pleasure or satisfaction which the other is unable or unwilling to give; and this theoretical realisation may in time transform itself into a social tradition, of a different kind from that expressed in most novels and newspapers of today. But that, if it comes, will not come quickly or without thought and practice: meantime, inconclusive as the conclusion may seem, I can only observe that in a changing world the oddest individual arrangements do seem to work, and to be compatible with loyalty, and suggest that, as the success of marriage appears more and more to depend, as we become more and more civilised and self-conscious, upon the fitting together of the personalities of individuals, we should more and more aim to be tolerant of the arrangements adopted, whether they seem to Puritans immoral, to feminists degrading, or to rationalists irrational, and not to

interfere with them, or even to take public cognisance of them, more than we can possibly help.

Eliot Slater and Moya Woodside, Patterns of Marriage, 1951

[143] Where two people are able to throw off the bonds of tradition, it is quite possible for happiness to be attained along paths normally thought impossible. We have one case where infidelity provided a turning point from unhappiness to happiness:

Mrs H. (89N) When I married I didn't want to marry him, but he threatened he'd die of a broken heart, so I thought I'd better . . . . For two years I was desperately unhappy. It was a great mistake. I hated sex relations . . . . All this time she was in the W.A.A.F. and only saw her husband once in three months. Then on one station she thought she had found THE man – and feels she would probably have married him if she hadn't been married already. She felt for him as she had never felt for her husband; but she told her husband, and was impressed by how wonderful he was about it. He was tolerant and gave her help and understanding . . . . She and her husband were reconciled again, and found 'we'd fallen in love with one another again, and everything was all right'.

Same-sex relationships, celibacy, and singleness generally

Writers suggest that the single woman might enjoy compensations, and there are hints that, with the advent of birth control, celibacy and chastity need not necessarily be combined. The possibility of good and creative friendships – even sexual relationships – between women continues to be argued, especially in the light of the numbers of 'surplus women' still to be found in British society. However, less positive images of same-sex relations persist.

Naomi Mitchison, Comments on Birth Control, 1930

[11] [T]here is something to be said for the view that the Nordic young should normally be allowed to have romantic affections for persons of their own sex up to the end of adolescence; these probably engage the emotions less violently and are more easily recovered from, but those who practise them must take care to grow up at the right moment and turn to the other sex when their bodies are fully developed, and that is sometimes difficult.

Margaret Kornitzer, The Modern Woman and Herself, *1932*

[225] Create a large body of persons who are permanently denied one of the chief means of life-expression and you promptly create a clot in the blood-stream of the community which eventually affects adversely every member of it. Such a body of persons, denied sex, produce a revulsion from it. The ardent need is turned back upon itself and curdled as it mills about under the consciousness. The canker spot spreads, and the pity of it is that the greater the potential richness, the stronger and more far-reaching the ill-effects of its repression.

Helena Wright, What is Sex?, *1932*

[136] During the years from fourteen to sixteen or seventeen boys and girls pass through a hero-worshipping stage for people of their own sex. This is a right and natural phase, and much good can come of it. Unfortunately, at present it is little understood. It is difficult to say whether this phase in development is emphasised by our present practice of separating the sexes each into schools of their own; possibly it is. However that may be, it is certain that all schools do contain strongly marked relationships of either girls to other girls, or of boys to boys.

The essential importance about these one-sexed [137] friendships is that they provide an outlet for emotion. Healthy boys and girls of fifteen and sixteen are people of strong affections and enthusiasms. If no suitable outlet is arranged for them, the energy of the feelings is so strong that they will find means of expression for themselves. At this age the kind of emotion is naturally romantic and not physical. The instinctive craving is for someone to admire and to copy. Girls fare better than boys in this respect. Public opinion at home and at school allows a girl to be affectionate, and does not necessarily laugh at her if she feels and expresses an ardent admiration for another, and generally older, girl. Consequently these relationships are often productive of great good. The physical side of them does not need to be predominant or excessive, because plenty of scope is allowed for romantic and even spiritual ways of expressing affection. The girl has her necessary emotional outlet and, while this stage lasts, she hardly realises that her sex capacity is quietly growing all the time.

Arabella Kenealy, The Human Gyroscope, *1934*

[219] Departure from the normal of this evolutionary objective . . . is seen in the reversion of our modern humans to degrees of hermaphroditism.

Known today as Sex-intergrades – mannish women and effeminate men
. . . . [220] This tide of degeneracy is being disastrously aggravated moreover, owing to the modern artificial manufacture of women sex-intergrades
excitating the development of those opposite characters which should
have remained recedent in them; but which thus evoked – by force of their
native dominance in physical differentiation, overpower and frustrate the
evolution of their natural woman-characters, physical and psychical. The
disastrous Feminist fallacy that masculine qualities are so superior to
woman-qualities that they should be duplicated in the sex to which they
do not properly belong, is prompting this mass-production, by our schools
and by other masculine training and employment, of these girl and women
sex-intergrades, in ever-increasing number and of increasingly masculine
qualities and bent. With lamentable consequences to modern social life
and civilised progress, and to the fitness of the race. It is readily induced
by masculine physical sports and the cult of male brain-faculties during the
plastic years of adolescence . . . .

[221] The mannish woman (as the effeminate man) may be, of course,
a 'freak,' or fluctuation, from the hereditary normal human; resulting
from non-eugenic matings of parents – ill-assorted marriages, with ill-
proportioned and deteriorate genetic variation in consequence. The
present-day mass-manufacture of these abnormal types is very much an
effort of abnormal culture, however.

Winifred Holtby, Women and a Changing Civilisation, *1934*

[128] The woman's movement of the past hundred and fifty years has
improved the social and economic status of the spinster, and, in some
still limited circles, removed her moral obligation of virginity. Teachers,
doctors, political organisers, artists and explorers may deliberately choose
to [129] remain unmarried in order not to be hampered in their work. In
some cases this means that they remain celibate; since the spread of
contraceptive knowledge, it generally means that they avoid motherhood.
But it is impossible . . . to call such women frustrated; most of them live
lives as full, satisfied and happy as any human lives can be . . . . It becomes
a matter of secondary importance whether they have also experienced the
enchanting flattery and relief of being loved; the exquisite intimacy of
physical contact, and the extension of personality which parenthood
brings with it.

[131] The spinster may have work which delights her, personal intimacies
which comfort her, power which satisfies her. She may have known that

rare light of ecstasy. In certain sections of society, it is possible that she will have had lovers . . . .

As for those unmarried women who remain virgins, some, highly-sexed by biological make-up, suffer physically. Their individual personality requires an activity which is has been denied. Others, never finding satisfactory occupation outside the domestic sphere, are constantly aware of the second-best position enjoyed by the unmarried woman in the home. But even more are affected, I think, by the pervasive and penetrating influence of opinion.

Laura Hutton, The Single Woman and Her Emotional Problems, 1935

[42] To many, no doubt, it will seem almost grotesque to compare two women's decision to throw in their lot together with a marriage between a man and a woman, and it will be thought that one can only be referring to definitely homosexual women. To such women certainly the situation does *feel* comparable to marriage; but in these days many women are driven, consciously or unconsciously, by the circumstances of their lives and their need for some more personal contact and intimacy than their work provides, to set up house with a congenial friend, and it scarcely seems an exaggeration, in view of the inevitability and magnitude of the emotional task that such a partnership will have to tackle, to compare it to marriage.

[86] It has already been suggested that sexuality may play a part in an intimate friendship between two women without their being aware of the fact. This must very often be the case, especially when the two friends live together and are in constant physical association, neither of them having any natural or direct outlet for the sexual part of their natures. The results of such *unrecognised* sexual stimulation are bound to be unfortunate. Tension and irritability will follow, on a substratum of perplexity, resentment and vague guilty feeling, the last particularly if the sexual nature of the emotional-*cum*-physical excitement is dimly divined. The first prerequisite for the management of the sexual element in any friendship is its frank recognition and acceptance. Nor is it to be regarded with horror and disgust. It offers certainly a problem to be worked out with care, but it is not necessarily something to be [87] eradicated.

[88] To the majority of women any notion of sexual contact with one of their own sex is wholly repugnant, and they are not likely themselves to feel any inclination to receive or give caresses of an openly sexual character. But many others, especially in these days of inevitable frustration

of their normal sexual instincts, may, in the course of their impulses to caress or be caressed by their most intimate friends, come quite naturally to a caress of a recognisably sexual character, such as, for instance, a kiss on the mouth, and discover with it a corresponding physical sensation of sexual pleasure. Such women are not necessarily [89] sexually inverted, nor in the least perverse. A natural mechanism of their psycho-sexual life is expressing itself.

[91] [T]he criticism is likely to arise that any mutual sexual stimulation between women must be bad (quite apart from being perverse), because the sexual organs are being used purely for the purpose of pleasure, and without any connection to their biological purpose – that of reproduction. Here, it seems, we come . . . to general principles of sexual morality common to both hetero- and homo-sexuality. It is absurd to say that all heterosexual caresses are intended to lead up to the act of procreation . . . . [92] [T]hat they should be the natural expression of *love* is the utmost that a morality of personal integrity (as distinct from social or conventional morality) demands, and this is surely the criterion that demands consideration in homosexual relations.

[99] [T]here are women whose frustrated desire for power has led them consciously to take up the role of initiator. The effect of such a woman's influence on an inexperienced girl is naturally likely to be much more damaging. Where such cases come to the knowledge of those in any way responsible for the welfare of the women concerned, interference on behalf of the younger woman may be justified, though it is a task to be under taken with great gentle- [100] ness, respect, and sympathy.

[101] [W]hat of the case of two mature women, with knowledge of life and of themselves, who may, in the course and development of an intimate [102] friendship, come to sexual expression of their love for one another? Surely it may be left to them to work this out along their own lines, with mutual respect and consideration – reassured as to the physical harm-lessness of genital caresses, if they have the impulse to such . . . . As to the emotional aspect of this physical expression of love, one may be perhaps allowed even to suggest that nothing but good need come from such a relationship, providing guilt, anxiety and conflict are absent, and the only desire is to give pleasure and relief from tension, as an expression of love and tenderness. These are, one must emphasise, extremely stringent conditions, but in so far as the sexual relations in a friendship of this kind are the expression of such intentions they raise the [103] masturbatory act from a purely auto-erotic, or at least self-centred, act to something more nearly approaching the normal use of sexual impulses, and they may thereby contribute, in a way that is entirely useful and constructive, to the

solving of the problem of the unmarried woman's frustrated biological fulfilment. To say this . . . is not by any means an attempt to give such sexual friendships a higher place in the solution of the problem of women's loneliness than friendships in which no such element enters or is dreamt of.

[109] Some sexually inverted women certainly suggest a physical element as part of their anomaly. They do appear to be, physically, transition types (of all degrees) between the wholly female and the wholly male human being . . . .

[110] Such types have been associated with certain degenerative factors . . . . From the point of view of psychic make-up it seems difficult to postulate such degenerative tendencies as general, however, for sexual inverts of this physical type are often characterised by special aptitudes. Intelligence, initiative, energy, courage, and creative power often mark them out from their average fellow-women . . . .

[111] Sexually inverted women of the type we have been describing feel towards members of their own sex all the emotions which a man feels towards a woman. In their love-life they feel like men, and fall in love in the full sense with women . . . . [112] But, as has been indicated, there are many degrees of transition, and there are sexual inverts who do not adopt this masculine style of dress and behaviour to any conspicuous degree, if at all . . . .

Sexual inverts of this type are by most people regarded as sexual perverts, and in [113] fact are often assumed to be inherently vicious. Such a judgement is not justified . . . . [114] It is fairer to describe such a woman as sexually abnormal (or anomalous) rather than perverted.

Sybil Neville-Rolfe, Why Marry?, 1935

[48] There is no evidence that a normal, balanced and mature personality becomes abnormal or reverts to emotional adolescence if physical sex expression is delayed or forgone, provided the individual does not live under conditions that create emotional conflict. There are, however, volumes of evidence of the physical, mental and moral disasters that follow in the train of promiscuity.

[95] Starving for love, deprived of homes and denied the joys of motherhood, many women found in friendship one with another some sort of substitute of these normal but lost relationships. Many of these friendships have mutually enriched the lives of the friends and, by giving emotional stability, have enabled them to make larger contributions to the welfare of society, and society, as expressed by public opinion, has

accepted the position. Unfortunately, however, under cover of a large number of normal and healthy friendships, an unnatural and perverted form of sex relationship between women has become more prevalent and more open in its expression.

[97] The friendship between girls in their teens is well known to all . . . . It is just [98] emotional play and a natural phase of development . . . . When, however, these emotional and possessive friendships persist after the young people have grown up, to the exclusion of any interest in the opposite sex, care is necessary . . . .

A girl who has no opportunity to meet members of the opposite sex may develop such an intense emotional relationship with another girl that when an opportunity does come for her to make men friends, she has lost all interest. If nothing occurs to break the close association between the two young women, an emotional bias may be created that will develop into a perverted psychological condition. In the majority of cases, however, intense friendships between young girls and young women fall into their natural place when opportunities for mixed friendships occur, and such girls and women usually marry happily.

It must be remembered, however, that the emotional side only can be engaged without danger. If girls, in ignorance of the significance of their acts, drift into physical practices that arouse their physical sex equipment to activity, then there is real danger that normal and mature development may be prevented . . . .

[99] [I]f . . . in ignorance, girls have drifted into physical practices, those in charge must remove the contributing conditions, but should not accentuate to the young people the importance of what has been happening. The object is not to attach emotional importance to it in the mind of the adolescent, lest the very psychological difficulties one wants to avoid should thereby be created . . . .

To become abnormal there must either be some physiological peculiarity or some emotional or psychological bias or serious emotional experience in early years. A phase of perversion can, however, be produced by the first awakening of physical sex by another woman; an isolated experience, however, will not necessarily do any permanent harm to a normal girl but should of course be guarded against carefully, and such cases can usually be helped and often cured by psychological treatment.

To turn . . . [to] an example of a real friendship between two mature individuals. For each partner in such friendships to gain full satisfaction, there are cer- [100] tain conditions that should be agreed to before starting a joint establishment. When neither has any other outlet for affection, there is a danger of undue possessiveness developing, which in its turn brings jealousy and a cramping of individual freedom.

[. . . .]

A balanced friendship . . . where each preserves [her] own independent mental life and worldly interests is one of the prizes offered by life.

[102] A few people are born with an abnormal sex equipment; the women of this group show some of the physical characteristics of the male . . . . Such cases are generally believed to be due to the sex glands not functioning properly . . . . In a few years probably the majority of cases of abnormality that are due to such causes will be able to receive satisfactory medical treatment. At present, however, they are physiologically abnormal from birth; but there are relatively few such persons.

There are, however, quite a number of people who have never grown up psychologically . . . . If such persons are put [103] into situations where their desire for power has to express itself through sex, and only members of their own sex are available, then, in ignorance, they develop a wrong and abnormal psychology or attitude of mind, because they never grow out of the adolescent stage in their emotional life.

[104] The confusion of thought today is due to the belief that the majority of these cases are due to inborn defect and that they are therefore incurable, while in fact many can be and are cured . . . .

Many people maintain today that we have no more right to condemn the sexually abnormal than had our forefathers to torture and burn as witches old women who were insane. This is quite true, but it must at the same time be recognised that women or men who are physically attracted by members of the same sex are abnormal, and that the abnormality is socially and racially very undesirable.

Those suffering from the condition should be looked upon as sick persons.

Irene Clephane, Towards Sex Freedom, *1935*

[235] [O]nce sex itself ceases to be regarded as shameful, its variant manifestations will earn not contumely, but indifference, or at most compassion. It is the 'sinfulness' of sexual abnormalities that is in many instances their attraction. Take away the idea of sinfulness, and substitute the idea that these manifestations are merely eccentric and not specially interesting ways of achieving a normal function – and they would often lose their attraction. Those beings who still needed some eccentricity of behaviour to achieve satisfaction would readily find partners of like mind in a condition of society in which there were no sex taboos – and no commercialised sex; and harm would be done to none, but only good to the exceptional few.

Marie Stopes, Change of Life, *1936*

[211] Some women become less feminine at the 'change of life' and find themselves lacking the permanent and protective love a truly masculine man gives to a truly feminine woman. Hence women who have been or even still are legally, wives, may be lonely and physically unsatisfied in marriage. There is then, in some, a tendency to fill the void with a homosexual love for a girl or younger woman. In various forms it develops more often than is generally recognised.

Ellen Dorothy Abb, What Fools We Women Be!, *1937*

[111] Probably every virgin has moments of wondering whether he or she has missed the biggest thing of all . . . . A pity to miss what at the lowest estimate is a pleasure, at its highest the fructifying ecstasy which underlies the whole of life and literature.

But isn't the spinster unnecessarily meek to let [112] the world tell her she is superfluous unless some man has in its eyes put the supreme seal on her for his own gratification? Is man always to be the sole arbiter of woman's usefulness or happiness? Is practice of a function which she shares with any savage to be the one criterion of her completeness?

We really have been a little too docile, not to say disloyal, in subscribing so humbly to this new-old doctrine and labelling as incomplete those women who still retain – for whatever reason – the despised virginity which was at one time regarded as a marvellous jewel.

[116] I am sometimes inclined to think that every woman should be married at twenty-one and have a child at twenty-two, so that she can then get on with the business of living, safe in the knowledge that she can never be sneered at now for being unwilling or incapable of 'doing what woman was brought into the world for.' The courtship period is particularly valuable, because it gives her confidence after a lifetime of inferiority so far.

But there would be fewer marriages if it was customary for single women who had had a proposal, to wear a kind of active service stripe that gave them half the prestige of marriage. It is marriage itself that attracts women, not merely the sexual experience it offers. Only the prostitute can make a living out of that.

[163] One can already hire quite a respectable gigolo. As divorce becomes more widespread, the well-off spinster may think it worth while investing in a temporary husband, or the working spinster may even save up for the respect-carrying title of 'Mrs.,' just as political honours can always be bought.

If reviving contempt for the spinster becomes more pronounced, as appears likely, husband purchase seems logically the next development . . . .

[164] On the other hand, now that matrimony is no longer the only career open to women, it is quite likely that the numbers of single women may remain relatively as high as they are now. Although marriage still offers the best prospects, there may be an increasing number of women whom independent means, a satisfying interest in life and love of freedom render disinclined to exchange all these for the position of second fiddle. Their advantages making them attractive, they will have sexual relationships if they want them. If they want children, they will have them too.

Melanie Klein, 'Love, Guilt and Reparation', 1937

[330] The strength of impulses and feelings . . . brings about very intense friendships between young people, mostly between members of the same sex. Unconscious homosexual tendencies and feelings underlie these relationships and very often lead to actual homosexual activities. Such relationships are partly an escape from the drive towards the other sex, which is often too unmanageable at this stage, for various internal and external reasons . . . . [331] At this stage of development, the increased homosexual tendencies, whether conscious or unconscious, also play a great part in the adulation of teachers of the same sex. Friendships in adolescence, as we know, are very often unstable. A reason for this is to be found in the strength of the sexual feelings (unconscious or conscious) which enter into them and disturb them. The adolescent is not yet emancipated from the strong emotional ties of infancy and is still . . . swayed by them.

In adult life, though unconscious homosexual tendencies play their part in friendships between people of the same sex, it is characteristic of friendship – as distinct from a homosexual love relationship[1] – that affectionate feelings can be partially dissociated from sexual ones, which recede into the background, and though remaining to a certain extent active in the unconscious mind, for practical purposes they disappear . . ..

Let us take as an instance a friendship between two women who are not too dependent upon each other. Protectiveness and helpfulness may still be needed, at times by the one, at other times by the other, as situations arise. This capacity to give and take emotionally is one essential for true

---

1   Klein footnoted this passage as follows: 'The subject of homosexual love relations is a wide and very complicated one . . . . I restrict myself, therefore, to mentioning that much love can be put into these relationships.'

friendship. Here, elements of early situations are expressed in adult ways . . . . A successful blending of a mother-attitude and a daughter-attitude seems to be one of the conditions for an emotionally rich feminine personality and for the capacity for friendship.

Mrs Cecil Chesterton, Women of the London Underworld, *1938*

[72] You will find in the more expensive ill-run night club a type of woman expensively dressed, well groomed, of early middle age and with a curiously unsexed look about them. They may have a mannish suggestion about their dress, or they may be feminine and fluffy in appearance. But male attention leaves them unmoved, though the sight of a pretty girl with a soft complexion and the look of genuine inexperience brings a light to their eyes. This type of woman is on the look-out for a companion of her own sex. Abnormal desires in the sex direction can always be gratified – given money and opportunity – and an appetite for abnormality can readily be satisfied in many night clubs in that quarter. It may often happen that the girl selected is utterly unsuspicious of what the older woman is after, and readily accepts an invitation to dinner, the theatre, or to a social evening. The advance in such a case in insidious, and the more ingenuous the girl the more difficult for her to distinguish between the evidences of a natural affection, and those of an unhealthy desire. Once a girl is debauched in this manner it is difficult for her to regain a normal view of sex. She is spoiled.

There are, we know, those who by inheritance [73] are unhappily deterred from normal sex relations. But for the most part these take their own ways of dealing with their problem. They are not often found on the prowl for the young and innocent. It is rather those women who, vitiated by excess of all description, look for untested experiences who are to be dreaded.

I have known girls who, warned by anxious relatives of the dangers of making acquaintance with strangers who may be white slavers, have quite innocently accepted friendly advances from women of whom they have not the least knowledge . . . . Emotionally speaking, once such an association is formed it is very difficult to induce a young girl to break it. Women of this type are very often brilliant intellectually with a power of fascination difficult for a young thing to resist. Extravagantly lavish, the older woman will endow her protégée with jewels, dresses, surround her with every kind of luxury. Sometimes the association drags on for years, long past the period when a girl might hope for marriage or a natural attachment [74] for a man. It happens, however, quite often that the connection is violently ruptured. The woman meets another more attractive girl and the former possessor of her interest and caresses is flung off. Deprived of all contentment with normality, her nerves wrecked, with a ravaged mind and body, the abandoned one may either take to drugs and drink, or an even worse fate – transfer herself to a fresh protectress . . . .

There is . . . no law against such relations between women, and all unsuspecting a girl may be deflowered of her innocence of mind and body by her own sex, without the malefactor suffering any punishment.

Prostitution and venereal disease

It is generally considered that outright commercial prostitution is increasingly being superseded by consensual relationships, although several writers point out that (particularly in a time of economic depression) prostitution is still resorted to and that a demand continues to exist. Though venereal diseases have declined enormously since the end of the Great War, infection rates rise once more with the outbreak of the Second World War.

Gladys Hall, Prostitution: A Survey and a Challenge, 1933

[28] [E]lderly and even aged women . . . having long ago (often prematurely) lost all personal attractiveness, offer themselves for a few pence, and often late at night when their younger colleagues have hours earlier obtained customers. Their method is frequently the offer of small articles for sale, such as studs or laces, etc., under cover of which they offer sales of a different nature. They may also be found furtively lingering near dark entries for no ostensible purpose but the one which is recognized by any customer who wishes to purchase . . . .

[A]n 'age curve' might be constructed, having its highest part somewhere between the ages of sixteen and twenty-four . . . . [T]he general opinion appears to be that the beginning of the highest part of the curve tends to occur at an earlier age than formerly.

[34] [I]t is often quite impossible for even a close watcher to perceive definite overtures between the prostitute and her customer. By some subtle glance or expression the invitation is indicated by one of the other and the response signified. Expression does, I think, mean a very great deal to the street habitués. It is not definable, but those accustomed to street work come to recognize it and clearly it is recognizable by prostitutes and customers. One may see the most fleeting glance from a prostitute serve to arrest the attention of her desired customer though it may be of no longer duration than the casual glance of another woman. Similarly one

cannot fail to recognize that there is some expression or expectancy about a man who is on the 'look-out' for a partner, which is significant to the prostitute. To some extent one may explain this mutual recognition by reference to a mutual readiness and watchfulness; but there remains a subtle recognition and understanding between individuals which constantly baffles expert observers.

The method of the young amateur is usually more crude and obvious. It consists frequently of a noisy and demonstrative manner designed to attract attention . . . .

Of the accosting of women by men remarkably little has been written, though it was clearly stated during the hearing of evidence by the Street Offences Committee in 1928 that [35] prostitutes themselves are very frequently the accosted rather than the accosting parties. Verbal accosting of women by men in the streets is of quite frequent occurrence . . . . [A] very usual method, and once which has attracted attention, is the accosting done by men from private cars.

[83] A combination of circumstances may most frequently be supposed to have led to promiscuous habits or professional prostitution . . . . Moreover, individual reactions to circumstances or combinations of circumstances are so different that it would be difficult to place a finger on any fact in any [84] record and say, 'Here was the cause.' Nevertheless, there are certain social and personal conditions which so frequently form the background to the promiscuous life as to leave no doubt that they are important factors.

[86] I have no evidence that women supplement, by prostitution earnings, wages insufficient to maintain them, but I have ample evidence that one or both forms of promiscuity are practised to supply what the witnesses describe as 'luxuries.' . . . . [F]or the purpose of the present discussion we may accept 'dress, drink, dainties, gay times' as the luxuries usually coveted.

[87] Many girls who are obliged to work away from home suffer intensely from loneliness. To have nowhere special to go, no one particularly interested in her whereabouts after [88] work, no one to whom to confide the little budget of news – the pleasant happenings or the irritating troubles – which the day has brought her, is a hard ordeal for many a girl when first transplanted. Her sense of utter unimportance may alter her whole sense of proportion. She is at the mercy, unless very well balanced, of the first influence which may first capture her attention in the new life. The mere desire for her natural share of fun and joy and companionship leaves her open to accept invitations which seem to lead to their provision, without knowledge of what the sequel may be.

[93] Again and again . . . there comes evidence of a belief in a 'prostitute type', having characteristics which lead inevitably to promiscuity . . . . [I]t gives colour to the idea that prostitutes are to be regarded almost literally as the natural provision for the polygamous needs of men. This idea does in fact appear to prevail among large numbers of women as well as among many men who would not themselves patronize prostitutes.

The truth seems to be that although there is 'no such thing as "la prostituta nata,"' there are at least three classes of [94] girls or women possessing tendencies which make them particularly prone to turn to prostitution in the absence of strong inhibition, social or personal. It seems possible to divide these groups thus: (a) individuals possessing a certain combination of characteristics certainly possessed by a large number of prostitutes and which appear to make promiscuity the most obvious course unless some counter-influence appears; (b) individuals temporarily (i.e. usually at puberty) possessed of either precocious or abnormally developed sex impulses; (c) individuals who by inheritance or some personal glandular development have what is commonly called an over-sexed constitution. The characteristics possessed by group (a) are those which are, more or less consistently, ascribed to the 'typical prostitute', namely vanity, greediness, indolence. The individuals in the second and third groups are characterized by their excessive readiness to be sexually stimulated, the main difference between them being that in one group it seems to be constitutional and in the other group due to temporary physical conditions . . . .

Although the tendencies of those in the first and second groups may make the adoption of promiscuity an easy course, there is nothing inevitable about such a development.

[96] The cause generally believed in and accepted by the public is the overwhelming male need to exercise, for his health's sake, the sex function, unbalanced by any similar need on the part of women. The inevitable result of this lack of symmetry is the existence of a body of women set apart to supply that [97] overwhelming male need, though by a curiously illogical process of thought, these women, while regarded as socially necessary, are at the same time classed with social offenders. This traditional inequality of sexual need between the sexes is the foundation on which is built the system of sex commerce . . . . Regarding the question of this overwhelming need there are two opinions . . . . But it is quite clear that such a belief takes no account of the possible variations between individuals, and has the result of grouping all men together and representing them as making a more or less united claim for a special service; and it is – perhaps because so commonplace – scarcely noticed that this suggestion is impressed upon boys and young men so early that they have little chance to discover for themselves the facts concerning their physical necessities.

[112] Are the venereal diseases inevitable results of promiscuity? Are they attributable only to promiscuity? . . . . [I]t may be said at once that venereal disease is not the inevitable sequel to promiscuity. Prophylactic treatment, following immediately after the risk of infection has been incurred, may be, and in many cases is, completely successful. But it must be added that no prophylactic treatment is absolutely reliable, and is least likely to be so when undertaken by the infected individual without expert guidance. [. . . .]

[113] [V]enereal infections may occur in some of the ways in which other infections may occur, namely by contact with an infected individual or with infected clothing, etc. But 'somewhere in the history of each venereal infection will be found an act of promiscuity as its origin.'

[165] Riotous and indecent behaviour by prostitutes is rare, nor do they, as a rule, importune; a breach of the peace in the accepted sense is unlikely to be caused by the average prostitute, however diligently and even obviously she may pursue her avocation; and the pleasantly worded or silent refusal of her overtures accorded to the prostitute by the average man accosted cannot with any truth be described as annoyance. Nevertheless, it is by the application of wording of this nature to behaviour which is not literally offensive and which is normally most discreet, that the police in Great Britain and most of the British dominions usually arrest women who solicit. The static or almost static condition of this type of legislation is clearly responsible for the inappropriateness of wording as applied to modern conditions.

Irene Clephane, Towards Sex Freedom, 1935

[212] Women's better economic status and increasing sexual freedom have made it unnecessary for the average man to seek prostitutes. The dying away of shame in sexual matters is leading to the fading away of that accompanying shame about sexual diseases which, since their nature and effects began to be better understood, has been one of the chief difficulties in the way of their effective treatment and diminution. So long as men and women are constrained by shame to [213] conceal these diseases until they reach a stage where concealment (or self-deception) is no longer possible, they can never be completely eradicated. Once all sense of shame can be dissociated from sex, it will be dissociated also from sexual diseases: save in so far as in that day, a man or woman will be ashamed to pass them on. Already, increased knowledge of their existence and of their baneful effects makes every man and woman with the smallest sense of responsibility take precautions to avoid them, by avoiding commercialised sex, and, if they have been unfortunate enough to fall victims all the same, to seek medical advice and cure at once.

Alison Neilans, 'Changes in Sex Morality', 1936

[213] [I]t is necessary to refer to an aspect of sex morality standards where the battle for equality in the law has not yet been successful, though it is still being continuously pursued. This is in regard to the woman described in the law as a 'common prostitute.' . . . [S]he is still the subject of special legislation and an outcast from [214] the protection of the ordinary law applicable to other people.

There seems to be an unyielding opposition in many men's minds against treating the woman who gives herself promiscuously for money as a human being . . . . [I]it seems almost impossible to make the average man realize, whether he be M.P., magistrate, policeman, or man in the street, that sexual promiscuity in a woman should no more cut her off from her full citizen right to legal justice than it does a man . . . . The resistance which this effort meets is probable psychological in its basis. The contempt which men feel for the prostitute, and the fact that they have always regarded themselves as far superior to her, even when they made use of her, suggests an attempt to rationalize the situation; it might be explained as an unconscious transference to the woman of the shame they feel for themselves in these relations. Many men accuse women of being harder in their judgement of the immoral woman than men are, but the facts show this is [215] not the case. Again and again, from 1870 onwards, the women who were fighting for equality have tried to help the woman of the streets and to secure for her legal justice.

Margaret Cole, Marriage: Past and Present, 1938

[158] [A]ny chapter dealing with the position of women and marriage in England today is incomplete if it makes no reference to the women engaged in the oldest of women's paid occupations . . . . [159] It is not a legal crime in England to be a professional prostitute . . . but it is a crime to proffer your wares, to solicit so as to be a nuisance . . . . [160] [T]he penalty for soliciting in facts puts the poor prostitute . . . entirely in the hands of the police in any particular district, and at the mercy of the attitude they choose to adopt to her . . . . She is even, in the laws which speak of 'common prostitutes', segregated into a class of persons whose rights are not the same as those of her fellow-creatures. This state of affairs, of which I should not imagine any reflective person could possibly approve, is made more easy by the very general social condemnation of the prostitute in the strict sense, i.e. the woman who makes or supplements her living by regular sale of her body, as distinct from the woman who is merely careless or nonconformist in her morals. The great disadvantage of violent social condemnation of a practice, however

well-deserved the condemnation may be, is that it results in pervading the whole subject with inhibitions and emotionalism, so that it is difficult to discuss the problems of the prostitute without becoming either violent or sentimental.

It is sometimes suggested that the partial breakdown of the 'double standard' of Victorian sexual [161] morality, producing on the one hand more 'immorality' among women and greater carefulness or fastidiousness among men, must have diminished the demand for prostitutes . . . . Some slight change there may have been, but I should doubt whether it was very great, or affected more than a few of those who take to prostitution or habitually visit prostitutes. The great majority of prostitutes . . . are poor, and have resorted to their trade either in order to supplement an inadequate wage or no wage at all during unemployment, or, at first at least, to get a little more fun out of life than virtue upon a pound a week offers; and so long as these conditions continue, so long will the supply be kept up. In so far as it has gone down at all, this is due much more to an improvement in the standard of life among the poorest than to any other cause . . . . But it would be well to get the social criticism of the system, whatever one's views about it, as much disentangled from the moral criticism as possible.

Dorothy Manchée, Social Service in the Clinic for Venereal Diseases, *1938*

[15] [P]atients infected with venereal disease, unlike other sufferers, are rarely able to speak of their trouble and so gain the relief and sympathy afforded to others, since they would, even if innocently infected, be punished by social ostracism. The emotional and mental stress thus intensifies their trouble, and these patients, more than any, need friendly understanding and help . . . .

Since treatment in the clinics is both free and confidential, patients are drawn from all classes of society and include a large percentage of married women and many of the professions and occupations.

[16] This first interview is of the greatest value, since if the right contact is established the patient will feel that she has a friend to whom she may turn. Since there is no such thing as 'an average patient,' approach in each case has to be individual, bearing in mind that as a rule considerable mental stress has already been endured before she summoned up sufficient courage to attend in the first place. With married women there is often an emotional outburst needing sympathetic handling, while the single girl, drawn from all ranks – bank clerks and nurses, factory hands, waitresses and domestics – is often badly in need of a helping hand, having no one in whom to confide.

Mrs Cecil Chesterton, Women of the London Underworld, *1938*

[22] Mary was duly installed in a smart West End flat, where the young man brought various men friends. It is an old story and with the inevitable sequel. The friends were clients out for a good time, and Mary was called on to 'entertain' them under threats. Still dominated by passion, she succumbed to her lover's persuasion and found herself a professional prostitute, receiving as many visitors as could be arranged.

The syndicate exploiting Mary run an ingenious racket. They rent and furnish West End flats where they install an attractive and, if possible, inexperienced girl, paying her a small percentage of her immoral earnings. This is one of the most profitable stunts of the underworld, and can be run with a minimum of risk and the maximum of profit. The victims, ignorant of the law, cannot escape. If they try to break away they are threatened with proceedings for arrears of rent, cost of food, clothes, etc.; and, bewildered and terrified, the girls remain in their masters' power, owned body and soul. This is the most immediate form of the white slave traffic, and unless the unhappy dupe is prepared to speak out and take the consequences of reprisal it is very difficult to unmask.

[152] There is a considerable profit to be made in a particularly dreadful trade. Men of abnormal sex desires, generally old and enfeebled by excess, pay large sums for strange sex indulgences. They get a repulsive ecstasy from flagellation and will hire young girls to whip them. Now it is difficult to arrange these matters in an hotel or apartment house, and for this reason there are women who rent a room and let it out for such indulgences. Furthermore, they supply the girl and the whip, and receive large sums for arranging the whole business. The girls in question are only paid a few shillings – the procuress makes the profit – but to the sexually curious the proceeding has an unhealthy fascination, and once launched on this particular sideline a general demoralisation usually follows. The girl becomes an expert in abnormalities, unable to find satisfaction in natural relations.

Dorothy Manchée, Social Service in the Clinic for Venereal Diseases, *1943*

[10] With all this disintegration of life as we know it, it is hardly surprising that the incidence of venereal disease should show an increase. It is the rapid rate of that increase, however, which is alarming to the authorities and forms a problem, the solving of which is in part the responsibility of every citizen.

[13] Excluded from the mobilization appears to be the 'professional prostitute.' A girl from bravado has only to give this as her occupation for the authorities to be baffled.[2]

[36] The world at large, busy with its own affairs, is all too ready to condemn the so-called 'prostitute' without pausing to consider how the girl reached that unhappy stage or how she is to escape from it without proper help.

There seems still a tendency on the part of society to regard with less tolerance the woman who has 'fallen from grace.' Disapproval without hope arouses only defiance, so often a tragic camouflage for despair. Since the profession would not exist were there no demand, men and women should take a wider view than the mere punishment of the woman.

Apart from these girls, there is what may be termed the 'unprofessional prostitute,' who while in a regular job is yet tempted, for various reasons, to add to her earnings. There is the girl of even more stability who 'sees no harm' in extra-marital intercourse, and the young and foolish wife who thinks it clever to be unfaithful.

Let us first consider the difficulties of the 'professional prostitute,' by which we mean the girl who has no visible means of support. She may be maintained in a flat in Mayfair [37] or be the veriest little camp follower; whatever her status, she was not always that, and with infinite care for her on someone's part there is no need for her to remain so.

What are the causes of such a condition? Destitution, vanity, laziness, what you will. It is both useless and cruel to blame a man for habitual drunkenness without seeking and helping, if it be within your power, to remove the cause. The same applies to the prostitute.

She may have lost her job originally and had nowhere to go; she may have 'got into trouble' and been turned out of her home with a baby in her arms; she may have become hopeless in the struggle to keep body and soul together, in the fight of the labour market where she has no tempting wares to offer; she may have found it 'impossible' to wear the shabby clothes which her wages provided when her contemporaries were so well dressed, had money to spend and were so apparently gay.

Once having adopted this mode of life, it is no easy matter to drop.

---

2 Strictly speaking, this was not true and there was no basis in law for this assertion. See Lesley A. Hall, '"The Reserved Occupation"? Prostitution in the Second World War', *Women's History Magazine*, no. 41 June 2002, pp. 4–9.

Louisa Martindale, The Prevention of Venereal Disease, *1945*

[55] The best method of prevention . . . lies in sexual morality. A campaign to make this easier would do more than any number of medical measures to make 'vice safe.'
[. . . .]
[56] The right campaign for prevention therefore must be on the following lines:

1 Sex instruction by medical men and women who have a real knowledge of the social and moral as well as the medical side of the subject.
2 A public demand for cleaner films and a higher standard in recreational broadcasts and literature.
3 Better housing and living conditions.
4 Plenty of healthy recreation, and
5 For those who have contracted Venereal Disease or fear that they may have done so, more Venereal Disease clinics of easy access . . . together with more almoners to help with the follow-up and to ensure ready attendance.

Birth control

The main struggle for the acceptability of birth control is over. Issues of the methods available, their acceptability and reliability, continue to be debated, and the question of the adequate dissemination of information and assistance to those who needed it most persists. Some radical figures in the movement move on to the next battle, joining Stella Browne in pleading for the legalization of safe surgical abortion. The wider social implications of birth control for women's lives are contemplated.

Naomi Mitchison, Comments on Birth Control, *1930*

[10] Birth control methods are used by three sorts of couples. By temporary or semi-permanent lovers who have at all costs to avoid having babies. By young married couples . . . who want to space their babies, or, more rarely, to avoid having any. And by couples married for some time who wish to have no more babies, or, more rarely, to go on spacing them.

So for the first of these three classes, the only alternative is abortion, which is apt to be dangerous, expensive and unpleasant, and is at present illegal. They must practise birth control. When two people are burning for one another, and anyhow probably having to get round or over all sorts of material obstacles before they can get their desire, this is only one more, and not perhaps a very important one.

[11] If two normal people want to live together permanently the probability is that one, or more likely both of them, want children. As I have said already there is a certain amount of propaganda about, advising that they should always wait first for a year or two in order to get used to one another. Quite apart from the desire for children . . . the suggestion seems to me most rash. The time for get- [12] ting used to one another, in all conscience, is before marriage. It is too late to discover afterwards – especially with our present divorce laws – that they cannot manage it.

Until lately there has been another difficulty . . . . [A] virgin girl, even when she faced the situation, could not think it possible that she would be able to wear any kind of check pessary. And most newly married lovers would prefer the risk of starting a baby at once, which is not perhaps so great as the normal risk, to having their delight and beauty marred by the use of any obvious contraceptive device by the man, a preference not merely of romantic sentimentality, but a moral and aesthetic choice of some importance.

[13] [O]ne of the problems which the young married couple must face . . . is this: are they the sort of people who want their children only when they are intended, or as happy and surprising accidents? It is quite easy to say that it is braver and nobler and more civilized to have only intentional children . . . . But there are others (whether we like it or not) who prefer the other thrill of the accident.

Janet Chance, The Cost of English Morals, *1931*

[52] [T]here is a seamy side to motherhood which it is inhuman to ignore. And that is the widespread approach of mothers, married and unmarried, in every class of the community at some time in their lives to self-inflicted abortion. Most have at some time wanted it, it would seem; many have attempted it; some have achieved it and yet not even the medical profession may face the facts.

It is not the thoughtless or debased woman who approaches the thought of abortion; it is the average, normal, woman; it is every second or third woman we meet. Attempts at abortion are commonly made even among those who have knowledge of the best contraceptives, and it would probably be difficult to find a [53] single uninstructed poor and fertile mother alive who has not made some crude and furtive attempt to get rid of an unborn child.

[71] *No one advocates abortion, any more than they advocate amputation.*

They only ask for the legalisation of all medically endorsed abortion. Amputation is legal. Yet women do not seek it foolishly; and if they did, their doctors would decline to perform the operation and no harm would be done. Why do we not trust the good sense of the women, backed by the professional standards of the doctors, in the matter of abortion? Only because we dare not face the truth. We dare not admit that our present morality has landed us with thousands of women so harassed and anguished by their present condition of married life that abortion seems to them the lesser of two evils.

Women do not enjoy abortions. They snatch at them in extreme despair.

Enid Charles, The Practice of Birth Control, 1932

[51] Ten women state they cannot obtain complete physical satisfaction when the sheath is used . . . . Several writers describe the sheath as too noticeable. A few more make use of adjectives such as inartistic, prosaic, and unromantic.

[52] The testimony to the bad effects of coitus interruptus is very strong. Most of the remarks are expressed in language which cannot be given an exact scientific meaning, but which undoubtedly indicates a very genuine reaction on the part of the individual testifying. In twenty-four cases the wife stated that she obtained no physical satisfaction. Several writers speak of the method as being unpleasant, harmful, or causing nervous strain. In the thirteen cases it was said to have caused a 'severe shock to the nervous system'. In four cases insomnia followed.

[56] Abstinence was said to be the sole means of family limitation in two cases. Of these two one was a missionary's wife who practised it over a period of twelve years . . . . The individual concerned states that she is happy and physically fit, and that she believes birth control to be socially and physically detrimental. The second case is that of the wife of a man holding a managerial post. The exact period of the abstinence is not stated, but the marriage extended over seventeen years. Three children were born. Abstinence was said to have been given up immediately before each conception. The opinion is expressed that artificial birth control is detrimental to love and respect and conducive to immorality. There remain fourteen individuals who combined abstinence over protracted periods with the use of contraceptive practice at other times. Two of the individuals concerned consider abstinence to be the healthiest and happiest way of spacing the births of children.

Gladys Hall, Prostitution: A Survey and a Challenge, 1933

[91] Knowledge of contraceptives . . . scarcely needs further emphasis . . . . [T]his knowledge . . . spread by ordinary commercial methods and available to all, has made possible a large amount of the amateur promiscuity which is advocated and practised. A worker, whose experience covers numbers of villages, described to me a talk which illustrates the fact of this widespread knowledge. When talking to an unmarried village girl of fifteen, who had unsuccessfully attempted to prevent pregnancy, the worker was told that all village boys and girls know all about contraceptives. 'Do you mean to say you talk about them?' asked the worker. 'Oh no,' replied the girl. 'We don't *talk* about them, but we tell each other, and that's that.'

Leonora Eyles, Commonsense about Sex, 1933

[89] It is wiser to space the family carefully so that the mother is able, physically and mentally, and the father financially, to cope with each child as it arrives . . . . [90] [O]ften the doctor advises them to have no more children and gives them merely the advice to occupy separate rooms. Surely even the most antediluvian doctor today knows the risk of such advice to people's nervous health? In the past six months I have known, in my correspondence, of only one doctor – and that a woman – who volunteered birth control advice of a scientific nature; the rest, if they gave any help at all, suggested the disastrous method of withdrawal.

[96] A further and, I think, highly important thing is that the preventive should be of such a type that it can be affixed much before love-making [97] begins and left untouched afterwards, and that it should be left entirely to the woman to manage it . . . .

The one great disadvantage of the rubber pessary is that it is quite unsafe to fix it for oneself. It must be done by a qualified person, because it is of extreme importance that it should fit tightly yet comfortably, and, in fact, not to be felt at all.

Winifred Holtby, Women and a Changing Civilisation, 1934

[67] To change a gamble with fortune [68] into a deliberate act subject to human will threatened a drastic upheaval of age-old expectation. If women were no longer subject to that instability, that dependence upon circumstance, which might at any moment visit them in the helplessness

of late pregnancy and childbirth, they could plan their lives and calculate possibilities with assurance equal to that of their male colleagues, and yet not buy this freedom with celibacy. The whole nature of women's attitude towards life, their place in society, their capacity and self-confidence could be changed. Instead of waiting upon time and tide and the rhythm of life's creative current . . . they could challenge chance and circumstance, fortune and misfortune, as well as any other human creature. Their mood might change from passive to active participation in life.

It is impossible to over-emphasise the psychological importance of this movement . . . .

[69] [T]he organisations conducting this campaign are, consciously or unconsciously, fighting the battle of the equal moral standard. They are making possible the independent and self-confident facing of the future by women who have hitherto been pawns of destiny – happy pawns most often, unaware of the inconvenience of their position, nevertheless. They are taking part in a revolution of which the fruits will be ethical and psychological as well as biological and economic; but the full nature of which we can still only prophesy by hazard.

[137] Nor is the use of contraceptives universal . . . . One woman worker in a London maternity clinic told me that when offering advice about birth control to women already exhausted by too many children, again and again they repelled her with the words, 'but it is so sordid!' The thought that it may be even more 'sordid' to bring into an already over-crowded home, without proper means for their support, children predisposed to be sickly, undernourished or unfit, has not yet overcome their traditional prejudice that forethought in sexual matters is indecent.

[140] One day we shall certainly think it barbarous that women in basement homes and squalid tenements, were permitted to torture themselves and jeopardise their lives with drugs and pills and all manner of inappropriate instruments, to prevent a sixth or seventh child coming to take the food from the mouths of the others, to prevent further malnutrition, mental deficiency or disease, to prevent, as they vainly hope, the permanent invalidism of the mother, because knowledge of contraception had been unavailable to her, and because the amenities of skilled attention were illegal.

In a perfect society no undesired child would be conceived. But this is an imperfect world, and when married couples sleep night after night together, constant abstention from intercourse exacts a nervous strain harmful to happiness and to the intimacy of human love; where methods of birth control are still imperfectly practised and, to many millions, unknown; where children, unwillingly conceived and resentfully carried, are born into poverty, disease and wretchedness . . . . At present the very word 'abortion' evokes a shock of nervous repugnance in most normal people. I cannot believe that this repugnance is divinely ordered or that its maintenance in ultimately essential for human welfare.

Dr Mary Denham, Planned Parenthood, 1934 (revised 1938)

[12] Only those children who have a reasonable chance of healthy, happy, and useful lives, and whose birth does not injure the health of the mother, should be born. Therefore those married people who already have as many children as they can rear with proper care and attention, and those who by reason of physical and mental defects are unlikely to produce healthy, normal children, should exercise their human intelligence and moral sense and refrain from further reproduction. Civilized people recognize the rights of individuals as well as those of the race, and child-bearing which injures the health of the mother, or is seriously detrimental to the welfare of the existing family, is now recognized as morally unjustifiable.

It is true that the reproductive habits of some humans are no better than those of animals; they breed without restraint, without thought for the [13] welfare of the children for whom they are responsible; but in the main, civilized human beings are coming to recognize more and more that it is their privilege and their moral duty to control reproduction in the interest of themselves, of their children, and of the race.

[19] Since any single act of sexual intercourse may result in pregnancy, it is not sufficient to limit intercourse even to once a year; husband and wife must refrain completely from the natural physical expression of their love for one another, even thought they may have to share a bedroom or to sleep in the same bed. Except in exceptional cases – such as continued ill-health or lack of normal sex feelings, or, for limited periods, during acute illness or the temporary separation of husband and wife – sexual abstinence as a means of family limitation must be condemned.
[. . .]

[20] It should be clearly recognized that the sex life of human beings differs from that of animals in one important respect, in that it has a double purpose. It is not only a means of reproduction, but also of the expression of the tenderness, sympathy, and devotion of two married people who love one another. There is an urge, an intense need for physical union, quite distinct from the desire for children; and sexual abstinence thwarts this perfectly natural instinct. The cost of leading such an unnatural life may be frayed nerves, insomnia, restlessness, and discontent, and the greater the love between husband and wife, the greater may be the penalty of the

frustration of the powerful urge to physical union. To refrain from stimulating the sex impulse, married people must refrain from physical contact, from those expressions of tenderness and love that find their natural outlet in caresses. Such a life is a travesty of marriage.

[22] Proper methods of birth-control provide the sensible alternative to frequent attempts to procure abortion; and it is to be hoped that, in the near future, facilities for all married women to be instructed in medically approved methods of contraception will be regarded as an essential part of our public health [23] services. It is common knowledge that the well-to-do may avail themselves – and do so freely – of the best medical aids for the spacing and limitation of their families by means of contraception. It is a matter of justice, as well as of public interest, that such aids should be available equally to the poor who most need them to save themselves from having recourse to repeated attempts to procure abortion. There is, of course, no question of compulsion, but help should be available for those married women, and especially for poor working mothers, who desire it.

[37] The regular practice of 'withdrawal' may cause definite physical and mental injury to both partners; and some cases of nervous and mental breakdown are attributed to it.

If, when the wife has been sexually excited, the husband withdraws before she reaches her climax (orgasm), she is left sleepless, restless, and dissatisfied, and her sex organs remain congested longer than is normally the case. The ultimate result of this state of affairs is that she becomes irritable and depressed, and she may develop insomnia; and it is not surprising that in time she develops a distaste for sexual intercourse which may grow to active loathing . . . . The physical effects on the wife, due to the prolonged congestion of her sex organs, may cause painful and profuse menstruation, backache, and other troubles.

Sybil Neville-Rolfe, Why Marry?, 1935

[141] Today, everyone accepts the principle that parenthood should be a responsible act. Some Churches advise their members to express the principle by abstaining from intercourse except when a child is desired, or only to have intercourse in what they term the 'safe period' . . . . If the plan of life of the married couple enjoins the first method, it must be remembered that physical contacts must be avoided if emotional conflict and serious strain is not to result . . . . The second method is to be deprecated, as on physical and psychological grounds it is bad for the woman and unsatisfactory for the man . . . .

For those who accept the responsibility of the new knowledge, the capacity to provide for welcome children [142] has enormously enhanced the happiness of married life. Intercourse as the love expression is freed from anxiety, while the necessary intervals between births can be secured.

F. W. Stella Browne, 'The Right to Abortion', 1935

[29] The woman's right to abortion is an absolute right, as I see it, up to the viability of her child. [30] It does not depend upon certainty of death for her . . . . It does not depend on damage or permanent injury to her physical or mental health . . . . It does not depend on the number of her previous confinements; the suggestion, put forward by some vigorous and veteran agitators for abortion law reform, that the woman should first supply a quota of at least two children, seems to me to disregard the individual needs, nature, and conditions of women. Neither does the right to refuse an unwanted child depend on economic conditions . . . . Neither does the right we claim depend on having obtained the sanction of the Law and the Church to live with some special man, to bear his name, and share his home and means. Abortion legal for married women only would be the final climax of the illogical absurdity of some respectability complex . . . .

The right to abortion does not depend on crimes which the conventions of romantic tradition deem worse than death . . . .

[31] Neither does the right to abortion *depend* on the uncertain and unpredictable result of possible genetic patterns in the child. Heredity is a much more intricate problem than pre-Mendelian Darwinism supposed.

[33] An adequate abortion law would also encourage *constructive* research . . . .

[34] The invention and circulation of a perfectly reliable and otherwise tolerable abortifacient – especially if it could be self-administered, either by the mouth or as injections, intravenous or intra-muscular – would be the greatest gift science could give to women.

[37] No contraceptive at present accessible to the public is 100 per cent reliable, and at the same time cheap, easy to store and to apply, otherwise non-injurious and aesthetically satisfactory. Moreover, there is almost incredible profiteering in the sale of these articles . . . . [38] Also, there is extreme individual diversity between one person and another in sexual matters, organically, functionally, and in psychic and emotional attitudes. Methods which work admirably between one couple of partners may and do fail dismally or disastrously with another, or may be successful for some time and then fail or become impracticable.

Miss E. V. Pemberton, Simple Advice to Those About to Marry, 1936

[36] [E]qually conscientious Christian people, with equally high ideals, hold opposite views on the subject. Some feel that the birth of children should only be restricted by abstaining from intimate relations, if necessary, altogether. Others feel that since intercourse has a very real purpose and value in married life, apart from bringing children into the world, the use of contraceptives may IN CERTAIN CIRCUMSTANCES, be preferable to INDEFINITE abstention. These differences of opinion, honest and sincere as they undoubtedly are, need to be frankly recognised, and all that can be done here is to give a brief summary of some of the more important facts which need to be taken into consideration by any couple who may be in doubt as to the right course to pursue.

Ellen Dorothy Abb, What Fools We Women Be!, 1937

[26] With the knowledge of birth control woman became mistress of her own body . . . . Within reason she could now plan her life in advance as much as a man. And she was also liberated from that cruel and blind emphasis on chastity as her one necessary attribute – a virtue which, [27] because linked up with the sacred rights of property, stood in man's mind as the highest virtue, the only virtue, woman's virtue itself.

Alice Jenkins, Conscript Parenthood?, 1938

[27] Ordinary knowledge of life proves that, although self-control may be one of the highest virtues, it is for many people an unsatisfactory method of regulating the number of offspring in family. It is estimated that last year in this country only 14,000 women learnt scientific birth control in Voluntary and Municipal Clinics, but there are nearly 100,000 abortions annually.

[29] If the mother is well-informed, and can afford the cost, she can be admitted to a nursing home, where a minor surgical operation is successfully performed without [30] friends being the wiser regarding its nature. For the news has spread that abortion can be procured painlessly and safely, and in this way the rich find a way to procure treatment denied to the poor . . . .

The uninformed woman, or the woman unable to obtain skilled help, sets about in desperation, sometimes with the help of a friend or neighbour, to end the un-welcome state of affairs, and often succeeds, by processes too nauseous to describe, with much permanent damage to herself . . . .

In one industrial area, by paying a weekly sum into an abortion club, women become entitled to unqualified assistance when necessary. When no abortionist is available in the area in which she lives, the woman requiring help travels for the purpose to another town. Ill-health often develops immediately, or, later, accounts for many internal operations of which the source is unsuspected.

Margaret Cole, Marriage: Past and Present, *1938*

[235] [T]he other reason why I am not discussing birth control at length here is that I believe that its battle is, in fact, won. There is, of course, much scope . . . in improving and cheapening appliances, in removing the various bans and restrictions, and in advising people on the technique, on how best to use the knowledge they have obtained. It will take a long time before the inhibitions of education and the hostility of various groups of [236] persons are finally overcome or reduced to negligible proportions. But I do not think there is the slightest question that that is the direction in which things are tending, and that we must therefore assume . . . that the use of contraceptives will go on steadily extending and that contraception will get steadily more efficient. It will not be a hundred per cent effective: it will certainly not be foolproof: and for some it will be more effective than for others . . . . I also believe – though this may be a little more open to dispute – that the use of contraceptives is extending and will extend among married and unmarried persons alike . . . . [237] In any event, it is going to be impracticable, however many efforts authorities may make, to confine birth-control knowledge to those who they think ought to have it.

Margery Spring Rice, Working-Class Wives, *1939*

[44] Contraceptive advice seems practically non-existent. A few women . . . speak of having been to the Birth Control Clinics, but there are dozens of women in obvious need of such advice either for procuring proper intervals between births, or to have no more children, who, although they have been told by their doctor that this is necessary, are not instructed by him in scientific methods and do not go to a Birth Control Clinic, even if there is one within reach.

[56] Medical Birth Control advice should be available for every working woman in order that she should be given at least the chance to protect herself, *and her family*, from the terrible state of attrition that is bound to

be the result of too quick successive pregnancies or pregnancies more numerous than the mother has strength to bear, or the father to provide for . . . . That such knowledge should not be available to women in the circumstances of the 1,250 under review is a serious indictment of the care given by the State to the mothers and children of the present generation.

Dorothy Thurtle, Abortion: Right or Wrong?, *1940*

[8] The practice of drug-taking to correct menstrual irregularities, or female irregularities as they are called, is extremely common. [9] When the menstrual period is overdue many women, in addition to taking drugs, indulge in violent exercise, or deliberately undertake heavy work about the house, such as the lifting of heavy furniture, and thus subject themselves to great physical strain (they have even been known to throw themselves downstairs) in an effort to bring on their period. Incidentally, it sometimes happens that women engage in this kind of violence unnecessarily, under the impression that they are pregnant, which in fact they are not . . . .

An impression strongly held by many organizations of women is that attempted abortion is much more common than is generally realized, and that very few women, normally fertile, have not, at some time in the course of their child-bearing lives, made some effort to dispose of an unwanted pregnancy, either by means of drugs, violent exercise, or more sinister methods such as will be described later

[18] There is a conspiracy of silence regarding what may be called polite or fashionable abortion. The medical prof- [19] ession . . . while admitting that certain practitioners carry on an illegal practice in procuring abortions, deny that this is a very common practice, and content themselves with deploring the fact that a few of the members of their honourable profession do not carry out the pledges they made on becoming qualified. . . .

Many modern practitioners sympathize with, and understand, the point of view of the modern woman who considers that she has a right to plan her family and her life for the greater happiness of the family she has helped to found. Unfortunately, they cannot express this sympathy in a practical form openly without coming in conflict with the law. They are, however, in a very strong position to help secretly, and they frequently do so.
[. . . .]

It is common knowledge that, providing a woman has the means, a properly controlled operation, involving negligible risk to her life or health, can be procured for her, carried out by medical practitioners of the highest skill . . . . [20] There is no doubt at all that for many years operations have been performed on wealthy women for reasons of slight ill-health, and even for quite frivolous reasons . . . .

No working woman would have been able to secure the same treatment for similar reasons. On the contrary, there are cases on record in which operation has been refused to poor women in conditions where few people would deny that the operation was justified.

[21] [T]he woman consults a specialist known to be complaisant in this matter, or she is referred to him by her own practitioner whom she has consulted for symptoms which she considers need a curettage. The word pregnancy need not be mentioned. The three parties, understanding the position, are discreet, and the woman [22] enters a nursing-home for dilatation and curettage, known as a *'D and C' operation*, and leaves it shortly afterwards with the pregnancy terminated.

If the woman is wealthy the operation will cost her, in either case, anything from 100 to 150 guineas.

A similar state of affairs is to be found among less wealthy women in suburban circles. The fees are naturally not so high, and 25 guineas is a sum more likely to be charged.

[31] To consider adequately the question of the legalization of abortion it is necessary to understand clearly that virtually every married woman in the country, leading a normal sex life with her husband, if they are both fertile, runs the risk of a pregnancy at least once every eighteen months to two years from the time of her marriage to the menopause . . . . This is the stark reality faced by all women, of every class.

Eliot Slater and Moya Woodside, Patterns of Marriage, 1951

[196] Mrs O. (100n), twenty-two, former machine operative in a factory, doesn't know about birth control and just takes a good dose of salts. Mrs. M. (41n), a respectable suburban housewife of thirty-five with a son of eleven, says she 'doesn't believe in birth control: it can harm your inside'. Her husband is 'careful' or she takes Beechams Pills . . . . Mrs L. (52n), says: 'We've never used preventives' and adds 'I don't understand birth control. Perhaps I'm rather simple?' Mrs K (32n), mother of two unplanned children, complains that a chemical contraceptive let her down. She won't go to a clinic to be fitted, as two of her friends have [197] been and that let them down too. Mrs M. (78c), aged thirty-eight with two children, doesn't know anything about birth control and says: 'I think it's most horrible. The very thought revolts me.'
[. . . .]

Mrs I. (32c), thirty-eight, two children, says she isn't keen on intercourse and has tried to discourage her husband as she is afraid of becoming pregnant . . . . Mrs Y . . . says she didn't want to start her family so soon or have them so quickly. She is now afraid she may have been 'caught' yet again and will be 'very annoyed' if this is so. Unenthusiastic about intercourse, she explains that this worry 'was always in the back of me mind. I was afraid'.

Mrs T (68n), thirty-eight, with four children, says she hasn't experienced orgasm since the birth of twins seven years ago, and puts this down to her fear of another pregnancy 'it's always in your mind' . . . . [H]er doctor sent her to a birth control clinic; but she couldn't be fitted as she was 'too slack' and nothing stayed in place. She does not like the idea of a chemical contraceptive. 'I'm afraid of them chemicals' . . . .

[204] Mrs E (88n), who suffers from heart trouble, severe chronic dysmenorrhoea, and increasing deafness of unknown origin, was referred by the doctor to a birth-control clinic after her first confinement. This was the day before the war started, and she never went. She bought one packet of [–] but 'never bothered' when it was finished . . . .

[205] Mrs D (84c), thirty-nine, has seven children and is again pregnant. She says she and her husband have mostly used withdrawal. She says she tried [–], but they let her down. After her last confinement the midwife advised her to 'go and get fitted'. She did intend doing so, but her husband was abroad at the time and she didn't bother . . . .

Mrs B (76n) . . . at first, only used one box; then withdrawal or no precautions ('I'm difficult to become pregnant', she thinks). Attended clinic after confinement and used a cap for some time, mostly without the chemical pessary. Isn't bothering about anything at present.

Ignorance and sex education

The same themes of early knowledge and the necessity for lack of embarrassment continue to be reiterated, as does the parlous state of general ignorance. Mary Cardwell demonstrates the extent to which the ideology of the necessity for some form of sexual enlightenment had extended even to Roman Catholics. We can note a shift from the perception of childhood masturbation as something to be prevented, even if gently, to being a normal manifestation of a child's exploration of world and self.

Helena Wright, The Sex Factor in Marriage, 1930

[25] Undoubtedly the best way to achieve a happy, well-balanced sex life is to learn all the facts of sexual anatomy and physiology in youth, long

before they have any individual [26] or emotional importance to the learner. Sex information would thus have time to become part of every-body's ordinary mental equipment, as familiar, beautiful, and friendly as any other piece of Nature's planning. Love and marriage could then hold no hidden terrors, as they too often do at present. Lovers would be free to go forward, knowing everything theoretically, each to make his own discovery of the magic of love's dictating.

Victoria E. M. Bennett and Susan Isaacs, Health and Education in the Nursery, 1931

[267] [I]t is quite indispensable to the child to have his questions frankly and simply answered, at the time when he asks them.
[. . . .]
If he gets no answer, or an evasive one, he is lost and bewildered by the sense that his grown-up friends either don't know the most important things that he [268] wants to understand, or (and this is the more probable) that they won't tell him. And if they won't tell him, *why* won't they? It can only be that there is something wrong and shameful about the knowledge they withhold. And indeed, the voice and tone and expression of mother when she told him to 'hush' and 'not to ask such things', or turned away and talked of something else, did suggest that there was something dark and strange about it. Then that means that behind this story of being small and growing, behind the question of where one comes from, behind the love of mother and father and even mother's love for the child himself, is something shameful and hidden, too shameful and hidden to be spoken of. What can it be? And in this way, the springs of life and love may be poisoned for the child.
[. . . .]
[269] When the child says, therefore, 'Where did I come from?' surely the only possible reply is the true one, put into simple words that he can understand. 'You grew in a warm nest inside me until you were big enough to grow without me, and so you were born.' And when he asks who looked after him when his mother was 'little', the answer is that he was not here then; he was not made, and had not begun to grow inside his mother. And all this can be linked up with the life of the animals he loves to play with, or to watch in the fields.
[. . .]
A great many mothers nowadays are dealing with the problem on these lines, and finding them most satisfactory. Many are keeping notes of all the questions their little children ask about babies, and of [270] how they take the knowledge that is given them in reply . . . .

Most people feel the father's part in procreation to be the most delicate and difficult aspect of the problems. There is no particular age at which children become interested in this. Some ask about it earlier, and some later; some never ask at all, but come to their own conclusions about things. The only guide for the parent is the child's own interest and questions. *If* he asks, then he must be answered about this, just as much as about the mother's part, and just as simply and truthfully. The father plants the seed which the mother shelters and nourishes, and which presently grows into the little baby.

[272] A point often raised is the age at which to give the child the true answer. Some people suggest that six or seven is better than three or four. But surely the only age is the one when the child asks! . . . . If the child does not ask until six or seven, well and good; but if he does . . . [273] then it can only do harm to postpone the answer, on grounds the child cannot possibly understand. To do so is to give a false weight to the curiosity, and will usually only make him hide it. If the child does ask at three, it means that he is unusually intelligent and observant, or that some special circumstance has drawn his attention to the problem . . . . That means he is ready for the answer, no matter how young he be.

Janet Chance, The Cost of English Morals, *1931*

[82] Sex knowledge and sex understanding are omitted, or suppressed, or even disgraced at home and at school . . . . [T]he essence of this education is secretiveness [83] and the people who suffer the most from it are the most afraid to speak of their condition or try to remedy it. At last, when the results have become serious and they must speak, it has sometimes to be to the judge in a divorce court, sometimes to an intimate friend with whom it is possible privately to confess to pain and failure, sometimes to a mental specialist.
[. . . .]
[I]nsufficient or faulty sex education robs young men and women of such genuine refinement of thought and dignity of bearing in sex life, of which they would otherwise be capable. It robs marriage in all classes of some of the finer aspects of love and passion. It lays on the prostitute a burden of social disfavour out of all proportion to her mistakes and follies. And wherever it is powerful this low-grade education robs women, in particular, of much freedom, richness and variety of development.

[84] Many parents hesitate to educate their children in sex matters as they think right because it lands them and their children in so many embarrassing situations and makes them at times so unpopular.

It may be easy enough for those who live in comparatively enlightened circles or are free to avoid antagonistic contacts, but for parents restricted to a tiny circle and without the backing of some opinion beside their own it demands considerable courage to follow their convictions.

It requires of them also the intelligence and tact to [85] go a step farther. They must let their children see quite clearly the differences of outlook that exist, so that they may learn to behave with some social sense; and yet they must do this without encouraging priggishness . . . .

Wise sex education is rare. Women as a rule begin that education, and women, as we have seen, are often not very balanced and informed in their attitude to sex.

[. . . .]

Sex is still, thanks to our moralists, a special subject – a marked subject. That is the whole trouble.

The average parent still makes some special, often some desperate, special effort to cope with the duty he or she acknowledges; the preparatory schoolmaster still hands out, almost with the boy's last return ticket home, a prophylactic packet of information and exhortation; the public school usually maintains in public a colossal silence, broken by an occasional expulsion; there is no provision made in the curriculum of the elementary schools for the teaching of the physiology of sex, nor [86] for the hygiene of sex, the most that is attempted being a certain amount of botany and some elementary Nature Study; any attempts made in the secondary schools are made on the initiative of some individual and can hardly be said to amount to sex education at all.

[. . . .]

Masturbation, homo-sexuality and irresponsible sex intercourse will not so easily prove pitfalls to those who in pre-passionate days have been given the scientific approach to sex questions.

And we should prepare to-day for the follies and stupidities of fifteen and sixteen year olds hence by accustoming children from infancy to hear sex facts acknowledged and opinions on sex conduct canvassed as occasion allowed, so that little by little they would build up . . . [87] a mental structure of knowledge, of acquaintance with adult opinion, and of moral judgements of their own in sex matters which would stand some stress and be of some use in a crisis.

Helena Wright, What is Sex?, 1932

[37] The pollen grains are the male cells, and the green case at the lower end of the pistil contains the female cells. The habits of these two are always the same; the female remains all the time in the same place where it began, safely protected until its work is finished. Unlike the male cells in

the lower kinds of water plants, pollen grains do not move by themselves, [38] but are blown or taken by insects; but the idea is the same. The female cells stays still; the male cell comes to it.

[69] The male frog has only testes and the female frog only ovaries. The clasping of the female frog by the male is a complete sex-act, because it is the immediate cause of the meeting of sperm and egg . . . .

Now . . . we can describe what is meant by copulation, and understand the meaning of what is said. It is the coming together of a male animal and a female animal in such a way that sperms from the male can directly meet and join up with eggs from the female.

[85] As the egg-cell remains inside the mother, it is obviously necessary that the meeting of the sperm and the egg must also take place in the mother's body. Here comes in the use of the projecting part of the sperm-tube of the male dog. In its ordinary condition the skin-covered visible part of the dog's penis is limp and short. Under the influence of sex excitement a change takes place which produces alterations of size and appearance. Running [86] along the length of the penis and surrounding the central tube are spaces in the tissues which are usually empty. When sex excitement occurs, blood is poured into these spaces and the whole organ becomes longer and thicker and firm in consistence, instead of being limp. The outside skin covering the penis seems able to stretch in width but not in length, and when blood-engorgement is complete, the end of the penis elongates and protrudes from the skin covered part for a distance which varies according to the size and type of dog. The protruding part has a covering of membrane which is smooth and pink and moist. When in this condition the penis is said to be erect. In copulation, the male jumps up behind the female and holds on by putting his forelegs on the female's shoulders. When the two animals are in this position, the projecting tube or penis is just opposite the opening of the vagina in the female and can easily fit into it. The tip of the erect penis is now some way inside the female's body, and the male dog begins a series of backwards and forwards movements of his hind quarters which apparently give pleasure to both partners. The movements continue for some minutes and [87] end in spasmodic contractions of the wall of the sperm-tube, which is thus able to eject the semen from the opening in the tip of the penis. By this means none of the semen is lost, but must all be safely received by the female.

[106] Surrounding the front part of the vaginal opening and extending forwards from it is a triangular area which is covered with the same kind of moist, delicate tissue as the tip of the penis; the apex of the triangle is towards the front and the base is formed by the front edge of the vaginal

opening. There is a fold of soft tissue running along each of the sides of the triangle, which meet at the apex in front, and fade away completely at the back at about the level of the vaginal opening. These folds are called the inner lips. At the point in front, where they meet, they form a kind of little hood which covers a small soft mass about the size of a pea. This is called the clitoris. From the point of view of development, it is in the same relative position as the penis in the male, and its function is the same as one of the purposes of the penis. Like the tip of the penis, the clitoris is covered with a moist, very delicate membrane. In the membrane are the same kinds of nerve-endings as there are in the penis and they have the same power – that of conveying the sensation of pleasure during copulation.

[108] A little reflection suggests the idea that there is a certain similarity between the sex-organs of the male and those of the female. Both sets can be divided into working parts and sensation-providing parts . . . . [109] The reason for the presence of organs whose only function is to provide sensations of pleasure is also understandable.

Copulation in man is performed in the same general manner as it is in the higher animals. The male embraces the female in such a position that the erect penis can easily slip into the vagina. Movements then take place which eventually result in a climax of pleasurable sensation to both, and the emission of semen into the vagina.

Enid Charles, The Practice of Birth Control, 1932

[164] [G]enuine biological education, which deals in an objective and ethically neutral manner with all the facts of animal life, including reproduction, may be hoped to encourage a matter-of-fact attitude to all human functions. If such an attitude exists to contraceptive technique, [165] appropriate precautions need not be more embarrassing than the use of suitable cutlery and table napkins when eating dinner.

Mary Borden, The Technique of Marriage, 1933

[28] [W]e have taught them, ever since they were in the nursery, to be afraid of sex. They have had it dinned into them that there was something mysterious, dangerous and unclean about sexual desire, so unclean that you couldn't mention it, and they have [29] grown up ignorant, bewildered, self-conscious, uneasy and morbidly curious. Now suddenly they are given to understand that it is the most beautiful, the most divine, the most reliable thing in the world, and they are told to bank on it, trust it as they might trust in God, There is something sacred about it.

Leonora Eyles, Commonsense about Sex, 1933

[135] [I]t might be well here to say a little about the babies who 'play with themselves.' I often get letters from mothers in terrible distress about this; one just this month told me that a ten month's old baby touched her genital organs when being bathed and was discovered doing so while asleep. 'I feel heart-broken,' writes the mother. 'Daddy says she will grow up to be a prostitute. Do you think I ought to put her into a strict Home before it is too late?' My reaction to that letter was to want to get out the car, rush to that home and kidnap the baby!

[139] It is difficult to say at what age children should be taught about sex. So much depends on the atmosphere of the home and the mentality of the children. In a home where people [140] are natural about their bodies, and procreation is referred to naturally, there is never a time when the children have to be taken aside and told . . . .

[T]he two younger ones cannot remember a time when they didn't understand it, because they were told when so young, while the eldest one remembers vividly that she was in a certain room with me, and what I was doing at the time – which shows that she was told very wrongly, since it should not have been such an impressive revelation to her.

[149] If we bring up young people to understand the biological processes of their bodies, if we teach them to use those bodies so that they will be proud of them, there will be none of this park-railing business, none of these unwanted babies of boys and girls who have no wish for parenthood, none of these marriages entered into without a trace of mutual respect, and none of these miseries of impotence and half-life.

Susan Isaacs, Social Development in Young Children, 1933

[345] [I]t should be widely realised that masturbation does frequently occur in early childhood amongst both boys and girls, and amongst children who nevertheless grow up quite happily and satisfactorily. It is important that this should be known, both because of [346] its great theoretical significance, and because of the need of the children themselves to receive wise treatment from parents and educators . . . .

It is quite untrue that masturbation in itself can cause such serious disturbances of mind or body as are here attributed to it. When it is associated with serious mental disturbance or bodily ill-health . . . the key lies in the *phantasies* which the act of masturbation expresses, and the excessive anxiety arising from these phantasies.

243

The public attitude towards masturbation in little children tends to take one of two directions. The first, which is by far the commonest and most traditional, is the view that masturbation is not only a harmful, but a wicked thing, and must be instantly stopped if moral and physical ruin is not to follow. Now this attitude, although completely exaggerated, and false in its exaggeration, does recognise the truth that masturbation has a psychological significance, and that its intention is anti-social. The second attitude, very modern, and found in far fewer people – those, mostly, who feel themselves emancipated from sexual prejudices – is that the act of masturbation has no significance at all and is a purely localised sensation reflex which need not be commented on by educators and will die away of itself as the child gets older. Now this view is a probably far safer attitude for parents to take.

Sybil Neville-Rolfe, Why Marry?, 1935

[118] If, from earliest years, children know something of the inter-dependence of body and mind and grow up with an objective attitude to all the functions of the body, it prevents the physical side of sex being pushed [119] into the unconscious, and thereby reduces the likelihood of the adolescent being overwhelmed by desire for purely physical sex experience over which he or she appears to himself to have no control. It also tends to prevent the persistence of infantile habits, such as masturbation, or perverted friendships with persons of their own sex, into adolescence and maturity, as these can be definitely recognised for what they are.

Training of the emotions presents difficulties to the conscientious but untrained parent, and yet the foundation for any guidance we give in sex behaviour and for selection in marriage must be given in childhood and youth. It must include the formation of ideals, the encouragement of admiration for essential qualities in the opposite sex; the setting of a standard in marriage relations and in home life; the building up of a sense of social and personal responsibility in sex conduct for the health and welfare of future children.

Gladys M. Cox, Youth, Sex and Life, 1935

[v] [Y]ears ago, I regarded sex instruction of children and adolescents as quite unnecessary; the very suggestion of such an idea rather shocked me. My ignorance of human affairs at that time, and the sex inhibitions resulting from a lack of proper sex instruction in early youth, led me to assume that such matters could and should be left to instinct, that really 'nice' people were not troubled by sex and in fact hardly gave it a thought;

and that even marriage itself called for no specific instruction in the [vi] large majority of cases. As the result of years of experience and observation in medical practice, and of correspondence with some hundreds of unmarried and married people of all ages, I have changed my views completely . . . . It will perhaps be useful to quote from a few of the many letters I have received.

[. . .]

I am to be married in September, and although I love my man and feel I cannot live without him, yet I loathe and dread the physical side of marriage. I know very little about this – only what I have overheard in conversations at different times. My mother died some years ago, and although the aunt with whom I live is a perfect dear and has done her best to take my mother's place, I feel I cannot discuss such matters with her, as she is unmarried and was very embarrassed when I asked her to explain about menstruation. Perhaps you could recommend a book to help me.

[vii] I am absolutely ignorant of anything concerning the physical side of marriage. I do feel this very much, but I have never been told anything about the facts of sex or marriage by my mother . . . I sometimes, when I think of my approaching wedding, feel absolutely terrified and appalled.

[. . . .]

Although I am now twenty-eight, when I hear some girls of 17 and 18 talking I go quite hot realising what a lot I don't know, and it's so very easy to get rotten ideas from queer-minded folk – although I try and not listen, some of the things stick in my mind and pop out rather disconcertingly at times – then I get worried and wonder if they are right. I feel it would be fairer to him if I got to know more about *my* side – because I do so want to make him happy, and if I get the right idea from the start I have more chance.

[. . . .]

At the moment, the idea both frightens and revolts me. How I wish I had been taught something about sex when I was young! I remember once asking my mother where babies came from, and she looked so embarrassed and annoyed with me that I felt I had done wrong to ask, and that there was something horrible about the subject.

[. . . .]

[viii] My mother . . . has never explained marriage or the natural facts of sex to any of us. Therefore I feel very much in the dark and quite unprepared for marriage. I have tried to talk to my mother, but I find it so difficult at this stage, and she looks so very uncomfortable when I refer to sex matters.

Mary G. Cardwell, Some Aspects of Child Hygiene, *1935*

[76] [T]here are two extreme schools – the one which would withhold nothing from the child, and would even let it fill its mind by unsupervised reading of books dealing intimately with sex, and the other which would withhold *all* information from the developing mind, and in addition would surround the subject with an aura of shame and secretiveness. Both err by giving sex a wrong perspective – by hanging it on a lamp-post, or hiding it in a mist of negation.

At probably no other period of child development has youth more need for the presence of a normal decent-minded and sexually sane teacher, who can guide the bewildered adolescent with the twin arms of wise friendship and intelligent sympathy, than at the period of early maturity.

To be shamed by sex is harmful, to be smeared by it is worse, and that man or woman is a teacher in the highest sense who can hand out to the pupil the simple [77] facts of sexual existence in just the right measure – neither too little nor too much, who can associate them indelibly with the idea of God and reverence for the body, and who can stand to youth as his 'guide, philosopher, and friend' in his questionings, his difficulties, his inhibitions, and his desire for liberty.

Of all the mistakes in sex education there is probably none greater than that of prevarication.

The child mind is itself essentially truthful and demands truth in return, and is very slow to forgive rebuffs, evasions and fairy tales when, later, the truth does reach it (so often in ugly guise). Moreover, it is essentially and naturally curious, and with the process of growth and with the occurrences of human life there come the simultaneous questions: What? How? And Why?

[. . . .]

Most frequently the question is worded thus: 'Where do babies come from?' or, 'How are babies made?'; but quite often it is expressed much more crudely, but the crudity is shorn of offence by its beautiful simplicity and unself-consciousness.

[. . . .]

[78] The parent is the natural and obvious person to answer the questions of the small child, and those arising later from the manifestations of puberty . . . but unfortunately many parents find themselves unable to do this either by reason of ignorance or self-consciousness, and so the task comes within the scope of the teacher.

[. . . .]

1. The *attitude* of the teacher is most important. She should equip herself with the simple facts of sex . . . and should be able to answer questions without embarrassment and in an impersonal manner. She must be perfectly clear that there is nothing shameful about sex properly used,

and that its manifestations are an indication of a healthy body and correct functioning.

2. The teacher should answer questions according to the age of the child's growth, avoiding unnecessary detail, and always associating reproduction with reverence for God and the parents, together with gratitude and affection for the latter.

[. . . .]

[79] 3. The teacher should avoid using sex information as a medium for warnings of possible horrors and a negation of values, for to do this is merely to divert the child's curiosity from a healthy into an unhealthy channel, and in the case of girl children may sow the seeds of future fear and dislike of natural functions and of the duties of marriage.

4. *No details as to the physical act of reproduction should ever be given to a class and only rarely to individual adolescents*, since they cannot understand this part of the subject at their stage of growth, nor is it desirable they should.

It is sufficient for them to know that the child is the product of a joint action on the part of the parents . . . .

One cannot sufficiently stress the importance of the teacher producing an atmosphere in which sex is seen through the eyes of beauty, perfection, reticence, and worship of the God who created so beautiful a mechanism.

Always the use of sex should be associated with ideals of right living, healthy thinking, and of community rights and responsibilities.

Merell P. Middlemore, 'The Uses of Sensuality', 1936

[65] [G]enital tension is relieved by mastur- [66] bation. It is a normal activity of the young child, an important one also, for it discharges general tension so that body and mind are left at ease to work their best . . . .

I would let a little child masturbate if he wants to, simply making sure that he has enough diverting things to play with and that he is encouraged to scramble about the house and garden seeking his own adventures.

[69] Supposing that compulsive masturbation lasts over a long period, it is an indication that the child's fantasies are painful enough to cause him severe emotional strain; then the parents would be wise to seek skilled advice. They can also give support by being consistent in their attitude towards the habit, but there is no single attitude that is 'right' for all children. It seems sensible to think of prolonged masturbation as a disability and to offer the child alternative pleasures; if he accepts them, well and good. If, however, he cannot relinquish any of his genital stimulation it is unprofitable to nag about it.

Nina Searl, 'Questions and Answers', 1936

[114] Should the child's questions about sex be answered? (Whether we know it or not, whether we like it or not, they will be taken as answered in some degree whether we treat them with silence or with lengthy explanations, with avoidances, or with eagerness. That is, the child will in any case become aware of our emotional attitude to them.)

Before we answer this with an unconditional affirmative we should consider more closely the nature of the situation in which his questions are [115] put. Is the child totally ignorant of sexuality, and does his question indicate a void to be filled up? Or has he some knowledge and is puzzled by certain aspects of the matter and therefore needs to get it straightened out in his mind? Or is he worried about some of his own sexual and emotional feelings and thoughts connected directly and indirectly with sexuality, so that he wants to be reassured that these sexual feelings are not dangerous or wicked in himself or his parents?

[119] [T]hey should not parade before him unnecessarily the facts an the pleasures of sexual relations from which he is excluded. But neither should they go to the other extreme and hide or ignore the pleasure factors by giving him the sexual facts for which he asks only in the guise of biology, for instance. We do not really deceive him by so doing, for, in so far as his mind is open to the truth at all, he has his own sensations and emotions to give the lie to such an attempt, and we therefore only shake his belief in our sincerity. After all, the mainstay of a secure relation between children and ourselves is honesty, which until recent years has been allowed small scope in dealing with their sexual problems.

Susan Isaacs, 'The Nursery as Community', 1936

[200] [W]e are often asked about the sexual play of little children, whether they should be allowed to admire each other's naked bodies or look at or touch each other's genitals, or to play those favourite lavatory games of 'doctor' and 'mother and baby'.

This is a very difficult question to answer and no simple and general rule can be laid down about it . . . . It is . . . [201] by no means easy to offer general advice, although it is certain that harsh interference with child's play and curiosities may make him afraid of all physical forms of love, unable to fulfil his normal sexual functions in later life, and uneasy in his social contacts. It may confirm his works fears about the badness of his own and other people's bodies, and of sexual impulses generally.

On the other hand, there is no doubt that it would not help the child to *encourage* his sexual plays, since it is always difficult to know just what these mean to him.

[. . . .]

Perhaps the best general rule is to turn a blind eye to the talk and play of little children in these directions, leaving it to them to work out their [202] problems for themselves, save where the sexual element becomes so blatant and defiant and directed to the grown-ups that it seems clear that the child is deliberately drawing attention to it.

Margaret Cole, **Marriage: Past and Present, 1938**

[174] I do not mean . . . that the parents can explain the universe to the child; very often they cannot explain it to themselves, and very often, too, they are not at all good at explaining anything, particularly to their own children. Where they are not, it is better that the actual explanation should be done by somebody else, such as a teacher (the obvious alternative), or a social worker, scout leader, or something of the sort, or even a friend who is older and just far enough removed from the family circle for the child not to feel embarrassed in talking and in asking questions. A good many children are shy of talking to mother or father – and not only upon matters connected with sex . . . . [175] I do think that, where parents can do it, it is much better that the explaining should be done by them – if only because it can be done casually and naturally, as it happens, during washing or upon a walk, and not made into a formal lesson. But, though it is a good function for parents to fulfil, if they can, it is not one for which they are indispensable.

[239] You can tell children how their bodies [240] are made and what their bodies are for – though you must be prepared for them to pay little attention to your teaching, and to forget it all quite soon; you can save a boy of fourteen from thinking that he has developed a new and loathsome disease after his first nocturnal emission or a girl who has been kissed at a dance from believing that she will instantly produce a baby . . . . [Y]ou cannot convey the sensations and emotions of sex to the sexually immature, any more than you can the sensations of toothache or religious ecstasy to one who has yet to experience them. You cannot teach – at least, I do not see how you can teach – a boy how to make love to his future wife so that she will enjoy it, or a girl how to live with a man who may have had a very different training. You could not, even if there were fewer inhibitions in the way, and if you were a good deal more certain than most people are what exactly you wanted to teach; and there is some risk in imagining that 'sex-education in schools' will turn the trick and will send out the half-grown boy or girl adequately equipped to cope with the problems of life.

[. . . .]

[241] Children need to be provided with information and with the best information which we can give them. But besides information they need, as soon as they come to years of indiscretion, counsel and some ethical guidance.

Chapter Five

꙰

Sex in the Welfare State, 1945–1969

Introduction

The post-Second World War period is often thought of as an era of 'flight into domesticity' during which feminism was at an all-time low and ideas of female sexuality were strongly affected by Freudian views about the primacy of the vaginal orgasm. Nonetheless, some women doctors working within the marriage guidance and family planning movements were emphasizing an empirically based approach to female sexual satisfaction within marriage which placed the clitoris as central to achieving this. However, while writers might not be telling their readers to 'lie back and think of England', there was a discernible trend to downplay the necessity of female pleasure and to exhort women to be agreeably compliant to their husbands' demands in the interest of the good of the marriage as a whole. Although there were attempts to move divorce (already made somewhat more accessible to a great percentage of the population through new Legal Aid provisions) onwards from the continuing adversarial paradigm of innocent and guilty parties, this was not achieved until 1970, in spite of the long-drawn-out proceedings of the Royal Commission which reported in 1956.

While sex educators expressed concern over pre-marital 'petting', the very regularity within which it appears in texts suggests that this, and a growing degree of premarital experimentation, were being practised by many young women. A committed monogamous relationship was seen as capable of validating lesbian relationships, which might be constructed as antithetical to stigmatized promiscuous and public male homosexual behaviour. Birth control was increasingly acceptable within marriage, but the difficulties in obtaining in and its unreliability meant that illegal and unsafe abortion was still common and demands to reform the law continued. In the early 1960s the Brook Clinics were established to give advice and fittings to unmarried women, but there were very few of these and only in large cities. It was not until the late 1960s that any change was made in the extremely limited terms (still based on the 1930 circular) under which contraceptive information was available under the National Health Service. There were several attempts to get Private Member's Bills legalizing abortion through Parliament before David Steel (with government support) achieved this in 1967.

Although in 1951 a number of civil rights from which she had formerly been excluded were restored to the prostitute, these were soon effectively taken back by the retrograde measures implemented in the wake of the recommendations of the Wolfenden Committee. However, prostitution seems to have largely fallen off the map as a burning issue of concern – given the perception that it had largely been superseded by a more general 'promiscuity', which tended to be blamed for the perceptible rise, after 1960, in venereal diseases. The few works that specifically tackled the problem were much more about observations of the prostitute and her world, from a social work or criminological perspective (or, in the case of *Streetwalker*, self-reporting by a prostitute, if this is an accurate description of the work), and framed within a 'deviancy' model, rather than being something that might happen to any unfortunate woman as a consequence of wider social ills.

There was significant progress in overturning some of the more rigorous censorship of literature and the media during the 1960s. Nonetheless there continued to be a good deal of caution remaining among publishers as to what they deemed permissible and appropriate, which placed constraints on what writers might say and how far they might go.[1]

Other recommended resources

Report of Royal Commission on Marriage and Divorce, 1955. The Medical Women's Federation contributed a section on lesbianism to the British Medical Association's evidence on homosexuality to the Wolfenden Committee, and see the Report of the Wolfenden Committee also on prostitution. Women's magazines at this period were addressing issues such as abortion and lesbianism in articles, as well as dealing with issues of sex in their health advice and 'agony' columns.

---

1   The continuing existence of these constraints was mentioned to me in conversation by Claire Rayner, October 2004.

Marriage

Many of the old problems remain: disastrous honeymoon experiences, the mismatch between husbands' demands and wives' desires. In spite of the voices still promoting the importance of female sexual pleasure, a disturbing trend appears in several of these texts with the downplaying of the importance of the female orgasm and the importance of compliance with the husband's 'needs' as an important element in marriage. Also disturbing is the reported tendency of women to consider their 'frigidity' as something wrong with them. Hubback notes that finding the time and energy for mutually gratifying sex constitutes 'work' for the wife.

Helena Wright, More About the Sex Factor in Marriage, 1947

[10] Happiness in marriage is of such universal and [11] fundamental importance in the life of a nation that everything possible should be done to improve unsatisfactory conditions. As a first step, it should be everybody's business to learn the truth about the present degree of failure to attain sexual happiness in marriage which is so widely prevalent. Speaking very roughly, it is an estimate that fifty out of every hundred wives still go through their years of married life without discovering that physical satisfaction can, and should, be as real and vivid for them as it is for their husbands.

Sybil Neville-Rolfe, Social Biology and Welfare, 1949

[48] Both begin their married life with the same idea, if, that is, the woman has *any* ideas; early experiences of intercourse prove that the husband always gets an orgasm, but that his wife, even with perfectly successful previous caressing of the erogenous zones, has to admit, if she is frank, that she feels nothing whatever that could called pleasant in her vagina. What happens next? Generally, nothing. The first experiences are merely repeated, and a characteristic attitude of mind becomes formed, amusingly different in each of the partners. The wife, when she finds that time does not alter matters, and that her vagina continues to be lacking in sensation, almost invariably blames herself. She feels inferior, she says to herself that she's a failure, and more often than not, she thinks that she is unique in her unhappy experience. The husband, with nothing to complain of in his own sensations, has no inclination to criticize himself . . . . [49] To neither of them does the vital question present itself, 'is the vagina the natural place where a woman should feel an orgasm at the beginning of her sexual experience?'

253

[145] If a high standard of adjustment within marriage is required, some failures are inevitable, but it is still to be proved that the increase in the number of divorces . . . that have been granted since the Matrimonial Causes Act widened the grounds for divorce, do in fact indicate any increase in broken homes due to marriage maladjustment. An additional divorce is not necessarily an additional broken home. The home may have been broken beforehand.

Joan Malleson, Any Wife or Any Husband, *1950*

[22] There are a great many women who are able and anxious to have intercourse, but do not experience real sexual feeling during the act, or have insufficient feeling to obtain a climax. Although some of these women are liable to develop symptoms of strain, many seem to be quite unaffected, and these can rest assured that neither they or their husband need worry about the matter. Fortunately, this condition usually allows full and happy sexual union and women of this sort can be entirely satisfactory partners to their husbands – sometimes even more so than women who have strong necessities of their own. This lack of response in no way interferes with childbearing, nor does it generally mean that a woman is not 'in love'; indeed, such women often get great gratification and tenderness from their sexual life.

[56] [W]omen are in general slower to be roused than men; their feelings are most stirred by courtship, intimate talk and personal attentions. They are liable to have great variation in their erogenous zones (the areas of the body from which pleasure is derived), and may therefore require a very individual approach before they are likely to be fully roused. Husbands who are not yet instructed on these points would be wise to learn . . . Most books on these subjects describe the discomfort and resentment of a wife who is left dissatisfied whilst her husband sleeps contentedly. The descriptions of suffering are accurate where the woman's capacity for orgasm has not been appreciated or satisfied by the husband. But of those without orgasmic capacity, fortunately it is but a very small minority who suffer in this way. It is well known that some women experience phases of increased desire at different times in their menstrual cycles . . . . The wise husband takes notice of such variations.

[92] [T]he modern overvaluation of orgasm is disturbing, since it puts a false emphasis on one limited factor in the whole sexual relationship. Such teaching tacitly implies that the mere presence or absence of orgasm should be the criterion of successful intimacy. Apart from the fact the orgasm is by no means possible for many women, people cannot measure

their deepest feeling by a physical response . . . .

[93] Such teaching tends also to belittle some of the deepest ties experienced by married people . . . . Many women value the intimacies of a rich sexual relationship and the experiences of childbearing far more highly than they do the attainment of orgasm.

Mary Macaulay, The Art of Marriage, 1952

[42] Whether or not the wife reaches what is known as the climax or orgasm, sexual intercourse between husband and wife can and should be utterly satisfying. This physical union between two people who love each other can have a significance far beyond its actual physical sensations . . .
.

[43] Many people, however, miss this free gift of love because they are seeking a physical thrill and satisfaction which often takes much longer to achieve . . . . It is, of course, ideal when the sexual side of marriage is mutually satisfying, and desirable for both husband and wife to learn to do all they can to make it so, but it often takes time.

Many husbands and wives indeed never experience the joy and comfort of physical love mutually satisfied. They miss something very precious . . . . Others, although they enjoy love-making, find it difficult to adjust to the point at which they both desire intercourse simultaneously, or are fully aroused together . . . . [44] In the meantime both husband and wife can appreciate and enjoy the blessing of the union they achieve even while learning the art of giving each other physical satisfaction.

Leonora Eyles, The New Commonsense about Sex, 1956

[53] Now to come down to more concrete and detailed snags in marriage. And first of all I would put the surprisingly general dislike of women for sexual expression of any sort. Out of, say, a thousand letters a week about people's troubles, six hundred would be from wives who said 'I love my husband, and we have a charming home and three wonderful children. But it is all spoilt for me because I do so hate bedtime and all it implies.'

[54] There are several general reasons for this state of things. Often the trouble starts very early in marriage through clumsiness and lack of knowledge . . . . Often it comes from the nasty, rather dirty ideas girls have got from other girls in their youth or from the mother's attitude towards the girl's body in childhood – but that trouble is not so common as it was in my youth . . . . But if she will read, and think, *really* think, and if her husband will be gentle and considerate these false ideas will disappear in time.

I have already dealt with the subject of boredom in intercourse and with the really shocking state of things when a husband demands sexual co-operation from his wife without making it desirable for her. After that cause, by far the commonest is the fear of pregnancy especially after a woman has had several children.

Morwenna Bielby, 'What is Christian Marriage?', 1956

[14] We must emphasize this fact about the true nature of sexual love, because Christians, perhaps Christian women especially, have often been so impressed by its dangers (and it *has* its dangers) that they have tended to minimize and even to deny its importance. This may be in part because some women still have a 'hangover' from the totally wrong idea that it was somehow not quite nice for a woman to enjoy sex (though nowadays there is a tendency for some books and some advisers on sex to go to the other extreme, and make loving wives, who find their greatest joy in the self-giving of marriage and in motherhood, feel guilty because according to the text-books they are 'cold'!).

Judith Hubback, Wives Who Went to College, 1957

[148] Sex fulfilment in marriage has the effect, among other things . . . of releasing various tensions and enabling the two partners to achieve the right amount of general, as well as immediate, relaxation. Its positive contribution to serenity is obvious. But the taboos which surround us on the subject are very considerable, so that it is not yet really openly and widely acknowledged that a normal sex life involves for some wives a considerable outlay of nervous and physical energy. Without sex they would be less happy, or at any rate live on a different plane. But with sex they must reserve a certain amount of liveliness for comparatively late in the evening. Tiredness, physical or nervous, is found by many wives to be one of the worst enemies of sexual pleasure and fulfilment. Therefore, the wife who wishes not only to derive the fullest pleasure from her husband's love but also to afford him the maximum satisfaction must normally reckon not to give herself to the full to her children and other daytime occupations. The difficulty of insuring this reserve of physical, nervous and emotional freshness for sex life is perhaps one reason for some wives' appearance of strain.

Doris Odlum, **Journey through Adolescence, 1957**

[155] The attitude to sex of a great many girls is extremely glamorous and unrealistic . . . . When they meet it in reality they often find that it falls far short of their expectations. Young women say to me: 'I thought it would be something wonderful but I can't see what they [156] make all the fuss about.' Unfortunately thousands of marriages are to a great extent spoilt by the fact that the wife does not fully participate in intercourse, and does not derive any pleasure or satisfaction from it.

[. . . .]

[157] [I]f she cannot enjoy her sex life she feels that she is letting her husband down, and also feels inadequate. Her resentment is then directed against him because he wants sex from her that she is apt to regard as a selfish and even lustful demand. She also feels self-pity and a sense of deprivation because he is enjoying something which she [158] is missing. Thus relationships between them almost inevitably become strained, however much affection and goodwill they may have for each other.

V. M. Hughes, **Women in Bondage, 1958**

[25] In most other species the female controls sexual activity and will not have courtship except for reproduction, which is kept strictly confined to a season . . . . In our species the female has no such authority; on the contrary, her muscular inferiority puts her at the mercy of the male, and so, unlike other male mammals, he can force his desires on the female. On the other hand, unless *he* wants indulgence, it cannot take place. No similar convenient dispensation of nature makes it impossible for him to have access to *her* person if she does not wish. He may even assault her, her mind may be filled with terror and loathing, but her treacherous reproductive system will be beyond control, as ready for fertilisation as if he were someone she loved . . . .

Even if civilised man does not always use his muscular superiority, that he must often employ some kind of moral threat is obvious from . . . the frequent masculine [26] complaint about the 'frigidity', or unwillingness, of women. Evidently much lovemaking is forced on women who do not want it.

It is always taken for granted that of course the woman is wrong in being 'frigid'. Even those 'enlightened' authorities who blame the man's methods of lovemaking and say he ought to 'woo' her, assume that her 'frigidity' is something that she should be persuaded out of. No-one seems to consider it natural, – something to which the man, rather, ought to accommodate himself by demanding satisfaction far less often.

Mary Macaulay, **Marriage for the Married,** *1964*

[34] Some brides and bridegrooms return from their honeymoon with the marriage still unconsummated because nervous apprehension has prevented one of them from being able to play his or her part adequately . . . . It is much more common, however, for a bride to confide in her friends that although she has not actually disliked her first experience of sex, she cannot understand what other people find in it that they think is so marvellous. Naturally, if this is how she feels about it, she and her husband are both disappointed. If they can be patient for a while and continue to make love they will soon find that time and practice bring them the satisfaction they seek.

One simple piece of advice would help all married lovers who are feeling a little disappointed – to make love freely and tenderly no matter whether the ultimate act of sex is successful or not. It is when intercourse is made an end in itself that it is most liable to fail. Love can be communicated through every touch, and to lie in each other's arms and caress one another without worrying about anything at all can give exquisite pleasure. Sometimes desire will arise gradually or suddenly and a union be completed quite unexpectedly when nervousness and inhibitions are forgotten.

[. . .]

[36] After a while a husband can usually learn to take more time and arouse his wife by making love to her in ways they will discover for themselves and she will be as ready for him as he for her before the final act of union. Adjustment of this kind takes time, the length of which varies from one marriage to another. Some couples need much patience before it is achieved.

Many women find that the joy they are able to receive from giving their husbands so much happiness is sufficient compensation for any disappointment in their own reactions. If a wife can be patient and welcoming and try to respond to her husband's lovemaking and learn how best to give *him* pleasure, she will forget about herself and in her self-forgetfulness will eventually lose her inhibitions and find her own sexual satisfaction. If, however, she lies like a dummy, feeling resentful and cheated, she will miss all she is longing to find. Even [37] 'trying to relax', which is so often advised, tends to fix her mind on herself whereas if she tries to study her husband and respond to his desire she will naturally move towards him instead of drawing away.

[91] Husbands and wives who are able throughout the years to bring warmth and ardour to their lovemaking, and lose themselves in the joy of happy sexual intercourse, have a safety valve which helps them to resolve all their other difficulties. Much of what has been written in recent years

about the sex act has been useful and helpful, but much less has been harmful or has been [92] wrongly interpreted so as to make lovemaking too self-conscious and technical.

[. . . .]

[93] Too much emphasis has been laid on the importance of female orgasm. Most women will eventually find themselves roused to climax if they enjoy loving their husbands, but for some wives this is not necessary in order to feel satisfied and happy. If they are physically roused so that they feel frustrated when they cannot reach a climax, it means they are very nearly at the point of orgasm, and stimulation of the clitoris will provide the solution for their difficulty.

Ann Allen, People on Honeymoon, *1968*

[44] [M]y disappointment was so great that now, years later, I still feel cheated and resentful.

The first night of our honeymoon, to my dismay, [45] my husband's sexual activities were over in a few minutes . . . . Having satisfied himself he promptly fell asleep. As the days passed it became obvious he thought this was something for a man to enjoy, but not a woman. All that he required of me was to be *there*. His love-making was non-existent . . . . For me, an ardent woman expecting to share his pleasure, his attitude was insulting beyond words.

[45] Englishmen have a reputation for acting like a bull in a china shop, and it is only too true, and that goes for their love-making and the rude, thoughtless way they go about sex. That night, for me, was shattering beyond words.

Helena Wright, Sex and Society, *1968*

[68] It is only comparatively recently that women have become aware that sexual enjoyment in marriage was a possibility for them. Whatever prospects of happiness marriage offered to brides before this awakening, physical satisfaction in intercourse was certainly not among them.

[. . . .]

A generation ago . . . a large proportion of wives who found no pleasure in intercourse made no complaint; they expected nothing better. Now the situation is almost the reverse. Largely owing to the initiative of the family planning movement, the spread of sexual education has revealed to women that their natural birthright is sexual equality in enjoyment and fulfilment.

[73] [T]he rapidity with which women are finding that they no longer need to be either unwilling mothers or unsatisfied partners is one of the most hopeful signs that social patterns of behaviour are capable of change for the better.

A new concept of stability and happiness in marriage and parenthood is on the horizon.

[99] [S]ociety should change its attitude and regard marriage as an attainment that has to be deserved, and whose possible success should be well tested beforehand for a reasonably long time . . . . The present arrangement . . . makes no allowance for the frequency with which a first sexual involvement proves to be of a transitory nature, and it fails to recognize the value of a mature judgement of partnership based on the comparison of several previous experiences.

The prevalence of ever-expanding Marriage Guidance Councils, and the growing necessity of providing sessions for consultations on marital difficulties found by family planning clinics, is eloquent evidence that successful marriage is a complicated and exacting enterprise. Surely it is reasonable to expect that if marriage were regarded with something of the seriousness that preparation for a profession always demands, the long-term results might be better?

It is to be hoped that in the course of time . . . a different conception of marriage from the present one will gradually emerge . . . . [100] [M]arriage will only be undertaken by partners who have given themselves enough experience of each other to have a reasonable prospect of staying happily together for life.

Rosalie Taylor, Inside Information on Sex and Birth Control, 1969 [unpaginated]

[Section 23] Sometimes the woman coming for advice on her problem of frigidity will tell me that she herself is quite content to be as she is – has no wish to become passionate for her own sake, but since her frigidity makes her husband miserable, she'd like for his sake to be altered so that he can be satisfied. 'I don't mind for myself at all as long as *he* is happy . . . .'

Of course, it may not really be so hopeless – behind this front of 'only for her husband's sake' she may really be wanting to have a good sexual experience for herself but does not feel she has a right to ask it for herself – she can only do so if she justifies it by an unselfish motive – to establish her husband's happiness for her husband's sake.

Desire, pleasure and satisfaction

This continues to be a problem, exacerbated, if anything, by women's increasing expectations of sexual pleasure. Although ideas of vaginal versus clitoral orgasm are present, and addressed in several of the texts excerpted here, the women writing them are usually not prepared to condemn clitoral orgasm but to see it as a good thing and a necessary stage towards the even more elusive vaginal variety. The persistence of the possibility of sexual desire and pleasure in the later years – and even the possible improvement of sex life at this time of life – also continues to feature.

Helen Wright, More About the Sex Factor in Marriage, *1947*

[14] *Women who expect nothing.*
'Do you enjoy having connection with your husband, as you should do?' If the patient belongs to the group under discussion, she usually looks quite blank and says nothing. The question is repeated. She realises that *something* is meant and asks 'Why, doctor? *What is there to enjoy?*' It is evident that it has never occurred to her, nor, presumably, to her husband, that she should have any part at all in sex-pleasure . . . .

[15] They endure intercourse quite patiently, for the sake of their husband's pleasure, but, when asked directly, they confess that they would be relieved if it never occurred again, and, as it is, they always hope that their husbands will want them as rarely as possible.

[16] [Extracts from letters received]
'He did what he came for speedily and left me. Not once did I get satisfaction, nor did it ever strike him that I could, or should. He merely used me and left me, and perhaps a baby might result! Occasionally I did begin to get some sensations just as he finished, and on one or two occasions was compelled to satisfy myself or I should have been unable to get to sleep. I soon got to hate his coming to me and to loathe the whole business.'
[. . . .]
[17] 'Although I have a great desire to "meet" my husband, when we are together it seems quite impossible to do unless I force myself, which is so unnatural. Yet when he is away at sea for a few weeks, I can dream I am with him. This dream can be so natural and everything normal as it should be. But when I am with him I can never get a full satisfaction of intercourse unless I force myself . . . My husband says I can buy tablets to help me, without having to force myself. Is this so?'

[46] There seem to be three misunderstandings which occur most frequently, and these are: failure to grasp the difference between sexual response in the erogenous zones, and an orgasm; lack of understanding of the unique rôle played by the clitoris, and a more or less unconscious adherence to a preconceived mental picture of what a woman *ought* to feel during sexual intercourse, which turns out to be based on the male instead of the female pattern.

[49] Attempts to follow the male pattern have been forcing women into making two fundamental mistakes; they have ignored the function of the clitoris, and just because the vagina is the natural stimulator for the penis, they have expected that it shall also be the region of primary female orgasm.

[52] [W]omen, even those who describe themselves as happy and satisfied in their marriages, often give the most curious answers when [53] asked where they feel an orgasm . . . [T]hey try to locate the memory of their feelings and after considerable thought they say, either, 'Oh! I feel it everywhere,' or, 'I feel it in my *head* of course,' or they point vaguely to the lower part of the abdomen and say in a puzzled tone, 'I think it's somewhere about here.'

[60] [I]t is . . . necessary to prove at first hand the truth of the statement that the clitoris does possess a unique kind of sensitiveness. It is best to do this with something other than the owner's finger, because the finger-tip is, naturally, itself sensitive to touch, and if it is used, there may be confusion of effect between the feeling finger and the part felt. Any small, smooth object will do, such as an uncut pencil, or a tooth-brush handle. The procedure is one of comparison of response elicited by a very light touch. One hand separates the outer labia without touching the inner ones, and the other hand holding the chosen object, touches first one inner lip and then the other, and then the clitoris, through or under its hood. If the hand movements are watched in the mirror it is easy to get the touches accurately in the right places, but without a mirror [61] and a good light, it is not easy, because an inexperienced woman has practically no sense of accurate position if she tries to use a finger unguided by her eyes. The effect observed is that the instant the clitoris is touched a peculiar and characteristic sensation is experienced which is different in essence from touches on the labia or anywhere else. This difference has to be experienced; it cannot be described in words.

A simple experiment of this kind will prove to everyone who tries it that the clitoris *is* an organ of unique sensitiveness. The next step is to discover what happens when it is given the right kind of stimulus necessary to produce its full functioning.

[63] [S]ince the clitoris is the essential organ of sexual sensation in women, and that rhythmic friction is the only stimulus to which it can react, orgasm failure at the outset of sexual experience is unavoidable if the clitoris is not discovered and correctly stimulated.

The full secret of sexual happiness for women will, however, only be revealed when the meaning of the word rhythm in this connection has been explained and thoroughly understood.

[66] That many couples, enlightened enough to know of the existence of the clitoris, and wishing to use it, do, in fact make attempts along these lines, is all too true. The usual result is painful embarrassment for the wife. [67] She is immediately aware of keen sensitiveness to touch in the clitoris region, and she gets fleeting seconds of genuine pleasure, but the irritating effect of movements that are sometimes right and sometimes wrong, gives her a predominant feeling of frustration.

The best way, therefore, to find the right rhythm is to use a method of finger-caressing which allows the wife to initiate and to guide the movements.

[73]The experience of wives who have succeeded in attaining vaginal sensitivity and who are also able to have an orgasm in the vagina whenever they wish, should be able to teach us a lot. Comparison of a number of such histories seems to suggest that there is a latent connection between the spontaneous, easy response of the clitoris, and the unawakened sensitivity of the [74] vagina . . . . [S]uccess in attaining a clitoris orgasm is the essential feminine experience which demonstrates sexual capacity, and that success automatically removes the haunting sense of inferiority and failure which is otherwise inevitable. Every wife who has learnt that the behaviour of her clitoris is reliable finds it easier to believe that one day her vagina might also become alive.

[87] Girls are generally unconscious of sexual desire until some man has [88] awakened their interest, and shown them, by the giving and receiving of physical affection, how vividly and joyfully their bodies can respond . . . .

This seems to be a natural condition, and without instruction and initiation, millions of women get no further in their sexual development. Here we have one of the most important reasons for the necessity of education in sexual matters. It is the inescapable duty and privilege of the older members of the community to teach young people the nature and the technique of feminine sexual response.

Leonora Eyles, Unmarried But Happy, 1947

[88] I have during the past twenty-five years had many confidences from single women . . . . [M]any of them spoke very frankly of . . . unbearable physical distress. This, I know, will shock some people; they do not accept the fact that women either married or single, can be physically distressed by [89] sexual desire.

[. . . .]

Very few married women will admit to any desire for sexual intercourse at all, though I have noticed . . . that women are getting much less reticent about it and even in some cases recognise it as a normal and natural thing. But most unmarried women would neither mention it nor admit it even to themselves . . . .

Centuries of civilisation have implanted in a woman . . . [90] the longing for everything that mating and motherhood brings – the sexual satisfaction, the mutual dependence of husband and wife, the joy and thrill of motherhood with its pride and its terrors and bitter disappointments. In the single woman these desires and needs are dammed back and can either cause intense unhappiness, even derangement, or be sublimated into channels that will bring happiness and self-fulfilment.

Violet D. Swaisland, 'The Adolescent Girl', 1949

[284] Most psychologists agree that there exists a natural barrier in the girl's mind against the first sex experience, and that this has to be broken down by her lover before she will willingly give herself to him. The strength of this barrier depends largely on external circumstances, but if from early adolescence the girl has developed a measure of fastidiousness, it is likely to prove, not indeed insuperable, but at least a restraining influence. Most girls, too, are aware that the first experience is likely to be accompanied by pain, and apart from this there is a natural fear of the unknown, and of taking a step which can never be retraced.

On the other hand many a girl, largely because of her maternal instinct, is inclined to give the man she loves what he asks for, and this desire tends to break down the barrier even where her own sexual desires have not been aroused.

Laura Hutton, 'The Unmarried', 1949

[427] Sexual desire is a normally recurring phenomenon in the body, and does not always wait upon the presence of a beloved person to make itself felt. Thoughts and fantasies may help to awaken it. What is the unmarried woman to do about this?

[. . . .]

The best advice that one can give to the middle-aged woman on the subject is to my mind the following: If from time to time you feel the need to relieve the physical stirrings of sex, do not worry or feel guilty about it. You are normal, and have the normal physical desires of a woman. Do not wage an endless war against them, getting more and more tense and miserable. If you can, relieve them, without dwelling too much on it. Then forget about it, and pass to the next job in hand. It is not wicked, for sex is not evil. It is not even important, except in so far as you worry about it.

Laura Hutton, 'Sex in Middle Age', 1949

[447] Many women assume that with the cessation of the periods, marking the end of the child-bearing period, all sex-life must end for them. Some are disconcerted and some are relieved to find that this is not so, but that sexual desire remains, and may even, in fact, be intensified and more frequent . . . . It is quite characteristic of this time of life that there is a flare-up of sexual desire, and with it a longing for romance and passion which [448] a woman may find very disturbing, and feel to be very reprehensible. [. . . .]

Many women, as a result of their upbringing, have a strong feeling that it is humiliating for them to feel more desire for their husbands than the latter appear to have for them, and hence they will do all they can to conceal this desire – at great cost to themselves. Both they and their husbands may be quite unaware that the intense irritability which so torments the home . . . is the result of frustration and of the unsatisfied need for a relaxation which only sexual expression can give.

In due course the fires will die down, but there is no rule as to the age at which this will happen.

Joan Malleson, Any Wife or Any Husband, 1950

[20] Many women are unable to get full satisfaction during the sexual act, and although in some cases this may not cause serious disappointment, occasionally symptoms of nervous strain begin to show. Very often lack of knowledge is all that is responsible for the difficulty.

Perhaps the most frequent cause of their dissatisfaction is due to failure to understand the structure and necessities of their [21] own bodies; or, alternatively, to lack of such knowledge on the part of the husband. A woman is usually slower in reaching sexual feeling than a man, and care and judgment may be required to arouse her . . . . Some people mistakenly believe that the straight-forward act of intercourse should be all that a woman requires to reach a satisfactory 'climax'. This seems to be true only in about one-third of all women. The majority find their greatest sexual feeling is situated in the front and outer part of the vaginal passage, at the sensitive small area which is medically termed the clitoris.

[. . . .]

The only purpose of these external parts is that when they are stimulated by gentle stroking with the fingertips, the woman's sexual feeling will be roused. Nature has placed them there entirely for this purpose – indeed, this is their only use – and the person who thinks that they are not to be enjoyed or touched is defying natural laws. Many wives are aware that the full use of the outer clitoral area will alone bring them satisfaction, yet they are too afraid either to ask, or to allow their husbands to touch this part of their body in the proper way.

[57] [T]here are some women who have feeling only when the cervix itself is stimulated. Such women may not get orgasm until they learn to relax and shorten the passage . . . or unless they try intercourse above the husband.

[. . . .]

[58] [I]n the vagina, movement or friction will – *when there is no inhibition* – arouse a special *quality* of feeling which is described as 'sexual desire.' Once started, the need is for this stimulation to increase until satisfaction is finally obtained.

Vaginal anaesthesia varies in degree and in persistence. In some women the passage remains completely without sensation throughout their whole adult life. Others may be astonished by an occasional dawning of feeling, perhaps during an erotic dream, or sometimes quite unrelated to sexual intimacy at all . . . . In other women a little feeling may be aroused if they are helped by a long and competent intercourse. In others, once or twice in a lifetime, orgasm may occur during [59] intercourse quite unaccountably, when neither the emotional nor the physical condition *seem* to have changed in any way.

[. . . .]

Women who have vaginal anaesthesia always feel reassured when they learn that their difficulty is a [60] common one. It is a help to them too, to know that little will be achieved by *trying*. Provided the knowledge of both partners – and as far as possible their technique – is adequate, it is much better for both that any effort to achieve orgasm should be abandoned. Women who so frequently assert that they have 'tried and tried' are happier when they cease in their attempt; indeed for many women, orgasm is an occasional chance by-product of a happy union, but not one which they claim as an established right. The woman who gives herself readily and with love is likely to have greater returns than one who seeks and seeks . . . .

Newly married women quite commonly have no vaginal feeling, a fact which is hardly surprising when one considers how completely the vagina has been protected from sight, touch and stimulation. Indeed, many girls grow up without consciously recognising its existence . . . . Hence, with newly married women some weeks or months may pass before the vagina learns to perceive normal sensation, and this should not cause surprise. If a woman is experienced and has borne children but has never known real sexual feeling in the passage, the chances that she may not do so are obviously considerable. Some women of this sort continue to value their sexual relations greatly and to moisten readily as though they were entirely responsive to their husbands . . . .

[61] The group of women most in need of help are those who get fully aroused but cannot achieve satisfaction either from vaginal stimulation or from the clitoris. For them the act of union may come to be a most disturbing experience, followed often by depression or irritability after a sleepless night. Congestion may cause an aching back and pelvis the next day. There is no doubt at all that if a woman, left in this situation, is capable of giving herself orgasm in any way, she should certainly do so.

[[64] [I]t may happen that a woman will say to the doctor: 'Our sexual life is all wrong,' or 'no good,' when all that she means is that she is one for whom the clitoral orgasm is possible, whereas a vaginal one is not. These doubts may be responsible, too, for a wide-spread belief that vaginal feeling will not be established if clitoral stimulation is permitted. I have found no evidence to support this view; but on the contrary have met numerous women who, after the establishment of vaginal orgasm, have partly or wholly abandoned the wish for clitoral stimulation.

[105] Many women believe that when they reach the change of life they will lose their sexual desire, or their capacity as a wife will in some way fail. Neither belief is true. It is possible for women of any age to enjoy sexual feeling; this will become less urgent and less vigorous, but it need not fail.

M. B. Smith, The Single Woman of Today: Her Problems and Adjustment, 1951

[37] The vital problem at the heart of the adjustment or non-adjustment of the spinster is that the reproductive urge ranks equally with the self-preservation instinct. They are the two most primitive, and therefore most powerful, forces in human life. They are deeply unconscious, and thus not easily controlled or sublimated. They find indirect and often dangerous outlets when repressed. It is acknowledged to be more difficult to divert or sublimate the sexual than the instinct of self-preservation.

Mary Macaulay, The Art of Marriage, *1952*

[54] Many inexperienced girls still seem to enter marriage in one of two frames of mind. Some are ignorant and afraid of sex . . . . The other group have read books on the sexual aspect of marriage, and expect to experience the most satisfying physical ecstasies immediately they enter married life. Most girls in the first group are reassured and comforted and gradually won over to a more receptive attitude . . . . Many of the others appear later in our consulting rooms complaining that they must have something wrong with them as, physically, marriage has been a great disappointment to them . . . .

The lack of sexual response in early marriage where there [55] is no conscious nervousness is due to inhibition, sometimes caused by fear or shame carried over from a childhood experience, but more often merely the result of a spartan British upbringing.

V. M. Hughes, Women in Bondage, *1958*

[26] Women's 'frigidity' is not unnatural . . . . [W]omen can have, can be expected to have, no instinct towards frequent lovemaking, and if they are to remember they are animals, they might as well remember the whole truth about animals, which is that [27] the female usually decrees when courtship shall take place, and decrees it only at certain seasons. Man has not only somehow obtained unnatural power over the female in this matter, so that he has her submitting to his desires all the time, but he actually has the effrontery to complain because she does not enjoy it.

Where women are 'odd' is not in being 'frigid', but in letting men dominate them, letting *men* decide how often they must submit to male desire and fertilisation, whatever their own wishes.

[30] Physical 'love', apart from these difficulties, is likely to mean to the woman something very different from what it means to a man. He always has satisfaction, she perhaps does not. Thus the process is, to her, not only without pleasure, but meaningless. She cannot understand what he sees in it, cannot understand the nature of his pleasure . . . .

Even if she has pleasure it is still questionable. Her body has on the first occasion to be heedlessly ruptured as though [31] it were a mere object for nature's use, and man's, not her instrument, as though her pain did not matter.

Mary Macaulay, **Marriage for the Married,** *1964*

[158] Wives who have been uninterested in sex in their youth are often much more responsive in their forties and many marriages are happier and better adjusted than ever before.

Claire Rayner, **Parent's Guide to Sex Education,** *1968*[2]

[38] Many girls find that they can bring about a very pleasurable orgasm . . . by manual stimulation of the clitoris. . . . [39] I would never suggest that a mother should let her daughter definitely know that she is aware that she masturbates . . . . However, if she can find some way of letting her know that this is a perfectly normal practice and one that virtually all women have used at some time or another (most commonly in puberty), she will help her a great deal.

[96] It is very necessary to explain to girls that, for a woman, sexual satisfaction is not made up only of sexual intercourse . . . . For her, total pleasure consists of sexual intercourse plus pregnancy plus childbirth plus the feeding of a baby. If a girl can be helped to grasp this idea, she will then see that intercourse with someone for whom she has no real emotional feeling, will not be completely satisfying . . . .

She needs to understand that however equal with men women may become in a social or professional sense, they can never be sexually equal.

[99] [A] girl needs to love her partner and build a relationship with him before she can really enjoy intercourse with him. So her drive appears to be much less. This is why so many people believe that a woman doesn't have a strong sex drive, but not only do they have one; it is sometimes stronger than a man's.

Helena Wright, **Sex and Society,** *1968*

[119] In women . . . the acquiring of pleasure in intercourse is a matter of learning and skill, and has nothing to do with the life of the egg-cell. There is, therefore, no reason why physical pleasure should be affected at all when fertility stops, and indeed there are reasons why it can be increased after the menopause. When fertility is finished, the whole stream of energy

---

2   Claire Rayner wishes to state that these comments should not be taken as representing her current (2004) views on the subject.

connected with child bearing in thought and action is released; fatigue and anxiety about care and education of the family are generally over, and the woman, for the first time since her first conception, is emotionally free to give energy and attention to skill and partnership in intercourse.

Rosalie Taylor, Inside Information on Sex and Birth Control, *1969 [unpaginated]*

[Section 3] Nowadays the much more active rôle of woman in lovemaking is both recognized and expected . . . . [I]n the sexual relationship she looks for an equally active pleasure and fulfilment. If she is not stirred or excited by lovemaking, she finds it difficult to reconcile herself to a passive rôle or indeed feels not only frustrated but often guilty and has a sense of personal failure.

However, her ability to give herself up to the enjoyment of lovemaking, and her capacity for a spontaneous welling up of sexual excitement, may be seriously handicapped if she is anxious or frightened, or preoccupied or suffering from some unacknowledged resentments or some uncertainty of herself as a woman. Then, instead of her vaginal entrance being soft, moist and yielding, it is dry, stiff, and held tight and resistant to man's penis, and penetration may be difficult and painful, and pleasure not achieved at all.

[Section 18] It is often easy for a woman to be aroused sexually and to receive an orgasm from the caressing of her clitoris but the feeling does not always come so easily from the vagina itself.

Since the clitoris is on the outside of the body, outside the vagina, it is somehow a familiar part of the body that has grown up with the little girl and into womanhood. The vagina, on the other hand, is the unknown hidden mysterious part of herself and the feeling that is released there, one knows not how and why, is frightening and mysterious too, unfamiliar and leaving her out of control of herself and vulnerable.

[. . . .]

It certainly does not seem that excluding and eliminating the sexual excitedness of the clitoris will help her to achieve vaginal excitedness. It is rather a question of bringing out and understanding the anxieties which block the progress of the feeling from the clitoris to the vagina, which might help.

[Section 21] Sometimes . . . a woman will explain that she does experience pleasure and even an orgasm from caressing of the clitoris but once her husband enters her vaginal passage, the feeling either goes altogether or does not come to anything, and leaves her with a sense of being cheated and frustrated when intercourse is over.

She may have grown increasingly anxious about this difficulty and some-times she is angry with her husband or herself. She tries harder and harder during intercourse to will her body into the right movements in the hope that they will evoke the 'right' feeling. She 'concentrates'. Unfortunately, the more she tries, the more the feeling eludes her.

[. . . .]

She may in fact already have experienced a lot of pleasure and comfort from a clitoral orgasm – but she is not content with this and may even forbid it. There seems to be a strange kind of 'morality' about 'good' and 'bad' sexual feeling – clitoral pleasure is felt to be 'bad', in some way immoral, and women will even forbid their husbands to give them this satisfaction from a fear that it would be habit-forming and stop them achieving the good, the moral 'vaginal' orgasm.

But the whole problem of reaching vaginal feeling is linked up with finding a way of achieving a kind of un-anxious passivity and acceptance – a giving up of watchfulness, of managing oneself and one's husband, so that in a relaxed quietness there might be the beginning of an unknown, uncontrolled feeling which could grow into a vaginal orgasm.

Heterosexual relationships outside marriage

During this period, considerable concern is manifested about the growing amount of premarital sexual activity, with the concomitant problem of illegitimate births occurring over a wide social spectrum There is also, perhaps paradoxically, anxiety about the prevalence of non-coital sexual practices ('petting') among the young. Questions about 'trial marriage' also feature. There is also some recognition of affairs of unmarried older woman with careers.

Leonora Eyles, **Unmarried But Happy,** *1947*

[15] The girl who 'lives with' a man today is often self-supporting. She is a woman who would, in a saner world, have married, had children and been a pillar of whatever social activity went on in her neighbourhood . . . . There is very little glamour about her life; she hasn't even the thrill of 'sinning gloriously' as sentimentalists [16] used to call it 'for love'. Because she doesn't believe in sin and soon begins to think she would willingly barter the glory for a little security.

Pearl Jephcott, Rising Twenty, *1948*

[90] Promiscuous and lengthy petting . . . is quite likely to be encouraged and regarded as a perfectly satisfactory activity for girls and fellows of 17 to 25. How far petting, done more or less in [91] public, is emotionally disturbing it is difficult to say: but when it is carried on with a succession of different people it at least seems to imply a lack of sensitiveness. The result of all this emphasis on sex means that when the girl really falls in love and starts serious courting she does it against a sex-drenched background that is unrelieved by other interests, or by a job in which she is doing relatively creative work . . . .

Quite a number suggest that though they regard fairly promiscuous petting as universal they don't much like it and have, anyhow meta-phorically, slapped the faces of numerous aspirants.

Laura Hutton, 'The Unmarried', 1949

[424] [D]esire does not in itself constitute a sufficient justification for entering upon a sexual relationship. Much more has to be taken into account. Here the problem becomes a very complicated one, and one with social as well as personal implications. There may be a very perfect relationship of love and mutual physical attraction between a woman and the man she longs to have as lover. But then there are the external circum-stances to consider. Are facts such as the risk to personal professional reputation, or the risk of pregnancy to be ignored?

More important still, should the chosen lover be married, is the question of his wife and, in many instances, his children.

[425] Further . . . is the full sexual relationship which is so greatly desired going to be worth all the risks and difficulties involved, when a real day-by-day life together may never be possible, and the most that can be hoped for is secret meetings and occasional week-ends together? . . . .

The only certain thing is that a sexual relationship entered into thought-lessly, irresponsibly, or even quite calculatingly just for the sake of the experience, is likely to bring a good deal of social trouble in its train, and may bring deep disillusionment, self-disgust and a crippling sense of futility to the individual . . . .

There are some women, of fairly tough psychological make-up, who can embark on an affair just as an experiment, and make a success of it, without much difficulty or distress; or even with an added self-respect engendered by the feeling that at least they now know what normal sexual experience is . . . .

Again, some women may have embarked on love affairs in passionate awareness of all that was entailed, have surmounted all the difficulties and distresses, including that of the inevitable final separation, and in spite of everything would not now be without their memories . . . .

[426] For a woman, sexual experience is not complete when it stops short at sexual intercourse. Pregnancy, childbirth and the nursing of the child are integral parts of sexual life for her, and these are almost necessarily excluded, or at least not desired, in the illicit love affair. Hence the normal woman is always to some extent dissatisfied in such an affair, and this fact should be reckoned with, before even a mature woman embarks on one.

Again, for a woman love cannot be localized. Just as her whole body responds in physical love, so her whole life is involved in the love of her heart, if it really is love. That is why so many affairs, entered on with joy, confidence and passion, so often lead to unhappiness, despair, and a greater loneliness than before. For an affair can almost never be combined with a real and secure life together, and a woman must always long for this security and permanency in a way not all men will fully understand.

Violet D. Swaisland, 'The Adolescent Girl', 1949

[282] [P]re-marital relationships between young people of the same social class are by no means uncommon, and are often entered into lightly and upon only the flimsiest emotional basis. The craving for sensation which is too often the result of an over-exhaustion of the nervous system plays an [283] important part in these affairs which, apart from their social consequences, tend to blunt the capacity for sustained emotion and may have a disastrous effect on the whole personality, making eventual adjustment to marriage and family life more difficult . . . .
[. . . .]
[T]he emotional strain and constant anxiety that such relationships must inevitably bring, often have quite a serious effect on a young girl's health. However great the precautions taken, the girl lives in constant fear that she may become pregnant.

Sybil Neville-Rolfe, 'The Misuse of Sex', 1949

[480] [T]he large number of casual non-commercial and irresponsible relationships, many of which consist only of an evening's companionship terminating in intercourse, which take place between young people . . . . differ from commercial prostitution on two points – they are based on some selection on the part of the individuals concerned, and no money passes. On both counts such behaviour is less degrading to the individual and somewhat less harmful to the community . . . .

[A] larger proportion are drawn from the normal young adults on whom present social practice imposes a delayed marriage age. Of these, many have more or less frequent sex adventures . . . . It may show the emergence of a better standard that the partners themselves, while prepared to admit promiscuity, are indignant at such adventures being classed as prostitution.

Sybil Neville-Rolfe, Social Biology and Welfare, *1949*

[87] [T]here is surely an objective difference between a single pre-marital sex adventure with emotional sanction but without parenthood or a single experience between adolescents [88] and the persistent promiscuity of an adult? There is as great an objective difference also between a single pre-marital experience and deliberate and persistent extra-marital relations.

[122] Just as developed personalities to-day recoil from prostitution, so will they in the future consider it an offence against themselves to enter into an incomplete and unsatisfying temporary relationship. The more fully the art of love is understood and the more fully individuals are developed as conscious personalities, the greater the depth attained in the mutual harmonies of the unique relationship.

[164] The temporary liaison may be anti-social and irresponsible and a source of unhappiness to two people, but at least it is entered into with emotional and often intellectual as well as physical satisfaction and therefore is one step further towards monogamy and not necessarily a barrier to it. For these reasons it is claimed the passing of prostitution is an advance in sex morals.

M. B. Smith, The Single Woman of Today: Her Problems and Adjustment, *1951*

[38] The enigma of the single woman in love with a married man . . . has a special significance in our times. It touches the roots of our social structure, and undermines the rule of family and the moral code by which we live; it is thus a sociological problem, but it is also a problem in social psychology, for these 'other women' are not essentially unmoral. They are subconsciously living out their normal drives towards fulfilment. They are being normal, and in many cases – almost all – the man is to blame. In some few cases there is a deep subconscious desire to play safe and avoid marriage.

Lena Jeger (ed.), **Illegitimate Children and Their Parents**, *1951*

[x] Unmarried mothers vary individually as much as married mothers – in fact rather more so, because some are pitifully young. But the one almost common factor is a background of unhappiness, of loneliness and emotional insecurity. Many come from broken homes of the most varied economic circumstances. In some cases there seem no obvious difficulties and these often need the most expert help.

But whatever the circumstances, a single mother is having to go alone through the experience of becoming a parent, an experience which was intended to be shared and in which the deepest emotional demands cry out for the missing partner. This can obviously be so psychologically disturbing that a girl's attitude to life in general, to men, to her child, to the possibility of a future successful marriage can be affected disastrously and a very great deal depends on how she is helped through this time.

Olwen Campbell (ed.), **The Feminine Point of View**, *1952*

[59] [C]asual liaisons between young people have certainly greatly increased. Though this must be felt to be the lesser evil, these short-lived connections imply a superficial attitude towards sexual experience on the part of many young people, and must tend progressively to endanger their standards of behaviour and lessen their chances of happy and stable marriage. Particularly for the woman these relationships tend to produce emotional disturbance and subsequent suffering . . . . [W]omen may fail both themselves and society if they use their newly-won freedom to adapt themselves to an unworthy male standard where they should be developing and upholding their own.

Mary Macaulay, **The Art of Marriage**, *1952*

[21] Some writers on sexual behaviour advise young people to carry their flirtations to a degree of intimacy which is most undesirable. It is very difficult for a couple to be able to stop what is known as 'heavy petting' at the right moment. They are bound to get so worked up emotionally and physically that only intercourse could provide the natural outlet; anything short of it seems unsatisfactory. Boys and girls who casually indulge in this sort of thing cheapen love-making, and are likely to bring shame and grief upon themselves and upon those who care for them.

[22] The question of premarital intimacy between those who eventually intend to marry each other has been much discussed. Some people think that a trial should be made before a couple undertake a lifetime companionship. But the essence of marriage is its permanence. No temporary arrangement can simulate [23] the security which makes it possible for a married couple to ride safely over the ups and downs . . . .

In spite of this, many young couples who have to wait a long time before they can marry are sexually intimate to a greater or lesser degree. But their relationship tends to be furtive and unsatisfactory, and they usually wish they had waited until they could come together freely and happily in the dignity of marriage. In fact in some cases it turns them against one another in a curious way. The girl is angry with the boy for making her afraid and ashamed of herself, and he comes to despise her for yielding to his importunities.

Leonora Eyles, Sex for the Engaged, 1952

[60] [A]s a general rule, once a girl has 'given way' to a boy, he is finished with her unless he has known her very well and got very friendly with her. But usually even then, he does not marry her. He has a deep suspicion of her.

But even if he wants her very much, the circumstances of pre-marital adventure are all against it. They may be taken unawares by their sudden flame of desire and lack of control; or, as is so common, the girl knows that if she doesn't 'give way' he will be finished with her because he can find plenty more. The stolen few moments . . . are attended by terror . . . .

Then, with actually engaged couples there is sometimes the stolen weekend in an hotel . . . . [61] It is almost always disappointing. There is no opportunity for real lovemaking. Desire must be linked with tenderness to make sexual intercourse a happy thing, and it should never be accompanied by fear or greed.

[71] A long engagement is an almost hopeless thing; kisses, caressing, the rousing of emotions should have their natural consummation in intercourse. Again and again passionate lovemaking has to be arrested midway and both young man and young woman wonder why they are getting nervy, why their precious snatched hours degenerate into squabbles, why in the end the engagement just drifts into indifference or the man clears off to make a hurried, unconsidered marriage with someone else.
[. . . .]
[72] [R]ather than let their engagement drift into squabbling and desirelessness, is there any reason why they should not be lovers? I don't think there is, except the reasons I have already gone into; it depends on their outlook, their own wisdom, their own self-control.

[74] [L]iving together, weekending together is no test for marriage because, no how 'emancipated' or unsentimental you think you are, there is a different 'feel' about it.

Leonora Eyles, The New Commonsense about Sex, 1956

[76] As a rule when a wife is unfaithful the urge does not come from inside her; it comes because she is feeling either bored or neglected; often she just wants to 'show him' and slips gradually into a love affair. There are a few cases where she really loves the new man and needs him. But much more often it is her husband's stupid neglect of her that has made her stray and if he takes her seriously and realises that she is more than an automaton to keep house, look after children and attend to his comforts, he can win her back. This naturally does not apply to those young wives who marry irresponsibly often for the wrong reasons, treat their children (when they have any) irresponsibly and are ready to have an affair with any young man who is thrilling, or, more often, who can give them a 'good time'.

Rose Hacker, The Opposite Sex, 1957

[98] The question of 'heavy petting' – that is to say the fondling and stimulating of the sexual parts to the point where sexual intercourse should be the normal end, yet is not – is therefore a burning one. Face up to the problems of sexual appetite and learn to control and use all your instincts to good purpose.
[. . .]
   [99] [F]ew girls realise the force of the glandular processes they themselves have aroused in the boys . . . nor do they see that the boys are impelled by something beyond their control to use any means to gain their end. Girls should know what happens to a boy's body when he gets excited and accept their own responsibility in the matter.
   In the same way, boys should know that although girls take longer to arouse, they too can be made equally desirous [100] and restless. They should be aware of how girls feel and, if they find themselves with girls who are young for their age or ignorant, they should be man enough not to take advantage of these feelings. It is a mean thing to take advantage of ignorance. Girls should understand that they should keep a watch on their own feelings as well as consider those of boys.

Doris Odlum, Journey Through Adolescence, 1957

[130] It is astonishing how often a girl believes a boy when he says that if she will consent to have intercourse with him he knows of some special way of avoiding any risk of her becoming pregnant. It is, however, not possible to avoid all risk of a pregnancy occurring even after incomplete intercourse. Mothers should make certain that their daughters are aware of this fact. There are many girls of sixteen or seventeen who are carrying on a practically independent existence . . . . They mix freely with men of all ages, yet have no clear knowledge of the exact nature of the sexual act or in what circumstances a baby may be conceived.

Virginia Wimperis, The Unmarried Mother and her Child, 1960

[55] [T]he large majority of the children's fathers were at conception either the fiancé or a friend of the mother's. In only some twenty cases was he a casual acquaintance. This information is based on the women's own statements, which are not necessarily to be trusted in every instance. There is, how- [56] ever, no obvious reason why such large numbers should state that they had known the father for many years if this were not true.

[68] Around 40 per cent . . . . are born to couples living stably together but debarred from marrying by the still-existing marriage of one or other partner. The study by the Midboro Health Department similarly found that at the actual time of conception about half of the mothers were living with the putative father, and that of those who were married, widowed or divorced, almost three-quarters were cohabiting; five years later the proportion still cohabiting was 44 per cent.
[. . . .]
    [69] It seems reasonable to assume that, at least in the cities, one in every two or three illegitimate births are to women cohabiting in a more or less permanent relationship.

[72] [T]he proportion of illegitimate children born to unmarried women not cohabiting was very roughly 25 per cent.

[73] It is a smaller group than that composed of stably cohabiting couples, but it is a group with much greater problems for everyone concerned . . . . The mother, in especial, can hardly avoid acute suffering. She has to face loneliness, shock, financial difficulties, her parents' attitudes, often social ostracism. She has the problems of whether to marry, and whether to keep or give up the child. Her position is in practice very different from that of a cohabiting woman.

[96] The stubborn reluctance of social workers in this country to accept this thesis that a majority of unmarried mothers are neurotic is . . . based on a very wide practical experience. They have watched difficult choices being made and have been impressed by the capacity of these women to triumph over handicaps and to bring up apparently healthy and happy children: they are not determinists. They claim no special knowledge of the psychology of the unconscious, but their impressions cannot be wholly written off.

Sociologists have also added their voice. Extra-marital intercourse, they stress, is very widespread. Are most of those who have extra-marital relations to be thought of as neurotic, or only those who conceive children outside marriage? Is failure to use birth control, and the ignorance of contraception among the young, always to be classed as neurotic?

Elizabeth Draper, Birth Control in the Modern World, 1965

[128] While new patterns are worked out the 'idea' of experiment filters through society generally, attracting like the Pied Piper a following of suggestible people, physically mature enough for coitus but not emotionally mature enough for marital responsibility, who do as fashion dictates, but without much gain and indeed sometimes with damage to themselves. Earlier physical maturation with its attendant sexual urge is perhaps adding to this problem, though appropriate upbringing and education may offset this by aiding earlier emotional maturation. Thus the new sexual trends towards greater liberty and experimentation have taken a hold on society and, in the absence of preventive measures such as specific birth control information, produce, despite an estimated two hundred to eight hundred abortions a day, an alarming crop of illegitimate and socially deprived children, and disillusioned and unhappy young people, saddled with responsibilities beyond their capacity to carry and still unable to sort out for themselves what it is all about.

Diana Dewar, Orphans of the Living, 1968

[137] Too many young people blind themselves to the fact that they are having sexual intercourse either because they are living in a dream world manufactured for the mass media or because they are extraordinarily ignorant. Intercourse seems unreal until later. Unfortunately, as yet there is no retroactive birth control pill for swallowing the morning after.

Another difficulty is that the level of communication between many young people is frequently so inadequate that they cannot talk about methods of birth control or the use of them. At the heart of a great many unwelcome situations in which young people find themselves is an unthinking and unrealistic attitude towards sex.

[. . . .]

In spite of our much publicised 'permissive society' not all young people now have sex before marriage but a large minority do. This appetite for sexual experience is openly encouraged by the commercial engineers of the teenage cult, the creators of sex symbols for the wider exploitation of the teenage market of money [138] and emotions. Unfortunately, the power of the erotic incitement generated by this style of commerce has not been sufficiently recognised as more than enough justification for frank and fearless sex education. As a result, young people are the more inclined to sexual experimentation and the more vulnerable to misadventure.

[144] With absurd lack of realism, girls still leave 'precautions' in sex to their boy friends. More often than not the boys do not bother: unprepared and unconcerned, they do not begin to understand the stupidity and cruelty of causing an unwanted baby to be born. It is encouraging, however, that some boys accompany their girl-friends to the Brook clinics.

Ann Allen, People on Honeymoon, 1968

[44] [A]fter a few months of getting to know each other, we were quick to sample the good things which married life has to offer. This we continued to do for the next five years. After this probationary period we decided to get down to the more serious business of getting married. To us this was merely the process of living and eating together.

[45] One great thing I regret was that we spent a week abroad together after getting engaged. I think that if some of the intimate and small things are not new to you the honeymoon is not as enjoyable; and all the extra excitement and happiness has gone.

I wasn't innocent when I married at 17. In fact, I had had a couple of 'small' affairs which I bitterly regretted. We had intercourse for about four months before we were married, and I told him about the others. Then he didn't seem to object, but later it was a different story.

Helena Wright, Sex and Society, 1968

[94] Now, at last, with the advent of contraception, freedom to express natural sexual energy within a new code of behaviour, is [95] offered to everyone who is prepared and able to accept the new discipline implied in the code.

Of the possible consequences of universal contraception, this is the one which is likely to meet with the most fierce opposition. It must be made clear, therefore, that the suggestion contains no thought of lessening the responsibility or the status of marriage. Rather might the effect of the open acknowledgement that marriage need not limit the sexual activities of the partners add emphasis to the condition of marriage.

[108] The right attitude to an accidental pregnancy, as an instance of deplorable carelessness, would have to emerge and have a strong effect in condemning irresponsibility. One of the tragic elements in the present situation among adolescents who are almost universally ignorant of contraception is that risking pregnancy by deliberate lack of protection is held among some of the participants to be a brave act of daring fate! . . . .

Thus, if unbroken discipline is observed in following contraceptive techniques, if the individual relationships are chosen wisely and un-selfishly, and if the parents concerned are broadminded enough to give sympathy and privacy, it is possible to imagine that immature experiments [109] in learning the difficult arts of love might turn out to be valuable preparation for serious adult responsibilities.

Claire Rayner, **Parent's Guide to Sex Education,** *1968*[3]

[101] Necking might not matter if it were an end in itself, if it only provided a little innocent pleasure and a safe outlet for the strong and normal sex drives of this age group. However, it isn't. It must be remembered that kissing and cuddling are enjoyable because they are a preparation for complete sexual intercourse. The more a young couple kiss and cuddle the more intense their desires become, so that necking *increases* the pressure of sex drives.

What happens when the couple reach a point when they must release the tension somehow, must experience some sort of sexual climax? Some couples, as we have seen, go all the way and have full intercourse. But there are many young people who are well aware of the value of avoiding intercourse until they are married but who still want to experience some sort of sexual satisfaction.

These young couples discover that it is possible to give each other satisfaction without going all the way to intercourse. They then feel obscurely that they are still chaste. That is, their necking becomes petting. Briefly, petting can be described as a form of love making in which each

3   See footnote 2.

partner brings about an orgasm for the other by handling of the sex organs. It is really mutual masturbation.

[. . . .]

[102] The first question I have asked myself is this: is petting harmful for a girl? Once again I am more concerned about the effect on girls rather than boys because it seems to me that girls are, in the whole, rather more easily disturbed in their total approach to sexuality than are boys.

There is some evidence that petting may be harmful to a girl. A girl who for many years becomes accustomed to reaching a sexual climax by means of petting with boys may find when she marries, and is at last free to enjoy normal intercourse, that she is not really able to enjoy it fully.

[. . . .]

[103] My own feeling is that the greatest drawback to petting is not a physical one but a psychological one . . . . The girl who regularly goes in for petting with different boys must inevitably come to value herself less and less.

Jean Pochin, Without a Wedding Ring, *1969*

[2] We have insight into hidden motives and unconscious drives that was not available to our grandparents, and this has produced in us a more realistic compassion. The common saying that 'it isn't the girls who *have* babies who are immoral, it's the ones who *don't*' shows at least [3] that the distinction between the unmarried mother and the prostitute has at last penetrated the public consciousness. The blanket of condemnation is being lifted from both.

[. . . .]

Another, more disturbing reason for the change of view is that unmarried motherhood has come home to us all, and lives now in our street. Condemnation has given places to a fear that after all it could happen in our family.

[. . . .]

Unmarried pregnancy certainly knows no bounds of age, social class or intelligence.

[. . . .]

[T]here may appear to have been an increase in unmarried pregnancies in the middle and upper-class social groups, although precise figures are not available, but in any case the overall illegitimacy rate continues to rise.

[. . . .]

In a way the increasing illegitimacy rate is puzzling. Contraceptives are now freely available, and even the most advanced advocates of [4] permissive morality still agree . . . that it is unethical to bring an illegitimate child into the world. Why, then, do more and more single girls have babies?

[9] [A] certain small proportion of women . . . quite deliberately set out to have a child without a husband and are prepared to face the consequences. There are others, more naïve, who give in to their boy-friends' advances because they hope it will lead to marriage if they do, and others again who trust their lovers' assurances that they 'won't do them any harm' . . . . Countless teen-agers experiment out of curiosity, happily convinced that nothing will happen to them . . . .

[T]he sources of illegitimacy may be found in drives and motives of many different kinds, conscious and unconscious. A pregnancy may be accidental in the sense that although intercourse was intended conception was not. On the other hand there are girls who seem predisposed to unmarried motherhood.

Same-sex relationships, celibacy, and singleness generally

During this period the numbers of individuals marrying in all age-groups reaches an all-time high, as the average age at marriage drops to an all-time low. The single woman thus becomes seen as a somewhat pathological failure rather than a victim of demographic imbalance.[4] However, writers continue to assert the value of balanced friendships between women, and to claim for the lesbian a higher moral standard and sounder monogamous relationships than her male counterpart.

Leonora Eyles, **Unmarried but Happy,** *1947*

[94] Accept the fact that sex is a powerful force in your life as in every other normal creature's; take comfort from the fact that, as you grow older the pull of the body becomes weaker, that years bring a greater pull of the mind and the spirit and bring with them some philosophic calm; most people can endure pain and stress if they know it will end some day . . . . [T]hey will not go on feeling as miserable as they do; as the organs of reproduction begin, in the natural course of things, to wither away, all the emotions connected with sex lose their power. And it is in a woman's own hands to end her unhappiness any day, even while she is young, by changing her attitude of mind, by dropping the sense of frustration, of having 'missed the bus'; by ceasing to envy the married woman the many things the single woman lacks . . . .

---

4   Though there must have been a sufficient number around to justify a new edition of Laura Hutton's *The Single Woman and Her Problems* in 1961.

[Y]ou have only to look round . . . to realise that marriage weaves no magic wand conferring miraculous happiness . . . .

[95] I am not saying that all the worries and agonies of married life and motherhood are not worthwhile; they are, a thousand times over. But the spinster has compensations and she will be wise to recognise them.

Laura Hutton, 'The Unmarried', 1949

[423] There are, it is true, many women who seem able to do without [sexual experience] entirely . . . . Many of the women whom we call perpetual adolescents never even seem to need it. Their ideals would in any case reject the idea, but not at any great cost in the way of self-denial and self-control. Their lives are filled with work and a multitude of interests and friendships. Their sexual instinct, probably never very strong, seems to be completely sublimated.

[428] Friendship, really affectionate friendship, offers indeed the best of all solutions and compensations to the unmarried woman, and for this reason her friendships with contemporaries, usually other women . . . are well worth taking seriously. Too often they are unstable and full of reverses, because the friends have not troubled to reflect on the situation, but have allowed their friendships to be the vehicle of all kinds of childish exactions, anxieties and jealousies, and of their, probably unrecognized, sexual frustration.

[429] Many of the passionate friendships discussed above are potentially homosexual, even where sex has never come to frank expression. Recognition of this fact may in some cases be necessary if the friendship is to continue as a useful factor in the lives of the women concerned, and such recognition should not necessarily mean condemnation of the friendship as a whole. Sex is for most people an inescapable factor in life, and a relationship between two people [430] that is both intimate and passionate is quite likely on occasions to arouse sexual feelings, even though these are not admitted as such . . . .

It is far better to know what one is dealing with, in order to come to some arrangement with oneself and one's friend about such feelings, and the situations that give rise to them, than either to pretend they do not exist, or to condemn them out of hand and perhaps break up a good friendship. Love is the criterion of what is worth-while in a friendship, not any purely physical manifestation.

Where the true invert is concerned – the woman who really feels she is a man in her inclination towards her women friends, and who usually has much that is typically masculine in her physical make-up – the management of sex in friendship may offer a serious problem, and much self-denial and self-control. It is a problem rather of responsibility towards other and particularly younger women. It is a grave responsibility to initiate a girl into sexual experience which is not normal. It may easily hold up her psycho-sexual development and thus be a factor in depriving her of normal fulfilment in marriage and motherhood.

Fortunately, in most inverts the sexual instinct (contrary to popular opinion) is not very powerful, and is very readily sublimated . . . . They are handicapped . . . by an anomalous psycho-sexual constitution, so that life will never be easy for them. But the anomalous is not necessarily the diseased any more than the abnormal is necessarily the vicious.

Sybil Neville-Rolfe, Social Biology and Welfare, 1949

[115] [A]ttraction to the same sex is normal, but if physical and emotional development do not keep in step during the adolescent period, and if through circumstances emotional development is arrested at the pre-adolescent stage, then serious maladjustment may result. With the normal person, as sexual capacity develops, the motivating desires and emotions associated therewith are heterosexual, that is, the attraction is to members of the opposite sex. Friendships, of course, remain from the adolescent period, and are often the greatest enrichments of life, but the normal friendships between men and between women are not linked with physical sex attraction. With the psychological homosexual, the emotional desires do not develop but remain anchored at the homosexual stage, and physical sex expression becomes related to members of the same sex and does not develop to the mature heterosexual stage.

Joan Malleson, Any Wife or Any Husband, 1950

[127] [A] girl retains much that is of value from an enduring affection to her mother, for later this leads to good relationships with her own sex. Such relationships can greatly enrich life for the average woman without in any way disturbing her heterosexual ties. Indeed, most women possess considerable capacities for tenderness towards women. When sublimated these form the basis of much valuable work . . . . Thus, although the small girl has to face more difficulties during emotional development than the boy, even where there has been considerable failure to attain maturity, she is left with other compensations.

[131] There has never been an equal prejudice against homosexuality in women . . . possibly because the retention of homosexual ties may be felt correctly to be more 'natural' in women than men. Active homosexual

practices are less common among adolescent girls than among boys. When they occur in adult women they are often found among normal and stable people. Moreover, these relationships tend to be more satisfactory and enduring than those made by most homosexual men. At times, when there is a surplus of marriageable women, some accept homosexual relationships in preference to celibacy or promiscuous unions . . . . Others turn to the practice if they have found disappointment in marriage. A small proportion of homosexual women show delinquent and alcoholic tendencies: such are classed as psychopathic personalities.

M. B. Smith, The Single Woman of Today: Her Problems and Adjustment, 1951

[22] To delude such a woman with the idea that she can lead a full life as a man's mistress, or in secret harlotry without any hope of motherhood, and with the organic idleness which constant use of contraceptives would bring, is cruel and heartless. There is no adequate or lasting satisfaction for any woman in a love affair, no emotional security against its cessation, and a constant dread of being 'found out'.

[. . . .]

[23] This business of facing life without a man is very difficult for most women. Some of them crack under the nervous strain and find themselves in mental homes, or suffering from psychosomatic illness of some kind; others suffer agonies of guilt from secret love affairs; others' masochism seems inexhaustible; others when in the society of those who are married have a ghastly sense of inferiority which hurts and even maims; others take to drugs or become 'good-time' drinking girls, hanging around pubs and 'clubs'; others drink in secret . . . . Loneliness and despair work havoc with them, and they clutch at anything that will relieve these. Ultimately, a section of them give way to the temptations of prostitution.

[46] The damming up of sex tension under the influence of social restrictions is often the cause of anxiety symptoms in the spinster. Psychotherapeutic treatment may alleviate these, and so make her life more tolerable, but this is still a subject matter for research . . . . [47] Psychopathology is being used in the treatment of the illnesses of the single woman in this country and in America, especially with reference to hysteria, epilepsy, obsessional neurosis, depression, manic schizophrenia, and nervous breakdown, but it is costly . . . . It would appear . . . that the problem of the spinster . . . has its aetiology in and before infancy. The traumata of babyhood, repressed from consciousness, though still active with the psyche, may well lead a woman to refuse, subconsciously, the duties and obligations of the mature state of married life.

Doris Odlum, Journey Through Adolescence, *1957*

[151] In the large majority of cases the first love is for a person of the same sex . . . . With girls . . . it usually fixes itself upon an older girl . . . or the games or gym mistress. One of the characteristics of the 'crush' . . . is that the adorers neither know nor wish to know very much about the personality or personal life of the beloved, nor do they particularly desire a very close relationship. A smile, or a nod of the head, or some brief word of greeting or commendation, keeps them happy for days; and in the case of girls, the acceptance of a gift by the beloved exalts them into the seventh heaven of bliss. The situation is created by the adolescent's need to fulfil itself in loving, and all that is required of the beloved is to maintain a somewhat remote god-like or goddess-like perfection and above all avoid exposing the feet of clay. In fact the role of the adored might be described as that of an emotional mannequin who permits himself or herself to be decked with all the rainbow hues of adolescent fantasy.
[. . . .]
  [152] Very few adults realise what a vitally important part this giving of love plays in the normal development of an adolescent. It would not be putting it too strongly to say that the success or failure of this first experiment in loving may well set the pattern for the individual's future attitude to love relationships, not only with those of the same but also of the opposite sex. If adolescents find satisfaction and fulfilment when they first give themselves unreservedly to another in this way, albeit only in fantasy, they have some grounds for believing that it is safe to love in reality without being wounded or rejected . . . . The more successful the first love affair, the more quickly they will be ready to pass on to the next stage and seek a love object on a more realistic basis and of the opposite sex.

'Streetwalker', *1959*

[47] I don't feel masculine, and I have no Lesbian tendencies, as far as I know. Very many of us develop them possibly to counterbalance the cankerous revulsion that results from continual contact with male lust, and possibly because an affection which seems truer and surer than one has learned to expect from men, and a physical pleasure stronger because of its contrast to the robot lovemaking of business hours, can be derived from an association with another woman.

Xenia Field, Under Lock and Key, *1963*

[28] Some women . . . seem to manage better . . . in adjusting themselves to live without the companionship of the opposite sex. As an alternative there are the 'crushes', 'pashes', jealousies and rivalries among the women, and there are love affairs that lead to lesbianism, but the emotional friend-ships are rarely long lasting. The atmosphere of a one-sex community is abnormal and unhealthy, and sex is an ever popular subject [29] in any prison. On occasion the prostitute is a lesbian, and therefore an unsuitable person to be locked up among numerous members of her own sex.

[58] Was a petty thief, more male than female, and the staff had some trouble in getting her to wear her skirt and remove [59] her thick working socks. She was an active lesbian and always in trouble as a result of her uncontrolled infatuations. Was prison the right place for her?

[62] Was a jumbled character of savage appearance who had always grabbed what she wanted. She fell in love with a fellow prisoner and became, anyway temporarily, a reformed character.

Helena Wright, Sex and Society, *1968*

[61] Female homosexuality is not recognized by the law. Despite the common concept of homosexuality as unnatural or perverted, in fact the occurrence of homosexuality in both sexes [62] at some stage of life is so common that it can hardly even be considered as abnormal.
   Transient homosexual attachments round about puberty are nowadays not seriously condemned, but it is still very common to find more permanent homosexual tendencies labelled as perversions . . . .
   On the contrary, this state of affairs is so usual in an otherwise psycho-logically normal person that it might more accurately be described as a natural phenomenon in the strictest scientific use of the phrase. As heterosexual and homosexual emotions are natural phenomena it is irrelevant to label them as either right or wrong.

[84] Homosexuals . . . are potentially as useful citizens as heterosexuals; they both need more sympathy and understanding, and that should be a challenge and not a reason for abuse and disrespect. The principle involved here is that sexual emotion is a driving force and it is capable of moving in several different directions. The direction it takes in any individual is, of itself, neither good nor bad. Nor is the direction necessarily fixed. Sexual valency can undergo changes, and in fact normally does so during the development from an adolescent into an adult.

Jean Pochin, **Without a Wedding-Ring,** *1969*

[29] The pregnancy of an intelligent, educated, mature single woman seems especially irrational; surely she at least ought to have had more sense? . . . .

[I]t may be that deeper, unconscious forces become more powerful. As she passes her thirtieth and thirty-fifth birthdays a woman knows well that her chances of marriage are lessening, and her unconscious urge towards motherhood, with or without a wedding-ring, may grow stronger. Also, and perhaps more likely, she may be consciously seeking security in the face of increasing loneliness . . . . A physical relationship with a lover does in fact seem to provide that security for many women, giving them the power and poise they need.

Prostitution and venereal disease

There is a general perception that resort to prostitution is continuing to be replaced by 'promiscuous' relationships, and the prostitute is increasingly characterized as a dysfunctional type rather than the victim of the social system. At first the problems of venereal disease are not foregrounded (given the perception that with the advent of antibiotics this age-old problem has finally been solved), but as the 1950s become the 1960s a discernible rise in the infection rate becomes apparent, and is particularly worrying in the younger age-groups.

Sybil Neville-Rolfe, 'The Misuse of Sex', 1949

[479] Those who come under the care of social workers, Local Authorities, or the police courts, are either of sub-normal mentality, have some glandular maladjustment that makes them physiologically over-sexed, or they come from broken homes, have been brought up in institutions, have step-parents, have lost their mother or both parents in early life, or show in their family histories certain hereditary traits. Poverty, which used to be thought the major cause, takes a low place in the scale of causation.

'Women of the Streets', 1955

[19] [D]epending on how the word 'annoyance' is interpreted, she may be arrested every time she speaks to a man or she may hardly ever be arrested. Neither course is desirable, and instead there appears to have arisen a system whereby prostitutes are charged at fairly frequent intervals roughly

in proportion to their persistence in soliciting, rarely more than once or twice a month, usually once every two or three months.

[37] May: ' . . . . but what do you think would happen on the streets if they cleared us away like that? It'd not be safe for respectable women to go about. The men demand it . . . .' Bessie: ' . . . . Men have to have a woman, a man without a woman is like a wild beast. So it'll be those little girls what'll get it. The men'll make a fuss of them, some one'll suffer.'

[50] Hyde Park is an area popular with those unable or unprepared to organize themselves with flats for business. Many young girls first try prostitution here, some move to other areas, but most stay, preferring the freedom of the Park; they can take customers inside the Park or go in cars on the North and South carriage roads. Prices range from ten shillings ('five shillings if you use your hands') to one pound in cars, and two pounds if the man is taken back to a room. Its population is young: 60 per cent are under thirty, 10 per cent under twenty-one. Nearly all of the girls there have had some sort of conviction before they commence soliciting . . . . I found all these girls very pleasant and co-operative; the number who refused to talk to me here was much lower than among West End prostitutes (a feature which was consistent: the lower the organizing ability of a girl and the poorer the area, the fewer refusals).

[51] Stepney also is predominantly a young prostitutes' district. It is one of the most popular resorts for absconders from schools, and girls who, having left their home towns, have come to London not knowing where to go . . . . The young girl in a state of social irrelation finds an uncritical, accommodating atmosphere here. She may take to living with various coloured men, existing in the intervals by prostitution; gradually these 'immigrant' white girls settle into the behaviour most acceptable to them, some evolve into fully professional prostitutes and move into other districts . . . . [T]he minimum price is ten shillings outside and one pound indoors for a short-time; usually only three pounds all-night, and many of the girls in pubs take only all-nighters. I was told that the large number of girls in this district ready to sleep with a man for nothing, or at least only for a bed, meant that the prostitutes frequently had blank evenings.

[56] A tradition of place and behaviour has grown up whereby a man, seeing a woman loitering in a certain street, may assume that she is a prostitute. The position is so well defined in some places that the girl feels that merely by standing she is doing enough . . . .

Against such a background the solicitation of prostitutes by men becomes a different action from the solicitation by prostitutes of men passing in the public streets.

It was this aspect of this social situation that I experienced [57] when I visited the carriage roads in Hyde Park . . . . This explains why I was accosted by men so often.

[59] Another variation which must be considered if the picture is to be complete, is in the form of sexual gratification supplied by the prostitutes. Place, to some extent, determines this, and of course the particular service the man is seeking. Masturbation is a fairly frequent variation outside; it is more convenient and [60] cheaper. 'Five shillings if you use your hands. Some of the men are very hard up and can't afford any more' . . . . Full intercourse often occurs outside, standing up in doorways, lying on the grass or on seats in the Park . . . .

Full intercourse does take place in cars and taxis, though it seems less frequent. Ena, who makes a practice of going in cars, said, 'Some men won't take a girl in a car if they think she won't allow full intercourse. Of course, you tell the man anything – it's the money you want – and then if he doesn't get what he wants it's too bad.' Car trade is sought by some girls who do not permit full intercourse.

Almost always perversions are only performed indoors; this explains to some extent the popularity of having a room, for the girl is thereby able to satisfy a greater variety of clients. It also explains why some girls prefer to remain outside: 'You pay perhaps seven guineas a week for a flat, then you have to undress and do all kinds of things'.

[77] [T]here is a definite market which is studied by the prostitute in order to obtain and maintain trade. In organizing a flat in which to work and a maid to help her she has veritably opened a shop . . . .

The women furnish their flats or rooms with the implements required for variations in normal sexual intercourse. They change their clothes for work, putting on high platformed shoes which, because they have become almost *de rigueur* for prostitutes, many dislike wearing . . . 'You've got to dress up for the part or it's not worth doing it. At night I always wear four-tiered, platform-soled shoes (that's why I'm wearing flatties now to rest my feet) and nylons. Some like fine silk stockings but I prefer nylons; men seem to like you like that'.

The prostitute often assumes not only a uniform but also a mask, the over-emphasized lips, etc., being familiar to everyone, though they are not often apparent in the day-time on the same women.

[79] The equipment of the prostitute's room, of course, varies according to her own versatility in the performance of perversions; nearly all have whips, canes, or improvisations for flagellation hidden away in otherwise empty drawers. Jean in addition has a supply of black lace underwear for the men who wish to dress up in women's clothing. High-heeled boots and

shoes to be worn by both men and women are often found in brothels
. . . . The most poorly equipped prostitutes can usually produce postcards,
photographs or drawings to show to customers; they sometimes sell these
to clients, but as the trade is illegal one hears less about it.

[82] It seems to me to be far from the 'easy life' it is reputed to be. Many
Park and Victoria women report that they stand for hours at a time without
customers, some Park girls for half and hour or more without a man
passing them. Ena, in Hyde Park, said she hoped to make £4 an evening
. . . but often did not as she became too tired . . . . She might solicit as
many as twenty men before she obtained a customer. Sally, another Park
girl, makes £4 or £5 at week-ends, but often only thirty [83] shillings on
other evenings; her friend Anne said she could make up to £15 a week, not
going out each evening; Sally insisted she would have to go out regularly
to do this. Avis limits herself to £3 each afternoon on South Carriage Road
'just two friends each afternoon; two thirty bobs and then I'm through'.
Winifred, a very attractive girl, told me she could make as much as £8
or £9 in an evening, but not often; this must mean very hard work.
[. . . .]
   The economic side of prostitution is not the cause of any woman's
becoming a prostitute, but there is no doubt that it is an important factor
in influencing her behaviour, and might be classed as a 'precipitating'
factor.

[93] Most of the women I knew in Stepney were irregular but continual
visitors to the local [VD] clinic. Their attendances were too [94] spasmodic
for satisfactory treatment . . . .
   The high incidence of V.D. at this end of the prostitutes' class structure
is in accordance with the view that V.D. is a problem of promiscuity rather
than of prostitution, for the girls in this group are only one degree
removed in age, personality and behaviour from the sexual anarchy of the
crowds of promiscuous girls who never become prostitutes . . . .
   Prostitutes from Mayfair, Soho, Hyde Park, Victoria and Waterloo
ascribed the spread of disease to this class of woman. Women who took
their clients to rooms also included in their censure prostitutes who
remained outside with men.

[97] Prostitutes insist on customers using rubber sheaths, both to avoid
infection and to prevent conception. For many prostitutes this seems to be
their only method of contraception. The practice is not popular with
clients, for the women receive offers of an extra ten shillings payment for
going 'without the rubber', requests which generally come from married
men. The use of condoms is customary with all prostitutes except the most
ignorant or the most impecunious;

[108] Once a girl has become a professional prostitute one perceives the phenomenon of stabilization in her personality and behaviour; this is both a psychological and a social process. She has openly renounced standards acceptable to ordinary society, she has acquired a profession where she is needed, and needed by men, where she has regular hours and colleagues, and most [109] important of all, where she finds herself in the company of people who are like herself in personality and outlook. She becomes a member of that society of which she had been on the fringe in her state of instability.

This prostitute society has its own class structure with varying standards of behaviour, the same qualities making for success in this as in any other professional sphere – charm, sympathy, intelligence, organizing ability, capital.

'Streetwalker', *1959*

[11] To be a successful prostitute, you've got to have at least one of three things: either outstandingly good looks and figure, and many of us are really beautiful; or the personality and individuality to make a man look at you twice, and then come back again and again; or the ability to talk or scare your clients, once you've got them back to your flat, into paying more than the original sum stipulated for extra attentions, or less ordinary functions – you must persuade them into something new, or roll them, steal from them.

If you possess all these assets, you have no business to be connected with commercial sex at all. Your place in the world is assured, if it is money and power that you want. If you have two of these qualifications, your best bet is to be a telephone number on an agency list, a hostess in a top rank club, or the mistress of wealthy men. Most of us, however, are endowed with only one of these qualities, and quite a large number have none at all.

A girl in this unfortunate position should really consider going home to her parents, or marrying the first reasonable man who comes her way, to whom she will probably make a passable wife. She certainly shouldn't waste her time on the streets, because unless you can earn £10 a night without much difficulty, it isn't worth it. The toll is much too heavy.

[16] [T]he hurried, the efficient and the businesslike are obviously favourites. Those who refuse to part with their money in advance must be got rid of, as must be those whose peculiarities did not reveal themselves at first meeting. The timid must be reassured of their safety or flattered into feeling that they are the men they want to be. The Don Juans, with prowess to display and achievements to be retailed, must be suffered with patience; the Galahads who, with immense condescension, allow you contact with

their persons, counting you lucky to have been favoured and expecting due appreciation for the honour, must also be supported.

Xenia Field, Under Lock and Key, *1963*

[41] They have no wish to co-operate, they do not settle down and they have no desire to work. Most of them mean to return to prostitution on discharge, so it is natural that they regard the whole experience in prison as waste of time.

It is against the Commissioners' principles to treat prostitutes as a special group, but the prostitute who enters prison for the first time is not normally treated as a 'Star' and is not allowed even if a first-offender to join the first-offender group. It appears that brothel-keepers are often out to recruit and are capable of making their way of life sound attractively adventurous as well as lucrative to the unwary young prisoner.

The individual prostitute may be aggressive while in prison, and there are a number who have made up their minds not to discuss their profession or background. 'You learn to be suspicious on the street', one woman explained. But once free again the majority of these women are very willing to talk frankly.

[43] The streets have been 'cleaned up' and the prostitute driven underground, but the situation is not necessarily improved, and we cannot even guess what the result will be. We can only be sure that the fear of penalties will not stop the trade. A prostitute will explain that her takings are unlimited, that more fines merely mean more work in order to pay them.

Street women can no longer afford to dawdle as they did. Many lead a poodle, pretending that they are taking their dog for a walk, while others stand at a bus stop as if awaiting transport.

There are people who would like to see a red-light district in all large towns, but this would be putting the clock back a hundred years. At the moment, the prostitute is still in a position to say 'no' to a prospective client if she should wish to do so.

[44] 'It's the money,' admitted a successful prostitute . . . . It was known that she was ready to be a party to perversion at a price, her aim being to buy a house and run a brothel. 'I get more in ten minutes than I should in a week in an office.'

[. . . .]

Some prostitutes may get only a few pounds an evening. But the Mayfair prostitute can make a hundred pounds or more a week, money that she could earn in no other way.

A prison psychologist has stressed the fact that the prostitute has on occasion urged other reasons than money . . . . Once they become accustomed to having it they find it difficult to do without it. Besides, this, the career suits many independent personalities.

Elizabeth Draper, Birth Control in the Modern World, *1965*

[129] Unhappily this experimentation and the fashions it produces have provided also the means of increasing the spread of venereal disease among young people and in particular among young girls who, once initiated into sexuality, often without fear of infection by their school-fellows, then satisfy their appetites, either sexual or for excitement, with older and sometimes infected men.

Claire Rayner, Parent's Guide to Sex Education, *1968*[5]

[70] The spread of venereal disease is alarming a great many medical authorities, and for good reason. These diseases spread like wildfire in a sexually promiscuous group, and their long term effects can be very unpleasant indeed.

[. . . .]

Don't assume that the fear of disease is a good deterrent against premature sexual experiment. For one thing, we need much better reasons than fear of disease to help young people see the value of sexual chastity and, for another, in the young, disease is not as alarming a thing as it is to older people.

[71] [F]or some teenagers, the possibility of getting a disease adds a spice to promiscuous sexual behaviour. Remember this, when talking to your children about venereal diseases, and try, if you can, to make it clear that this is not a 'glamorous' thing, that brings with it years of dismal dreariness. Emphasise the nasty and dull aspects of it, and you will avoid making the diseases seem even remotely attractive.

Birth control

By this time, birth control has become a default assumption, although there are perceived to be problems as to its reliability and the extent to which it is actually being used by everyone who might benefit, not to mention persisting inaccurate ideas of what constitutes a method of

---

5   See footnote 2.

contraception. The problem of abortion and demands for law reform continue.

Sybil Neville-Rolfe, 'The Misuse of Sex', 1949

[485] Although local authorities may now provide free information on contraception to married women whose health would be impaired by further pregnancies, these facilities are by no means available in all parts of the country. A large number of married women still try various ways of procuring miscarriages, as do also unmarried girls to whom it often appears essential that they should escape maternity.
[. . . .]
[486] There still remain certain conditions under which the legal termination of pregnancy is the lesser evil

Sybil Neville-Rolfe, Social Biology and Welfare, 1949

[305] The popularization of the use of relatively effective contraceptive methods has given to those with sufficient intelligence . . . a long step towards personal, social and economic freedom. Some attribute the decline in population and in family size primarily to this practice. While it has undoubtedly reduced the numbers of births in the family, a larger proportion of those born now survive . . . .
To-day, as science has clarified the physiological processes of repro-duction, the technique of contraception will inevitably become increasingly effective and foolproof until practically every birth by a person of normal intelligence may within measurable time be conscious and deliberate.
[. . . .]
Already public opinion in educated communities is expecting the individual to exercise conscious responsibility for parenthood.
[. . .]
[306] The suppression of information and facilities for contraception, even if it were practicable, would not rectify the position. Not only would this be an impossible task, but it would also remove a valuable agency in human progress. The more responsible the individual parent, the greater the desire that children should be born under the best conditions.

Joan Malleson, Any Wife or Any Husband, 1950

[22] Some women control or 'hold back' their sexual feeling, believing that in this way they will not become pregnant. It is known for certain that

suppressing the climax makes no difference to the likelihood of a pregnancy following, for if no preventatives are used the seed is just as likely to reach the womb whether a climax occurs or not. It is almost impossible for the practice of 'holding back' to leave the woman's health unimpaired.

Olwen Campbell (ed.), The Feminine Point of View, 1952

[57] [T]he old narrow marriage pattern is already changing, mainly through the spreading knowledge of effective methods of contraception. For the first time in history married women have some choice of work and way of life. It cannot be too clearly recognised that family planning (by whatever methods) whether by contraception or abstinence, has enormously improved the position of women and also of children. The unwilling pregnancy, the unwanted child . . . need no longer exist. Instead, we may look for children eagerly desired and responsibly planned for.

In this connection the members of this Conference feel bound to register the opinion that the authoritative condemnation of any form of family planning on religious grounds is a tragic obstacle [58] to human progress.

Judith Hubback, Wives Who Went to College, 1957

[149] The deeper emotions aroused by married life have considerably altered since birth control in one form or another became a normal habit for many couples. It is not only the obvious change that the fear of unintentional pregnancies is now almost conquered – the gain in sex life is certainly very great – it is also that, once the family has reached its planned size, wives can consider sex in a different way from that in which they have seen it until then: it will gratify their immediate needs and release the sexual tension which married life has shown them they, as well as their husbands, experience, but if they are wise, on the emotional plane, they will face up to the fact that they must consciously cut the reproductive urge out of love and sex. . . . . The wife experiences sexual pleasure without her part in reproduction – conception – being played: the two are physically separable, but emotionally they are closely linked.

It is fairly common for a woman who has had a child or children to find that sexual intercourse is more satisfying emotionally without contraceptive protection than when practising birth control.

V. M. Hughes, Women in Bondage, 1958

[65] [S]he often conceives in spite of precautions, for there is no absolutely reliable contraceptive. She is now like a rat in a trap . . . . She is supposed to be committing a 'crime' if she even employs an instrument on her own body in order to terminate the pregnancy . . . .

[66] [N]o possible legal penalty can deter the woman who is prepared to risk a terrible death . . . . Society is as directly responsible for the deaths of all women who die of amateur abortion as if it had itself murdered them . . . . [T]his does not 'serve her right', but is due to nothing more than a mere law, made in men's interests, and one that must be bad because it brings about tragedies like this.

[. . . .]

[67] It is natural and understandable for women to wish not to be wholly at the mercy of their own and men's fertility, and the law forbidding it is a tyranny . . . . Men have morally no right to influence here, much less to dictate to women what shall happen to their bodies.

[72] It is sometimes hinted that if women indulge in physical union they must take the consequences. But often the woman is unwilling, or only half willing, for submission. She is raped, or her lover taunts her with not 'loving' him, with 'frigidity', or her husband pesters her . . . . It is the last straw for men to round on women after using them thus, with, 'Well, if you don't want babies all the time, you shouldn't have physical relations.'

Even if the woman has voluntarily indulged in lovemaking, this view is still shamelessly unfair, for she gets all the physical consequences and in many cases a good deal less of the pleasure than the man.

Alice Jenkins, Law for the Rich, 1960

[28] The consultant had said, referring to his wife who was some distance away, 'Laura is over there. Looks well, you think? Yes, our three are flourishing, and we've just avoided trouble. She conceived another, but as our eldest is under four years old we just couldn't face a fourth and I arranged for a termination.'

[29] Hearing this from my husband nearly robbed me of breath, and when I listened to further details it seemed, to use a biblical expression, 'as though a great light had burst upon my vision'. Here at last was the safe way out, for which my mind had groped in the dark. This was *reformed law in practice*, being exercised illegally by someone empowered to do so. I asked myself the question, 'If a woman tired with the cares of her existing family could thus have an unwelcome pregnancy safely terminated, could this help not be extended to poverty-stricken women in the lower income

groups? Or must safe surgical termination remain the prerogative of the rich?'

[36] [N]o threat of penalties will deter the intelligent working woman from seeking her own way out when she is faced with a larger family than she feels she can cope with . . . . Pills and drugs having failed, she follows the well-trodden path and discovers the hitherto unknown person who can give here the relief she is seeking. Many of these amateur operations seem to be successful, but others entail years of broken health or end suddenly in the hospital mortuary.

[40] Some opponents of legal termination imagine hordes of women clamouring for this medical service, ignoring the fact that the operation, although safe, is not exactly a picnic. Moreover, the respectable mother of three or four children (for nine out of ten women asking for termination belong to this category) is unlikely to persist in taking risks which will periodically require her hospitalisation for a few days, thus depriving her family of her presence.

Elizabeth Draper, **Birth Control in the Modern World, 1965**

[88] It has been hoped by widening grounds for legal termination under medical and hospital care to reduce the number of more or less unskilled procurers, some of whom operate purely for gain while others do so with little or no financial benefit out of compassion for those unable, for lack of legal grounds or money, to get medical help. Despite their sometimes good intentions it is by these practitioners that the greatest misery is caused and the greatest damage frequently done.

[139] There are many who use birth control but are not altogether happy in practising it . . . . What of the thirty per cent who do not use any method at all even in this country of easy access to contraceptive appliances? Ways of reaching them have yet to be devised for if they are not reached, how can a balanced community be achieved? They need to be motivated and activated and helped to think well of contraception.

[201] It further handicaps public spending that lip-service is lingeringly paid, in public if not in private, to the idea that, as self-control ought to be possible, a birth-control service is a form of self-indulgence which ought to be paid for by the individual as are other luxury goods. A further embarrassment . . . is the relatively unchallenged theory that availability of contraceptives will encourage immorality. There is a very general desire

to reduce the number of [202] illegitimate babies, but by means only of stemming the rising tide of extra-marital intimacy. Those who would introduce other estimations of cause and effect, and at least other means of amelioration, have uphill tasks

Claire Rayner, Parent's Guide to Sex Education, *1968*[6]

[82] It is possible to tell adolescents about contraception in such a way that they are given all the information they will ever need about it while at the same time making it difficult for them to obtain the sort of contraception they might use themselves. There are so many different methods of contraception today that it is possible to point out to children, with complete truth, that the best methods are the ones that are supervised by doctors. If emphasis is put on these methods, clearly it will be more difficult for adolescents to make use of them before marriage.

However, it must be remembered that even if you do use this method of teaching your children about contraception, it is becoming more and more common for contraceptive advice to be given to the unmarried.

Ignorance and sex education

Still there is a pervasive amount of ignorance, still there are pleas for earlier better sex education. Still the association between ignorance and early and unfortunate sexual experiences is made.

Pearl Jephcott, Rising Twenty, *1948*

[87] This obsession with sex . . . seems to be influenced by the fact that practically none of the hundred girls, except for the dozen or so who were at secondary or central schools, ever had any formal teaching about it. Most, though not all, were familiar with the bare physical facts by the time they were 17, but they varied greatly in the amount and exactitude of further knowledge. While one 16 year old Londoner says impatiently, 'You know what a tart is, don't you?' and has a supply of bawdy jokes, another girl as old as 18 may still be quite ignorant of the meaning of birth control. The regulation instructions on V.D. given to the Services of courses get round to the girls, while the implications of the V.D. poster and press

6   See footnote 2.

campaign have probably spread knowledge about some aspects of sex to circles which it would not previously have reached . . . .

[88] From what sources have the girls obtained their knowledge of sex, apart, that is, from feminine friends of their own age and that other most fertile source of guidance, the elder sister? A few attended films and lectures through a youth organisation like the Women's Junior Air Corps, and much appreciated them. Some say they acquired most of their knowledge from their mother, though certain Londoners . . . reject this scornfully, 'Your mother wouldn't tell you anything.' Very few seem to have used books for fact-finding . . . . One of the North Country girls . . . sent for the books about sex mentioned in the [89] correspondence columns of a widely read and respected woman's magazine, and found them helpful. She is strongly of the opinion that fewer girls would 'go wrong' if they knew more about sex; and she wishes that written matter was more readily available. The booklets of the British Social Hygiene Council seep round. In one case they are still circulating, with all the spice of a clandestine literature, among a set of girls one of whom first got hold of them several years ago. The approval of these highly critical readers of their publications would rejoice the heart of the Council.

Susan Isaacs, Troubles of Children and Parents, 1948

[229] [T]he most helpful plan is to answer the child's questions on the subject of birth at the time when they are asked . . . . Young children of, say, from three to five years of age, often ask such questions spontaneously, whereas older children, of from seven to eight years onwards, are more shy and less openly interested in these matters. Indeed, boys and girls in the later years of childhood are sometimes embarrassed and awkward when talked to on this subject . . . .

I should certainly give your little girl a copy of *How a Baby is Born* as a present. The delightful illustrations would be very likely to start a number of questions, and you could then either answer these yourself or read her the text of the book . . . . [I]t would be better to tell her about it yourself than to let her hear in some secret or frightening way from another child. But I would not read the book to her in a solemn or didactic way. Let her have the book and follow her interest in it in whatever form it takes, making clear anything she wants to know in a simple and frank way, and telling her that you would like to answer any questions she wants to ask about it.

Marjorie C. Hume, 'Sex Education in the Home', 1949

[211] Parents must first think the matter out thoroughly for themselves – if possible the mother and father should do this together – and then make a coherent plan, based on certain large, fundamental principles, to cover the whole period of the child's life from infancy to maturity. The alternative, to leave the child to pick up sex knowledge for himself, with the possible assistance of a few meagre scraps of information grudgingly given, is to court almost certain disaster.

There are still plenty of parents to be found who say airily: 'Oh, well they'll pick it all up soon enough. I don't need to bother.' True, the majority of children will pick up a certain amount of knowledge, but it will be garbled, twisted, distorted, incomplete knowledge, probably acquired in thoroughly undesirable ways and from thoroughly undesirable sources.

[216] The cabbage patch, the gooseberry bush, and the doctor's black bag are not so popular nowadays as they were a generation ago, as answers to children's questions, but fibs and fairy stories are still all too common, and so are evasions and putting off – 'Oh, I'll tell you when you're older.' Nothing is safe which leaves the child's natural curiosity unsatisfied, or which gives him the impression that there is something queer and different about sex matters. He is quick to realize that his mother (or father) is embarrassed by certain questions, and is unwilling to talk about them, and this soon begins to build up in his mind that feeling of shame and guilt in association with sex which we have already discussed.

Leonora Eyles, Sex for the Engaged, 1952

[54] Many parents and teachers think that they have taught young people all they need to know on that subject, given them books and even shown them diagrams. The fact remains that many young people even after a talk with mother or father, or a lecture or two at school, seem strangely ignorant; if they have been told in an awkward and shame-faced way probably they have repressed it . . . .

I read recently that every boy or girl should, at puberty, be taken to a good doctor who would explain the facts of life clearly. I cannot think of anything more mistaken. To surround the facts of reproduction, of love, with the atmosphere of the consulting-room is taking it all out of its right place . . . . The right way to explain these things to children is to begin very young, as soon as the child asks questions; some modern young parents are able to answer such questions frankly and without embarrassment but many are still very muddled themselves . . . .

If children have not been told in childhood, and the parents do not know how to tell them, it is best for them to learn at school – if the school treats this as a subject to be explained, as some do. If none of these methods is available, it is best to read a sane, non-sentimental book and get the facts straight. The most dangerous thing is to listen to young friends who have usually got it all wrong

Dr Esther Waterhouse, 'What Shall We Tell Our Children About Sex?', 1956

[41] [W]e should approach the task in a humble attitude of mind, so that with God's help we shall be able to show to our children some of the wonder of the story. There is a difference between giving scientific instruction and trying to show the child the right attitude of mind. That is why teaching given in the home, by the parents, is valuable to the child. Everyday life in the home gives ample opportunity for simple teaching to be given.

[42] [L]et us imagine some possible questions and answers . . . .

Q. Where did I come from? Where do babies come from?
A. You grew – you started as a little egg and grew.
Q. Where did I grow?
A. You grew in a special little house inside Mummy's body.

[. . . .]
You remember that Mummy told you about the little passage way through which you came, well [43] before you began, Daddy had to put a special seed into Mummy's body and he put it in that passage, and he used a penis to do this . . . . The seed is called a sperm, and it swam up the passage inside the little house in Mummy's body and there it met a special cell which Mummy made, called an 'ovum'.

[44] If possible let the family keep pets . . . . [I]t is usually quite simple to give teaching to the owners of these pets, so that they begin to have a grasp of the subject of reproduction . . . .

Many children are keen gardeners, and will appreciate the different parts of the flower, especially if a magnifying glass is used. So you can show them the stamens and the stigma and the box where the seeds develop, and the pollen on the stamens, and explain to them that the pollen from one flower of the same species has to be deposited on the stigma of another flower before the fruit or seed develops . . . .

The opportunities which may arise while bathing or dressing. All children take an interest in their own bodies and also in those of other people, and thus they will ask questions about them. By using these questions as a 'jumping-off ground', you can amplify a child's knowledge of the facts of sex.

Rose Hacker, The Opposite Sex, 1957

[37] Some parents think the keeping of pets is enough to enlighten any child, not realising that children quite often do not imagine any likeness between animals and human beings. Some children do not like to ask questions . . . . A few parents shirk the whole business and think that questions are best answered at school. But not every teacher is equipped to teach such a subject, and children quickly recognise the fact.

Most youngsters seem to think that parents should tell the facts of life to their own children and not leave them to pick up their information from others, but some children realise that this is not easy for many parents who, as one teenager put it, 'have no language about sex that would not make them blush'.

Doris Odlum, Journey Through Adolescence, 1957

[21] A curious mixture of fear, false modesty, and resistance to change still surrounds the whole question of what we should tell our children about their own physical and psychological development as well as about the sexual relationships of human beings and the part that they play in the life both of the individual and the community. Here again the ostrich attitude is extremely dangerous because the development is occurring and has to be dealt with. The urges towards sex are deeply ingrained in the pattern of human nature because they are vital for the continuance of the species, and it is only by understanding them and facing up to them that we can hope to influence or control them so that they are used for the benefit both of the individual and the community. It is the absolute duty of parents to make sure that their [22] children know the facts of reproduction from a very early age, and that they are taught them in such a way that they will not appear in any way unpleasing or indecent. All children, by the age of six or preferably younger, should know where babies come from and have some idea of how they are born, so that they do not imagine inaccurate and impossible methods of birth, as many children did in the past, with terrifying effects.

[24] Parents are often afraid that if their children know about sex they will want to experiment . . . . [T]he dangers of leaving growing children in ignorance of the nature of their own emotional urges, and those of the

opposite sex with whom, in the modern world, they mix freely and without any adult guidance or control, are leading to even more disastrous results. This is another case where knowledge is the road to understanding and wisdom.

Doris Odlum, The Mind of Your Child, 1960

[98] Sex teaching should never be accompanied by warnings or any suggestion that sex in itself is wrong or dangerous. Otherwise we may frighten children into feeling a disgust for the sexual aspect of marriage and parenthood. We should make it clear that sexual love is natural to man and the method by which we become parents and have children to carry on the race. From this good start it is easy to point out how important it is to use such a valuable gift wisely and to realise what a great contribution both men and women can make to the welfare of the community by building up a happy family. Children who feel they can talk freely about sex to their parents will be much less likely to go with bad companions or get into difficulties later on.

Elizabeth Draper, Birth Control in the Modern World, 1965

[133] There is . . . a common problem in all teaching . . . on this subject. It can so easily take on that unacceptable quality of the old and experienced lecturing in terms of final assessment and evaluation – but on the basis of *their* experience, pre-conditioning, and values – with a too easy assurance which is unpalatable or even disturbing to the sensitive, seeking, developing, and often idealistic young person. It is not uncommon to find teenagers who are quite accustomed to discussion about sex and family planning . . . being thoroughly upset by a lecture in this idiom at school. The content of the lecture is probably irreproachable and accurate, but the manner of discussing it, and the personal attitudes which this manner betrays to a sensitive audience, can be traumatic in effect. It is of all subjects one in which the teacher must be alive to the frame of mind and emotions of the learner and must be fully aware of the possible influence to which the latter has been subjected . . . .

[134] It is one thing to have this information even in quite detailed terms in a remote and academic context . . . It is quite another to relate it to one's own feelings and activities. It is here that the individual's needs are so diverse and so sensitive that the most valuable teaching is probably in the context of the small group discussion or individual consultation; and it is difficult for the outside visiting teacher to be able to succeed in giving this.

A better method probably, once the basic facts have been imparted, is to allow the children to bring up their own points for discussion, and it may sometimes be essential for them to do this anonymously.

[136] Venereal disease has been one of the hazards in sexual relations for many generations, and the greater the range of sexual activity the greater the hazard. It is wholly proper to give it its place in discussions of this subject, but knowledge alone will not avoid it altogether. Neither is there much hope that factual knowledge will change or restore the 'moral' aspects of sexual activity and reduce promiscuity

Diana Dewar, Orphans of the Living, *1968*

[138] There is much freer discussion about sexual matters but it is seldom carried on between adults and children with the maturity and under-standing required for real communication across the growing gulf between the generations. Many young people are never invited to talk about sex at school or at home, nor do some of them feel free to do so. The majority first learn how babies are born from their friends. Usually through jokes .... [B]y twelve or thirteen most children know, or think they know, the facts of life. Much of this information comes from their friends and much is inaccurate and crude. Unhappily, when informed sex education comes later these children are often disinclined to listen because they think they know it all, and the misunderstandings and prejudices which have taken root early remain.
[. . . .]
[139] [T]he main reason so many working-class parents will not talk to their children about sex is that they literally cannot find the words. It is doubtful whether they could give a coherent and correct explanation of the sexual act to anyone, let alone a mystified child.
[. . . .]
The widespread ignorance, confusion, and embarrassment surrounding sex must be dispelled among many parents if they are to help their children in any meaningful way. There is no substitute for the help of mature loving parents in this or any other role, and children will listen to their parents about sex if only they make sense of it!
Schools appear to be more concerned to give sex education to girls than to boys .... Most of the girls received biological and physiological instruction. Some were also given moral advice but few received any technical information.

Helena Wright, Sex and Society, 1968

[75] As possession of the answers to the fundamental inquiries about the facts of sex gradually becomes universal among children, the harm still being caused to young minds by clandestine and inaccurate sexual gossip will gradually be eliminated. Thus, the biological teaching, which should be obligatory in all schools, could be begun in the youngest classes on the foundation of simple knowledge acquired at home.

When it becomes accepted that elementary biological teaching will be part of all school curricula right from these youngest ages, the relation of home instruction to school teaching will be clearly defined and understood. Up to the age of five it is the parents' privilege to provide the groundwork in their answers to all the questions of their children. After that age, parents ought to be able to trust schools to go on building smoothly and to give appropriate biological information as interestingly and competently as information on any other subject.

[78] In considering all the different kinds of emotional involvements that can bewilder and torment girls and boys as they try to understand the new ideas and apply them to themselves, their mentors must remember that heterosexual attachments are not the only ones which will need advice and guidance. Homosexual relationships involve just as much responsibility in behaviour as do heterosexual ones. It would be advisable for all teachers who are willing to be approached in this way to inform themselves about the salient facts of normal psychology as they apply to quite young girls and boys. Knowledge of this kind would help advisers to detect sexual tendencies of which the individuals are as yet unaware. Kindly explanations of the various phases that are normal in adolescents could save anxiety and bewilderment, and help in understanding and control.
[. . . .]

[I]t must be emphasized that during the description of sexual psychology the chief objects of sexual experience, pleasure and power must be allowed their full, true importance. It must also be made clear that women are potentially just as capable as men of achieving complete sexual satisfaction, but that, unlike men, their capacity for sexual pleasure is generally slow in developing.

The chief difficulty in this stage of the sex education of adolescents is how to choose a method which will convey adequately and honestly the strength of the instinctive urge to experience sexual pleasure, balanced against the necessity for the individual control and self discipline in all sexual relations which is so essential for the continuance of civilized society.

[86] The only motive of parents who now, unfortunately, think it their duty to prevent infantile physical sexual enjoyment, can be that the parents

connect physical enjoyment with some vague idea that it is 'wrong' or dangerous for the infant. The opposite idea should motivate the parents, that sexual pleasure is in itself 'good' and healthy. Thus, they would be doing all they could to prevent their children connecting sex pleasure with guilt.

Claire Rayner, Parent's Guide to Sex Education, *1968*[7]

[1] [S]exual intercourse and reproduction are natural functions – but this doesn't mean that every individual is born with an instinctive knowledge of how his or her body works, how to help it work best, and above all, how to *enjoy* it.

I believe it is possible to teach children about sex, to discuss it freely, without for one moment invading individual privacy. One of the most valuable things that has come out of our modern willingness to discuss matters of sex freely and easily is that it has been 'cleaned up.'

[4] Some people have thought that if children are not answered when they ask, if sex is never discussed in their presence, they will lose interest and just not think about it until they are much older. That is a false idea if ever there was one. Even very small children learn quickly what sort of things must not be talked about with their parents, and shut up accordingly – but the interest is still there, underneath the surface of their minds. In fact, it is *increased*. [5] Adult secrecy on what seem to a child a perfectly normal thing to talk about . . . alarms them. It makes them think there is something wicked, dirty, shameful, about their own bodies. And this can be a very dangerous idea for a child to get hold of.

[11] [T]he woman who secretly thinks sex is horrible and disgusting, and no joy, will pass the same attitudes on to her daughters . . . .

This is why it is so important for married couples to enjoy their sex lives. Not only do they themselves lose much if there are unresolved sex prob-[12] lems in their relationship; they can't really help their children to grow up into completely happy adults.

[65] [I]t is usually best to leave it to your children to ask the first questions about these problems rather than sitting down solemnly to 'have a little talk.' . . . . [T]here is one subject that may have to be brought up by adults, and that is the behaviour of sadists, child molesters and so on. Sometimes there will be news items that will bring the questions up, but if there are

7   See footnote 2.

no such triggers, then obviously it is essential that children be told about these things anyway . . . .

[S]mall children can be given a blanket warning about not talking to strangers and not accepting gifts or sweets, without being told that these people are dangerous because they are sexually deranged. A blanket warning is not, however, enough for teenagers. They need to know *why*.

[80] [E]ven if your adolescents accept the idea that chastity before marriage is a worthwhile way to live, they will still need to know about birth control and accept the idea [81] that it is a good thing in itself, to arm them for the day when they will marry and become potential parents themselves.

As for the idea that telling young people about contraception will encourage them to embark on experiments themselves – I believe that this idea cannot be supported. I am quite sure that many young people embark on sexual experiment as a way of gaining information that they so desperately need.

Appendix

Ϩꙮ

Biographical notes on authors

Organizations with which writers were associated

ALRA	Abortion Law Reform Association (f. 1936)
BSSSP	British Society for the Study of Sex Psychology (1913–1947)
FPA	Family Planning Association (previously National Birth Control Association, f. 1930)
FPSI	Federation of Progressive Societies and Individuals, later Progressive League (f. early 1930s)
FS	Fabian Society
FW	*The Freewoman* and its associated discussion circles (1911–1913)
ML	Malthusian (from 1921 New Generation) League, first birth control organisation in the UK (f. 1878)
MWC	Men and Women's Club (1880s)
NCCVD	National Council for Combatting Venereal Diseases, later known as British Social Hygiene Council (f. 1914)
NKWWC	North Kensington Women's Welfare Clinic, birth control clinic set up in 1924
NUWSS	National Union of Women's Suffrage Societies (the constitutional suffragists)
WBCG	Worker's Birth Control Group (f. 1924)
WFL	Women's Freedom League, broke away from the WSPU in protest at its autocracy
WSPU	Women's Social and Political Union, founded by the Pankhursts, the militant suffragettes

Sources for additional information

DNB   *The Dictionary of National Biography*[1]
FCLE   *The Feminist Companion to Literature in English*
ODNB   *The Oxford Dictionary of National Biography* (the revised and expanded version published 2004)
WSM   *The Women's Suffrage Movement: A Reference Guide*, edited by Elizabeth Crawford
WWW   *Who Was Who*

Authors cited

Ellen Dorothy Abb (fl. 1930s)
No information found.

Ann Allen (fl. 1960s)
Journalist, agony aunt, *Sunday Mirror*, author of history of the NSPCC and a handbook for teenage girls. Married, four children.

Lady (Florence Elizabeth) Barrett (née Perry) CH CBE, MD, MS (1867–1945)
Distinguished obstetrician and gynaecologist. Sympathy with early suffrage movement but condemned militancy. Profound religious beliefs. Married Sir William Barrett FRS in 1916.
DNB.

Victoria E. M. Bennett (fl 1930s)
Child psychologist.

Annie Besant (1847–1933)
Freethinker, trade unionist, theosophist, supporter of Indian independence. ML, MWC.
Annie Besant: An Autobiography (London: T. Fisher Unwin, 1893). Numerous biographies, DNB.

Morwenna Bielby (fl. 1950s)
Methodist. Writer of religious drama.

---

1   The women who appear in this also appear, usually with revised and expanded entries, in the ODNB (2004). Inclusion in the original DNB tends to indicate a certain degree of recognition of a woman's achievements in her lifetime.

Elizabeth Blackwell (1821–1910)
Pioneering doctor: first woman on UK Medical Register (qualified in USA). MWC.
Several biographies, DNB.

Catherine Booth (1829–1890)
'The Mother of the Salvation Army': married General William Booth.
Several biographies, DNB.

Mary Borden (Lady Spears) (1886–1968)
Born in USA, educated at Vassar, married G. D. Turner, three sons, divorced, ran a field hospital in France during the Great War, married English soldier, later MP and diplomat, Edward Spears. Numerous novels.
FCLE, ODNB.

Maud Churton Braby (fl. 1900s)
'New Woman' novelist, corresponded with G. B. Shaw.

Mary Katherine Bradby (fl. 1920s)
Psychoanalyst, poet.

Vera Brittain (1893–1970)
Novelist, autobiographer, pacifist. FPSI.
Paul Berry and Mark Bostridge, *Vera Brittain: A Life* (London: Chatto & Windus, 1995), DNB.

Stella Browne (1880–1955)
Radical feminist socialist sex reformer, founder of ALRA.
ML, BSSSP, WBCG, FS, FPSI, ALRA.
Lesley A. Hall, *Strong Red Rag: Stella Browne, Radical Feminist, Socialist and Sex Reformer* (London: I. B. Tauris, forthcoming), ODNB.

Josephine Butler (née Grey) (1828–1906)
Leading Victorian feminist and leader of the campaign for the repeal of the Contagious Diseases Acts.
Jane Jordan, *Josephine Butler* (London: John Murray 2001), DNB.

Olwen Ward Campbell (née Ward) (1890–1952)
Daughter of the Cambridge philosopher Professor James Ward. Biographer and writer on literary subjects. Married Professor A. Y. Campbell. Persistent ill-health.

Mary G. Cardwell MD (fl. 1910s–60s)
Qualified in medicine 1918. Catholic writer on hygiene, etc. Lecturer on Hygiene at the Mount Pleasant Training College, Liverpool.

Janet Chance (née Whyte) (1886–1953)

Rationalist, birth control supporter, established Sex Education Centre. Married, children. Committed suicide by throwing herself out of a window while under treatment for depression after her husband's death. FPSI, ALRA.

Dr Enid Charles (1894–1972)

Statistician and demographer, Communist. Daughter of the Rev. James Charles of Denbigh. Educated at Newnham College Cambridge, and University of Liverpool. Married Professor Lancelot Hogden, 1918, four children, marriage dissolved in 1957. Later worked with World Health Organisation.
WWW, ODNB.

Mrs Cecil Chesterton (née Ada Elizabeth Jones, known as 'Keith') OBE (*c*. 1870–1962)

Daughter, sister, aunt and wife of men associated with newspapers and periodicals, and herself a prolific journalist. Married Cecil, brother of G. K. Chesterton, in 1917, who died shortly afterwards. Voluntarily lived as a down-and-out in London, the experience which led to her founding the Cecil Houses for Homeless Women.
WWW, ODNB.

Jane Clapperton (1832–1914)

Socialist, freethinker.
ML, MWC, Legitimation League, WFL, WSPU.
WSM, ODNB.

Irene Clephane (fl. 1930s)

Journalist, author, and translator.

Margaret Cole (née Postgate) (1893–1980)

First Class Honours in Classics Tripos, Girton. Taught, then worked for the Fabian (later Labour) Research Department, married G.D.H. Cole (d. 1959): commuting marriage, three children. In same circle as the Mitchisons, also wrote detective stories, biography. FS.
Betty Vernon, *Margaret Cole 1893–1980: A Political Biography* (London: Croom Helm, 1986), DNB.

Geraldine Coster (1882– ? Still publishing 1968)

Nurse, psychoanalyst. Also wrote on Wychwood School, geography, and yoga.

Gladys M. Cox (fl. 1920s–1960s)
Qualified in medicine 1925. Married. Medical Officer of Infant Welfare and Birth Control Clinics. Wrote on contraception and women's health issues. Health editor, *Modern Woman*.

Clemence Dane CBE (Winifred Ashton) (1888–1965)
Author (*Regiment of Women*, 1917), playwright. Studied art, tried acting, taught in a girls school, and became a writer (mention in obit of 'woman friend "E.A." who stood by her in her new venture').
DNB.

Dr Mary Denhan, *see* Gladys Cox.

Diana Dewar (1927–1984)
Writer mainly on religious matters. Married to regional TV manager for BBC West. Three sons. Journalist, later in life freelanced on sociological, educational and moral topics.
Died 'by falling from the Clifton suspension bridge'.

Elizabeth Draper (b. 1915)
Methodist background. Married twice. Assorted career experience: advertising and market research, work in rehabilitation of psychiatric casualties, General Secretary of the Institute for the Study and Treatment of Delinquency. From 1960–1964 secretary and investigator to a research group advising the FPA on how its work might 'be brought further into line with present requirements'.

Edith Havelock Ellis (née Lees) (1861–1916)
Wife of Havelock Ellis. Known lesbian. Novels, plays, essays. Biographical information in biographies of her husband. FW, WSPU.
Her posthumously published *Stories and Essays* (Berkeley Heights: The Free Spirit Press, 1924) contains biographical reminiscences by friends and colleagues, including by Stella Browne, q.v. See also biographies of Havelock Ellis, FCLE.

(Margaret) Leonora Eyles (née Pitcairn) (1889–1960)
Daughter of the owner of a Staffordshire pottery works. Married twice. Spent some time living in a working-class neighbourhood. Journalist, novelist, autobiographer, socialist, 'agony aunt' of *Modern Woman*.
Autobiographies *The Ram Escapes: The Story of a Victorian Childhood* (London: Peter Nevill, 1953), *For My Enemy Daughter* (London: Victor Gollancz, 1941), FCLE, WWW, ODNB.

Letitia Fairfield (1885–1978)
Qualified doctor and barrister. Roman Catholic. First Senior Medical Officer of the London County Council. Sister of Rebecca West.
WSPU, FS, NCCVD.
ODNB.

Xenia Field MBE, JP (1894–1998)
'Prison reformer and horticulturist'.
ODNB.

Rose Hacker (née Goldbloom) (b. 1906)
Marriage Guidance Council.
Autobiography, *Abraham's Daughter* (London: Deptford Forum Publishing, 1996).

Charlotte Haldane (née Franken) (1894–1969)
Biographer, novelist, twice married, the second time to J. B. S. Haldane, brother of Naomi Mitchison, following controversial divorce case.
Judith Anderson, *Charlotte Haldane: Woman Writer in a Man's World* (Basingstoke: Macmillan, 1998), ODNB.

Gladys Mary Hall, MA (fl. 1930s)
No information found.

Cicely Hamilton (Cicely Mary Hammill) (1872–1952)
Actress, writer, suffragist (WFL), birth control and abortion reform. Autobiography. WSPU/WFL, BSSSP, ALRA.
Cicely Hamilton, *Life Errant: Autobiographical Reminiscences* (London: J.M. Dent, 1935), Lis Whitelaw, *The Life and Rebellious Times of Cicely Hamilton, Actress, Writer, Suffragist* (London: Women's Press, 1990), FCLE, WSM, ODNB.

Mary Agnes Hamilton (née Adamson), CBE (1884–1966)
Journalist, novelist and biographer, politician (Labour MP, 1929–1931) and public servant. 'Her marriage, which was unfortunate, lasted only a very little while, and she seldom referred to it'.
Autobiographies *Remembering My Good Friends* (London: Jonathan Cape, 1944) and *Up-hill all the way* (London: Jonathan Cape, 1953), WWW, ODNB.

Winifred Holtby (1898–1935)
Writer, feminist, anti-racist, socialist. FPSI.
E. E. M. Jardine, *Winifred Holtby as I Knew Her; A Study of the Author and her Works* (London: Collins 1938), Vera Brittain, *Testament of*

Friendship: The Story of Winifred Holtby (London: Macmillan and Co., 1940), Marion Shaw, *The Clear Stream: A Life of Winifred Holtby* (London: Virago, 1999).
DNB.

Jane Ellice Hopkins (1836–1904)

Social purity worker.
Sue Morgan, *A Passion for Purity: Ellice Hopkins and the Politics of Gender in the Late-Victorian Church* (Bristol: Centre for Comparative Studies in Religion and Gender, University of Bristol, 1999), DNB.

Ettie Hornibrook (née Rout) (1877–1936)

New Zealand anti-VD worker, birth control, sex reform generally.
Jane Tolerton, *Ettie: A Life of Ettie Rout* (London: Penguin 1992), ODNB.

Judith Hubback (b. 1917)

Writer, analytical psychologist. Cambridge graduate, 'mother of three young children'.

Violet Marjorie Hughes (fl. 1950s)

No information found.

Marjorie C. Hume (fl. 1940s)

General Secretary, Marriage Guidance Council.

Isabel Hutton (née Elmslie) (d. 1960)

Doctor, psychiatrist.
Autobiography, *Memories of a Doctor in War and Peace* (London: Heinemann, 1960). WWW, ODNB.

Laura Hutton (1889–1974)

Doctor, physician at the Tavistock Clinic, London.

Susan Isaacs (née Sutherland) CBE (1885–1948)

Psychoanalyst and educational psychologist. Married twice. 1933 started department of advanced study of the education and psychology of young children at the University of London Institute of Education. Wrote weekly answers to parents in *Nursery World*.
Lydia A.H. Smith *To Understand and to Help: The Life and Work of Susan Isaacs, 1885–1948* (Rutherford: Fairleigh Dickinson University Press, 1985), ODNB.

Lena (Baroness) Jeger (née Chivers) (b. 1915)
Journalist, Labour MP.

Alice Jenkins (1888–1968)
Born in Yorkshire, started her career as a pupil teacher, married William Jenkins, one daughter. Only surviving founder of ALRA to see the passing of the 1967 Act. WBCG, FPA, ALRA.

(Agnes) Pearl Jephcott (1900–1980)
Organizer of Girls' Clubs. Worked for PEP (Political and Economic Planning) and then Department of Social Science at Nottingham University, later LSE. Participant social observation, e.g. in *Girls Growing Up*, and other surveys on needs of youth, juvenile delinquency. Unmarried.
ODNB.

Arabella Kenealy (1859–1932)
Practised medicine, 1888–1894, until diphtheria left her with delicate health, and she became a writer, producing novels (*Dr Janet of Harley Street*, 1893, includes a sympathetic lesbian figure), articles in magazines, and works on medical and scientific themes. Strongly anti-feminist, saw woman as eugenic regenerators of the race; interested in occultism. Never married.
FCLE, ODNB.

Melanie Klein (née Reizes) (1882–1960)
Born in Vienna, her father a Polish Jewish doctor, her mother from Hungary. Married, later divorced, children. Became a psychoanalyst working particularly with children. Came to England in 1926 and was a major influence on the development of psychoanalysis in Britain.
Biography and numerous studies of her influential theories, DNB.

Margaret Kornitzer (fl. 1930s–1960s)
Authority on adoption, also writer of children's books.

Constance Long (d. 1923)
Qualified in medicine 1896. Studied psychoanalysis and was one of first British Jungians. Associated with the Brunswick Square Clinic set up by May Sinclair before the First World War. Female partner. BSSSP.

Barbara Low (1884–1958)
Socialist, feminist, Became involved in psychoanalysis. FW, BSSSP, FS.

Mary Macaulay (1902–)
Born India, Liverpool Medical School, 18 years in general practice with

her husband, two sons also doctors, 1930–1956 medical officer to Liverpool Branch, Family Planning Association, helped to found Merseyside Branch of the Marriage Guidance Council. FPA.

Joan Malleson (née Billson) (1900–1956)
Married the actor and author Miles Malleson while still a medical student, qualified as a doctor 1925, two children, later divorced. Moving spirit behind the Bourne test-case that created case-law enabling doctors to perform abortions on the grounds of risk to woman's physical or mental health. Involved in birth control and sex therapy. NKWWC, FPA, ALRA.
ODNB.

Dorothy Manchée (fl. 1930s–1940s)
Almoner, St Mary's Hospital, London.

Ethel Mannin (1900–1984)
Prolific novelist, journalist and autobiographer. Born in a London suburb, educated at the local council school and started work at 15 in advertising. Generally interested in progressive causes. Married twice, one daughter.
Several volumes of autobiography and reminiscence, FCLE, ODNB.

Norah March, BSc, FRSanI (d. 1946)
Hygiene educator, secretary of National Baby Week Council, editor of *Mother and Child*, secretary, Health and Cleanliness Council. BSSSP, NCCVD.

Louisa Martindale CBE, JP, MD BS, FRCOG (1872–1966)
Surgeon. Life partner of another woman, Ismay Fitzgerald. Suffragist. Continuing interest in the problems of venereal diseases. NUWSS.
A Woman Surgeon: An Autobiography (London: Victor Gollancz, 1951), WSM, ODNB.

Annette M. B. Meakin (1867–1959)
Translator, biographer, traveller. Studied music, in First World War qualified as a chemist's assistant. With her mother the first woman to cross the Trans-Siberian Railway.

Dr Merell Philippa Middlemore (d. 1938)
Qualified in medicine 1923. Author of *The Nursing Couple* (1941). Died suddenly of cardiac failure, leaving a bequest to Joan Malleson, 'desiring . . . that she will apply the same in favour of any needy person, charity or cause in which she is interested'.

Naomi Mitchison (née Haldane) (1897–1999)
Author, traveller, autobiographer, Mass Observer, socialist, wife of MP, sex reformer, free love, birth control. NKWWC, FPSI.
Small Talk, All Change Here and *You May Well Ask: A Memoir 1920–1940* (London: Victor Gollancz, 1973, 1975, 1979). Jill Benton, *Naomi Mitchison: A Century of Experiment in Life and Letters* (London: Pandora, 1990). Jenni Calder, *The Nine Lives of Naomi Mitchison* (London: Virago, 1997), ODNB.

Doris Langley Moore (1902–1989)
Born in South Africa. Married. Novelist, biographer, fashion historian, writer on etiquette. Founder of Museum of Costume.
WWW, ODNB.

Alison Neilans (1884–1942)
Organizer for the WFL, from 1913 General Secretary of the Association for Moral and Social Hygiene, 'fearless application of equal moral standards' and Editor of *The Shield*. WFL.
WSM.

Sybil Neville-Rolfe (née Burney) (1887–1955)
From a naval family. Married first, at 20, Lt. A. C. Gotto, and widowed young, later marrying Cmdr C. Neville-Rolfe (by whom she had children). A founder of the Eugenics Education Society (1908) and subsequently a leading figure in the NCCVD, also involved in establishing the National Council for the Unmarried Mother and her Child. A 'eugenic feminist'.
ODNB.

Harriet Nokes (fl. 1890s)
Prostitute rescue worker.

Helena Florence Normanton (Mrs Gavin Bowman Watson Clark) QC (1883–1957)
Admitted as a student to the Middle Temple in 1919 (first woman), first woman called to English bar, 1922, and one of the first two (1949) to be made a King's Counsel (take silk).
ODNB.

Doris Odlum (1890–1985)
One of the outstanding child psychiatrists of the day, with a Diploma of Education as well as medical qualification, DPsychM. Involved in many organizations related to mental health.
ODNB.

Dame Christabel Harriett Pankhurst (1880–1958)

The eldest daughter of Emmeline Pankhurst, with whom and her sisters she founded the WSPU in 1907. A leading figure in the militant suffrage movement.

Autobiography (posthumously published), *Unshackled: The Story of How We Won the Vote* (London: Hutchinson and Co., 1959). Several biographies, DNB, WSM.

E. V. (Vera) Pemberton (d. 1980s)

Rector's daughter: ran Ingatestone Boys' Club for over 50 years. Published various pamphlets on sex education and marriage guidance, worked with church groups such as the Mothers' Union. Unmarried.

Jean Pochin (fl. 1960s)

Secretary of Carlisle Diocesan Council for Social Work.

Helena Langhorne Powell FRHistS (1874–1942)

Historian, educationalist. Headmistress of Leeds Girls' High School, Principal of Cambridge Training College and of St Mary's Training College, Lancaster Gate.

Claire Rayner (b. 1931)

Nurse, agony aunt, novelist, popular health writer.
How Did I Get Here from There? (London: Virago, 2003).

Lucy Re-Bartlett (d. 1922)

Studied Indian philosophy in India with Anne Besant. Married D. Emilio Re of Rome and promoted the Italian cause in England. Never a suffragist.

(Agnes) Maude Royden CH, DD (1896–1956)

Daughter of a former Mayor of Liverpool. Educated at Cheltenham Ladies College and Lady Margaret Hall, Oxford. Worked in a women's settlement in Liverpool before going to help the Rev. G. W. Hudson Shaw in his country parish. 1908 joined the National Union of Women's Suffrage Societies. One of the first women pastors in England, and a mistress of pulpit oratory, in spite of troubles in finding a pulpit. Pacifist. Married Hudson Shaw, then over 80 and retired, 1944: he died very shortly afterwards. NUWSS.

Maude Royden, *A Threefold Cord: Autobiographical Reminiscences* (London: Victor Gollancz, 1947), Sheila Fletcher, *Maude Royden* (Oxford: Blackwell, 1989), DNB, WSM.

Dora Russell (née Black) (1894–1986)
Feminist intellectual, sex reformer, progressive educationalist, socialist, pacifist, wife of Bertrand Russell (open marriage): marriage dissolved. Four children, two by Russell, two by Griffin Barry. WBCG, FPSI, ALRA.
The Tamarisk Tree (3 volumes of autobiography) (London: Elek, 1975, Virago, 1980, 1985), FCLE, ODNB.

Dame Mary Scharlieb (née Bird) (1845–1930)
Wife of European magistrate in India, one of first women to qualify in medicine in UK, leading figure in social purity movement. NCCVD.
Reminiscences (London: Williams and Norgate, 1925), DNB.

Olive Schreiner (1855–1920)
South African, novelist, author. Close friend of Havelock Ellis. Married Samuel Cronwright. MWC.
Several biographies and critical studies, DNB (subentry to that of her brother).

Nina Searl (fl. 1930s)
Psychoanalyst.

M. B. Smith (fl. 1950s)
'Herself a single woman'.

Margery Spring Rice (1887–1970)
Feminist, birth controller, part of Mitchison circle. A founder of NKWWC, also involved in starting the Birth Control Investigation Committee. NKWWC, FPA.
ODNB.

Margaret Stephens (fl. 1910s)
No information found.

Marie Stopes (1880–1958)
Botanist, traveller, playwright, poet, feminist (second generation), advocate of birth control and the sexual rights of women. Retained her maiden name on both of her two marriages (the first annulled on the grounds of non-consummation, which led her to write *Married Love*). WFL, FS.
Several biographies, DNB.

Violet D. Swaisland (fl. 1940s)
Lecturer in social hygiene, writer of works on sex education. NCCVD.

H. M. (Helena Maria Lucy) Swanwick (née Sickert) (1864–1939)
Born in Germany to a German-Danish father and English mother, came to England in childhood. Married 1888, no children. Feminist, socialist, pacifist. Editor of *Common Cause*, journal of the NUWSS, and a founder of the Union of Democratic Control. WSPU, NUWSS.
I Have Been Young, etc: An Autobiography (London: Victor Gollancz, 1935), DNB, WSM.

(Rosa) Frances (Emily) Swiney (née Biggs) (1847–1922)
Born in Indian to a military family, married to a major-general, six children. Extreme social purity feminist, interests in theosophy and food reform, founded the League of Isis. ML, NUWSS, WSPU, WFL.
WSM, ODNB.

Rosalie Taylor (1906–1999)
Born in Pinsk, Russia, came to UK aged 8. Qualified in medicine Royal Free Hospital 1931. Gynaecologist and founder member of the Institute of Psychosexual Medicine, worked in birth control, marriage guidance and studied non-consummation. Twice married, two children. FPA.

Dorothy Thurtle (née Lansbury) (d. 1973)
Daughter of Labour politician, George Lansbury, married to Ernest Thurtle, MP (d. 1954), local Labour councillor. WBCG, ALRA.

Dr Esther Waterhouse (1908–1995)
Methodist doctor.

Dr Helen Webb (fl. 1880s–1900s)
Qualified in medicine, 1888.

Mrs Rosalind Wilkinson
'An experienced social research worker'; investigated prostitution and gave evidence to the Wolfenden Committee, also talked about it on BBC *Woman's Hour*.

Virginia Wimperis (fl. 1960s)
MA Cantab.

Moya Woodside (b. 1907)
Research psychiatric social worker. Also involved in birth control movement.

Helena Wright (née Lowenfeld) (1887–1982)
Doctor, former medical missionary, open marriage, birth control

movement, marital therapy. Jewish by birth, became member of Church of England, spiritualist interests. NKWWC, FPA.

Barbara Evans, *Freedom to Choose: The Life and Work of Dr Helena Wright, Pioneer of Contraception* (London, 1984), DNB.

≷

Further reading

Paula Bartley, *Prostitution: Prevention and Reform in Britain, 1860–1914* (London: Routledge, 1999).

Lucy Bland, *Banishing the Beast: English Feminism and Sexual Morality, 1885–1914* (London: Penguin Books, 1995).

Lucy Bland and Doan, Laura (eds), *Sexology in Culture: Labelling Bodies and Desires* (Oxford: Polity Press, 1998).

Barbara Brookes, *Abortion in England, 1900–1967* (London: Croom Helm, 1988).

Hera Cook, *The Long Sexual Revolution: English Women, Sex, and Contraception 1800–1975* (Oxford: Oxford University Press, 2004).

Laura Doan, *Fashioning Sapphism: The Origins of a Modern English Lesbian Culture* (New York: Columbia University Press, 2001).

Paul Ferris, *Sex and the British: A Twentieth-Century History* (London: Michael Joseph, 1993).

Lesley Hall, *Sex, Gender and Social Change in Britain since 1880* (Basingstoke: Palgrave, 2000).

Emily Hamer, *Britannia's Glory: History of Twentieth-Century Lesbians* (London: Continuum, 1995).

Angela Ingram and Patai, Daphne (eds), *Rediscovering Forgotten Radicals: British Women Writers 1889–1939* (Chapel Hill, NC: University of North Carolina Press, 1993).

Sheila Jeffreys, *The Spinster and Her Enemies: Feminism and Sexuality 1880–1930* (London: Pandora Press, 1985).

Audrey Leathard, *The Fight for Family Planning* (London: Macmillan, 1980).

Claudia Nelson and Sumner Holmes, Ann (eds), *Maternal Instincts: Visions of Motherhood and Sexuality in Britain, 1875–1925* (London: Macmillan Press, 1997).

Alison Oram and Turnbull, Annmarie, *The Lesbian History Sourcebook: Love and Sex between Women in Britain from 1780 to 1970* (London: Routledge, 2001).

Roy Porter and Hall, Lesley, *The Facts of Life: The Creation of Sexual Knowledge in Britain 1650–1850* (London: Yale University Press, 1995).

Constance Rover, *Love, Morals and the Feminists* (London: Routledge and Kegan Paul, 1970).

Mary Lyndon Shanley, *Feminism, Marriage, and the Law in Victorian England, 1850–1895* (Princeton, NJ: Princeton University Press, 1989).

R. A. Soloway, *Birth Control and the Population Question in England, 1870–1930* (Chapel Hill, NC: University of North Carolina Press, 1982).

R. A. Soloway, *Demography and Degeneration: Eugenics and the Declining Birthrate in Twentieth-Century Britain* (Chapel Hill, NC: University of North Carolina Press, 1990).

Martha Vicinus, *Intimate Friends: Women Who Loved Women, 1778–1928* (Chicago: University of Chicago Press, 2004).

Judith R. Walkowitz, *Prostitution and Victorian Society: Women, Class and the State* (Cambridge and New York: Cambridge University Press, 1980).

Judith R. Walkowitz, *City of Dreadful Delight: Narratives of Sexual Danger in Late-Victorian London* (London: Virago, 1992).

Jeffrey Weeks, *Coming Out: Homosexual Politics in Britain from the Nineteenth Century to the Present* (London: Quartet, 1977).

Jeffrey Weeks, *Sex, Politics and Society: The Regulation of Sexuality since 1800* (London: Longman, 1981).

Ina Zweiniger-Bargielowska (ed.), *Women in Twentieth Century Britain* (London: Pearson Educational, 2001).

Bibliography of works cited

Ellen Dorothy Abb, *What Fools We Women Be!* (London: Cassell and Co., 1937).

Anne Allen, *People on Honeymoon* (London: Daily Mirror, 1968).

[Anonymous] *Downward Paths: An Inquiry into the Causes which Contribute to the Making of the Prostitute. With a Foreword by A. Maude Royden* (London: G. Bell and Sons, 1916).

[Anonymous] *Streetwalker* (London: The Bodley Head, 1959).

Florence E. Barrett, *Conception Control: And its Effects on the Individual and the Nation* (London: John Murray, 1922).

Victoria E. M. Bennett and Susan Isaacs, *Health and Education in the Nursery* (London: George Routledge & Sons, 1931).

Annie Besant, *Marriage, as it Was, as it Is, and as it Should Be: A Plea for Reform* (London: Freethought Publishing Company, 1882).

Annie Besant, *The Law of Population: Its Consequences, and its Bearing upon Human Conduct and Morals* (London: Freethought Publishing Company, 1889).

Morwenna Bielby, 'What is Christian Marriage?', Margaret Statham (ed.), *Young Wives Talk Together: A Symposium for Leaders of Young Wives Groups* (London: The Epworth Press, 1956), pp. 13–21.

Elizabeth Blackwell, *Counsel to Parents on the Moral Education of their Children* (London: Hirst Smyth & Son, 1882).

Elizabeth Blackwell, *The Human Element in Sex, Being a Medical Inquiry into the Relation of Sexual Physiology to Christian Morality* (London: J. & A. Churchill, 1894).

Elizabeth Blackwell 'Purchase of Women: the Great Economic Blunder', *c.* 1890, *Essays in Medical Sociology*, vol. 1 (London: Ernest Bell, 1902a), pp. 133–174.

Elizabeth Blackwell, 'Rescue Work in Relation to Prostitution and Disease: An Address given at the Conference of Rescue Workers held in London, June 1881', *Essays in Medical Sociology*, vol. 1 (London: Ernest Bell, 1902b), pp. 113–132.

Mrs [Catherine] Booth, *The Iniquity of State Regulated Vice: A Speech Delivered At Exeter Hall, London, on February 6th, 1884* (London: Dyer Brothers, 1884).

Mary Borden, *The Technique of Marriage* (London: William Heinemann, 1933).

Maud Churton Braby, *Modern Marriage and How to Bear It* (London: T. Werner Laurie, 1908).

M. K. Bradby, *The Logic of the Unconscious Mind* (London: Henry Frowde Hodder and Stoughton, 1920).

Vera Brittain, *Halcyon or the Future of Monogamy* (London: Kegan Paul, Trench, Trubner, 1929).

Vera Brittain, 'The Failure of Monogamy', in Norman Haire (ed.), *World League for Sexual Reform: Proceedings of the Third Congress, London, 1929* (London: Kegan Paul, Trench, Trubner & Co., 1930), pp. 40–44.

F. W. Stella Browne, *The Sexual Variety and Variability Among Women and Their Bearing Upon Social Re-construction* (London: Publication no. 3 of the British Society for the Study of Sex Psychology, printed for the Society by C. W. Beaumont and Co, 1917).

F. W. Stella Browne, 'The Right to Abortion', in Norman Haire (ed.), *World League for Sexual Reform: Proceedings of the Third Congress, London, 1929* (London: Kegan Paul, Trench, Trubner & Co., 1930), pp. 178–181.

F. W. Stella Browne 'The Right to Abortion', in F. W. Stella Browne, A. M. Ludovici and Harry Roberts, *Abortion* (London: George Allen & Unwin, 1935), pp. 13–50.

Josephine E. Butler, *The Constitution Violated: An Essay* (Edinburgh: Edmonston and Douglas, 1871)

Josephine E. Butler, *Some Thoughts on the Present Aspect of the Crusade Against the State Regulation of Vice* (Liverpool: T. Brakell, Printer, 1874).

Josephine E. Butler, *Social Purity* (London: Morgan and Scott, 1879).

Olwen W. Campbell (ed.), *The Report of a Conference on the Feminine Point of View* (London: Williams & Norgate, 1952).

Mary G. Cardwell, *Some Aspects of Child Hygiene: A Book for the Use of Training Colleges and Practising Teachers* (London: Sir Isaac Pitman & Sons, 1935).

Janet Chance, 'A Marriage Education Centre in London', in Norman Haire (ed.), *World League for Sexual Reform: Proceedings of the Third Congress, London, 1929* (London: Kegan Paul, Trench, Trubner & Co., 1930), pp. 37–39.

Janet Chance, *The Cost of English Morals* (London: Noel Douglas, 1931).

Enid Charles, *The Practice of Birth Control: An Analysis of the Birth-Control Experiences of Nine Hundred Women* (London: Williams & Norgate, 1932).

Mrs Cecil (Ada Elizabeth) Chesterton, *In Darkest London* (London: Stanley Paul, first published 1926, 4th edition 1927).

Mrs Cecil (Ada Elizabeth) Chesterton, *Women of the London Underworld* (London: Readers Library Publishing Co, 1938).

Jane Hume Clapperton, *Scientific Meliorism and the Evolution of Happiness* (London: Kegan Paul, Trench & Co., 1885).

Irene Clephane, *Towards Sex Freedom* (London: John Lane The Bodley Head, London, 1935).

Margaret Cole, *Marriage: Past and Present* (London: J. M. Dent & Sons, 1938).

Geraldine Coster, *Psychoanalysis for Normal People* (London: Oxford University Press, first published 1926, 3rd edn [1932]).

Gladys M. Cox, *Youth, Sex and Life* (London: C. Arthur Pearson, 1935).

Clemence Dane, *The Women's Side* (London: Herbert Jenkins Limited, 1926).

Mary Denham, *Planned Parenthood: A Guide to Birth Control* (London: George Newnes, 1934, revised 1938).

Diana Dewar, *Orphans of the Living: A Study of Bastardy* (London: Hutchinson, 1968).

Elizabeth Draper, *Birth Control in the Modern World: The Role of the Individual in Population Control* (Harmondsworth: Penguin Books, 1965).

Edith Havelock Ellis, 'The Love of Tomorrow', *c.* 1914–15, in *The New Horizon in Love and Life* (London: A. & C. Black, 1921a), pp. 1–10.

Edith Havelock Ellis, 'A Noviciate for Marriage', *c.* 1892, in *The New Horizon in Love and Life* (London: A. & C. Black, 1921b), pp. 11–22.

Edith Havelock Ellis, 'Semi-Detached Marriage', *c.* 1915, in *The New Horizon in Love and Life* (London: A. & C. Black, 1921c), pp. 23–31.

Edith Havelock Ellis, 'Marriage and Divorce', *c.* 1914–1915, in *The New Horizon in Love and Life* (London: A. & C. Black, 1921d), pp. 32–37.

Edith Havelock Ellis, 'Eugenics and the Mystical Outlook', *c.* 1911, in *The New Horizon in Love and Life* (London: A. & C. Black, 1921e), pp. 38–54.

Edith Havelock Ellis, 'Eugenics and Spiritual Parenthood', *c.* 1911 in *The New Horizon in Love and Life* (London: A. & C. Black, 1921f), pp. 55–69.

Edith Havelock Ellis, 'Blossoming-Time', *c.* 1914–15, in *The New Horizon in Love and Life* (London: A. & C. Black, 1921g), pp. 70–79.

Leonora Eyles, *The Woman in the Little House* (London: Grant Richards, 1922).

Leonora Eyles, *Women's Problems of To-day* (London: The Labour Publishing Company, 1926).

Leonora Eyles, *Commonsense about Sex* (London: Victor Gollancz, 1933: reprinted 1939).

Leonora Eyles, *Unmarried But Happy* (London: Victor Gollancz, 1947).

Leonora Eyles, *Sex for the Engaged* (London: Robert Hale Limited, 1952).

Leonora Eyles, *The New Commonsense About Sex* (London: Victor Gollancz, 1956).

Letitia D. Fairfield, 'The State and Birth Control', in Sir James Marchant (ed.), *Medical Views on Birth Control* (London: Martin Hopkinson & Co., 1926), pp. 104–131.

Xenia Field, *Under Lock and Key: A Study of Women in Prison* (London: Max Parrish, 1963).

Rose Hacker, *The Opposite Sex (Telling the Teenagers)* (London: Pan Books, 1960, first edition published by André Deutsch, 1957, as *Telling the Teenagers*).

Gladys Mary Hall, *Prostitution: A Survey and a Challenge* (London: Williams & Norgate, 1933).

Charlotte Haldane, *Motherhood and its Enemies* (London: Chatto and Windus, 1927).

Cicely Mary Hamilton, *Marriage as a Trade* (London: Chapman & Hall, 1909).

Mary Agnes Hamilton, 'Changes in Social Life', in Ray Strachey (ed.), *Our Freedom and its Results by Five Women* (London: The Hogarth Press, 1936), pp. 231–285.

Winifred Holtby, *Women and a Changing Civilisation* (London: John Lane The Bodley Head, 1934).

(Jane) Ellice Hopkins, *The Power of Womanhood or Mothers and Sons: A Book for Parents, and Those in Loco Parentis* (London: Wells Gardner & Co., 1899).

(Jane) Ellice Hopkins, *The Story of Life: For the Use of Mothers of Boys* (London: The Walter Scott Publishing Co., 1902).

Ettie Hornibrook, *Practical Birth Control: Being a Revised Version of Safe Marriage* (London: Heinemann, 1931) [see also Rout, Ettie].

Judith Hubback, *Wives Who Went to College* (London: William Heinemann, 1957).

V. M. Hughes, *Women in Bondage* (London: Torchstream Books, 1958).

Marjorie C. Hume, 'Sex Education in the Home', in Sybil Neville-Rolfe (ed.), *Sex in Social Life* (London: George Allen & Unwin, 1949), pp. 210–242.

Isabel Emslie Hutton, *The Hygiene of Marriage* (London: William Heinemann (Medical Books), 1923, 3rd edn 1930).

Laura Hutton, *The Single Woman and Her Emotional Problems* (London: Baillière, Tindall and Cox, 1935).

Laura Hutton, 'Sex in Middle Age', in Sybil Neville-Rolfe (ed.), *Sex in Social Life* (London: George Allen & Unwin, 1949a), pp. 440–451.

Laura Hutton, 'The Unmarried', in Sybil Neville-Rolfe (ed.), *Sex in Social Life* (London: George Allen & Unwin, 1949b), pp. 414–434.

Susan Isaacs, *Social Development in Young Children: A Study of Beginnings* (London: George Routledge & Sons, 1933).

Susan Isaacs, 'The Nursery as Community', in John Rickman (ed.), *On the Bringing Up of Children by Five Psycho-analysts* (London: Kegan Paul, Trench, Trubner & Co., 1936), pp. 167–232.

Susan Isaacs, *Troubles of Children and Parents* (London: Methuen & Co, 1948).

Lena M. Jeger (ed.), *Illegitimate Children and Their Parents* (London: National Council for the Unmarried Mother and Her Child, 1951).

Pearl Jephcott, *Rising Twenty: Notes on Some Ordinary Girls* (London: Faber and Faber, 1948).

Alice Jenkins, *Conscript Parenthood: The Problem of Secret Abortion* (London: George Standring, 1938).

Alice Jenkins, *Law for the Rich* (London: Victor Gollancz, 1960).

Arabella Kenealy, *Feminism and Sex-extinction* (London: T. Fisher Unwin, 1920).

Arabella Kenealy, *The Human Gyroscope: A Consideration of the Gyroscopic Rotation of Earth as Mechanism of the Evolution of Terrestrial Living Forms, Explaining the Phenomenon of Sex: Its Origin and Development in Significance in the Evolutionary Process* (London: John Bale, Sons & Danielsson, 1934).

Melanie Klein, 'Love, Guilt and Reparation' [1937], in *Love, Guilt and Reparation and Other Works 1921–1945* (London: The Hogarth Press, 1975), pp. 306–343.

Margaret Kornitzer, *The Modern Woman and Herself* (London: Jonathan Cape, 1932, reissued 1934).

Constance E. Long, *Collected Papers on the Psychology of Phantasy* (London: Baillière, Tindall and Cox, 1920).

Barbara Low, *Psycho-Analysis: A Brief Account of the Freudian Theory* (London: George Allen & Unwin, 1920).

Barbara Low, *The Unconscious in Action: Its Influence Upon Education* (London: University of London Press, 1928).

Barbara Low, 'Sexual Education: Some Psycho-Analytical Considerations', in Norman Haire (ed.), *World League for Sexual Reform: Proceedings of the Third*

Congress, London, 1929 (London: Kegan Paul, Trench, Trubner & Co., 1930), pp. 368–373.

Mary Macaulay, *The Art of Marriage* (Harmondsworth: Penguin Books [1957]; originally published 1952).

Mary Macaulay, *Marriage for the Married* (London: Delisle, 1964).

'Medica' [Joan Malleson], *Any Wife or Any Husband: A Book for Couples who Have Met Sexual Difficulties and for Doctors* (London: William Heinemann, 1950).

Dorothy Manchée, *Social Service in the Clinic for Venereal Diseases* (London: Baillière, Tindall & Cox, 1938).

Dorothy Manchée, *Social Service in the Clinic for Venereal Diseases* (London: Baillière, Tindall & Cox, 1943)

Ethel Mannin, 'Sex and the Child', in Norman Haire (ed.), *World League for Sexual Reform: Proceedings of the Third Congress, London, 1929* (London: Kegan Paul, Trench, Trubner & Co., 1930), pp. 374–378.

Norah March, *Sex Knowledge* (London: W. Foulsham, *c.* 1922).

Norah March, *Towards Racial Health: A Handbook for Parents, Teachers, & Social Workers on the Training of Boys and Girls* (London: George Routledge & Sons 1915, 3rd edn 1920).

Louisa Martindale, *Under the Surface* (Brighton: The Southern Publishing Company, Limited, 1908).

Louisa Martindale, *The Prevention of Venereal Disease* (London: Research Books, 1945).

Annette M. B. Meakin, *Woman in Transition* (London: Methuen & Co., 1907).

Merrell P. Middlemore, 'The Uses of Sensuality', in John Rickman (ed.) *On the Bringing Up of Children by Five Psycho-analysts* (London: Kegan Paul, Trench, Trubner & Co., 1936), pp. 57–85.

Naomi Mitchison, *Comments on Birth Control* (London: Faber & Faber, 1930).

Naomi Mitchison, *The Home and a Changing Civilisation* (London: John Lane The Bodley Head, 1934).

Doris Langley Moore, *The Technique of the Love Affair* (London: Rich & Cowan, first published, 1928, revised and enlarged edition, 1936).

Alison Neilans, 'Changes in Sex Morality', in Ray Strachey (ed.), *Our Freedom and its Results by Five Women* (London: The Hogarth Press, 1936), pp. 173–230.

Sybil Neville-Rolfe, *Why Marry?* (London: Faber and Faber Limited, 1935).

Sybil Neville-Rolfe, 'The Misuse of Sex', in Sybil Neville-Rolfe (ed.), *Sex in Social Life* (London: George Allen & Unwin, 1949a), pp. 452–487.

Sybil Neville-Rolfe, *Social Biology and Welfare* (London: George Allen & Unwin, 1949b).

H. N. [Harriet Nokes], *Thirty-Two Years in a House of Mercy* (London: Society for Promoting Christian Knowledge, 1895).

Helena Normanton, *Everyday Law for Women* (London: Ivor Nicholson and Watson, 1932).

Doris Odlum, *Journey Through Adolescence* (London: Delisle, 1957).

Doris Odlum, *The Mind of Your Child* (London: W. & G. Foyle, 1960).

Christabel Pankhurst, *The Great Scourge and How to End It* (London: E. Pankhurst, 1913).

E. V. Pemberton, *Simple Advice to Those About to Marry* (first published by the author, 1936).

Jean Pochin, *Without a Wedding-Ring: Casework with Unmarried Parents* (London: Constable, 1969).

Helena Powell, 'The Problem of the Adolescent Girl', in Mary Scharlieb (ed.), *Sexual Problems of To-day* (London: Williams and Norgate, 1924), pp. 97–117.

Claire Rayner, *Parent's Guide to Sex Education* (London: Corgi, 1968, Dolphin Books Doubleday NY edition, 1969).

Lucy Re-Bartlett, *The Coming Order* (London: Longmans, Green & Co., 1911).

Lucy Re-Bartlett, *Sex and Sanctity* (London: Longmans, Green & Co., 1914).

Ettie A. Rout [I.e. Ettie A. Hornibrook], *Safe Marriage: A Return to Sanity* (London: William Heinemann (Medical Books), 1922).

Ettie A. Rout [I.e. Ettie A. Hornibrook], *The Morality of Birth Control* (London: John Lane The Bodley Head 1925a).

Ettie A. Rout [Mrs F. A. Hornibrook], *Sex and Exercise: A Study of the Sex Function in Women and its Relation to Exercise* (London: William Heinemann (Medical Books) 1925b).

A. Maude Royden, *Women and the Sovereign State: The State and Prostitution* (London: Headley Bros. Publishers, 1917).

A. Maude Royden, *Sex and Common-Sense* (London: Hurst and Blackett, first published 1921, 8th edn *c.* 1922).

Dora Russell, *Hypatia, or Woman and Knowledge* (London: Kegan Paul, Trench, Trubner, 1925).

Dora Russell, 'Marriage and Freedom', in Norman Haire (ed.), *World League for Sexual Reform: Proceedings of the Third Congress, London, 1929* (London: Kegan Paul, Trench, Trubner & Co., 1930), pp. 25–29.

Mary Scharlieb, *The Bachelor Woman and Her Problems* (London: Williams & Norgate, 1929).

Mary Scharlieb, *Womanhood and Race-Regeneration* (London: Cassell & Company, 1912).

Mary Scharlieb, *What It Means to Marry; or, Young Women and Marriage* (London: Cassell and Company, 1914).

Mary Scharlieb, *The Seven Ages of Woman* (London: Cassell and Company, 1915).

Mary Scharlieb, *The Challenge of War-time to Women* (London: National Council of Public Morals for Great and Greater Britain, 1916a).

Mary Scharlieb, *The Hidden Scourge* (London: C. Arthur Pearson, 1916b).

Mary Scharlieb, *What Mothers Must Tell their Children* (London: The National Council for Combating Venereal Diseases, 1917).

Mary Scharlieb, *Straight Talks to Women* (London: Williams and Norgate, 1923).

Mary Scharlieb, 'Courtship and Marriage', in Mary Scharlieb (ed.), *Sexual Problems of To-day* (London: Williams and Norgate, 1924), pp. 118–146.

Mary Scharlieb, 'The Medical Aspect of Conception Control', in Sir James Marchant (ed.), *Medical Views on Birth Control* (London: Martin Hopkinson & Co. 1926), pp. 48–68.

Mary Scharlieb and Barbara Butts, *England's Girls and England's Future* (London: The National Council for Combating Venereal Diseases, 1917).

Mary Scharlieb and F. Arthur Sibly, *Youth and Sex: Dangers and Safeguards for Girls and Boys* (London: T.C. & E.C. Jack, 1913).

Olive Schreiner, *Woman and Labour* (London: T. Fisher Unwin, 1911).

Nina Searl, 'Questions and Answers', in John Rickman (ed.), *On the Bringing Up of Children by Five Psycho-analysts* (London: Kegan Paul, Trench, Trubner & Co., 1936), pp. 87–122.

Eliot Slater and Moya Woodside, *Patterns of Marriage: A Study of Marriage Relationships in the Urban Working Classes* (London: Cassell & Company, 1951) (Report of Investigation during 1943–6).

M. B. Smith, *The Single Woman of Today: Her Problems and Adjustment* (London: Watts & Co., 1951)

Margery Spring Rice, *Working-class Wives: Their Health and Conditions, Being the Survey of the Conditions of 1,250 Married Working Women, Based on Information Collected by the Women's Health Enquiry Committee* (Harmondsworth: Penguin Books, 1939).

Margaret Stephens, *Woman and Marriage: A Handbook* (London: Duckworth, 1910, reissued 1935).

Marie Carmichael Stopes, *A Letter to Working Mothers: On How to Have Healthy Children and Avoid Weakening Pregnancies* (London: The Mother's Clinic for Constructive Birth Control, 1918a [1925 reprinting]).

Marie Carmichael Stopes, *Married Love: A New Contribution to the Solution of Sex Difficulties* (London: A.C. Fifield, 1918b).

Marie Carmichael Stopes, *Wise Parenthood: A Sequel to 'Married Love', a Book for Married People* (London: A. C. Fifield, 1918c).

Marie Carmichael Stopes, *A New Gospel to all Peoples* (London: The Mothers Clinic, 1920).

Marie Carmichael Stopes, *The Truth about Venereal Disease* (London: G. P. Putnam's Sons, 1921).

Marie Carmichael Stopes, *The Human Body* (London: Gill Publishing, 1926a).

Marie Carmichael Stopes, *Sex and the Young* (London: Gill Publishing, 1926b).

Marie Carmichael Stopes, *Enduring Passion: Further New Contributions to the Solution of Sex Difficulties, Being the Continuation of Married Love* (London: G. P. Putnam's Sons, 1928)

Marie Carmichael Stopes (ed.), *Mother England: A Contemporary History, Self-Written by Those Who Have Had No Historian* (London: John Bale, Sons & Danielsson, 1929).

Marie Carmichael Stopes, *Marriage in My Time* (London: Rich and Cowan, 1935).

Marie Carmichael Stopes, *Change of Life in Men and Women* (London: Putnam, 1936).

H. M. Swanwick, *Women in the Socialist State* (Manchester, London: The National Labour Press, 1921).

Frances Swiney, *The Awakening of Women or Woman's Part in Evolution* (London: William Reeves, 1905, 3rd edition, 1908).

Frances Swiney, 'The Sons of Belial', in *The Sons of Belial and Other Essays on the Social Evil* (London: C.W. Daniel for the League of Isis, *c.* 1912), pp. 7–33.

Frances Swiney, 'State Regulation of Vice', in *The Sons of Belial and Other Essays on the Social Evil* (London: C.W. Daniel for the League of Isis, *c.* 1912), pp. 38–42.

Rosalie Taylor, *Inside Information on Sex and Birth Control* (London: The Dickens Press, 1969).

Dorothy Thurtle, *Abortion: Right or Wrong?* (London: C. A. Watts & Co., 1940).

Esther Waterhouse, 'What Shall We Tell Our Children About Sex?', in Margaret Statham (ed.), *Young Wives Talk Together: A Symposium for Leaders of Young Wives Groups* (London: The Epworth Press, 1956), pp. 41–48.

Helen Webb, *Life and Its Beginnings* (London: Cassell and Company, 1913).

Rosalind Wilkinson [research worker], *Women of the Streets: A Sociological Study of the Common Prostitute Edited by C.H. Rolph for and on Behalf of the British Social Biology Council* (London: Secker & Warburg, 1955).

The Women's Co-operative Guild, *Maternity: Letters from Working-Women* (London: G. Bell & Sons, 1915).

Helena Wright, *The Sex Factor in Marriage: A Book for Those Who Are, or Are About to Be, Married* ([London]: Noel Douglas, 1930).

Helena Wright, *What is Sex?: An Outline for Young People* (London: Williams & Norgate, 1932).

Helena Wright, *More about the Sex Factor in Marriage* (London: Williams and Norgate, 1947).

Helena Wright, *Sex and Society* (London: George Allen and Unwin, 1968).

Index

Abb, Ellen Dorothy: *What Fools We Women Be!* 189, 214–15, 233
abnormality 39, 56–7, 213, 216–17, 223
abortifacients 232
abortion 7, 149, 298–9; Browne 95, 142, 152, 168, 225; class 298–9; illegal 252, 298, 299; legalisation 79, 227, 236, 252; medical operation 235–6; rape 152, 298; repugnance 230; right to 232; self-administered 78, 143, 144, 147, 151, 152, 226, 229, 233–4, 296; statistics 233, 279
Abortion Law Reform Association 168
abstinence: as contraception 73, 106–7, 233; family planning 74, 227, 230, 297; involuntary 104; nervous strain 229–30
adolescence: homosexuality 288; ignorance 278; infatuation 287, 288; same-sex relations 206, 207, 212, 285; sex drive 46; sex education 302–3, 309
The Adult 6, 12
adultery 11, 14, 15, 20–1, 95, 171
affairs: casual 190, 199–200; class 203; experience 199; health 200; personality 194; seduction 196–7; sexual desire 272–3; techniques 200–2
age factors: passion 182; prostitutes

217, 290; sex education 88–9, 239, 243; sexual desire 174, 283–4; sexual intercourse 269; *see also* menopause
age of consent 20, 21
Allen, Ann: *People on Honeymoon* 259, 280
Arnold, Matthew 22
arousal 254, 264, 265–6, 277; clitoris 110, 180–1, 183, 242, 251
Association of Moral and Social Hygiene 6, 12
attraction 105, 125, 175, 185
auto-eroticism 60, 128; *see also* masturbation

Barrett, Lady: *Conception Control* 99, 146–7
Bartholin's glands 180
Bennett, Victoria E. M.: *Health and Education in the Nursery* 237–8
Besant, Annie 3, 16, 33n1; *The Law of Population* 17–18, 28, 32–3; *Marriage* 13–14, 20–1
Bielby, Morwenna: 'What is Christian Marriage?' 256
biology: reproduction 85; sex education 79–80, 92, 241, 306, 307; venereal disease 140–1; *see also* botany
birth control 3, 7, 37, 74–5, 225–6; advice 142–3, 145, 167, 234–5;

chastity 233; clinics 233, 234; communication between partners 279–80; consequences 147–8; Depression and war era 225–37; family planning 78, 231; fidelity 185; health of woman 74–5, 149–50; methods 32–3, 234; morality 139, 147–8; reliability 251–2, 295–6; sexual equality 202; single women 121; Stopes 95; Stopes era 142–52; Suffrage era 37, 73–9; Victorian era 31–3; welfare state era 295–300; *see also* contraceptives

bisexuality 4, 60

Blackwell, Elizabeth: *Counsel to Parents on the Moral Education of their Children* 16–17, 20, 26–7, 34; *The Human Element in Sex* 18–19; 'Purchase of Women' 28–30; 'Rescue Work in Relation to Prostitution and Disease' 25–6, 34

bodily ignorance 32, 90, 92–3, 97–8, 303–4

Booth, Catherine: *The Iniquity of State Regulated Vice* 21, 27–8

Borden, Mary: *The Technique of Marriage* 172–4, 242

botany: pollination 79, 85, 158, 165, 240–1, 303; sex education 85, 87, 92, 159

Bourne case 168

Braby, Maud Churton: *Modern Marriage, and How to Bear It* 44, 49–50, 74, 81

Bradby, M. K.: *The Logic of the Unconscious Mind* 135–6

Bradlaugh, Charles 33n1

Breach of Promise 191

brides: disgust 101, 171, 174; ignorance 38, 41, 42–4, 93, 97, 101, 106, 113–14, 172; pregnant 190; virginity 198

British Medical Association 252

British Social Hygiene Council 3, 5, 301

British Society for the Study of Sex Psychology 3, 4

Brittain, Vera: 'The Failure of Monogamy' 107–8; *Halcyon* 96, 105–6, 122, 163–4

Brook Clinics 252, 280

Browne, F.W. Stella: abortion 1, 3, 4–5, 95, 142, 152, 168, 225; 'The Right to Abortion' 152, 232; same-sex desire 37; *Sexual Variety and Variability among Women* 47–8, 53, 59–60, 72–3, 78–9, 91

Butler, Josephine 3, 4, 11, 96; *The Constitution Violated* 19–20, 22–3; marriage 13; *Social Purity* 13, 24–5; *Some Thoughts on the Present Aspect of the Crusade against the State Regultion of Vice* 23–4

Butts, Barbara: *England's Girls and England's Future* 53, 93–4

Campbell, Olwen (ed.): *The Feminine Point of View* 275, 297

car trade 291; *see also* joy riding

Cardwell, Mary G. 237; *Some Aspects of Child Hygiene* 246–7

Casti Connubii 167

casual sex 273–4, 275

celibacy 7; Depression and war era 206–17; enforced 114–15, 125, 183; gratification 108; health 54; insanity 44; positive/negative 55; procreation 142; radical 37; religion 142, 143; single women 208; Stopes era 123–34; Suffrage era 54–60; as unnatural 17–18; voluntary 58–9; welfare state era 283–9; widows 19

censorship 252

Chance, Janet 4; *The Cost of English Morals* 170–1, 182, 226–7, 239–40; 'A Marriage Education Centre in London' 108, 164

Charles, Enid: *The Practice of Birth Control* 227, 242

chastity 24, 26–7, 58, 194, 233

Chesterton, G. K. 149

Chesterton, Mrs Cecil: *In Darkest London* 120–1, 139–40; *Women of the London Underworld* 204, 216–17, 223

child-bearing: abstinence 73, 106, 233; excessive 15–16, 32, 37, 102, 144, 235; free choice 151; health of mother 74, 230; leaving to chance 226; planned 146; *see also* pregnancy

children: fantasies 153; infatuation 129–30; masturbation 157, 237, 243–4, 247; questions answered 165, 238, 248; right to life 75, 117;

sex education 88–9, 153–5, 239, 243, 301; sex organs 161; sexuality 156, 248–9; *see also* girls
Christianity 72–3, 256
Church of England Lambeth Conference 167
Clapperton, Jane 16; *Scientific Meliorism* 14–15, 17, 28, 31, 35
class: abortion 298–9; affairs 203; chastity 26–7; pre-marital sexual intercourse 273; prostitutes 292; sex manuals 5
Clephane, Irene: *Towards Sex Freedom* 185, 198–9, 213, 220
clitoris: arousal 110, 180–1, 183, 242, 251; orgasm 115, 181, 259, 261, 262–3, 267, 270–1; stroking 263, 266, 269
co-education 117–18
co-habitation 271, 278–9
coitus interruptus 75, 143, 227, 231, 237
Cole, Margaret: *Marriage: Past and Present* 178, 189, 204–6, 221–2, 234, 249–50
condoms 227, 292
conjugal rights 97, 100–4, 152, 171, 173
constipation 114, 157
consummation 171, 177
Contagious Diseases Acts 5–6, 11, 12, 25–6, 139
contraception 8, 145, 242, 299–300; clinics 150; freedom 208; illegitimacy 282–3, 300; knowledge about 48, 228; morality 198; promiscuity 48; race 149; reliability 232, 234, 298; responsibility 281; rhythm method 148, 150, 231–2; sexual equality 198, 280–1; sexual experimentation 309; Stopes era 142–52; unmarried women 252, 300; *see also* birth control; family planning
contraceptive advice 234, 252, 300
contraceptives 76, 145; acceptability 228, 229; distaste for 226; experience 190; genital organs 147; satisfaction 297
copulation 169, 241, 242
Coster, Geraldine: *Psychoanalysis for Normal People* 131–2, 162–3
courtship 112, 184, 214

Cousins, Sheila (pseudonym) 168
Cox, Gladys M.: *Youth, Sex and Life* 185–6, 196–7, 244–5
crush: *see* infatuation
custody of children 11

Dane, Clemence 4, 95; *Regiment of Women* 97; *The Women's Side* 129–31
Denham, Dr Mary: *Planned Parenthood* 230–1
depravity 30, 101, 127
Depression and war era 8, 167–8; birth control 225–37; celibacy 206–17; extra-marital heterosexual relations 190–206; ignorance 237–50; marriage 168–79; prostitution 217–25; same-sex relations 206–17; sex education 237–50; sexual desire 179–90; sexual pleasure 179–90; single women 168, 206–17; venereal disease 217–25
deviancy model 252
Dewar, Diana: *Orphans of the Living* 279–80, 306
dilatation and curettage 236
disgust 170–1, 174
divorce 123, 199; accessibility 251; adultery 11, 14, 171; equality 11, 13–14; inequalities 37; limitations 204–5; love 100; Matrimonial Causes Act 254; sexual mismatches 164; social status 178
Divorce Act (1923) 95
divorce laws 38–9, 168
double standards: intimacy 53; morality 12, 16, 23–5, 30–1, 49, 66, 202, 222; prostitution 12, 63, 71–2; seduction 49
Downward Paths 46–7, 52, 68–70, 90
Draper, Elizabeth: *Birth Control in the Modern World* 279, 294–5, 299–300, 305–6
dreams 188, 266
dysmenorrhoea 237

economic freedom 22, 45, 65, 119; lack of 47; men/women 99; monogamy 105–6; prostitution 67; sexual freedom 220; Socialism 137; women's movement 108
education 11–12, 117–18
effeminacy 208

ejaculation 113
Ellis, Edith Lees 12; 'Blossoming Time' 86–7; 'Eugenics and Spiritual Parenthood' 56–7; 'Eugenics and the Mystical Outlook' 55–6; 'The Love of Tomorrow' 43; 'Marriage and Divorce' 43; 'A Noviciate for Marriage' 15, 21–2, 35; same-sex desire 37; 'Semi-Detached Marriage' 44
Ellis, H. Havelock 60
emotions 205, 238, 244, 305–6
engaged couples 118, 276–7
erogenous zones 254, 262
erotic 124, 185, 280
ethnocentrism 5
eugenics 31, 35, 37, 56
Evans, Barbara 4
experience 2, 117, 189, 190, 199
extra-marital heterosexual relations 7, 20, 122–3, 137–8, 172, 279; Depression and war era 190–206; Stopes era 116–23; Suffrage era 49–53; Victorian era 19–22; welfare state era 271–83; see also pre-marital sexual relations
Eyles, Leonora 5, 6, 97; *Commonsense about Sex* 174–5, 183, 193–4, 228, 243; *The New Commonsense about Sex* 255–6, 277; *Sex for the Engaged* 276–7, 302–3; *Unmarried but Happy* 264, 271, 283–4; *The Woman in the Little House* 101–2, 118, 147, 155–6; *Women's Problems of Today* 150–1, 161–2

Fairfield, Letitia D.: 'The State and Birth Control' 150
family 32, 33
family planning 143, 144–5, 225–6, 228, 296; abstinence 227, 230, 297; see also birth control
family size 32
fantasy 153, 186–7, 243–4, 247
fathers: daughters 131–2; discounted 51; reproduction 32, 157–8, 162–3, 239
Federation of Progressive Societies and Individuals 3
feminism 1, 37, 202–3, 251
fidelity 40, 107, 185, 205
Field, Xenia: *Under Lock and Key* 288, 294–5

flagellation 223, 291
flowering plants 79, 84, 158, 165, 240–1, 303
free love 12, 21–2, 43, 49–53
freedom: contraception 208; political 50–1; sexual 51, 52, 53, 220; spinsterhood 215; see also economic freedom
The Freewoman 3, 6, 38
Freud, Sigmund 47, 97, 251
friendship: affectionate 284; intimacy 215–16; in marriage 107–8; obsessive 134; passionate 284; romance 118; same-sex relations 60, 95–6, 123, 124, 125–6, 129, 134, 209; sexuality 124, 209; as substitute 211–12
frigidity 268; husband's satisfaction 260; masturbation 114; morality 182, 184; pseudo 113–14; self-control 117; wives 171, 173, 175, 253, 257
frustration 194, 263, 284

Garner, Leslie 38n1
genital organs 104–5, 147, 180–2
gigolos 214
girls: bodily ignorance 92–3; responsibility 93–4; sex education 81, 154, 159
glands, sexual 180, 213, 277
glandular compounds 133
gonorrhoea 41, 67, 71, 138–9
gratification 54, 65–6, 73, 108; see also satisfaction
guilt 186, 308

Hacker, Rose 4; *The Opposite Sex* 277, 304
Haldane, Charlotte 4; *Motherhood and its Enemies* 121–2, 141, 151
Hall, Gladys: *Prostitution: A Survey and a Challenge* 175, 192–3, 217–20, 228
Hall, Lesley A. 224n2
Hall, (M.) Radclyffe: *The Well of Loneliness* 3, 97
Hamilton, Cicely 4; *Marriage as a Trade* 39, 45, 54–5, 64, 74–5
Hamilton, Mary Agnes: 'Changes in Social Life' 203
happiness 14–15, 253, 260
health: affairs 200; birth control 74–5,

149–50; celibacy 54; child-bearing
15–16, 74, 230
Herbert, A. P. 168
heredity 232
hermaphroditism 207–8
hero-worship 129, 130, 207
Hinkle, Beatrice 4
Holtby, Winifred 4; *Women and a
Changing Civilisation* 208–9,
228–30
homosexuality 2; adolescence 288;
causes 57, 59–60, 124–7; male 251,
283; sex education 240; sexual
pleasure 210; shame 127; teachers
128–9, 132; *see also* inverts;
lesbianism
honeymoon 172–3, 176, 253, 258,
259; *see also* wedding night
Hopkins, Ellice: *The Power of
Womanhood* 15, 22, 30–1, 33;
prostitutes 28; *The Story of Life*
79–80
Hornibrook, Ettie 4; *Practical Birth
Control* 182; *see also* Rout, Ettie
Hubback, Judith 253; *Wives Who Went
to College* 256, 297
Hughes, V. M.: *Women in Bondage*
257, 268, 298
Hume, Marjorie C.: 'Sex Education in
the Home' 302
husbands: extra-marital relationships
122–3; patience 170, 174, 258;
possession of wives 176; purchase
of 215; sexuality 179; wives'
compliance 178–9, 251, 253, 268
Hutton, Isabel 4; *The Hygiene of
Marriage* 103, 112–13, 147–8,
182–3
Hutton, Laura: 'Sex in Middle Age'
265; *The Single Woman and Her
Emotional Problems* 186–7,
199–200, 209–11, 283n4; 'The
Unmarried' 264–5, 272–3, 284–5
Hyde Park 204, 290, 291, 292
hygiene 65, 116, 138, 145, 161, 240

ignorance, sexual 7; adolescence 278;
brides 38, 41, 42–4, 93, 97, 100–1,
106, 113–14, 172; Depression and
war era 237–50; innocence 80, 83,
84–5, 91, 163; menstruation 245;
modesty 90; passion 170;
physiology 103; promiscuity 196;

Stopes era 153–66; Suffrage era
79–94; Victorian era 34–6; virtue
164; welfare state era 300–9; *see
also* bodily ignorance
illegitimacy: co-habitation 278–9;
contraception 282–3, 300; enforced
marriage 203–4; fidelity 205;
infidelity 118; reasons for 119–20,
279; social status 20; stigma 202;
war-babies 118, 122; *see also*
mothers, unmarried
impotence 187–8
incest 49
infanticide 75, 149
infants, sexuality 243, 307–8
infatuation: adolescence 287, 288;
children 129–30; same-sex 59,
127–8, 129–30, 207
infidelity 118, 206, 277
innocence 80, 83, 84–5, 91, 163
insanity 44, 111
intimacy 53, 193, 215–16, 255,
275–6
inverts 6, 57, 59–60, 123, 211, 284–5;
see also homosexuality
Isaacs, Susan: *Health and Education
in the Nursery* 237–8; 'The Nursery
as Community' 248–9; *Social
Development in Young Children*
243–4; *Troubles of Children and
Parents* 301

Jeffreys, Sheila 1
Jeger, Lena (ed.): *Illegitimate Children
and Their Parents* 275
Jenkins, Alice: *Conscript Parenthood?*
233–4; *Law for the Rich* 298–9
Jephcott, Pearl 5; *Rising Twenty* 272,
300–1
joy riding 204

Kenealy, Arabella: *Feminism and
Sex-Extinction* 98, 110, 124–5, 136,
153–4; *The Human Gyroscope* 175,
195, 207–8
kerb-crawling 193, 204
Key, Ellen 51–2
Klein, Melanie: 'Love, Guilt and
Reparation' 215–16
Knowlton, Charles 33n1
Kornitzer, Margaret: *The Modern
Woman and Herself* 172, 183,
191–2, 207

Ladies' National Association 5, 11, 12
Lambeth Conference, Church of
    England 167
Legitimation League 6, 12–13
lesbianism 4; British Medical
    Association 252; father–daughter
    relationship 131–2; friendship 209;
    legal status 288; monogamy 251,
    283; power 210; prejudice 285–6;
    in prison 288; Stopes 132–3
libido: see sex drive
local authority welfare centres 167
Long, Constance 4; *Collected Papers
    on the Psychology of Phantasy*
    123–4, 153
love: divorce 100; lust 98; marriage 14,
    39–40, 41, 105–6; monogamy 43;
    morality 35; naturalness 305;
    passion 16–17, 110, 115–16;
    physicality 39–40, 43; platonic 126,
    134; sex education 85–6; sexual
    intercourse 145, 230–1, 232
lovers, married 272, 274
Low, Barbara: *Psycho-Analysis* 153–4;
    'Sexual Education' 164–5; *The
    Unconscious in Action* 132, 163
lubrication 109, 112, 180–1, 185
lust 44, 98, 174

Macaulay, Mary: *The Art of Marriage*
    255, 268, 275–6; *Marriage for the
    Married* 258–9, 269
Malleson, Joan 168; *Any Wife or Any
    Husband* 254–5, 265–6, 285–6,
    296–7
The Malthusian 6, 12
Malthusian League 3, 12, 31
Manchée, Dorothy: *Social Service in
    the Clinic for Venereal Diseases*
    203–4, 222, 223–4
Mannin, Ethel: 'Sex and the Child'
    165–6
March, Norah 4; *Sex Knowledge*
    99–100, 127–8, 144–5, 155;
    Towards Racial Health 59, 88–9
marital rights: see conjugal rights
marriage 7; age at 28; anticipated 118;
    companionate 195; Depression and
    war era 168–79; desertion 197–8;
    economics 64, 100, 171, 197;
    fidelity 40, 107; happiness 14–15,
    260; lifelong contract 22, 42, 98;
    love 14, 39–40, 41, 105–6;

preparations for 163–4; prostitution
    61, 171; rape 11, 13; refused
    119–20; sacredness 39, 154; sexual
    intercourse 176–7; status 37, 214;
    Stopes era 97–108; Suffrage era
    38–44; venereal disease 41;
    Victorian era 11, 13–16; welfare
    state era 253–60; *see also* brides;
    conjugal rights; husbands; wives
marriage, types: cross-cultural 5;
    enforced 203–4; experimental 39,
    43, 44; open 168, 169, 190; trial 50,
    193, 195–6, 271
marriage education centres 164
Marriage Guidance Councils 260
Marsden, Dora 6
Martindale, Louisa: *The Prevention of
    Venereal Disease* 225; *Under the
    Surface* 49, 63
masturbation: children 157, 237,
    243–4, 247; fantasy 186–7, 243–4,
    247; frigidity 114; guilt 186;
    morbidity 60, 82–3; mutual 282;
    orgasm 114–15; phantasies 243–4;
    prostitutes 291; relief of tension 48,
    185, 247; same-sex relations
    210–11; sex education 89, 166, 240,
    244, 269; single women 265; wives
    114–15
*Maternity: Letters from Working
    Women* 37, 77–8, 89–90
Matrimonial Causes Act 254
Meakin, Annette M.B.: *Woman in
    Transition* 61
Medical Women's Federation 252
men: conservatism 96; effeminacy 208;
    ignorance 100–1; as prostitutes 66;
    sexual desire 219; sexual pleasure
    170, 253; sexual purchases 64–5;
    see also fathers; homosexuality;
    husbands; prostitute-users
menopause: same-sex relations 214;
    sexual desire 179, 265, 267,
    269–70; sexual pleasure 115,
    181–3, 187–8
menstruation 235, 237, 245
Middlemore, Merrell P.: 'The Uses of
    Sensuality' 247
miscarriage 151
mistresses 286, 293
Mitchison, Naomi 4; *Comments on
    Birth Control* 169, 179, 190, 206,
    225–6; *The Home* 175–6, 184–5

Modern Woman 6, 97
modesty 32, 90
monandry 47
monogamy: conjugal rights 97; economic freedom 105–6; failed 107–8; lesbianism 251, 283; love 43; lust 44; sexual techniques 164
Moore, Doris Langley 190; *The Technique of the Love Affair* 200–2
moral education 87–8, 306
moral hygiene 90
morality: birth control 139, 147–8; contraception 198; double standards 12, 16, 23–5, 30–1, 49, 66, 202, 222; ethical guidance 250; extra-marital relationships 172; frigidity 182, 184; love 35; nation 27–8; schools 34; sexual desire 188
motherhood, refused 75, 77, 149
mothers: children's sex questions 238; daughters 285–6; fitness 75; health 15–16, 74, 230; rights 117; sex education 91, 92, 156, 158–9, 162; unmarried 116, 119–21, 275, 278–9, 282–3; urges 289

National Birth Control Association 167–8
National Birth-Rate Commission 38, 97
National Council of Public Morals 38, 97
National Health Service 252
nature study: *see* biology
Neilans, Alison: 'Changes in Sex Morality' 202–3, 221
Neville-Rolfe, Sybil 5; 'The Misuse of Sex' 273–4, 289, 296; *Social Biology and Welfare* 253–4, 274, 285, 296; *Why Marry?* 176–7, 195–6, 211–12, 231–2, 244
New Generation 3
The New Generation 6, 168
nocturnal emission 249
Nokes, Harriet: *Thirty-Two Years in a House of Mercy* 30, 36
non-monogamy 168–9
Nordic youth 206
Normanton, Helena: *Everyday Law for Women* 171, 191
nymphomania 47

obscenity 67
obscenity trials 33n1

Odlum, Doris: *Journey through Adolescence* 257, 278, 287, 304–5; *The Mind of Your Child* 305
onanism 60
orgasm 108, 112–13, 114–15, 181, 185–6, 253; clitoris 261, 262–3, 267, 270–1; *coitus interruptus* 231; dreams 188; female 253; lack of 179, 254; men 253; mutual 109–10; overvalued 254–5, 259; sexual positions 266; vaginal 251, 253, 261, 270–1
ovum 303

Pankhurst, Christabel: *The Great Scourge* 41, 50–1, 57–8, 66–8, 77
parents/sex education 239–40, 249, 301, 302, 304–5, 308–9
passion: age 182; depravity 101; ignorance 170; love 16–17, 110, 115–16; lust 44; mutual 108; power 46; sexual experimentation 53
Paul, Saint 104
Pemberton, E. V.: *Simple Advice to Those About to Marry* 177–8, 187, 233
penis 110, 112, 181, 241–2, 262, 270, 303
personality 193, 194, 274
perversion 212, 291
pessary 145, 226, 228
petting 251, 271, 272, 275–6, 277, 281–2
phantasies: *see* fantasy
physicality 16–17, 39–40, 43
physiology: education 153, 156, 158, 159, 237–8, 240; ignorance 103; reproduction 44; sexual 87–8; *see also* sex education
Plan: The Journal of the Federation of Progressive Societies and Individuals 168
Pochin, Jean: *Without a Wedding Ring* 282–3, 289
pollination 79, 84, 165, 240–1
Powell, Helena: 'The Problem of the Adolescent Girl' 158–9
power 46, 210
pre-marital sexual relations 190, 251, 271, 273, 276, 280
pregnancy: avoidance 278; fathers 148–9; fear of 236–7, 256, 273, 296–7; gender of child 55, 129;

health of woman 15–16, 74, 230; ignorance 89–90, 249; pre-marital 190; underage 30; unplanned 142, 281; unwanted 76, 78–9, 178, 194, 229–30, 298–9; *see also* child-bearing
prison 288, 294–5
procreation 56, 142, 146, 239
promiscuity: consequences 195, 211; contraception 48; emotions 205; ignorance 196; personality 274; prostitutes 70, 192, 218; prostitution 113, 135, 137, 192–3, 252; venereal disease 220
property rights 11
prostitute-users 135–6, 175, 293–4
prostitutes 23, 61, 219, 221; age 217, 290; amateur 121, 192; background 29–30, 69, 224, 289; class 292; condoms 292; costumes 291–2; criminality 71; deviancy model 252; economic factors 64, 292, 294–5; exploitation 71–2; hygiene 65; legal justice 221; London 28; male 66; mentally deficient 70, 136, 138; motivation 70, 218; prices charged 290; prison 294–5; professional 121, 122, 141, 192, 221–2, 293; promiscuity 70, 192, 218; servant girls 68, 140, 141; services 291; sexual desire 47, 219; soliciting 217–18, 221–2, 289–90; unsuccessful 69–70; venereal disease 65, 292; and wives, compared 135; working conditions 62, 139–40
prostitution 3, 5, 7, 25; car trade 291; Christianity 72–3; community conscience 21; Depression and war era 217–25; double standards 12, 63, 71–2; economic arguments 66–7, 71–2, 136; feminism 37; forced 63; marriage 61; passing of 274; promiscuity 113, 135, 137, 192–3, 252; regulation 4, 27–8; as safeguard 290; seduction 26–7, 46–7, 52, 192; sex drive 67; social responsibility 68–9; Stopes era 135–41; Suffrage era 61–73; as temptation for women 26–7, 29–30, 286; unmarried mothers 121; venereal disease 11, 22–31, 62–3; Victorian era 22–31; welfare state

era 289–95; white slavery 29–30, 223
psychoanalysis 3, 95
psychology, male–female 123–4, 126
pupil–teacher relations 128–9, 132

race 5, 149
rape 11, 13, 101, 152, 191, 298
Rayner, Claire: *Parent's Guide to Sex Education* 269, 281–2, 295, 300, 308–9
Re-Bartlett, Lucy: *The Coming Order* 40–1, 45–6, 55, 76; *Sex and Sanctity* 42–3, 51, 58–9, 85–6
religion 142, 143, 231–2; *see also* Christianity
repression, sexual 111, 114–16, 125, 136, 183, 197
reproduction 88–9; animals 80, 85, 92, 303; father's role 32, 157–8, 162–3, 239; fitness for 84, 139; instinct for 75, 161–2; physiology 44; *see also* biology; botany; sex education
reputation 199
rescue workers 69
responsibility 93–4, 240, 277, 281
Rhondda, Lady 6, 97
rhythm method 148, 150, 231–2
Roman Catholicism 167, 237
Rout, Ettie: *The Morality of Birth Control* 103–4, 113, 139, 148–9; *Safe Marriage* 137–9, 145; *Sex and Exercise* 104–5, 113–14; *see also* Hornibrook, Ettie
Rover, Constance 1
Royal Commission on Marriage and Divorce 37, 38, 251, 252
Royal Commission on Venereal Diseases 38, 72
Royden, Maude: *Sex and Common-sense* 100–1, 111, 117–18, 125–7, 146, 156–7; *Women and the Sovereign State* 71–2, 92–3
Russell, Dora 1, 4, 96; *Hypatia* 119, 149, 159; 'Marriage and Freedom' 107

safe period: *see* rhythm method
same-sex relations 7; abnormality 216–17; adolescence 206, 207, 212, 285; Depression and war era 206–17; friendship 60, 95–6, 123, 124, 125–6, 129, 209;

independence 215–16; infatuation 59, 127–8, 129–30, 207; inverts 211; masturbation 210–11; power 210; seduction 216–17; Stopes era 123–34; Suffrage era 37, 54–60; welfare state era 283–9; *see also* homosexuality; lesbianism
satisfaction 104–5, 269; contraceptive devices 297; in marriage 255, 256; sexual equality 307; strain 265–6; *see also* gratification; sexual pleasure
Scharlieb, Mary 96, 160n3; *The Bachelor Woman and Her Problems* 122–3, 133–4; 'Courtship and Marriage' 104; *England's Girls and England's Future* 53, 93–4; *The Hidden Scourge* 53, 68, 90–1; 'The Medical Aspect of Conception Control' 149–50; *The Seven Ages of Woman* 43–4, 87–8; *Straight Talks to Women* 118, 148, 157–8; *What It Means to Marry* 42, 51–2, 77; *What Mothers Must Tell their Children* 72, 92; *Womanhood and Race-Regeneration* 83–4; *Youth and Sex* 46, 84–5
schools 34, 249; *see also* teachers
Schreiner, Olive: *Woman and Labour* 40, 45, 55, 64–5
Searl, Nina: 'Questions and Answers' 248
seduction: affairs 196–7; double standards 49; legislation 191; prostitution 26–7, 46–7, 52, 192; same-sex relations 216–17; shame 63
self-abuse: *see* masturbation
self-control 94, 117, 133, 146, 150
sensuality 45–6, 47
servant girls 26–7, 29, 68, 140, 141
sex drive: adolescence 46; age 45; enforced celibacy 114–15, 125, 183; glandular compounds 133; prostitution 67, 135; selectivity 73; spinsterhood 130–1, 267, 286; women 108–9, 111, 269
sex education 7, 244–5; adolescence 302–3, 309; biology 79–80, 92, 241, 306, 307; children 88–9, 153–5, 239, 243, 301; Depression and war era 237–50; emotions 238, 305–6; ethical guidance 250; girls 81, 154,

159; homosexuality 240; language 81, 91, 304, 306; love 85–6; masturbation 166, 240, 244, 269; moral advice 306; mothers 91, 92, 156, 158–9, 162; parents 239–40, 249, 301, 302, 304–5, 308–9; physiology 153, 156, 158, 159, 237–8, 240; schools 249; sexual desire 81; sexual pleasure 108; Stopes era 96, 153–66; Suffrage era 37, 79–94; teacher 246–7; venereal disease 72, 93–4, 140–1, 225, 295, 300–1, 306; Victorian era 16–17, 34–6; welfare state era 300–9
sex hygiene 158
sex-intergrades 208
sex manuals 5
Sex Reform Group 3
sex/violence 184
sexology 2
sexual desire 7, 190, 219; abnormality 39, 223; affairs 272–3; age 174, 283–4; arousal 264; cycles of 109, 187, 189, 254; Depression and war era 179–90; disgust 114, 170–1, 174; gratification 54; menopause 168, 179, 265, 267, 269–70; mismatched 253; morality 188; prostitutes 47, 219; sex education 81; single women 264–5; spinsterhood 133–4; Stopes era 108–16; Suffrage era 44–8; tiredness 256, 257; unsatisfied 57–8, 133–4; Victorian era 16–19; welfare state era 261–71; women 48, 168, 177–8, 185, 264–5
sexual equality 198, 202–3, 280–1, 307
sexual experimentation 49–53, 309
sexual harassment in workplace 52, 193
sexual instinct: *see* sex drive
sexual intercourse 45, 169; age 269; dislike of 101–2, 255–6, 261; engaged couples 276–7; fear of pregnancy 236–7; frequency 177, 178; hygiene 145; love 145, 230–1, 232; marriage 176–7; menopause 182–3, 187–8; non-penetrative 181, 258; rejected 97–8, 207; sacredness 153, 242; self-control 99; technique 163–4, 166; timing 184–5; willingness for 257; women's active role 270; *see also* conjugal rights

sexual offences 38
sexual organs 17, 161, 180, 183
sexual play 248–9
sexual pleasure 7; Depression and war
    era 179–90; guilt 308;
    homosexuality 210; men 170, 253;
    menopause 115, 181–2, 188; sex
    education 108; Stopes era 108–16;
    Suffrage era 44–8; Victorian era
    16–19; welfare state era 261–71;
    wives 112–13, 169–70; women 37,
    96, 168, 251, 253, 259–60, 263
sexual response 268
sexuality 2; children 156, 243, 248–9;
    Christianity 256; friendship 209;
    women 1, 2–3, 16–17, 95
sexually transmitted diseases: see
    venereal disease
Shafts 12
shame 63, 127, 220
sheath: *see* condoms
Shelley, P. B. 22
The Shield 5, 12
Short Homes 30
Sibly, F. Arthur: *Youth and Sex* 46,
    84–5
Sibthorpe, Margaret Shurmer 6, 12
single women 7; birth control 121;
    celibacy 208; contraception 252,
    300; Depression and war era 168,
    206–17; independence 119–20;
    married lovers 274; masturbation
    265; as mistress 286; motherhood
    119–20; post World War I 95–6;
    prostitution 286; sexual desire
    264–5; social status 125, 283, 286;
    Suffrage era 54–60; welfare state era
    283–9; *see also* spinsterhood
Slater, Eliot 169, 178–9; *Patterns of
    Marriage* 178–9, 190, 206, 236–7
slavery 28–30
Smith, M. B.: *The Single Woman of
    Today* 267, 274, 286
social purity 3, 12, 24–5, 31
social status: divorce 178; illegitimacy
    20; single women 125, 283, 286;
    spinsterhood 54–5, 209, 214, 215
Socialism 137
sociologists 279
sperm 303
spinsterhood: compensations 215,
    284; economic status 208; freedoms
    of 215; job satisfaction 208–9; sex

drive 130–1, 267, 286; sexual desire
    133–4; social status 54–5, 209, 214,
    215; virginity 208; voluntary 58;
    World War I 123
Spirochaeta pallida 140–1
Spring Rice, Margery: *Working-Class
    Wives* 234–5
Steel, David 252
Stephens, Margaret: *Woman and
    Marriage* 39–40, 45, 75, 81–3
Stepney 290
Stopes, Marie 1, 3, 4, 5, 6, 8, 95;
    Change of Life 187–8, 214;
    Enduring Passion 105, 114–15,
    132–3; *Letter to Working Mothers*
    144; *Marriage in My Time* 197–8;
    Married Love 2, 95, 97–8, 108–10,
    135, 142; *Mother England* 106–7,
    115–16, 151–2, 163; *A New Gospel
    to All Peoples* 98; *Sex and the
    Young* 119–20, 128–9, 140–1,
    160–1; *The Truth About Venereal
    Disease* 116, 137, 154; *Wise
    Parenthood* 142–3
Stopes era 95–7; birth control 142–52;
    celibacy 123–4; extra-marital
    heterosexual relations 116–23;
    ignorance 153–66; marriage
    97–108; prostitution 135–41;
    same-sex relations 123–34; sex
    education 153–66; sexual desire
    108–16; sexual pleasure 108–16;
    venereal disease 135–41
Street Offences Committee report 97,
    218
Streetwalker 252, 287, 293–4
sublimation of sex 186, 284, 285
Suffrage era 37; birth control 37, 73–9;
    celibacy 54–60; extra-marital
    heterosexual relations 49–53;
    ignorance 79–94; marriage 38–44;
    prostitution 61–73; same-sex
    relations 54–60; sex education 37,
    79–94; sexual desire 44–8; sexual
    pleasure 44–8; single women
    54–60; venereal disease 61–73
suffrage movement 3, 8, 37, 51, 95
suppository 145
Swaisland, Violet D.: 'The Adolescent
    Girl' 264, 273
Swanwick, H. M.: *Women in the
    Socialist State* 99, 111, 137
Swiney, Frances: *The Awakening of*

Women 38–9, 49, 54, 62–3, 73–4, 80; 'The Sons of Belial' 65; 'State Regulation of Vice' 65–6
syphilis 41, 71, 138

Taylor, Rosalie: *Inside Information on Sex and Birth Control* 260, 270–1
teachers 128–9, 132, 246–7
Thurtle, Dorothy: *Abortion, Right or Wrong?* 178, 235–6
Time and Tide 6, 97
transvestism 291–2

unmarried women: *see* single women
Urania 6, 38

vagina: lubrication 109, 112, 180–1, 185; orgasm 251, 253, 261, 262, 270–1; penis 241–2, 270; sensation 181, 263, 266–7
Venereal Disease clinics 225, 292
venereal diseases 4, 7, 222, 223–4; consequences 93, 94, 137; Contagious Diseases Acts 25–6; Depression and war era 217–25; husbands infecting wives 41, 62–3, 68, 71; hygiene 116, 138, 161; prevention 225; promiscuity 220; prostitutes 65; prostitution 11, 22–31, 62–3, 66, 71; sex education 72, 93–4, 140–1, 225, 295, 300–1, 306; spread of 141, 295; stigma 220, 222; Stopes era 135–41; Suffrage era 37, 61–73; treatment 77, 138–9, 222, 289; welfare state era 289–95; *see also* gonorrhea; syphilis
Victorian era 8; birth control 31–3; extra-marital heterosexual relations 19–22; ignorance 34–6; marriage 11, 13–16; prostitution 22–31; sex education 34–6; sexual desire 16–19; sexual pleasure/satisfaction 16–19
violence/sex 184
virginity 48, 121, 197–8, 208, 214
virtue 164, 233
Voluntary and Municipal Clinics 233

wage levels: insufficient 121, 141, 218; pressures 70; supplementing 29, 68

war-babies 118, 122
Waterhouse, Dr Esther: 'What Shall We Tell Our Children About Sex?' 303–4
Webb, Dr Helen: *Life and its Beginnings* 84
wedding night 168, 174, 259
welfare state era 8; birth control 295–300; celibacy 283–9; extramarital heterosexual relations 271–83; ignorance 300–9; marriage 253–60; prostitution 289–95; same-sex relationships 283–9; sex education 300–9; sexual desire/pleasure 261–71; single women 283–9; venereal disease 289–95
white slave trade 223
widows 19
wild oats metaphor 50, 51
Wilde, Oscar 55
Wimperis, Virginia: *The Unmarried Mother and her Child* 278–9
withdrawal method: *see coitus interruptus*
wives: frigidity 171, 173, 175, 253, 257; husbands' pleasure 258–9, 260, 268; infidelity 277; masturbation 114–15; own pleasure 112–13, 169–70; possession 176; and prostitutes, compared 135
Wolfenden Committee 252
'Women of the Streets' 289–93
Women's Cooperative Guild 3, 4, 5, 37
women's magazines 252
Woodside, Moya 169, 178–9; *Patterns of Marriage* 178–9, 190, 206, 236–7
Workers' Birth Control Group 4
workplace/sexual harassment 52, 193
World Congress for Sexual Reform 96
World War I 8, 53, 123
Wright, Helena 4; *More About the Sex Factor in Marriage* 253, 261–3; *Sex and Society* 259–60, 269–70, 280–1, 288, 307–8; *The Sex Factor in Marriage* 169–70, 180–2, 237–8; *What is Sex?* 207, 240–2

Youth and Sex report 38